GUIDING GLOBAL ORDER

T0386602

The G8 and Global Governance Series

The G8 and Global Governance Series explores the issues, the institutions and the strategies of participants in the Group of Eight network of global governance, as well as the other actors, processes, and challenges that shape global order in the twenty-first century. Many aspects of intensifying globalization, once considered domestic, are now moving into the international arena, generating a need for broader and deeper international co-operation, and demanding new centres of leadership to revitalize, reform, reinforce, and even replace the galaxy of multilateral institutions created in 1945. In response, the G8, composed of the world's major market democracies, including Russia and the European Union, is emerging as an effective source of global governance. The G8 and Global Governance series focuses on the new issues at the centre of global governance, covering topics such as finance, investment, and trade, as well as transnational threats to human security and traditional and emerging political and security challenges. The series examines the often invisible network of G8, G7 and other institutions as they operate inside and outside established international systems to generate desired outcomes and create a new order. It analyzes how individual G8 members and other international actors, including multinational firms, civil society organizations, and other international institutions devise and implement strategies to secure their preferred global order.

Also in the series

Shaping a New International Financial System
Challenges of governance in a globalizing world
Edited by Karl Kaiser, John J. Kirton and Joseph P. Daniels
ISBN 0 7546 1412 3

Hanging In There
The G7 and G8 Summit in maturity and renewal
Nicholas Bayne
ISBN 0 7546 1185 X

The G7/G8 System
Evolution, role and documentation
Peter I. Hajnal
ISBN 1 84014 776 8

The G8's Role in the New Millennium
Edited by Michael R. Hodges, John J. Kirton and Joseph P. Daniels
ISBN 1 84014 774 1

Guiding Global Order

G8 Governance in the Twenty-First Century

Edited by

JOHN J. KIRTON
University of Toronto

JOSEPH P. DANIELS
Marquette University

ANDREAS FREYTAG
University of Cologne

Routledge
Taylor & Francis Group

LONDON AND NEW YORK

First published 2001 by Ashgate Publishing

Reissued 2018 by Routledge
2 Park Square, Milton Park, Abingdon, Oxon OX14 4RN
711 Third Avenue, New York, NY 10017, USA

Routledge is an imprint of the Taylor & Francis Group, an informa business

Notice:
Product or corporate names may be trademarks or registered trademarks, and are used only for identification and explanation without intent to infringe.

Publisher's Note
The publisher has gone to great lengths to ensure the quality of this reprint but points out that some imperfections in the original copies may be apparent.

Disclaimer
The publisher has made every effort to trace copyright holders and welcomes correspondence from those they have been unable to contact.

A Library of Congress record exists under LC control number: 00111400

ISBN 13: 978-1-138-63487-9 (hbk)
ISBN 13: 978-1-138-63489-3 (pbk)
ISBN 13: 978-1-315-20480-2 (ebk)

Contents

List of Tables

List of Figures

List of Contributors

Donald J. S. Brean is professor of finance and economics at the Rotman School of Management at the University of Toronto. Professor Brean is a graduate of the University of Toronto and the London School of Economics and Political Science. His research deals with international finance, foreign investment, and economies in transition. Recent publications include two edited volumes, *Taxation in Modern China* (Routledge, 1998), and *Research in International Portfolio Management* (2000) with John Hull.

Joseph P. Daniels is Associate Professor of International Economics at Marquette University, Milwaukee, Wisconsin, and was Visiting Professor of Economics and International Relations, University of Toronto, in 1997–98. An established scholar on the G7 Summit process, he has published widely on international economic policy processes. He is co-editor of *The G8's Role in the New Millennium* (Ashgate, 1999) and *Shaping a New International Financial System* (Ashgate, 2000).

Barbara Dluhosch has been a lecturer at the University of Cologne since 1998, where she was a research associate sponsored by the German Research Foundation from 1995 to 1997. She is also a Visiting Professor of Economics at the University of Munich for 1999–2000, and was a visiting researcher at Stanford University from 1995 to 1996, and a research associate at the Bank of Spain in 1994. Her main research interests are international macroeconomics, trade theory, and policy.

Juergen B. Donges is currently Professor of Economics and Director of the Institute for Political Economy at the University of Cologne. He served as Vice-President of the Kiel Institute of World Economics from 1983 to 1989. From 1988 to 1991, Dr. Donges was chairman of the German Commission on Economic Deregulation and has been a member of the German Council of Economic Experts since 1992, serving as chairman since March 2000. He has written extensively on international economic issues.

Klemens Fischer has been Minister Counsellor at the Permanent Representation of Austria to the European Union since 1995. For the two previous years he was a member of the negotiating team for the accession of the Austrian Mission to the European Union in Brussels. He has been a lecturer at the Institute for Communication and Media at the Technical University in Berlin, the Institute for Political Science at the University of Siegen, the Centre for European Studies at Maastricht, and the Rotman School of Management at the University of Toronto. He is the author of *Lobbying und Kommunikation in der Europäischen Union*, published by A. Spitz in Berlin in 1997.

Andreas Freytag is Senior Economist and Managing Director of the Institute for Economic Policy at the University of Cologne. He has been a Visiting Scholar at the Faculty of Economics and Politics at Cambridge University, and has published widely on international economic relations and globalisation. He is currently working on the political economy of international monetary policy.

Pierre Marc Johnson is Senior Counsel with the Canadian law firm Heenan Blaikie. A former premier of the province of Quebec, he has taught law at McGill University and lectures in various fora and participates regularly in many United Nations negotiations. He is an advisor to the North American Commission on Environmental Cooperation, and was vice-chair of the National Round Table on the Environment and the Economy and chair of its foreign policy committee from 1990 to 1997. Dr. Johnson is coauthor of *The Environment and NAFTA: Understanding and Implementing the New Continental Law* (Island Press, 1996) and has published many articles on development and globalisation. He is a member of the Professional Advisory Council of the G8 Research Group.

John J. Kirton is Director of the G8 Research Group, Associate Professor of Political Science, Research Associate of the Centre for International Studies and Fellow of Trinity College at the University of Toronto. He has advised the Canadian Government on G7 participation and international trade and sustainable development, and has written widely on G7 summitry. He is co-author of *Environmental Regulations and Corporate Strategy: A NAFTA Perspective* (Oxford University Press, 1999) and co-editor of *The G8's Role in the New Millennium* (Ashgate, 1999) and *Shaping a New International Financial System* (Ashgate, 2000).

Razeen Sally is a lecturer in international political economy at the London School of Economics and Political Science and author of *Classical Liberalism and International Economic Order: Studies in Theory and Intellectual History*

(Routledge, 1998). His research interests concentrate on trade policy-making in developing countries and countries in transition, the World Trade Organization and developing countries, and the history of economic ideas, particularly the theory of commercial policy.

Helmut Schieber is President of the Land Central Bank in Baden-Württemberg. From 1992 to 2000, he was a member of the board of the Deutsche Bundesbank, during which time he was responsible for international relations, financial markets, credit, and foreign exchange. A member of the Central Bank Council of the Deutsche Bundesbank since 1992, he is the author of *Was ist der Wert des Geldes wert?* (with Heinz Rapp, published by Europäische Verlagsanstalt in 1977) and has lectured extensively on monetary and economic policy issues.

Christoph Schwegmann is a doctoral research fellow of the Fritz-Thyssen Foundation at the Stiftung Wissenschaft und Politik in Ebenhausen and Berlin. He received his master's degree from the University of Mannheim. His research interests include modern concerts in international relations and European foreign and security policy.

Martin J. G. Theuringer works with Juergen Donges at the Department of Economics at the University of Cologne. He holds the Certificate of Advanced Studies from the Kiel Institute of World Economics and has worked at the Institute for Empirical Economic Research in Munich. He has published articles on international trade policy, development, and transition, as well as labour economics.

Peter Tillmann is a research assistant at the Department of Economics of the University of Cologne. He is currently at work on his doctoral thesis in the field of international finance and empirical macroeconomics.

George M. von Furstenberg holds the Robert Bendheim Chair in Economic and Financial Policy at Fordham University in New York. He was previously the Rudy Professor of Economics at Indiana University in Bloomington, Indiana. The president of the North American Economics and Finance Association, Dr. von Furstenberg has published widely on international and finance issues, including a chapter on 'Transparentising the Global Money Business: Glasnost or Just Another Wild Card in Play?' in Karl Kaiser, John Kirton, and Joseph Daniels (eds.), *Shaping a New International Financial System* (Ashgate, 2000). He is a member of the Professional Advisory Council of the G8 Research Group.

Preface and Acknowledgements

Guiding Global Order, the fifth in Ashgate Publishing's series on the G8 and Global Governance, expands the focus of the series in three important ways. First, this volume deals comprehensively with the major issues, across the economic, transnational relations, and political-security spectrum, that lie at the core of the Cologne Summit of 1999 and also of the Kyushu-Okinawa ministerial and leaders meetings in July 2000. Second, it widens the focus on the G8 to include the other international institutions and processes that the G7/8 has spawned, or that are a key component of the G7/8 itself. Third, and most expansively, it examines the role of the G7/8 in the broader context of global order. The book examines the important changes to that order already underway at the beginning of the twenty-first century as well as the fundamental challenges that exist in guiding the emerging order in ways that reflect the needs of the global community as a whole. Previous volumes in this series have explored in detail the major contributions of the G7/8 system to shaping international order in more stable and just ways; *Guiding Global Order* addresses the broader question of the overall global order itself, concentrating on key dimensions and critical issues areas such as finance, trade, sustainable development, and security.

This book thus considers the work of the G7/8 beginning at the 1999 Cologne Summit as well as the broader challenges of guiding global order that have become clear at the start of a new century. These challenges have been dramatically highlighted by the assaults from some civil society actors on the long established and accepted procedures of global governance at the late 1999 ministerial meeting of the World Trade Organization (WTO) in Seattle, and subsequent gatherings in 2000, including the United Nations Conference on Trade and Development (UNCTAD) in Bangkok, the World Economic Forum in Davos, and the meetings of the International Monetary Fund (IMF), World Bank, and G7 finance ministers in Washington DC and Prague. It is the broader and more fundamental set of questions arising from these events that have lent an urgency and defined an intellectual direction for this volume.

Guiding Global Order has its origins in several activities. The first is the Academic Symposium that took place in Cologne on 17 June 1999, immediately following the meeting of the G8 foreign ministers in Cologne and the G7 finance ministers in Frankfurt, and immediately before the opening of the G7 and G8 Summits themselves on 18 June. The symposium, sponsored jointly by the G8 Research Group based at the University of Toronto and the Institute for Economic Policy of the University of Cologne, took as its theme 'The Economic Agenda and Challenges of the G7/G8 Cologne Summit'. It assembled several younger scholars from Germany and North America, including Mexico, to discuss with those at the University of Cologne and from the G8 Research Group the central issues on the Cologne Summit's economic agenda. This volume contains the extensively revised versions of most of the papers presented at the symposium. We are grateful to Barbara Dluhosch, Martin Theuringer, Joseph Daniels, and Peter Tillmann for their contributions in this regard.

The volume also contains chapters based on the presentations at an open town hall Citizens Forum on the evening of June 17. At this forum, three leading international economic and finance authorities discussed with the citizens of Cologne the core finance issues dealt with at the Summit. Professor George von Furstenberg, a member of the G8 Research Group's Professional Advisory Council, participated, together with Professor Juergen Donges, the Director of the Institute for Economic Policy at the University of Cologne, and Helmut Schieber, a member of the Directoriums der Deutschen Bundesbank. Their contributions in this volume flow from their remarks that evening. We acknowledge with thanks their initial and subsequent work.

A third set of chapters, from specially invited contributors, is designed to deal with the broader array of core political, security, and other issues dealt with at or flowing from the Cologne Summit. We are grateful to Razeen Sally, Christoph Schwegmann, Klemens Fischer, and Donald Brean for contributing in this fashion.

The fourth type of contribution stems from the ongoing work of the G8 Research Group on issues closely related to the evolution of the G7/8 system of international institutions and the broader issues of global order it must address. Here we thank Dr. Pierre Marc Johnson, a member of the G8 Research Group's Professional Advisory Council, for his chapter.

This volume contains some of the early research related to the University of Toronto's Centre for International Studies' project on 'Securing Canada's Environmental Community Through International Regime Reform (EnviReform)'. Financed by the Social Sciences and Humanities Research Council of Canada (SSHRC), through its strategic grant programme on 'Globalization and Social Cohesion in Canada', the EnviReform project identifies effective ways for Canadians to participate more directly in the international trade systems that affect their natural environment, food, health, and safety. The project analyses the social and environmental impacts of existing trade liberalisation on Canadians and explores new strategies for regulation and risk assessment, environmental information, voluntary standards setting, and participation by civil society. These strategies aim to allow Canadians to participate in shaping trade and finance regimes in more unified and socially sustainable ways. The contributions in this volume of John Kirton and Pierre Marc Johnson in particular emanate from the initial stages of this research.

Taken together, *Guiding Global Order* thus explores its broad subject from several vantage points. It contains contributions from those based in most of the G8's constituent regions. The contributors come from the disciplines of economics, political science, management studies, and law, and from universities, leading research institutes, private legal practice, and government. As a group, they have experience with many of the core governmental and intergovernmental institutions in the field. They thus bring a wide variety of perspectives, analytic approaches, and judgements to bear. In particular, this book brings a new generation of younger scholars, based largely in Europe, into the ongoing debate about G7/8 and global governance — a group with fresh and often more sharply critical perspectives on the G7/8, stemming from a wide variety of intellectual vantage points.

Given the rich diversity of views contained within these chapters, no effort has been made to embrace all in a single theoretical tradition, interpretative framework, or concluding consensus. Rather, *Guiding Global Order* begins with a review of the G7/8's activity as it confronts the core challenges of global governance in the twenty-first century. It then offers various views in each of the three sections that follow on the G87/8 and the international community's economic agenda, the broader transnational and political agenda, and moves to involve and relate to new actors in the central processes of global governance.

Assembling such a volume had left us with a deep debt to those who contributed in many different ways to this enterprise. Our first debt is to those members of the G8 Research Group's Professional Advisory Council, led by George von Furstenberg and Pierre Marc Johnson, who served as speakers and contributors and provided advice and support in the Academic Symposium, Citizens Forum, and design of this volume.

We owe much to our partners at the University of Cologne's Institute for Economic Policy for joining us in this important project. This debt begins with Professor Juergen Donges, who first saw the promise in this venture, who contributed an important chapter and who gave us constant and firm support throughout.

We are most grateful to those organisations that provided the material resources, both financial and in kind, to make possible the activities on which this volume is based and the associated program of the G8 Research Group. The City of Cologne, the Cologne Chamber of Commerce, and the United States Information Service sponsored the Citizens Forum in Cologne and included our members in it. The Office of the Chancellor in the Government of Germany fostered critical connections. The Canadian Embassy in Germany, its outstanding ambassador Gaetan Lavertu, and its impressive public affairs officer Agnes Pust facilitated this joint venture in Canadian-German intellectual co-operation. Our financial sponsors for the G8 Research Group's 1999 field program include the Canadian Department of Foreign Affairs and International Trade, Siemens Corporation, and the City of Toronto. The SSHRC, through the EnviReform project, financed the final editorial stages of this book. Our in-kind sponsors, for the Symposium, and for the innovative webcasting program that broadcast it to the world, were eCollege.com, Media One, Hewlett Packard, Sony, Kodak, the German government's host broadcaster for the Cologne Summit, Canada's *National Post*, and the *Washington Times*. Together they joined with the G8 Research Group to produce, using the Symposium program and other material, the world's largest online classroom ever, engaging close to 5000 students from over 1000 educational institutions in 72 countries around the world.

We owe a special word of thanks to two individuals. The first is Paul Jacobelli, whose dedication, initiative, persistence, and skill were vital in drawing together the sponsorship consortium that made the Academic Symposium and thus this volume possible. The second is Madeline Koch, the Managing Editor of the G8 Research Group, whose managerial and editorial skills were essential in ensuring that initial thoughts and rough drafts offered in English and German were transformed into a polished single book in a timely and elegant fashion. More broadly, we note with deep appreciation the indispensable contribution of Jillian Bannister, the 1999 Director of Communications of the G8 Research Group, Sandra Larmour, the Director of Development of the G8 Research Group, Nancy Scott as a legal advisor, and Heidi Ullrich of the London School of Economics and Political Science.

We are further grateful to the members of the G8 Research Group, and particularly those who were able to join us for the Academic Symposium and the G7/8 Summit in Cologne. While all contributed in so many ways, we must thank in particular Diana Juricevic for her devoted editorial assistance and Ivan Savic, Gina Stephens, Marilena Liguori, Klaudyna Osika, and Bob Papanikolaou for helping see the manuscript through to completion.

At the University of Toronto, we are grateful for the continuing support of our colleagues at the Centre for International Studies: Professor Louis Pauly, its director, who oversees our research activities, and Professor Peter Hajnal, who assumed the onerous but necessary task of securing the anonymous referees who reviewed our draft manuscript and collectively approved it for publication. We owe much to the comments of our reviewers, whose often trenchant but ultimately supportive comments have been taken fully into account. At Trinity College, we acknowledge the critical support of provost Tom Delworth, bursar Geoffrey Seaborn, head librarian Linda Corman, who oversees the development of the G8 Research Collection, and Professor Robert Bothwell, Co-ordinator of the International Relations Program. At the Department of Political Science, Professor Robert Vipond, Chair, and professors Ronald Deibert and Ronald Biener have provided constant encouragement. At the University of Toronto Library, chief librarian Carole Moore, internet director Sian Miekle, and project manager Marc Lalonde have been indispensable. And at the Office of Public Affairs, Cheryl Sullivan has cheerfully and effectively assisted us with publicity and promotion.

Perhaps our greatest gratitude is reserved for our series editor, Kirstin Howgate, and her colleagues at Ashgate. It was Kirstin who had the vision to see the virtue of producing this volume and who worked effectively to ensure a smooth adoption and publication of the manuscript.

Finally, we acknowledge the understanding, patience and support of our families as we laboured to convert raw drafts into publish text. We are also indebted to our students and the alumni of the G8 Research Group who provided constant inspiration as we pursued our work. It is to this next generation of scholars on the G7/8 and global governance that we dedicate this book.

John J. Kirton, Joseph P. Daniels, and Andreas Freytag
January 2001

List of Abbreviations

ADB	Asian Development Bank
AMF	Asian Monetary Fund
APEC	Asia-Pacific Economic Cooperation
ASEAN	Association of South-East Asian Nations
BIS	Bank for International Settlements
CAP	Common Agricultural Policy
CCL	Contingent Credit Line
CCP	Common Commercial Policy
EC	European Community
ECB	European Central Bank
EFTA	European Free Trade Association
EMS	European Monetary System
EMU	European Monetary Union
ERM	Exchange Rate Mechanism
EU	European Union
FAO	Food and Agriculture Organization
FDI	Foreign Direct Investment
FRY	Federal Republic of Yugoslavia
FSF	Financial Stability Forum
G7	Group of Seven
G8	Group of Eight
G10	Group of 10
G20	Group of 20
G22	Group of 22
G77	Group of 77
GAB	General Arrangements to Borrow
GATT	General Agreement on Tariffs and Trade
GDP	gross domestic product
GNP	gross national product
HIPC	Highly Indebted Poor Countries
IBRD	International Bank for Reconstruction and Development, also known as the World Bank
ICFY	International Conference on Former Yugoslavia

IFIs	International Financial Institutions
IFOR	Implementation Force
IGO	intergovernmental organisation
IMF	International Monetary Fund
IMFC	International Monetary and Financial Committee
IUCN	World Conservation Union
KLA	Kosovo Liberation Army
KVM	Kosovo Verification Mission
LDCs	Less Developed Countries
LLDCs	Least of the Less Developed Countries
LTCM	Long-Term Capital Management
MAI	Multilateral Agreement on Investment
MEA	Multilateral Environmental Agreement
MFN	Most Favoured Nation
NAB	New Arrangements to Borrow
NAFTA	North American Free Trade Agreement
NATO	North Atlantic Treaty Organization
NGO	non-governmental organisation
NIEO	New International Economic Order
NPV	net present value
ODA	Official Development Assistance
OECD	Organisation for Economic Co-operation and Development
OPEC	Organisation of Petroleum Exporting Countries
OSCE	Organization for Security and Co-operation in Europe
PV	present value
PRC	People's Republic of China
SALs	Structural Adjustment Loans
SDRs	Special Drawing Rights
SHAPE	Supreme Headquarters, Allied Powers Europe
SFOR	Stabilization Force
TEC	Treaty Establishing the Economic Community
TEU	Treaty on European Union
TNC	transnational corporation
TFP	total factor productivity
TRIPs	Trade-Related Aspects of Intellectual Property
UN	United Nations
UNCTAD	United Nations Conference on Trade and Development
UNDP	United Nations Development Programme
UNEP	United Nations Environmental Programme

UNESCO	United Nations Educational, Scientific, and Cultural Organization
UNHCR	United Nations High Commissioner for Refugees
UNIDO	United Nations Industrial Development Organization
UNMIBH	United Nations Mission in Bosnia and Herzegovina
UNPROFOR	United Nations Protection Force
UNSC	United Nations Security Council
WTO	World Trade Organization

1 Introduction

JOHN J. KIRTON, JOSEPH P. DANIELS, AND
ANDREAS FREYTAG

The June 1999 G7 and G8 Summit in Cologne, Germany, marked the end of the first quarter century of the operation of this unique international institution. Far more importantly, it set the stage for the much more ambitious and effective form of global governance that the G7/8 system is called upon to provide to meet the heightened challenges that the twenty-first century brings. The Cologne Summit's outline of a blueprint for reforming the international financial system pointed to a much more transparent, domestically intrusive, internationally inclusive, and effective regime for governing global finance in an era of intense globalisation. The Summit's landmark achievement — the Cologne Debt Initiative — marked a significant step forward in an 11-year effort to relieve the debts of the world's poorest countries. In doing so, it highlighted the additional obstacles these countries face if they are to integrate into the global economy in a way that secures sustainable and-widely shared growth. The Cologne Summit's decisive role in successfully ending the war to liberate Kosovo and in mobilising the reconstruction effort to secure a genuine, multiethnic democracy foreshadowed the new demands faced by G8 members and others for major military and humanitarian intervention efforts on a global scale and for rebuilding domestic societies and polities to accord with evolving global norms. And in several other fields, from multilateral trade to education and the environment, the Cologne Summit set the direction for the major international regime-building exercises that shape global order today.

Beneath these individual achievements there lies a more profound change in the intellectual core and legitimate processes for shaping and managing global order in the coming era. What might be called the new 'Cologne consensus' marked the end of an unchallenged two-decade-long agreement on neoliberal principles as a guide to global and international governance and a shift toward a more socially sensitive and inclusive approach to globalisation. Whether this is a real and enduring change — and, if so, whether it is one for good or for bad — is the subject of analysis and debate in the policy world, among scholars, and in this book. Moreover, as affirmed by the presence of many thousands of citizens who came to Cologne to call for the relief of the

1

debt of the poorest, the 1999 Cologne Summit marked a major escalation of the demand for the more effective influence and direct inclusion of civil society in the emerging centres of global governance. Furthermore, the creation of the new G20, and subsequent calls by the 1999 G8 chair Gerhard Schroeder and the 2000 chair, Japanese prime minister Keizo Obuchi, for China to participate in the G8 Summit demonstrated a broadening effort to expand the G7/8's inclusiveness and representativeness, and thus the legitimacy of the global order it guided.

These historic achievements at Cologne, as carried forward to and through the July 2000 Okinawa G7/8 Summit, point to a future that will by no means unfold inevitably or easily. Indeed, the task of constructing a stronger, more modern, more socially sensitive international financial system remains a slow, complex, cumbersome and still highly contested project. The post-Cologne difficulties in constructing a tolerant civil society in Kosovo, in maintaining respect for human rights in Russia amidst the ongoing conflict in Chechnya, in including China in the network of G7/8 governance, and in launching a new Millennium Round of multilateral trade negotiations clearly demonstrate how much of a struggle it will be to insert new principles and processes into well-entrenched patterns of governance. The depth and difficulty of the challenge have been dramatically highlighted by the disruptions from civil society actors to the long-established procedures of global governance at the November/December 1999 ministerial meeting of the World Trade Organization (WTO) in Seattle and subsequent gatherings in 2000 of the United Nations Conference on Trade and Development (UNCTAD) in Bangkok, the World Economic Forum in Davos, and the International Monetary Fund (IMF), World Bank, and G7 finance ministers in Washington and Prague. The accomplishments of Cologne must thus be evaluated and built upon in response to this formidable set of voices, and their challenge to the longstanding essentials of neoliberal orthodoxy and state sovereignty. The challenge is to create a more inclusive, legitimate, and socially safeguarded consensus at the core of the emerging global order.

The Approach

Guiding Global Order addresses this ongoing struggle to define a new socially safeguarded and more legitimate and inclusive global order for the twenty-first century. It can be taken for granted that this goal is shared by most citizens, politicians, and analysts, whether they are economists or political scientists and regardless of what epistemic, professional, or national community they come from. There are, however, very different opinions about the best or even possible way to achieve this goal. This book adds to the existing literature and debate over this 'best way', since two general opposing views of the Cologne consensus have flourished, and are represented at the core of this work.

Political scientists generally welcome this change because they see the large and beneficial potential of both nation-states and global governance to improve the social situation of the people via co-operative political action. Moreover, they are sceptical about whether the market will solve the distribution problem properly. In other words, they see a contradiction between neoliberal economic policy and social cohesion. The empirical evidence thus far cannot allow one to reject this view entirely.

In contrast, economists are generally more optimistic. They tend to argue that the open markets and nondiscrimination brought by globalisation will add to social cohesion. To start with, they would question the view that there have been two decades of unchallenged agreement on neoliberal principles. As for liberal policy, much of it seems to be lip service from politicians, rather than the practical realisation of liberalism in economic policy. In addition, economists, in particular those trained in political economy, have less trust of governments than political scientists.

These two opposing views, collected in one book examining the current challenges of G8 and global governance, can be very useful for both groups. Although they deal with the same topic and agree on the same eventual goal, political and economic scholars often do not understand each other. This makes it awkward for satisfactory discourse and thus difficult for an analytic consensus to emerge that is relevant to policy. The debate on global governance can greatly improve if people better understand each other's analyses and priorities. There is much to be learned. It is to be hoped that *Guiding Global Order* will contribute to this learning process, and thus in a small way fulfil the commitment contained in the Cologne Summit's charter on life-long learning. This dialectical approach does have its shortcomings, however. The most obvious is that many pure political scientists or economists might be offended by the other discipline's contributions. Nevertheless, costs remain the exception rather than the rule.

Beginning with the Cologne Summit of June 1999, the book explores the extent to which the emerging global order at the beginning of the twenty-first century is, should be, and can be marked by a major shift toward a new consensus that gives widely shared prosperity, social and environmental safeguards, and greater inclusiveness and representation an equal place with raw growth, market liberalisation, and managerial efficiency. To do so, it considers the changes taking place across a broad spectrum of the major issues dealt with by the G7/8 at the Cologne Summit and on the road to and through the Kyushu-Okinawa Summit of July 2000. This spectrum ranges from the high politics of winning the war in Kosovo to the low politics of international macroeconomic policy co-ordination and debt relief. Moreover, *Guiding Global Order* looks outward at the expansion of the G7/8 system through the advent of new international institutions such as the G20, through a closer association with the emerging major power of China, and with the centre of supranational governance in the European Union (EU).

In each case, this work conducts several tasks. First, it examines the steps forward made at Cologne and the extent to which they represent major changes in new and innovative directions, as opposed to marginal advances or reversions to an older *status quo*. Second, it explores the underlying causes of the new directions set by Cologne and on this basis offers judgements as to their future course and cadence. Third, it critically assesses the quality of those major decisions and subsequent directions to determine if the Cologne consensus will be effective in accomplishing its ambitious targets or if more radical reform is required. Fourth, it judges how adequate these evolving new principles and processes in global governance will be in addressing the challenges brought by the rapidly changing world of the twenty-first century and what new paths and policies are still required in response.

The point of departure for these explorations is an analysis of the work of the G7/8 system itself and its activity at Cologne and beyond. But its central concern is the much larger and more fundamental issue of global order itself. The book thus deals with the work of the G7/8 at the 1999 Cologne Summit, the group's subsequent activity, and the broader challenges of guiding global order that have become clear as the twenty-first century opens. It examines the major economic, transnational relations, and political-security issues that were fundamental not only to the Cologne Summit of 1999 but also to the Kyushu-Okinawa ministerial and leaders meeting in July 2000. But the examination extends to the other international institutions and processes that have grown out of the G7/8 and expands further to consider the role of the G7/8 in the wider context of global order at this historic moment.

To conduct this examination, *Guiding Global Order* combines the talents of authors from several disciplines: economics, political science, and management studies. It brings together the work of professional scholars and those who serve as practitioners in central policy-making institutions. It embraces the perspective of those located in several of the G8 members' countries and regions. Yet, this book has a particular emphasis. Many of its authors come from Europe and Germany, and include some of the leading authorities in their fields. Many are writing, often in critical fashion, on the G7/8 and its issues for the first time. This work thus offers the contribution of a new generation of European scholarship on the G7/8, and one that will be particularly timely, given the G8's return to Europe in the year 2001.

This work uses three major analytic tools from the disciplines of economics and political science. First, it draws on the insights of game theoretic and rational expectations and public space approaches in economics to assess the sustainability, effectiveness, and wisdom of the approaches pursued at Cologne to pressing policy problems. Second, it employs the various strands of international regime theory to consider whether changes in formal principles extend into norms, rules, decision-making procedures, and the actors' conceptions of their interests and identities. Here the work focusses substantively on whether the departures from the prevailing neoliberal orthodoxy evident at Cologne mark a return to an earlier 1945-like consensus of embedded liberalism or a move into a new, durable, and effective normative system more appropriate to the needs of a rapidly globalising world. Third, the work enters and extends the ongoing scholarly debate on the causes and consequences of G7/8 governance, by exploring the relevance of the existing causal models in the new conditions of the twenty-first century, and the way the G7/8 system relates to other, competing forms of global governance (Kirton and Daniels 1999).

The Analyses

'Part I: The Core Economic Issues' deals with the economic questions that have been central to the G7's operation during its first quarter century and that remain vital in the globalised economy of the twenty-first century. These issues of macroeconomic policy co-ordination, monetary policy, and finance, and the systems that govern them, and of multilateral trade and its international institutional galaxy, have acquired a new prominence and complexity in this much more tightly integrated world. They have also drawn the G7/8 and other international institutions ever more deeply into the task of domestic governance.

This examination of the core economic issues begins, in Chapter 2, with Andreas Freytag's 'Internal Macroeconomic Policies and International Governance'. This chapter builds on the work of those who explore the politics of macroeconomic co-ordination (Dixit 1996, Iverson 1999). It takes up the question of where and when international policy co-ordination is appropriate and what the proper role of the G7/8 is in this process. Noting the difference between those scholars who express great faith in the effectiveness of the G7/8 as an instrument of comprehensive policy co-ordination and those who prefer a stable rules-based alternative to discretionary crisis response management, Freytag considers in turn the concept of state sovereignty, international policy co-ordination in commercial policy, and the resulting lessons for macroeconomic policy, and takes the specific domain of monetary policy as a critical example. He concludes with suggestions about how to incorporate the G8 process more effectively into the resulting model of improved policy co-ordination.

Freytag's central conclusion is that international co-operation can be very useful in disciplining governments that might be tempted to pursue destabilising macroeconomic policies or that have actually done so. While governments are naturally reluctant to surrender sovereignty to international institutions, in practice they have limited sovereignty in the face of rent-seeking behaviour by domestic actors and can thus usefully look abroad for ways to install a longer term perspective and recapture their domestically lost sovereignty. In the field of international commercial or trade policy, international co-operation can protect citizens against their own governments by offering a set of internationally agreed rules that should be entrenched in the domestic constitution. Similarly, in the field of macroeconomic policy, domestic political pressures tend to produce bad policies, such as inflation, that can only be broken with a credible commitment grounded in an international agreement, especially if it is again entrenched domestically. In the field of monetary policy, an application of both adaptive expectations and rational expectations theory suggests that inflation is a domestic problem caused by government failure where a credible commitment made internationally and constitutionally enshrined domestically would be useful, even in the absence of significant international inflationary spillovers in the real economy. The G7/8 can play the useful role of lowering inflation among outside countries by offering a monetary policy framework that is binding among them and open for voluntary adoption by those countries, and that is again domestically established within the constitutions of all.

In Chapter 3, 'Challenges for the Global Financial System', Juergen B. Donges and Peter Tillmann begin with what they see as the major outstanding challenge to the world economy and the G7/8 — securing financial stability amidst the continuing lack of knowledge about the causes and consequences of the crises that imperil it. They ask: With such crises spreading globally and threatening so much and so many, where should economic policy intervene to contain and counter them, and what role should national governments and international organisations play? In answering these questions, they offer an overview of the major tasks, including inflation control and central bank independence, that summiteers will face at future G8 meetings (Laubach and Posen 1997). They provide some guidelines for dealing with these central issues on the agenda of international finance.

In offering these guidelines, Donges and Tillmann counter the emerging conventional wisdom among politicians that globalisation weakens national governments and thus demands stronger, more interventionist forms of global governance. They argue, rather, that globalisation puts pressure on national governments to shape an efficient and sustainable policy mix that brings credibility in international capital markets. This task begins by adopting a concept of 'good governance' that has at its core a monetary policy aimed at price stability, prudent fiscal, debt and wage policy, an exchange-rate regime that does not eliminate risk for investors or require high interest rates to maintain, and transparency in the banking sector, with precautions to prevent moral hazard. These precepts remain relevant for combating financial crises like those of the 1990s, which will happen from time to time, but which now feature much greater global contagion and short-term thinking. The proper response is for the G7/8 to craft a strengthened international financial system that features much greater transparency and accountability, more efficient banking regulation, and a limited role for the IMF. This role should focus on catalysing private-sector restructuring packages in the face of financial crises and refusing to serve as a lender of last resort. The perennial proposals that financial crises raise as solutions — a Tobin tax on international capital flows and a target-zone regime for exchange rates — should be firmly rejected. Especially because globalisation is such a profound and irreversible process, it is national, and not international authorities, with a consistent, stability-oriented economic policy at home, who are central to securing a stronger international financial system. G8 Summits should certainly discuss such subjects, but decide to instruct national governments, within and without, to get on with this job.

In Chapter 4, George M. von Furstenberg discusses 'U.S. Dollarization: A Second-Best Form of Regional Currency Consolidation'. This analysis is important to the international community and the future role of the G7/8 for two reasons. Most broadly, it may be that the future international order will be shaped more by regionalisation and regional governance arrangements rather than globalisation and direct global governance (for background see Cohen 1998, Strange 1998, and Kirshner 1995). How North America and the Western

Hemisphere react to the lead set by the EU will determine whether such a process is marked by conflict or the compatibility and co-operation that will make global convergence ultimately possible. More specifically, as Chapter 10 explores further, especially if the Western Hemisphere, following the lead of Euroland, should adopt a single currency, the G7 may give way in the monetary and even macroeconomic field to a G3 that could affect the prospects for successful G7 co-ordination, and the relevance of Britain, Canada, and Russia in the club.

To provide background to this looming challenge, von Furstenberg traces the history of dollarization, first inside the United States to the 1973 completion of full national dollarization, and then externally, where many countries during the 1990s in Europe, in transition economies, and in Latin America moved to adopt or use the Deutschmark, Euro, and then U.S. dollar as their own. Identifying the reasons behind the disappearing small brands of money, von Furstenberg examines the alternatives small countries face, focussing on unilateral monetary union and a multilateral alternative. He then considers the case for multilateralism, and the recent moves of the U.S. government to make dollarization more attractive to outside countries.

The bold conclusion is that the free international movement of capital, free trade, and e-trade in financial services make regional currency consolidation inevitable. The trend is already in evidence, with consequential groups in many countries of the Americas voicing support for some form of formal dollarization. Yet, von Furstenberg concludes that while complete dollarization may be useful for the immediate future, it is second best in the short run and unsustainable in the long run in the Western Hemisphere. Unilateral dollarization requires paying a very high financial tribute to the United States, a price that many will find onerous once they have reaped the short-term advantages of securing monetary stability and low inflation through unilateral dollarization. They will then reclaim co-ownership and collective management of their monetary assets by forming a multilateral union with like-minded countries, as many states in Europe have done with the creation of the Euro.

In Chapter 5, 'Looking Askance at Global Governance,' Razeen Sally addresses the growing view that global problems require global solutions and that it is thus global governance replete with sustainable development and social democracy, rather than national governance grounded in neoliberal fundamentals that is now required. He first examines the wisdom from the classic economic theorists of the past three centuries, followed by a review of the quite different forms of global governance embedded in and offered by the IMF and World Bank, the United Nations socioeconomic agencies and

UNCTAD, the Organisation for Economic Co-operation and Development (OECD), the WTO, and the G8. He then considers the future of global governance, indeed, whether it will have, and should have, a future at all.

Sally argues that the current conventional wisdom about global governance in general and the concrete form of international economic policy co-ordination in most international fora, including the G7/8 Summits, must be subjected to scrutiny. Such close criticism reveals that most arguments for global governance are based on bad economics and even worse political economy. He asserts that most post-1945 international policy co-ordination has increased the discretionary political power and discretionary spending of governments, and thus government failure in the international system. Soft policy co-ordination focused on deliberation, policy surveillance, and hard research, and strict and simple international rules that limit the power of national governments play a useful role. On the whole, however, national governance rather than global governance has diminished in neither importance nor effectiveness since 1945. It should remain the first and last foundation for international economic policy action in the future.

'Part II: The Broad Agenda' addresses the transnational and high, hardsecurity issues that have become ever more central to the G8. These are subjects on which the G8 has made some of its most path-setting advances since meeting at Cologne. These include debt relief for the world's poorest countries, a process pioneered by the G7 during the previous 11 years, and the protection of the global ecosystem, where countries of Europe have often been in the lead within the G8. It also includes the defining issue of the Cologne Summit — the process of bringing peace and reconstruction to the Balkans and Kosovo, and the role played by the G8, other forms of concert governance, regional institutions such as the EU, and multilateral institutions in this task.

The exploration of the broad agenda begins in Chapter 6 with Barbara Dluhosch's examination of 'The G7 and the Debt of the Poorest'. Noting the vast debt accumulated by the world's Least of the Less Developed Countries (LLDCs), she starts by examining the Highly Indebted Poor Countries (HIPC) initiative launched in 1996, its record in actually relieving debt through to 1996, and the effort of the G8 at the Cologne Summit to put a much-enhanced debt-relief package into place. She then explores how much of a real burden the debt actually represents for Less Developed Countries (LDCs) and takes a searching look at whether debt relief is the right remedy for the problem. She concludes by considering the G8's contribution to debt relief and sustainable development and the alternative instruments of trade and aid that it has available to accomplish its objectives.

Dluhosch notes that there are considerable doubts about whether the strategy of debt relief affirmed and enhanced at the Cologne Summit constitutes an effective remedy. She suggests that trade, rather than this form of aid, might be a better cure, for trade does not contain the principal-agent problem embedded in the debt-relief approach. The 1996 HIPC initiative, launched in response to the growing debt burden of the LDCs, had by 1999 lessened the debt of only seven of the identified 41 countries, leading the G8 at Cologne to authorise a much deeper and broader HIPC program. Yet, while at first glance this debt burden looms large, it must be considered against factors such as the long time frame for its repayment, its heavy concentration in principal rather than interest, the growth and inflation in the recipient economies, the way the initial loans have been allocated, the willingness of recipient governments to reform, and the stable and low share of short-term debt to total debt. In such a situation, neither the efficiency-enhancing argument, in its four dominant variants, nor the distributive rationales for debt relief are compelling. Rather, the key interest of the G8 lies in catalysing rapid and sustained growth in the LDCs. Here the key instruments are a greater opening to international trade on the part of the LDCs themselves and a co-ordinated effort in trade liberalisation, particularly in such sensitive areas as agriculture, on the part of the G8.

Christoph Schwegmann's Chapter 7 is titled 'Modern Concert Diplomacy: The Contact Group and the G7/8 in Crisis Management'. Schwegmann examines the concept of modern concert diplomacy and the impact of such diplomacy in recent regional crisis management. He contrasts the concept of modern concert diplomacy with other concepts of multilateral co-operation, especially international regimes and international organisations. He then assesses the role played by modern concert diplomacy in contemporary international relations by conducting a critical case study of great power diplomacy in Bosnia-Herzegovina and Kosovo within the framework of the Contact Group and the G7/8. On this basis, the chapter enriches the current understanding of the Contact Group's and the G8's role in ending the hostilities among the ethnic parties and in shaping the post-war order in Bosnia and Kosovo. It concludes by providing an outlook on future tasks and roles of concert diplomacy in general and in particular of the G7/8 in the management of violent international crises.

Schwegmann argues that concerts are institutions that rely on few informal rules and that serve mainly to co-ordinate policy. In this sense, concerts differ from international regimes and organisations explicitly established for a rule-guided management of international relations. His two critical cases confirm that the G7/8 and the Contact Group are both based on the same underlying logic, and demonstrate the use and effectiveness of modern concert diplomacy for high-security crisis management. Both were lightly institutionalised arenas for policy co-ordination among an exclusive group of powerful states that aimed to act as lead nations in the international community of states. Their reference to international principles, rules, and norms gave their efforts legitimacy in the eyes of outside states, while within the concert, the participation of the EU gave lesser states a substantive role. While both concerts were born of crisis, the willingness of their great-power founders to transfer subsequent activities to established international organisations shows how concerts reinforce the existing institutionalised order rather than replace it. In future crises, great-power management under a G8 flag rather than Contact Group flag would offer greater apparent legitimacy and place a regional crisis into a broader global context. But it would also give the unwanted impression that the G8 feels responsible for crisis management all over the world in ways that meet neither the G8's capacities nor its intentions.

In Chapter 8, Klemens Fischer takes up the question of globalism and regionalism from a European perspective by examining 'The G7/8 and the European Union'. For the purpose of analysing the complex relationship between the two institutions, he first compares international organisations such as the G8 to supranational organisations such as the EU. After a short overview of the structure of the EU, which is of particular interest for American and other non-European readers, Fischer investigates its relations with the G8. His focus is on those countries that are members of both organisations. For this purpose, he first analyses the role Germany played during its EU presidency and as host of both the European and the G8 summits. He concludes that Germany was a perfect host and honest broker. He then proceeds by comparing the outcome of both summits. His focus is on two policy fields treated by both the EU and by the G8: environmental policy and trade policy.

Fischer finds that whereas the EU goes further in the field of environmental policy than does the G8, it is the opposite for trade policy. The G8 tries to foster multilateral integration in particular by considering the least developed countries; the EU is careful in this respect. This result is not unexpected, given that the EU must struggle with structural change once the negotiation results of the Uruguay Round are translated into action. These differences, however, do not indicate that members of both the EU and the G8 are contradicting themselves, because the EU is much more responsible for economic policy than the G8. Thus within the G8 politicians are able to formulate long-term objectives without being immediately bound to them. This is not the case within the EU. Fischer concludes that membership in both international institutions poses no problem for European countries.

'Part III: New Directions in Global Governance' examines the evolution of global governance at the dawn of the twenty-first century, by looking at several central developments that are being generated by, or are affecting, the work of the G7/8. The first is the expansion of the G7's work on reforming the international financial system to a greater level of inclusiveness. This will be achieved through the creation, at Cologne, of a new G20 that embraces many of the world's consequential middle powers and emerging economies, and more broadly through the potential expansion of the G8 itself, with the recent call for and movement toward a closer, institutionalised association with China. The second is the advent of supranational governance on a regional basis, with the advent of the Euro in the EU and its impact on the process of G7 monetary and macroeconomic policy co-ordination. The third is the impact on actors, notably the way the G7 and bodies such as the OECD in the area of corporate governance, are affecting the work of international business with ever more directness and detail. The fourth is the much larger issue of whether the current course and cadence of globalisation and the global governance that guides it is sustainable.

These analyses commence with John J. Kirton's Chapter 9, 'The G20: Representativeness, Effectiveness, and Leadership in Global Governance'. Here Kirton examines the sudden and widespread moves at the end of the 1990s to expand the G7 through the creation of new forums for the governance of international finance. His focus is on the G20, the most important of these new fora and the one that some see as having the potential to supersede the G7 itself. He begins with a review of existing analyses of the fledgling G20 and explores the logical international institutional 'trilemma' of representativeness, effectiveness, and leadership that the G20 faces. He then examines the emergence of the New Arrangements to Borrow (NAB), the G22, the Financial Stability Forum (FSF), the Cologne Summit 'GX,' and the G20 itself. He proceeds to analyse the G20 during its initial year in operation, from the G20 deputies meeting in November 1999 through the December 1999 Berlin ministerial, the March 2000 deputies review session, the Washington IMF-World Bank, G7, and the IMF's International Monetary and Financial Committee (IMFC) meetings in April 2000, and planning for the October 2000 G20 Montreal ministerial. Kirton finally looks ahead to the future of the G20 and draws conclusions about its importance and role.

Kirton argues that the G20 is likely to become an effective and legitimate source of leadership, but only if its founding custodians give it the authority of leaders themselves and the full breadth, novelty, and ambition of the agenda that leaders demand. In any event, the G20 will remain important as a way of reinforcing the leadership and legitimacy of the G7/8 by ensuring that the latter's initiatives are understood and accepted by a broader group of consequential countries, and by ensuring that the G7/8 operates with richer sensitivity to the perspectives of the wider international community. The G20, more than its leading new institutional competitor — the IMFC — has the characteristics that will enable it to emerge as the key centre of legitimisation, sensitisation, and timely, well-targeted action and leadership in the emerging international system. Moreover, its current custodians show signs of forwarding the vision required to endow the G20 with the political authority and the broad, innovative, and ambitious agenda required to render it effective as a leading centre of global governance.

In Chapter 10, Martin J. G. Theuringer deals with 'International Macroeconomic Policy Co-operation in the Era of the Euro'. This chapter analyses how the introduction of the Euro and the third stage of the European Monetary Union (EMU) will affect the G7 process of macroeconomic policy co-operation, as seen through a German lens. Some argue that the EMU will make it even more difficult to reach explicit agreements within the G7 framework than before and that the European Central Bank (ECB) will have fewer incentives to participate in policy co-ordination than the Bundesbank did. Theuringer dismisses the arguments given by the European Commission in favour of more policy co-ordination. Following his analysis, G7 policy co-operation in the future will remain focused on exchange-rate targeting.

However, in contrast to widespread fears in Germany, Theuringer concludes that the European Commission's Ecofin Council will not be able to misuse the G7 to undermine the independence of the ECB via exchange-rate policy through Article 109(2) of the Maastricht Treaty. His argument is based on political economy considerations: the Ecofin Council has to act unanimously; its exchange-rate policy must consider the objective of price stability; and it is generally assumed that potential exchange-rate co-ordination will be rather loose, as with the Louvre accord.

In Chapter 11, 'The G7/8 and China: Toward a Closer Association', John J. Kirton begins with the call by Germany and Japan, the 1999 and 2000 G8 hosts, to include China in the annual G8 Summit. He examines in turn the scholarly and analytic debate over how far, by what formula, and on what logical foundation China should be associated with the G7/8, the changing attitude of G7/8 leaders to China from 1975 to the 1999, China's assistance in combating the 1997–99 global financial crisis and constructing a new international financial system, and China's role as an associate of the G7 in the new G22,

G20, and FSF. He concludes by specifying how the G7/8 should best move to associate with China in the near term.

Kirton argues that the existing debate among those who see China as an object, associate, or actual member of the G7/8 is tilting in favour of China's position as an associate, given the change in attitude of the G7/8 toward China from 1975 to 1999. China's responsible position in the 1997–99 financial crisis, its approach to international financial system reform in ways that co-incide with the position of some G7 members on some core issues, and its contribution to the G22, G20, and FSF warrant a move toward association with the G7/8 itself at the leaders level. The proper move, Kirton concludes, is to invite China's leader to join G8 leaders for a pre-Summit dinner dialogue.

In Chapter 12, Donald J. S. Brean examines 'Corporate Governance: International Perspectives'. He discusses the important question, just coming on to the agenda of the OECD and the G7, of whether globalisation has consequences for corporate governance, particularly as the growing number of mergers leads to an increase in multinational enterprises. This issue of corporate governance is one of increasingly direct and growing importance for the G7/8. For the past 15 years, the G7/8 has examined microeconomic matters with ever more attention and ever more detail, to the point where it has come to address the behaviour of large multinational firms themselves. The entire process of democratic and market transformation in Russia has come to depend importantly on inculcating a stable rule of law for companies, and fostering a corporate culture that gives investors and other stakeholders confidence that rational market-oriented behaviour is replacing the gangster capitalism of old. Similarly, as the analysis in Chapter 11 in this volume confirms, the global financial crisis of 1997–99 and the ensuing G7-led effort to create global codes of good conduct to govern the behaviour of financial institutions and other corporations in developing and emerging economies has brought the issue of corporate governance to centre stage (Kaiser, Kirton, and Daniels 2000). And the newer emphasis, from Cologne through Okinawa, on transparency and accountability, on combating money laundering and tax evasion, on having corporate behaviour promote the new priorities of human security, and on setting the rules to shape the information technology revolution has made corporate governance of core concern to the G8 over a broad policy terrain. The issue is growing beyond the consensus-oriented analysis of experts in the OECD into one requiring the political attention of G7 and G8 leaders themselves. Indeed, the global community is fast moving into an era where the G7/8 may emerge not only as an effective global centre of domestic governance but of corporate governance as well.

Given that both the culture of corporate control and the legal framework differs within multinationals and within the countries where they are based, there is a high probability of potential conflict among G8 countries over the issue of corporate governance. Brean first shows that poor corporate governance has serious consequences for the whole economy. In a second step, he distinguishes two different systems of corporate control, the market or outsider model versus the institutional or insider model. Brean concludes that the outsider model is superior to the insider model. He predicts that in future mergers the outsider model will increasingly dominate as the relevant model. However, as the empirical evidence proves, it is clear that an international merger is a very difficult undertaking with respect to corporate governance.

Although Chapter 12 refers to the process of global governance only indirectly, it gives rise to a very interesting comparison. If it is true that globalisation will lead to a widespread use of the outsider or market model of corporate control, a conclusion that seems very plausible, it may also be the case that globalisation will lead to an increase in the use of markets as a device for global governance. This would show that the relevant question in economic policy is not whether we need a neoliberal or a socially sensitive economic policy model but how to make a market-oriented economic system more socially sensitive.

In Chapter 13, 'Creating Sustainable Global Governance', Pierre Marc Johnson shows that the global agenda does not end with transnational corporations' behaviour, trade policy, and the financial architecture. Instead, other policy areas such as environmental and development policy as well as human rights are of vital interest. In particular, Johnson is convinced that these policies need to be treated through integrated international co-operation. In other words, he aims at a comprehensive strategy to meet all the objectives, partly by accepting their links among one another. Thus, he argues that, for example, trade and the environment cannot be treated separately. In addition to international organisations, civil society should participate in the relevant decision making.

By advocating a comprehensive agenda for global governance, Johnson favours harmonisation in a variety of policy areas, such as environmental standards. He also argues that the developing world should be equipped with more financial and technological resources to cope with the new — obviously high — environmental standards. Although not explicitly stated, he takes a long-run perspective. This chapter shows one way to a world with higher distributional justice, sustainable growth and democratic participation.

Part IV of the book, containing Chapter 14, offers a conclusion that integrates these chapters and the judgements they make in regard to the four central tasks identified at the outset of this introduction. Chapter 14 thus offers an overall assessment from the chapter contributors and the editors' own judgements of the degree, direction, and durability of the contribution made by the G7/8 at and after the Cologne Summit to new principles and processes of global governance, and how appropriate these are to the challenges faced by the international community at the outset of the twenty-first century. The concluding chapter also relates the legacy of Cologne to the agenda, process, and path to and through the Japanese-hosted Kyushu-Okinawa Summit in July 2000, in order to better assess the depth and sustainability of the new Cologne consensus.

The book ends with four appendices. The first is a statement by Helmut Schieber, president of the Land Central Bank in Baden-Württemberg and a member of the board of the Deutsche Bundesbank from 1992 to 2000, given at the Citizens Forum on the eve of the Cologne Summit, on 'New Challenges for the International Monetary System'. In his brief analysis, he notes several recent trends in the global economy — the growth of monetary aggregates, monetary turnover, financial integration, and financial volatility, which is much faster than the growth of the real economy. He argues that the resulting global systemic risks lend urgency to the task of creating resilient financial institutions, through such measures as international co-operation among prudential supervisors through the new FSF. There is a further need to adjust the current approach to capital account liberalisation and strengthen the role of the International Financial Institutions (IFIs) in crisis prevention and resolution. Their emphasis on promoting transparency and disclosure can do much to prevent crises, while a shift in emphasis from massive injections of financial aid to a catalytic role in organising private-sector participation is the key to successful crisis resolution.

The remaining three appendices contain several official documents of the Cologne Summit. These will allow the reader to check some of the judgements offered in this book, and explore other aspects of the changes initiated at Cologne.

Conclusions

As outlined in detail in the concluding chapter, the analyses contained in this volume offer a diverse and multidimensional array of views on the central questions of guiding global governance at the outset of the twenty-first century. The book thus demonstrates the quite different points of departure and perspectives on global order and the G8's role in it between currently mainstream economists and scholars of management studies on the one hand

and political scientists and scholars of law on the other. It reveals similar differences between analysts based in North America and those in Europe, and between established analysts of the G7/8 and a new generation of younger scholars taking up this subject for the first time.

Yet amidst these vigorous disagreements, it enriches the scholarly and policy debate in several ways. It provides detailed, innovative, empirically, and analytically grounded treatments that demonstrates the G7/8's very real accomplishments and impact in guiding global order. These accomplishments range from the realm of macroeconomic policy co-ordination, a subject that remains at the heart of the G7/8's work and promise, to the most fundamental issues of war and peace. This book is often sharply critical of the direction the G7/8 has set at Cologne. It thus features a lively debate between those endorsing the shift to a socially sensitive, safeguarded, and thus sustainable, more inclusive approach, and those challenging the credibility and wisdom of the new direction.

Above all, the analyses in this book reveal a considerable underlying faith in the role of the G7/8 as the central institutional system for guiding global order in the new era. They do so both directly, by explicit endorsement of the new directions set and new decisions taken at Cologne and, indirectly, by offering a multitude of recommendations about the new path the G7/8 system, broadly defined, is taking and should take in substantive policy and institutional process, in the coming years. In doing so they have advanced a scholarly and policy debate that contains one of the central analytical challenges of our times, and one on which the contributions of a widening circles of analysts and citizens are needed.

References

Cohen, Benjamin (1998), *The Geography of Money*, Cornell University Press, Ithaca, NY.

Dixit, Avinash (1996), *The Making of Economic Policy: A Transaction-Cost Politics Perspective*, MIT Press, Cambridge, MA.

Iversen, Torben (1999), *Contested Economic Institutions: The Politics of Macroeconomics and Wage Bargaining in Advanced Countries*, Cambridge University Press, Cambridge.

Kaiser, K., J. Kirton, and J. Daniels (eds.) (2000), *Shaping a New International Financial System: Challenges of Governance in a Globalizing World*, Ashgate, Aldershot.

Kirshner, Jonathan (1995), *Currency and Coercion: The Political Economy of International Monetary Power*, Princeton University Press, Princeton.

Kirton, J., and J. Daniels (1999), 'The Role of the G8 in the New Millennium', in M. Hodges, J. Kirton, and J. Daniels (eds.), *The G8's Role in the New Millennium*, Ashgate, Aldershot, pp. 3–17.

Laubach, Thomas, and Adam Posen (1997), *Disciplined Discretion: Monetary Targeting in Germany and Switzerland*, International Finance Section, Department of Economics, Prineton University, Princeton

Strange, Susan (1998), *Mad Money*, Manchester University Press, Manchester.

Part I
The Core Economic Issues

2 Internal Macroeconomic Policies and International Governance

ANDREAS FREYTAG[1]

Introduction

Today, international policy co-operation is perceived being important as never before in world politics. There is much hope that contemporary problems can be solved via co-operation and co-ordination. Economic policy is one such field, given that economic welfare is still distributed very unevenly among the different regions of the world. In addition, globalisation has contributed to a greater need for international co-operation. Consequently, an international meeting such as the G8 Summit is an appropriate opportunity to emphasise international co-operation. Some authors, such as John Kirton (1999), have great confidence in the effectiveness of the G8 process to co-ordinate economic and other policies. However, as Michael Hodges (1999, p. 69) has rightly put it, the 'G7/G8 is a forum, rather than an institution'. Obviously, different observers expect entirely different outcomes from international economic policy co-operation.

There are at least two ways to look at the G8 process. The first is to regard it as a kind of international economic fire brigade on hand every time a crisis occurs. This fire brigade requires discretionary power to intervene suitably. Several questions instantly come to mind. To name just two: who controls this fire brigade? Who pays for the interventions? The other way — probably the one Hodges had in mind — is to provide a set of rules, a framework for economic policy designed to stabilise expectations and, thereby, to smooth economic fluctuations.

According to Henning Klodt (1999), international co-operation makes sense in those policy areas where international spillovers are great and where there is a high degree of certainty about the effect of international co-operation on world-wide economic welfare. Klodt (p. 8) applies a system of co-ordinates (with four quadrants) with international spillovers in a very precise and appealing picture that effectively points to a first-best economic policy. Hence, Klodt derives very clear policy conclusions from this picture. Trade policy, competition policy, and global environmental policy are treated fruitfully

21

through international policy co-operation. Monetary policy, social policy, and local environmental policy are better left to domestic policymakers.

This chapter discusses the relationship between internal economic policy and international economic policy co-operation from a political economy, or positive, perspective. It argues that international co-operation can be very useful in disciplining governments that may be tempted to pursue destabilising macroeconomic policies or have already done so. For this purpose, the problem of sovereignty will be briefly discussed, followed by an explanation of how international policy co-operation is organised in commercial policy. Subsequently, some lessons for macroeconomic policies are drawn from these considerations and monetary policy is discussed, along with some general suggestions of how to incorporate the G8 process into this policy model.

The Issue of Sovereignty

The title of this book — 'Guiding Global Order' — touches on a very important issue, namely the issue of sovereignty. One of the main problems with international economic policy co-operation is that it normally ceases when national governments must give up large degrees of freedom in decision making. Governments are not partial to sharing their supremacy with foreign institutions, be it on a bilateral or on a multilateral level. Moreover, international co-operation may result in tradeoffs. In monetary policy, for instance, a fixed exchange rate system benefits all member countries, if they follow a similar monetary policy in regard to internal stability. For instance, under the Bretton Woods system, inflation in the United States was higher than that in Germany. There was constant pressure on the Deutschmark to appreciate. The Bundesbank was only able to keep the exchange rate stable by intervening on the market for foreign exchange, that is by buying U.S. dollars. This caused a rapid but unwelcome increase in the money supply, which was incompatible with the Bundesbank's policy objectives. In turn, Germany inflated more than it wished to. In this respect, its sovereignty was restricted. International policy co-operation demands a compromise.

However, governments only have limited sovereignty, regardless of whether they participate in international economic co-operation. Governments do not operate in isolation from society. Their power is restricted legally by rent-seeking activities. These activities cause governments to deviate from a rational and desirable economic policy and pursue a policy that is economically doubtful but politically rational. The reason for this deviation from first-best policies is that the ability to exert influence on the political process is distributed unevenly among pressure groups. The success of lobbies negatively correlates with the size of their membership, positively with the opportunity cost of lobbying (producers are more interested in high prices for their products than consumers are in low prices for these goods), and negatively with the ability of a sector to cope with structural change (Olson 1965, Freytag 1995). To summarise, in theory the most successful rent-seeking groups are the declining industries with a small number of big firms. This proposition normally holds even if the government is determined to pursue an economic policy that does not favour some groups at the expense of others. There is overwhelming empirical evidence for this view both in commercial policy and in macroeconomic policy. Thus, internal economic policy also demands a compromise.

Obviously, there is a dilemma: a deviation from a first-best solution is politically appealing. International governance forces decisions upon governments that regularly result in trade-offs between the external policy objective and the internal target. National governance is also unable to meet economic policy objectives because of logic of the political market. How can this dilemma be solved? An adequate solution should combine the advantages of international co-operation and domestic governance. It requires looking for a way to give international economic policy co-operation a long-term perspective that would enable governments to regain sovereignty domestically as well as externally.

The Use of International Co-operation in Commercial Policy

International policy co-operation and co-ordination both have their merits. One particular function of international policy co-operation is not at the centre of public debate, although it is the most important, if not the only relevant, function. This is the use of international policy co-ordination as a way to protect citizens from their government. Through international policy co-operation, a government can be forced to pursue policies that are in the best interests of the country as a whole by giving that government the possibility of declining the demands of special interest groups. International commercial policy after World War II has implicitly taken this route. Governments can apply the Most Favoured Nations (MFN) principle and extend national treatment to foreign suppliers of goods and services within the framework of the General Agreement on Tariffs and Trade (GATT) and its successor, the

World Trade Organization (WTO), thus guaranteeing their citizens the right to make their purchases where they desire. Of course, unilateral free trade would be sufficient, but there is always the danger that it is reversed when industries that produce goods that compete with the imports — being unwilling or unable to adjust to structural change — lobby for trade barriers (Kawamoto 1997, p. 90f). According to the WTO, an open market can be secured by a reciprocal and multilateral agreement.

However, the GATT's success story is not complete. The principle of reciprocity has caused a somewhat mercantilist atmosphere to prevail in trade policies. Despite its generally beneficial effects, to open the domestic markets for foreign competition is nearly always and everywhere perceived as a concession (Krugman 1997). This tendency has led Jan Tumlir in his writings to promote a domestic underpinning of international agreements. His argument is based on the distinction between two concepts: the concept of the 'international' economy versus the concept of the global economy. The former concept interprets international economic activities as an exchange between countries that are seen merely as spots, as opposed to the latter where international exchange takes place between individuals. Following this approach, there is no methodological difference between international activities and intranational economic ones. Whereas the former demands international governance, the latter works with domestic governance and was favoured by Tumlir. As a consequence, he suggests laying down the MFN principle as a civil right in the domestic constitution and giving the citizens the right to take their government to court if it does not adhere to the international treaties it has concluded.[2] Governments would thus regain internal sovereignty toward domestic interest groups. Free trade and open markets become both politically and economically rational. The basic argument can be transferred to macroeconomic policy as well.

Application to Macroeconomic Policies

The 1990s have witnessed a variety of macroeconomic crises all over the world. In general, the problem of systematically bad macroeconomic performance is caused neither by foreign powers nor by inadequately co-ordinated international policy. Permanently high levels of inflation or unemployment can always be traced back to poor domestic macroeconomic policies,[3] either because of a lack of policy instruments (i.e., the Tinbergen rule[4] is not obeyed) or because of a dynamic inconsistency that enables policymakers to deviate from an announced policy target after the public has reacted to the announcement. Again, the problem for policymakers is rooted in the character of political markets. Inflation, for instance, can create a political business cycle that increases the chances of the government in charge to win the next election. Dynamic inconsistency can be overcome by credible commitment to a certain policy or policy regime (Blackburn and Christensen 1989). There are several ways to make a credible commitment, for example, implementing an internationally co-ordinated economic policy. Renegotiating it would mean breaking international agreements.

From this perspective, international economic policy co-operation can be used to support the government in its attempt to pursue an economically sound domestic economic policy. The international agreement or organisation plays the role of a scapegoat that can be made responsible for unpopular but efficient policy measures. The government can overcome special interests by arguing that the policy measure in question is part of a package deal that benefits the country as a whole. Thus, criticism is due to the international agreement or organisation. Put another way, the latter is doing the 'dirty work' for the domestic government (Vaubel 1991).[5]

This logic has been applied regularly to those countries facing a financial crisis. The International Monetary Fund (IMF) normally gives support only conditionally, after a government has agreed on a reform package or at least certain clearly defined elements of macroeconomic policy. Only after the willingness to pursue a sounder macroeconomic policy has been explained (but, unfortunately, not proven), are IMF funds granted. Thus, the government can avoid the pressure groups and give the impression that the IMF has forced the adoption of the new policy regime. However, the G8 process of international policy co-ordination is not only helpful to countries facing severe macroeconomic problems; it is also useful for helping the G8 countries themselves co-ordinate macroeconomic policies. This co-ordination must pay attention to the fact that bad macroeconomic performance is caused by domestic policy failure rather than by international phenomena. As a consequence, policy co-ordination means agreeing on policy rules.[6] For instance, monetary policy rules can be co-ordinated so that as a result of the rules, not of any interventions, exchange-rate fluctuations shrink.

This well-known function of international macroeconomic policy co-operation can even be improved when the government commits itself not only externally but also internally. A rule in international macroeconomic co-ordination along the lines of Tumlir's suggestion in trade policy first means that countries internationally agree upon an economic policy framework committed to stability. Second, this framework must be made a legal provision in each country, giving the citizens the right to sue the government if it does not follow the agreement. This would certainly strengthen the commitment to stability and would be a strong disincentive to favour certain interest groups at the expense of others. It would not, on the other hand, deprive the government of the necessary flexibility to react to shocks. Thus, as in commercial policy, the international track is a device to protect the public from its own government in the sense that the government is forced to pursue policies that are in the interests of the economy as a whole. There may be a great deal of support within a country to implement Tumlir's rule because citizens today agree on an economic order that may offer an uncertain distributive outcome but is regarded as being fair. *Ex ante*, everyone can support this order. Once there are distribution effects, rent-seeking activities will alter this outcome.

It must be emphasised that there is no need for international co-operation to introduce this rule domestically. Every country can implement the constitutional right of compliance with international treaties on its own. Unilateral implementation has a great advantage: one central argument against Tumlir's rule is that the scope of international treaties may be considerably restricted as governments want to generate or keep discretionary power. This danger cannot be ruled out if the introduction of this rule is subject to 'international' co-operation and negotiation. However, this danger can be mitigated through unilateral action.

The Example of Monetary Policy

Monetary policy is a good example of the useful interaction of domestic policies and international macroeconomic co-operation. The two main motives for inflation acknowledged in the literature are the employment motive and the revenue motive (Cukierman 1992, chapters 3 and 4, Newlyn 1962, pp. 148–166). Monetary policymakers are seen as individuals with personal interests (Persson and Tabellini 1990). These interests are incorporated in an objective function of the following general form:

$$Z = f\,(\pi, N, S, ...)$$
$${-}\;\;{+}\;{+}$$

Z denotes the utility of the policymaker, p, the rate of inflation, N stands for employment, and S denotes seigniorage. The policymaker is assumed to maximise Z with respect to p.[7] Thus, it can be taken for granted that, in most cases, inflation is created deliberately by governments that apply monetary policy to achieve objectives other than those monetary ones that are part of Z.[8] Obviously, such policymakers lack policy instruments or face distortions so that these objectives cannot be met without the help of monetary policy.

Under the employment motive, the government makes use of the assumed 'money illusion' among a public that does not immediately recognise the inflationary surprise. If this is true, the supply of labour will then rise and employment will increase and a short-run Phillips curve relation exists. Especially before a general election, it would seem attractive sometimes to practise monetary expansion in order to create a political business cycle.[9] To put it differently, policymakers act as if they believe in the 'money illusion' of the public (Mueller 1989, p. 286). B. McCallum (1997) suggests that a considerable part of the inflation from the 1960s through the 1980s can be explained by the widespread belief among politicians in a negatively sloped Phillips curve. Inflation on grounds of the employment motive of policymakers can lead to more employment through two channels. One is adaptive expectations, that is, the public forms expectations only by considering the past. If the government raises inflation every year, the public never will be able to expect next year's inflation rate properly. Thus, employment will remain above its natural level.

However, the adaptive expectation hypothesis has only limited explanatory power. Assuming rational expectations, instead, leads to the second channel of inflation. The policymaker has private information about the economic environment and about her or his own attitude and properties that the public does not have. In this case, it might be possible to cheat the public, at least in the short run.[10] Theoretical analyses and empirical observation suggest that monetary policy is an inappropriate means to raise employment permanently. In other words: the long-run Phillips curve is not negatively sloped (e.g., Friedman 1987, p. 25f; Broaddus 1995).

The second motive for policymakers is their inability to balance the public sector's budget. Especially in countries with hyperinflation, a high and persistent fiscal deficit, in other words the urgent need for seigniorage, has contributed chiefly to inflation. Other sources of revenue are insufficient or expenditure is too extensive to be covered by revenues. Therefore, it becomes necessary to finance public expenditures via monetary expansion. This is usually done by using credit from the central bank to fill the gap between expenditures and revenues. The revenues generated through monetary expansion are usually called seigniorage.

Both enhancing employment and revenue seeking via monetary policy depend on the formation of public expectations. A public that forms adaptive expectations can be misled for a longer period. Otherwise, monetary expansion has no real stimulative effects. As long as the public anticipates every monetary expansion correctly, only prices for commodities and factors will change. That is the economy will be neither positively nor negatively affected. But it is rather improbable that the public will be able to foresee the effects of expansive monetary policy correctly. It is especially difficult to incorporate every future surprise inflation into long-term lending contracts, for example. Thus, inflation is very harmful for economic prospects.

Under rational expectations, monetary policy announcements may not be credible due to time inconsistency. The core of a dynamic inconsistency problem is the following: the government announces a certain policy in period t for the following period $(t + 1)$, which is optimal from its point of view. After the announcement, the public reacts by choosing wage contracts. These reactions cause the initially announced policy to become sub-optimal in period $t + 1$ from the government's standpoint. The government, therefore, has an incentive to deviate from the initially announced policy (Kydland and Prescott 1977, Calvo 1978). Monetary policy becomes endogenous in the political process. If the government indeed chooses an inflation rate that differs from the declared one, the public will no longer trust the government's policy announcements. It will become even more difficult to reach stability.

These remarks indicate that inflation is a purely domestic problem caused only by governmental failure. At this point commitment enters the fray. The public can be protected from being exploited by the government through a commitment by the government to pursue a rule-based monetary policy. A credible commitment causes political costs for the government if it does not stick to its announced policy rule. Thus, such a commitment enables the government to resist pressures to increase money growth beyond the economically justified path, thus keeping in line with the quantity theory of money.

Monetary policy does not affect foreign countries, at least not in the medium or long run. Therefore, without any significant spillovers, there seems to be no argument for international economic policy co-operation (Klodt 1999). Nevertheless, there is a case for international action. Commitments can be made credible in two ways: first, the government signs an international agreement to pursue a monetary policy dedicated to stability. This commitment could be either made unilaterally, namely in the case that the country is suffering from high inflation in the recent past. Or it could be made multilaterally: many governments recognise the need for monetary stability but feel unable to pursue it unless backed by an international agreement. To make sense, however, the agreement should not be directed at a certain exchange rate, interest rate difference, or other target variable, no matter how vaguely formulated. It should rather focus on policy rules. Governments should agree on a certain monetary regime, for instance creating a central bank system with certain minimum elements. Second, the commitment can be fixed internally by giving the citizens the right to sue the government in case it does deviate from the international agreement. Tumlir's rule can be formulated very generally, by specifying that it holds for any international agreement the government has concluded. It should be laid down in the constitution.

To be sure, both elements can be used on their own. Either the government commits domestically to an independent central bank with or without a nominal anchor, or it fixes the monetary regime externally without domestic backing on a constitutional level. However, empirical evidence suggests that the pressures by special interests, including the government's own interests, can become overwhelming. By committing both internationally and domestically, the country's citizens can effectively be protected from governmental failure.

What Can the G8 Do to Improve Monetary Policy at Home and Elsewhere?

For a considerable time now the G7 countries have not had monetary problems that would require external co-operation with domestic constitutional backing. Other countries have suffered from high inflation, including Russia. Yet, there have been increasing efforts to combat inflation all over the world in the 1990s, some of them successful, others not. Not surprisingly, this experience shows that a credible commitment plays a crucial role in reducing inflation.

The G8 could trigger disinflation in the world by providing a framework for monetary policy that binds member countries and that can be voluntarily adapted by others. This framework could be interpreted as an open standard that could contain the commitment to guarantee a high degree of central bank independence, to use monetary policy only for the objective of price stability, to require some transparency, and so on. There are three considerable advantages for the G8 in this approach: first, the process would demonstrate political leadership on an important policy issue. Second, the political cost for the G7 would be zero, because its members' central bank statutes and laws already contain these elements; Russia is a little different and still must improve its central bank law. Third, such a standard would raise the political costs of abusing monetary policy for other objectives, even in G8 countries. The main advantage, however, is that other countries in which the credibility of monetary commitment has recently been low could use this standard as an anchor. They could thus increase the credibility of their monetary policy and lower future inflation remarkably.

In addition to this possible G8 initiative, such a standard could be backed domestically by introducing Tumlir's rule for any international treaties, both inside and outside the G8. This track, however, is left to national constitutional decision making. If both tracks are followed, an international agreement launched by the political and economic powers in the world can protect citizens in the rest of the world from the misbehaviour of their governments.

Notes

1 Helpful comments by Stefan Mai are gratefully acknowledged.
2 For an overview, see Sally (1998, chapter 8) as well as Freytag and Sally (2000). See also Tumlir (1979, 1983, 1984, 1985).
3 This does not necessarily exclude the possibility that short-term fluctuations are caused internationally.
4 To solve the problem of determination, Tinbergen (1952) demands one policy instrument for each economic policy objective.
5 Schneider and Wagner (1999) even suggest delegating monetary policy to an international organisation.
6 This reasoning also holds for microeconomic policy. Take the recommendations of the *Basle Capital Accord*, which forms a minimum standard of rules, and the Köln Charter, 'Aims and Ambitions for Lifelong Learning', which is not justified by any international spillovers.
7 The arguments in the objective function can be interpreted as proxies for the utility of the policymaker in charge. A policymaker's personal utility may depend on being in office or on the preferences of her or his constituencies (Alesina and Tabellini 1988).
8 This is a very crude and general description of monetary policy. For a more detailed analysis, see the papers in Mayer (1990), especially the contribution by Hetzel (1990).
9 See Belke (1996, pp. 7–157) for a comprehensive overview. See also Alesina and Tabellini (1988).
10 For a survey on this strand of literature, see Alesina and Tabellini (1988, pp. 543–546).

References

Alesina, A., and G. Tabellini (1988), 'Credibility and Politics', *European Economic Review*, pp. 542–550.

Belke, A. (1996), *Politische Konjunkturzyklen in Theorie und Empirie: Eine kritische Analyse der Zeitreihendynamik in Partisan-Ansätzen*, Mohr, Tübingen.

Blackburn, K., and M. Christensen (1989), 'Monetary Policy and Policy Credibility: Theories and Evidence', *Journal of Economic Literature*, vol. 27, pp. 1–45.

Calvo, G. (1978), 'On the Time Consistency of Optimal Policy in a Monetary Economy', *Econometrica*, vol. 46, pp. 1411–1428.

Cukierman, A. S. (1992), *Central Bank Strategy, Credibility, and Independence: Theory and Evidence*, MIT Press, Cambridge, MA.

Freytag, A. (1995), 'The European Market for Protectionism: New Competitors and New Products', in L. Gerken (ed.), *Competition among Institutions*, Macmillan, Houndmills, pp. 231–258.

Freytag, A., and R. Sally (forthcoming), 'Globalisation and Trade Policy: 1900 and 2000 Compared', *Jahrbuch für Neue Politische Ökonomie*, vol. 19, Mohr Siebeck, Tübingen.

Hetzel, R. L. (1990), 'The Political Economy of Monetary Policy', in T. Mayer (ed.), *The Political Economy of American Monetary Policy*, Cambridge University Press, Cambridge, pp. 99–114.

Hodges, M. (1999), 'The G8 and the New Political Economy', in M. Hodges, J. Kirton, and J. Daniels (eds.), *The G8's Role in the New Millennium*, Ashgate, Aldershot, pp. 69–73.

Kawamoto, A. (1997), 'A Regulatory Reform on the International Trade Policy Agenda', *Journal of World Trade Law*, vol. 31, no. 4.

Kirton, J. (1999), 'Explaining G8 Effectiveness', in M. Hodges, J. Kirton, and J. Daniels (eds.), *The G8's Role in the New Millennium*, Ashgate, Aldershot, pp. 45–68.

Klodt, H. (1999), *Internationale Politikkoordination: Leitlinien für den globalen Wirtschaftspolitiker*, Institut für Weltwirtschaft, Kiel.

Krugman, P. A. (1997), 'What Should Trade Negotiators Negotiate About?', *Journal of Economic Literature*, vol. 35, pp. 113–120.

Kydland, F., and C. Prescott (1977), 'Rules Rather Than Discretion: The Inconsistency of Optimal Plans', *Journal of Political Economy*, vol. 85, pp. 473–491.

Mayer, T. (ed.) (1990), *The Political Economy of American Monetary Policy*, Cambridge University Press, Cambridge.

McCallum, B. T. (1997), 'Crucial Issues Concerning Central Bank Independence', *Journal of Monetary Economics*, vol. 39, pp. 99–112.

Newlyn, W. T. (1962), *Theory of Money*, Clarendon Press, Oxford.

Olson, M. (1965), *The Logic of Collective Action*, Harvard University Press, Cambridge, MA.

Persson, T., and G. Tabellini (1990), *Macroeconomic Policy, Credibility, and Politics*, Harwood, Chur, Switzerland.

Sally, R. (1998), *Classical Liberalism and International Economic Order: Studies in Theory and Intellectual History*, Routledge, London.

Schneider, F., and A. Wagner (1999), The Role of International Monetary Institutions after the EMU and after the Asian Crisis: Some Preliminary Ideas Using Constitutional Economics, Paper presented at the Annual Meeting of the Public Choice Society, New Orleans, 13–15 March.

Tinbergen, J. (1952), *On the Theory of Economic Policy*, North-Holland, Amsterdam.

Tumlir, J. (1979), 'The New Protectionism, Cartels and the International Order', in R. C. Amacher, G. Haberler, T. D. Willett (eds.), *Challenges to a Liberal International Economic Order*, American Enterprise Institute, Washington DC, 1979.

Tumlir, J. (1983), 'International Economic Order and Democratic Constitutionalism', *ORDO* 34, pp. 71–83.

Tumlir, J. (1984), *Economic Policy as a Constitutional Problem*, Institute of Economic Affairs, London.

Tumlir, J. (1985), *Protectionism: Trade Policy in Democratic Societies*, American Enterprise Institute, Washington DC.

Vaubel, R. (1991), 'A Public Choice View of International Organizations', in R. Vaubel and T. D. Willett (eds.), *The Political Economy of International Organizations*, Westview Press, Boulder, CO, pp. 27–45.

3 Challenges for the Global Financial System

JUERGEN B. DONGES AND PETER TILLMANN

Introduction

Since the 1998 G8 Summit in Birmingham, the world economy has produced some remarkable accomplishments. Economic growth in the United States has continued to be strong. The Euro has been successfully launched in 11 countries in the European Union. Inflation has remained low. Furthermore, the globalisation of production and capital markets has proceeded. This has given an additional push to trade in goods and services and to international investment. But there is one major outstanding challenge: to secure global financial stability. Meetings such as the G8 Summit in Cologne in 1999 are frequently seen as a vehicle to achieve this goal through co-ordinated national action and enhanced international co-operation.

Recent financial and currency crises in emerging countries have made it dramatically clear that there is still a lack of knowledge about the causes and consequences of financial turmoil. In particular, in spite of the extensive research that has been carried out in this field, questions about why crises emerge, how they spread to other countries, whether they can be predicted and prevented, and how they can be managed are not yet adequately answered.

If a financial crisis in tightly linked international markets is not limited to one region and, consequently, the rise in unemployment and the fall of real income are not restricted to the latter but can be observed in other economies as well, there arises the question of how and where economic policy should intervene to prevent such developments. The answer is not a simple one. There is confusion about the responsibility for the financial crises. Should the national governments be made liable and forced to solve their problems without assistance or should international organisations such as the World Bank or the International Monetary Fund (IMF) react to fight the negative effects of the crises? Some politicians have asserted that national economic policy does not have enough capacity to influence developments given the volume and the pace of international capital flows in a globalised market. This is definitely not true. Globalisation does not weaken national policy. Rather, globalisation pressures governments to shape an efficient and sustainable policy mix so that credibility in capital markets can be (re-)established.

Given these realities, this chapter provides an overview of the main tasks that the G8 leaders might face at future summits. It offers some brief guidelines for dealing with the current agenda of international finance.

The Concept of Good Governance

Every country, including each industrialised one, is called upon to try to protect itself autonomously from failure in its economic policy, as well as to pay attention to the requirement of consistent and sound economic policy. This is the prerequisite for the axiom of so-called 'good governance'. Corresponding to the recent development and acceptance of the concept of good governance, emerging market countries must take the following items into account.

Monetary policy plays a leading role. It must be a policy designed to implement price stability as investors react sensitively to excessive and — above all — volatile inflation rates. Trust in monetary policy cannot be enforced; it must be earned. Support by a prudent fiscal policy is of utmost importance and requires that public spending be kept at a rate that can be financed without creating capital market turmoil. Governments that allow public debt to increase beyond levels of sustainability may be tempted to put pressure on the central bank to accelerate monetary growth so that inflation will eventually reduce the real burden of that debt. Furthermore, wage policy must accomplish the goal of price stability by enforcing collective agreements that keep the total labour costs per worker at a constant level. The institutional measure to discipline fiscal and wage policy is to grant the central bank independence from governmental intervention and to set rules to enforce a stability-oriented policy.

A second issue of good governance involves the exchange rate regime: Pegging the domestic currency to a stable foreign currency with unrestricted capital flows may be a possibility for making a stability-oriented economic policy more credible. Credibility can also be achieved by the instalment of a currency board regime (as in Argentina) or even by full dollarization (as Ecuador is striving for), provided the pegging currency can pursue its economic policy in harmony with the policies abroad.

Before a decision on the exchange rate regime can be made, one must examine whether a system of fixed exchange rates can deal with speculative attacks or withstand conflicts between domestic and foreign macroeconomic goals. Nothing could be worse for the credibility of economic policy than the creation of an illusion of a fixed exchange rate being riskless. The collapse of a currency would shatter the trust of citizens and investors in the future prospects of the economy, especially if the government tried to counteract the depreciation of the home currency with a marked interest rate rise or a restriction of capital outflows.

High interest rates interfere with economic activity. A sudden restriction of the convertibility of the national currency cuts the country off from foreign direct investment, as the national currency turns out to be what Wilhelm Röpke terms a 'mousetrap currency' (Röpke 1954). There is always the possibility that a fixed exchange rate could not be sustained in a crisis. In this case the exchange rate should fluctuate from the beginning or at least as soon as a crisis looms. An example of this path is Taiwan's policy in autumn 1998. Taiwan was not infected by the currency turbulence in the region, as the possibility of riskless foreign exchange speculation against the central bank was entirely ruled out.

In the context of the principles of good governance, transparency in the banking sector is indispensable. Financial intermediaries must not expect automatic and unlimited assistance from the government, i.e., the central bank, in case of a liquidity crisis. Otherwise problems of moral hazard occur due to asymmetric information. Insolvent banks should be able to go bankrupt. This strengthens the credibility of a country's economic policy and is necessary both so that the banks can calculate the risks of loans and financial investments very carefully and so that the depositors can pay thorough attention to the differences in the solvency of individual institutions. Governments of industrialised countries must resist the temptation of offering guarantees to their banks for investing in emerging countries. Such precautions should be taken within the financial system before the flow of capital to and from emerging countries is liberalised. Then the national financial position would be less vulnerable to speculative attacks from abroad.

The New Features of the 1997–99 Crises

The 1997–99 financial and currency crises in a number of Asian countries and in Russia and Brazil are not unique. Such crises occur from time to time. The 1970s witnessed the collapse of the Bretton Woods system of fixed exchange rates. The 1980s saw the world debt crises start in Poland and Mexico and then spread through Latin America and beyond. The early 1990s saw the crisis of the European Monetary System (EMS) (just after the Treaty of Maastricht was agreed on), forcing Italy and the United Kingdom to leave the Exchange Rate Mechanism (ERM). The mid 1990s were shaken again by an exchange market turmoil, this time in Mexico.

Financial crises that begin locally can quickly become global. In the changing context of globalisation, capital markets tend to react rapidly with the help of continuous improvements in payment technologies and information technology. This is indeed something new. Moreover, international investors have become much more selective in choosing potential countries to invest in. There is a trend toward short-term thinking in capital flows. Financial innovations (such as derivatives) create significant leverage in the international financial system, in particular when business is done beyond regulatory jurisdictions (for example, in offshore centres or on the cross-border internet). There is a continuous referendum in capital markets about the credibility of economic policies. Bad policies are punished sooner or later by a withdrawal of capital and a substantial depreciation of the home currency (often overshooting its future equilibrium level) and a risk premium on interest rates for government bonds. Deteriorating macroeconomic fundamentals (particularly the inconsistency between monetary and fiscal policies and the official exchange rate as pointed out by first-generation crisis models) are relevant. So too are structural deficiencies such as rigidities in goods and labour markets (which do not allow the economy to adjust smoothly to external shocks) and weak financial structures with inadequate regulatory and prudential supervision, as international investors seem to be prone to herd behaviour.

Against this background of globalisation, the ongoing discussion on strengthening the international financial architecture has become very prominent in political and academic circles (Kaiser, Kirton, and Daniels 2000). In February 1999, the G7 countries established the Financial Stability Forum to work out ideas on how to deal with challenges for the financial system (Tietmeyer 1999). The question is not whether future financial crises can be avoided once and for all. This is not possible, as no government can cope with every turbulence. Conventional early warning indicators, important as they are, do not always give the right signals (e.g., Berg and Patillo 1998). Second-generation crisis models emphasise the role of the switching expectations of a regime shift and of the sunspots that serve as a co-ordination mechanism of these expectations. Jeanne (1997) and Obstfeld (1996) show that the potential occurrence of crises are, to a certain extent, unrelated to a country's fundamentals. Reliable early warning indicators will thus not be at hand in the near future. It is therefore essential to consider strategies that are capable of minimising the inherent risks.

Minimising the Risk of New Crisis Creation and Contagion

To reduce the risk of new crises emerging and then spreading to other countries ('contagion effects'), three main responses are required.

Transparency and Accountability

First, greater transparency and accountability are needed, so that all relevant financial market information can be analysed comprehensively and systematically by investors (when assessing and pricing the risk), by national regulatory authorities (when monitoring developments in banking, insurance, and securities) and by governments (when shaping policies). There should be open communication on polices across the world. It is important to know what others do. But there is no reason to have formal international co-ordination of monetary and fiscal policies, either at G8 Summits or in other places.

It is not helpful when, at the start of a crisis, governments react with rigorous restrictions on capital outflows (e.g., Malaysia) and one-sided debt moratoria (e.g., Russia). These only cure the symptoms. The root of the problem is ignored and, as experience shows, capital flight is not restrained — indeed, it is even accelerated. Far worse, investors receive the negative signal that comprehensive economic and institutional reforms are not to be expected. The result is an additional loss of confidence, making the way out of the crisis increasingly difficult, quite apart from the future costs to be carried by the country in case it wants to regain access to international capital markets. The results are high-risk premiums and a lower credit rating compared to countries that solved the crisis reasonably well.

There is consensus at the political level as well as among scholars that industrialised countries must also play a role in stabilising the financial system. This seems clear when exogenous shocks to emerging economies originate in industrialised countries. In this context the financial crisis looming in Japan for years and the repeated devaluation of the yen probably were important aspects in the development of crisis expectations in neighbouring countries such as China and South Korea, which kept their currencies pegged. Moreover, there are areas of responsibility for the industrialised countries stemming from self-interest. In general, economic policy must produce a suitable framework for sustained economic growth. This includes the openness of international trade according to the principles of multilateralism, non-discrimination, and Most Favoured Nation treatment set out in the General Agreement on Tariffs and Trade (GATT) and the World Trade Organization (WTO). They give incentives to emerging market countries to specialise according to their comparative advantage. Opening markets and liberalising trade in the industrialised countries are essential aspects in an internationally co-ordinated approach to the stability of the financial system.

Efficient Banking Regulation

Second, the world needs a banking system with a sound structure. Prudential regulation and supervision are of primary importance. Substantial improvement is required in emerging economies. The Core Principles for Effective Banking Supervision set out by the Bank for International Settlements can be used as a guideline (see Folkerts-Landau and Lindgren 1998). Existing systems for banking regulation must suit dynamic financial innovation and must be supplemented with transparent decision structures.

In terms of the principles of good governance discussed above, such rules in financial systems should be established before the capital market is liberalised. The national financial system would then be more resistant to speculative attacks and vulnerability to self-fulfilling bank runs would be reduced. When liberalisation takes place too fast, as was the case in a few emerging countries struck by financial crises, the national government must rapidly establish a solid framework for the banking sector. Imposing capital controls is the wrong therapy.

The right incentives must be set for banks operating internationally. Governments of industrialised countries must withstand the temptation of assisting national private banks operating in emerging market countries that are in financial trouble. Such assistance cannot but create moral hazard and put a burden on taxpayers. The principles of competence and responsibility in the market economy must be fully respected. On the one hand, banks can profit from advantageous decisions about allocating credits or investments in emerging market countries. On the other hand, they must not escape the consequences of their mistakes. For this reason, private lenders must definitely be involved in the mechanisms of crisis management. If borrowers default, credit claims must be written off.

Since the crisis in Asia, it is a known fact that the credit and market risks in emerging economies are high in comparison with others. They can instantly turn virulent. Furthermore, the possibility of spillover effects is very high in a system of fixed exchange rates and interdependent financial markets. Hence, private banks must carefully choose which countries to operate in and weigh the risks appropriately. They can protect themselves against losses by imposing proper risk premiums. Competent risk management should be able to produce a thoroughly diversified portfolio, especially in emerging countries.

The Role of the International Monetary Fund

Recently, the role of the IMF in surveillance, crises prevention, and crisis resolution has become the central focus in the discussion. After the Asian crisis, the IMF was criticised by all sides. One of the main points of criticism was the fact that it had offered financial help too fast and without consulting others, thus acted as a lender of last resort, although the systemic risk of a breakdown of the world economy was negligible.

Another major point of disapproval was that macroeconomic programmes of austerity were imposed throughout the region hit by the crisis. This happened in spite of the fact that conventional crisis indicators such as high public deficits and inflation rates were not viewed as the main underlying sources of the problem, even if economic growth had already slowed down. The criticism was based on the continuing currency speculation after reforms were announced and internal civil unrest broke out due to increasing unemployment and a massive loss in real income (especially in Indonesia).

What conclusions can be drawn from these criticisms? The most radical answer is to abolish the IMF completely. This would overcome the problem of moral hazard and would avoid conflicts with the claim to sovereignty of national governments in economic policy. Yet, there is no answer to the question of what the international financial order would then be based on. Globalisation neither makes international institutions unnecessary nor requires new regional institutions to prevent financial turbulence.

The pragmatic answer is to force the IMF to assume a surveillance and catalytic function only. Such surveillance would consist of running a detailed analysis of countries on the macroeconomic level and incorporating the economies' institutional framework on a microeconomic level. The results and the economic recommendations made by the IMF should be published in order to stabilise private-sector expectations.

The catalytic function would consist of proposing an adequate solution in case of a crisis and co-ordinating the completion of the ensuing restructuring and adjustment programs with governments, banks, and private investors. The

IMF could preserve its resources in the future and secure a sufficient disbursement capacity with the given credit facilities. Thus the catalytic role can be accomplished efficiently. Rules must be laid out beforehand, obliging participants (especially private investors) to take over joint financial responsibility.

In no case should the IMF act as a lender of the last resort. Doing so would give way to moral hazard on the part of both governments in emerging market countries and international investors. Moreover, contrary to a national central bank, which can print money, the IMF will always have only limited resources at its disposal and could easily run out of funds if it overextends its lending activities. This would deepen the problem. Whenever financial rescue operations are required, the IMF should bear only the absolutely necessary part of the rescue package. Other large parts would have to be borne by private agents and the governments concerned. IMF emergency loans should be provided at an interest rate above the market rate and be collateralised to the largest extent possible.

The Tobin Tax and Target-Zone Proposals

In the discussions of the financial and currency crises, two proposals appear time and again: the Tobin tax on capital flows and the adoption of target zones for exchange rates (see, for example, Davanne and Jacquet 2000). Both are badly flawed ideas.

The Tobin tax constitutes a 'therapy' of merely dealing with the symptoms of the trouble. Beyond that, the distinction between 'good' and 'bad' capital flows beforehand is simply not possible to make, as Claessens, Dooley, and Warner (1995), amongst others, have shown empirically. Apart from this, the tax would be followed by allocative distortions on capital markets if it is not implemented multilaterally. It would mean a major setback, especially for emerging economies competing for internationally mobile portfolio capital and foreign direct investment. If the tax is ignored (which should not be difficult considering recent financial innovations), the inefficiency can be identified directly in the volume of the administrative costs.

Two points can be advanced against the concept of an exchange-rate target zone. One is the fundamental technical problem of determining equilibrium exchange rates. How should such an exchange rate be computed? When should it be adjusted? There is hardly a field where the knowledge is so far from being complete as in the field of equilibrium exchange rates. The other point of concern is that credible target zones require not only synchronous business cycles and homogeneous policy targets among countries but also a readiness to defend the parity against every sort of attack. In reality, however, the defence of the peg can severely endanger the aim of price stability, which must be neglected in order to defend the parity. Drafting currency reform rules with an immense 'pretence of knowledge', to use Friedrich von Hayek's (1974) phrase, leads to what Otmar Issing (1996) terms an 'illusion of co-ordination'. It can hardly be seen as a policy to restrain financial crises in the future. The only promising way to secure stability in international capital flows and currency relations is to stabilise expectations in the market via a consistent and coherent economic policy at home. Such expectations on the part of global financial markets can be channelled institutionally by functioning banking supervision and co-operation among the supervisory authorities of all the countries, including the emerging markets. International regulation need not be increased and autonomous self-regulation of the financial sector need not be reduced.

Therefore, a new exchange rate system is not needed, nor is a reintroduction of capital controls. Target zones for the exchange rates of the industrial countries will simply not work because no country is willing to subordinate its monetary and fiscal policy to another country. Extending such a regime to emerging economies will not be appropriate either, as fixed exchange rates, which are commonly used throughout East and Southeast Asia (in different ways), played a key role in the recent financial crises. New restrictions on capital movements, particularly capital outflows, would be counterproductive. They delay reforms of the domestic financial sector and shake the confidence of foreign investors, thereby having a negative effect on the desirable inflow of foreign direct investment. Moreover, such restrictions usually are not very effective, because of the great incentive on the part of market participants to circumvent them.

Conclusion

In conclusion, primary responsibility for effective crisis prevention lies with the national authorities in every single country. This adds to the challenges facing the international monetary system. Those challenges include the creation of low inflation, sound fiscal budgets, sustainable current account deficits (or surpluses), realistic exchange rates, open access to goods and services markets, and flexible labour markets. Stability begins at home, with credible domestic policies. Credibility is the only instrument that governments and central banks can use to attain the confidence of international capital markets.

Overcoming as well as preventing exchange rate crises will remain a difficult task in the presence of globalised financial markets. Globalisation is an irreversible process. The judicial decision on the quality of economic policy and the domestic institutional framework is made on capital markets. Problems of improper institutional arrangements cannot be solved with the help of international cartels, an idea much favoured by some politicians. A solid economic order at home and a consistent stability-oriented economic policy are the ways to participate in the welfare-increasing nature of open capital markets. Such a policy may in the future have greater prospects than in the past.

Gatherings such as the G8 in Cologne and Okinawa are doubtless good places to reflect on and discuss financial turmoil. Yet, strengthening financial regulation, developing macroeconomic policies, and improving crisis management would better be left to countries to handle internally. To strengthen and reform existing international financial institutions and arrangements according to the axioms of good governance is a promising way to go.

Following the logic of Mancur Olson (1982), regional finance and currency crises may be needed to enforce efficiency in economic policy and clear up deadlocks in the society and the economy. In this respect, perhaps the latest currency crisis had a positive side.

References

Berg, Andrew, and Catherine Patillo (1998), 'Are Currency Crises Predictable? A Test', IMF Working Paper, No. 98/145, International Monetary Fund, Washington DC.

Claessens, Stijn, Michael P. Dooley, and Andrew Warner (1995), 'Portfolio Capital Flows: Hot or Cold?', *World Bank Economic Review*, vol. 9, pp. 153–174.

Davanne, Olivier, and Pierre Jacquet (2000), 'Practising Exchange Rate Flexibility', in Karl Kaiser, John Kirton, and Joseph Daniels (eds.), *Shaping a New International Financial System: Challenges of Governance in a Globalizing World*, Ashgate, Aldershot, pp. 153–186.

Folkerts-Landau, David, and Lindgren, Carl-Johan (1998), *Toward a Framework for Financial Stability*, International Monetary Fund, Washington DC.

Hayek, Friedrich A. von (1974), 'The Pretence of Knowledge', in Nobel Lectures (Nobel Memorial Lecture) in Bank of Sweden, *Nobel Lectures: Economic Science*, World Scientific Publishing Company, Singapore.

Issing, Otmar (1996), 'Reform des Weltwährungssystems?', *Zeitschrift für Wirtschaftspolitik*, vol. 45, pp. 316–322.

Jeanne, Olivier (1997), 'Are Currency Crises Self-fulfilling? A Test', *Journal of International Economics*, vol. 43, pp. 263–286.

Kaiser, Karl, John Kirton, and Joseph Daniels (eds.) (2000), *Shaping a New International Financial System: Challenges of Governance in a Globalizing World*, Ashgate, Aldershot.

Obstfeld, Maurice (1996), 'Models of Currency Crises with Self-fulfilling Features', *European Economic Review*, vol. 40, pp. 1037–1047.

Olson, Mancur (1982), *The Rise and Decline of Nations*, Yale University Press, New Haven.

Röpke, Wilhelm (1954), *Internationale Ordnung – Heute*, Rentsch Verlag, Stuttgart.

Tietmeyer, Hans (1999), 'International Co-operation and Co-ordination in the Area of Financial Market Supervision and Surveillance', Report to the Finance Ministers and Central Bank Governors of the G-7 Countries (26 February 1999).

4 U.S. Dollarization: A Second-Best Form of Regional Currency Consolidation

GEORGE M. VON FURSTENBERG

Introduction

Free international movement of capital, free trade, and e-trade in financial services have combined to make regional currency consolidation inevitable. In light of this prospect, advocacy of rapid dollarization, in some cases throughout the entire Western Hemisphere, has spread beyond the United States. Business and government groups in countries from Argentina to El Salvador and Mexico have openly expressed interest in formal dollarization. While complete dollarization may indeed be a useful step for the period immediately ahead, it is distinctly second best in the short run and unsustainable in the long run, even in the Western Hemisphere.

Specifically, uncooperative unilateral monetary unions, such as those brought about by formal dollarization, are inferior to the multilateral sharing model of monetary union pioneered in Europe. Dollarization involves paying a very high financial tribute to the United States. Countries become reluctant to continue paying billions of dollars' worth in forgone seigniorage once they have become accustomed to monetary stability and internalised the virtues of low inflation. Rather than paying indefinitely for this, they will reclaim co-ownership and co-management of their monetary asset by forming a multilateral monetary union with like-minded countries.

The Business of External Dollarization

As the paper dollar was coming into its own by being issued and accepted as a pure fiat money in its home market, it was also beginning to be accepted for transactions and store of value functions in foreign countries. A brief look at history is warranted before evaluating the advanced stages of this development that could soon lead to formal dollarization or the unilateral adoption of the U.S. dollar as sole legal tender by other countries in the Western Hemisphere. In this glance backward, the 1904 adoption of the U.S. dollar as in effect the sole medium of payment by Panama is considered exceptional because it is doubtful that the new state had any choice in the matter.

For centuries, countries obtained most of their money by mining or panning for it or by importing the precious monetary specie in return for goods or by means of foreign loans at great expense. In the twentieth century, national monetary sovereignty became the norm, as links to commodity standards were cut in crisis-driven spurts of reform and replaced by discretionary policy management of the growth of fiat money. In the United States, for instance, the demonetisation of gold in 1973 — by lifting the requirement that Federal Reserve notes must be 40 percent backed by a fixed amount of artificially valued gold in the U.S. Treasury — completed the process of internal or national dollarization by cutting the last ceremonial links to an external or international standard. Henceforth the dollar was a pure fiat money whose 'production' was entirely subject to national control and to whatever internal disciplines by which U.S. policymakers cared to abide.

Informal external dollarization, with the U.S. dollar circulating side by side with the respective national currency abroad without benefit of legal tender rights, had become widespread in the aftermath of World War II, particularly in the occupied countries. It then receded as foreign monetary systems were rebuilt in Europe and Japan in the 1950s and as the dollar proved weak against some of the other major currencies in the 1960s and 1970s. External dollarization started to advance again after the United States credibly rededicated itself to the virtues of hard money in the early 1980s. Also, post-communist transitional economies and economies emerging from other disasters, particularly in Latin America, provided more liberal access to U.S. dollars in the 1990s. By the end of the century, dollarization had become a hot issue from Mexico to Argentina, with informal, partial dollarization progressing. At the same time, formal or complete dollarization, under which the U.S. dollar would become the sole legal tender in the adopting country, was being ever more openly debated in business and government.

National currency, being subject to strictly enforced government 'copyright', can be viewed as part of a country's marketable and exportable intellectual property. Foreign use indirectly involves the payment of 'royalties' to the United States. Even though paper money costs the U.S. monetary authorities next to nothing to produce physically, foreigners must pay full value in goods to acquire it, or relinquish interest earnings or make interest payments as long as they hold it. (Of course, U.S. taxpayers do not get the greenbacks for nothing either, but whatever seigniorage profits and interest savings they provide for their own government they get back in lower taxes.) So while external dollarization is good business for the United States, the question is whether is it also the best the Americas can do by and for themselves in the long run.

Initial guidance comes from a Scottish economist who wrote 276 years ago about the nature and causes of the wealth of nations. Adam Smith recognised that wealth arises from value-creating activities and not from government fiat or hoards of shiny things. So too with national money: It has value because a country produces goods and services that can be usefully transacted with it under non-inflationary conditions. Let the price level explode or production implode and the value of money is destroyed. But just because the value of a national monetary asset can be ruined by mismanagement or calamity does not mean that each nation should not aspire, and lay claim, to its monetary wealth potential either by itself or jointly with others.

Not just the fool's gold of monetary policy sovereignty but genuine national income is lost when financially small countries end up importing or renting the money they use. They then pay in goods and services exports and through interest payments on foreign loans for something they could have, by prudent policy and international co-operation, for free. A member of the Board of Governors of the Federal Reserve System recently rejoiced that 'with about $300 billion of U.S. currency in the hands of foreigners, the United States earns roughly $15 billion per year in seigniorage'.[1] The last figure is twice the current U.S. budget for non-military foreign aid[2] and could soon be triple or quadruple. Net, this foreign aid could be flowing the wrong way.

The Disappearing Small Brands of Money

In principle, every country, regardless of size, has a right to its own, home-made monetary base by virtue of the national product of its citizens that gives transactions value to this base. Yet if the country is small and wide open to international financial flows, it may have great difficulty exercising that right for its national currency if it acts alone. Such a currency denomination is simply of little use and ultimately uncompetitive. It may still be needed to pay wages, taxes, and retailers, and local banks may have to keep it on their balance sheet if the government says so. Yet all the big financial transactions and contracts will eschew denomination in an internationally obscure and volatile denomination that has little liquidity or accounting use. Buffeted and made expensive by country and currency risks even when kept on a strict regimen of internationally prescribed best practices, the small currency loses out to a currency that is in wide international use.

No matter how small countries decide to roll with the punches of open capital markets with their own money and exchange rates, small really is not beautiful in matters of money. Inflation targeting for a small country with flexible exchange rates is a frustrating exercise with frequent misses: Mexico was down to 7 percent inflation before the crisis that started in December 1994 forced it to crash and float. Six years later, its inflation rate is only just edging back to single digits, having come down painfully and slowly from over 50 percent during 1995. Currency boards offer good shelter from inflation as long as the exchange parity with the dollar or backing by the Deutschmark or Euro can be maintained. But long stretches of sunny weather tend to be punctuated by severe storms that require costly, and politically risky, interest-rate defences. When Argentina's sovereign debt rating was reduced by Moody's in early October 1999, the agency cited the country's fixed exchange rate with the dollar: The deterioration in Argentina's terms of trade with Brazil, which had given up on a less committed dollar peg in January 1999, and then also with Chile, was making the present downturn of its economy 'particularly difficult'. A peso interest-rate surcharge of 500 basis points or more over U.S. dollar claims issued by the same Argentine banks in 1999 showed that the market is far from convinced that the Argentine peso is as good as the U.S. dollar or that the program of 'convertibility' at a rate of one to one is here to stay.

Whether garaged in a currency board or out on the curb, small moneys thus no longer can expect to survive without protection in their limited areas of circulation. Here 'small' means financially small with a currency denomination that is not fit for the international capital market, and not necessarily geographically small, like El Salvador. But currency protection itself is up against more and more rules of international finance and investment and trade-in-services liberalisation. Even the citizens of a financially small country of issue (of course, Switzerland is not small in that sense) frequently require extra compensation to hold their own money voluntarily on deposit because they view it as an inferior brand. Loan customers get a correspondingly costly quote in the national money, if they are large and connected enough to get any quote at all, and turn to foreign-currency lenders, mostly foreign-owned institutions, both inside and outside the country if they can. Thus there is creeping Euroization at the eastern and south-eastern periphery beyond the 11 current members of Euroland and creeping U.S. dollarization in many other countries, particularly in the Western Hemisphere. It is not fair, but lack of fairness is not an effective defence against natural currency oligopolies on the make.

Not that the oligopolies are particularly customer friendly or the least bit co-operative in public. Federal Reserve chairman Alan Greenspan intends neither to inhibit nor to facilitate the dollarization of an economy that seeks it. Hence if Argentina were to go from about 60 percent average dollarization of its bank balances in 2000 to 100 percent formal dollarization in 2001, it will do so by its own resources and initiatives. It would sacrifice an estimated $750 million in annual interest earnings to start with. Its peso banknotes would have to be taken out of circulation and exchanged for greenbacks purchased by Argentina's central bank with the proceeds from the sale of U.S. treasury bills or other interest-bearing securities. When Kosovo recently was declared a Deutschmark (future Euro) zone, the Deutsche Bundesbank, too, held that to be none of its operational or policy concern. Hence countries that desire a strong international currency to use as their own can do so only through a costly unilateral act unless they are allowed to become partners in a multilateral monetary union.

Unilateral Monetary Union and the Emergence of a Superior Alternative

Unilateral monetary union is the distinctly second-best choice that is left for countries that can not do any better than embrace an established dominant currency as their own without formal co-ordination with its issuer. Such a union is much safer than enduring the stresses of bimonetarism under widespread partial dollarization. When banks have large amounts of both foreign and domestic currency assets and liabilities on their books, the quality of their dollar claims on domestic obligors tends to be undermined, worst of all by contractive exchange crises. So economic vulnerability to any crisis of confidence in a country is less with formal, complete dollarization than with informal, half-baked dollarization that is never robustly hedged. But formal dollarization itself is worse than being allowed to accede to a multilateral union in the region. Such a co-operative solution is not on offer in the Western Hemisphere, but was adopted in Europe at the start of 1999. Instead of importing a defence against a small country's monetary identity problems that seems more like surrender, it invites countries to hold out for something better by co-producing and co-managing their own pool of megamoney.

One way of explaining the difference between unilateral and multilateral monetary union is to think of what happens when a minor national airline company gets such a bad reputation that almost all air travellers, foreign and domestic, prefer to fly on other carriers. Eventually that bankrupt airline and all its local airbussing and landing rights are sold to a foreign carrier for a penny, and good riddance.

But what if the small national airline had in fact been well run but now was unable to overcome the enormous network and code-sharing externalities that it could not enjoy as long as it remained on its own? It would then seek a timely business combination, such as a friendly merger, that did not imply being closed down and declared dead for foreign vultures. Even if the small airline were to lose its national identity through an exchange of shares in the surviving carrier, there would then be full maintenance of value and, indeed, the creation of new value, for both the acquired and acquirer, through an economically efficient merger. By contrast, if the acquirer refused a timely merger, declined to give anything of value, and rather waited until the small national carrier had gone belly-up, then one has a picture of the industrial-relations equivalent of what happens under unilateral monetary union.

Many applaud complete dollarization, the least adaptable and least forgiving form of monetary union, as more stable and efficient than carrying on with heavily protected, poorly maintained, and ultimately doomed mini-carriers of monetary services, particularly in South and Central America and in the Caribbean. Others would say that taking a dangerous toy away from a small country is all to the good without acknowledging that the country's customer base should be worth something. By definition, Pyrrhic victories do not last, but neither do those that are completely unrestrained. Historically, on the European continent, commanders could often lay siege and starve out a free city rather than come to terms with its citizens if theirs was the only army and cavalry in the field. A few far-sighted field marshals chose the latter course, sparing the city. They tend to be remembered as builders of history.

Multilateral union is much kinder to small countries than is joining a monetary union unilaterally, as with unassisted formal dollarization. It does not expropriate their national monetary asset through annihilation and foreign replacement. Rather, it transforms this asset from a national to a multinational form and makes it whole in the process. For even if a country had lost part of the domestic component of its monetary base, and hence part of its national seigniorage, through currency substitution to the dominant international currency in the region, its seigniorage share would be based on estimates of all of the common currency circulating within it after monetary union. The Deutschmark notes, which account for 10 to 20 percent of Poland's currency supply, together with U.S. dollars and zloty, now still yield a flow of seigniorage benefits to

Germany — via interest saved on the debt that the German government otherwise would have issued. However, this foreign fraction will become part of Poland's own Euros and seigniorage share once Poland joins the European Monetary Union, as well may happen in the course of this decade. In addition, the head of Poland's national bank will then have a seat on the European Central Bank Council, like every other member, thus acceding through a merger of equals. Financial and banking systems, once cleaned up and properly provisioned and mutually supervised, will start to mesh throughout a wider European monetary region, so that even country risk will drop sharply. Poland, incidentally, has had a per capita gross domestic product (GDP) that was about the same in 1997 as that of Mexico at the prevailing average exchange rates. Hence monetary union need not be exclusive to rich countries.

The Reckoning

Countries clearly are in a bind if they cannot profitably keep their own small currency and not gain accession to a multilateral union either. But those with the dominant currency may want to beware of taking and keeping all. A unilateral monetary union is not anchored in international treaties or binding undertakings but predicated on the convenience of the adopting country. Once the 33 member countries of the Organization of American States to the south of the United States will have been completely U.S. dollarized long enough to be used to world-standard stable prices, there may be nothing, not even the market, to stop them from eventually seeking to leave the unsettled state of unilateral monetary union with the United States.[3] To recapture their seigniorage, they may try to form a multilateral sub-union of their own by creating popular demand for changing legal tender, tax, and unit-of-account rules. They may thus be able to induce U.S. dollars held by the public to be swapped for a freshly minted common currency by some future Latin American and Caribbean system of central banks. Alternatively, they may join an existing multilateral monetary union that gives better terms than the United States.

Once having been led on the path of monetary rectitude, why pay royalties to the U.S. dollar forever for a lesson well learned? It is unrealistic to think that the likes of Brazil, Argentina, and Chile will accept and then stay with U.S. dollarization for much of the present century, no matter how 'American' that century will be. Even Mexico, which is showing ever less determination to keep the dollar portion of its money supply down, could eventually come to resent dollarization, which would tax it more than $1 billion per year off the bat, and then more each year as its economy and monetary base keep growing, compared with enjoying the flow of seigniorage from all the currency used inside the country.[4]

Once the Latin American and Caribbean countries work out a superior alternative among themselves or with an established multilateral union, they will undollarize jointly. They will stop paying rent for the use of foreign currency and turn it in for income-yielding investments and also for U.S. goods and services down the road. Uncooperative unilateral union in which the external currency-customer be damned may thus get its eventual comeuppance: If the dollar should ever come to reign from Seattle to Santiago or from Alaska to Antarctica, as famous alliterators have recommended, that reign will be shorter than the half-life of James Monroe. The model of shared control and ownership of the type pioneered in Europe is more sustainable because it contributes to the wealth of a plurality of nations and does not just make the monetary wealth flow *e pluribus ad unum.* It is time for the United States to take a careful look at Europe's multilateral model of monetary union and to develop a variant that would remain beneficial for the Western Hemisphere as a whole in the long run. Until then, there is no bridge that leads from European monetary union to an American monetary union, or from EMU to AMU (Beddoes 1999, pp. 8–13).

First Steps to Making Dollarization More Attractive

The *International Monetary Stability Act* of 1999 was introduced on 8 November 1999 and referred to the Senate Committee on Banking, Housing, and Urban Affairs (1999). This act is the first indication that the U.S. Congress could be willing to encourage dollarization actively. The Act recognises that official dollarization of the Western Hemisphere is not easily attained or subsequently sustained without some financial consideration to the dollarizing countries. It is emphatic about the Federal Reserve System having no obligation to act as lender of last resort or to consider the economic conditions of dollarized countries when formulating or implementing U.S. monetary policy. But it offers partial conditional compensation for the loss of seigniorage by the dollarizing country.

Compensation is to be given for 85 percent of the interest forgone by a country that exchanges its own holdings of U.S. Treasury securities for Federal Reserve notes (currency) for the purpose of official dollarization and obtains consols (perpetuities) in return. In other words, no compensation is to be granted for seigniorage lost by pre-existing informal dollarization of a country, and the compensation to be offered for going all the way with dollarization is fractional. Compensation is also inadequately adjusted for the especially rapid growth of currency holdings expected in dollarized developing countries. Furthermore, the spirit of unilateralism prevails in some other respects on the U.S. side as the consols to be issued to the dollarizing country may be declared null and void under certain conditions. These conditions are unlikely to remain fixed at the hands of the U.S. Congress and the Administration when penalising or pressuring an officially dollarized country becomes politically attractive for any reason. For instance, when Panama became a target of U.S. official wrath in 1988/89, it was caught in a financial stranglehold by the United States using its control of dollar flows and of assets with U.S. banks. Interest on the consols may also be attached to what could be a broadening list of conditions.

Although representing progress toward a concept of making formal dollarization less costly to the adopting countries in certain respects, the Act thus still would leave dollarization a distinctly second-best form of currency consolidation. Europe has shown that there is a more tolerant, multilateral model of achieving such needed consolidation by right of treaty, rather than by staying on the right side of Uncle Sam.

Notes

1 Meyer 1999.
2 Budget of the United States Government Fiscal Year 2000, p. 143: The spending proposed for international development and humanitarian assistance is US$7.6 billion.
3 As detailed in von Furstenberg (2000), Canada is in a special class.
4 Mexico's monetary base, consisting almost entirely of peso currency, has been equal to about 3.5 percent of Mexico's GDP in recent years (Banco de México, 1999, p. 237). Adding U.S. dollar bills in Mexico would raise this to around 5 percent. At an interest rate of 5.5 percent otherwise earned on U.S. government securities, the annual cost of complete dollarization would be equal to 0.275 percent of Mexico's GDP. With that GDP estimated at $460 billion for 2000, the annual loss of seigniorage would start at $1.25 billion. This figure could be expected to rise every year at the same rate as GDP so that the current discounted value of all the seigniorage lost under just three decades of dollarization could easily be more than 20 times as large.

References

Banco de México (1999), *The Mexican Economy*, Dirección de Organismos y Acuerdos Internacionales of Banco de México, Mexico.

Barro, R. J. (1999), 'Let the Dollar Reign from Seattle to Santiago', *Wall Street Journal*, Midwest edition, 8 March, p. A18.

Beddoes, Z. M. (1999), 'From EMU to AMU?', *Foreign Affairs*, July/August.

Meyer, L. H. (1999), 'The Euro in the International Financial System', *Federal Reserve Bank of Minneapolis The Region*, vol. 13, no. 2, pp. 25–27, 58.

U.S. Senate Banking Committee on Banking, Housing, and Urban Affairs (1999), *Citizen's Guide to Dollarization*, Committee Documents Online, 106th Congress, <www.senate.gov/~banking/docs/reports/dollar.htm> (September 2000).

von Furstenberg, George M. (2000), 'Does North America Need an Amero?', *Policy Options/Options politiques*, vol. 21, no. 7, pp. 55–58.

5 Looking Askance at Global Governance

RAZEEN SALLY

Framing the Debate

For some time, it has been *de rigueur* to advocate global governance, or what is more modestly called international policy co-ordination. Problems, one is told, are increasingly global and ever less susceptible to resolution at the national level. Global governance, therefore, must intervene across a broader range of policies for which national governance is found decreasingly effective.

Most global governance enthusiasts tend to reinforce a global-problems–global-solutions thesis with noticeable elements of social democracy. A purely neoliberal approach to globalisation, they hold, would be socially disruptive within and between nation-states. Policy co-ordination between governments, therefore, should venture beyond narrow, technical economic issues to cover social and environmental policies in order to achieve sustainable development and social justice, presumably meaning intra-national and international equity.

This chapter casts a very sceptical eye at these general arguments in favour of global governance, and at concrete manifestations of policy co-ordination in international organisations and intergovernmental fora such as G8 summits. Its thrust is confined to international economic policies. It does not broach security issues.

Most arguments for global governance are in fact bad economics and even worse political economy. There is a case for 'soft' policy co-ordination in some areas, essentially restricted to intergovernmental talking shops, information disclosure, policy surveillance, and, perhaps, some hard research. There is also a case for 'harder' co-ordination by means of strict and simple international rules that limit rather than expand the discretionary powers of national governments. However, a great deal of post-1945 international policy co-ordination falls into neither category. It has increased discretionary political power, accompanied, of course, by increased discretionary spending. This only grafts government failure onto the international system. It should be rolled

55

back, not extended. It is striking that this is precisely the type of policy co-ordination promoted by global governance enthusiasts.

One last point deserves emphasis. Even allowing for acceptable forms of soft and hard policy co-ordination, the role of such co-ordination should be modest. In contrast to the global governance thesis, national governance has diminished neither in importance nor in effectiveness. It remains, and should remain, the first and last instance of international economic policy action.

To develop this argument, this chapter first selectively examines the core logic of the leading classical economic theorists of the past three centuries. It then reviews the different forms of global governance offered by the International Monetary Fund (IMF) and the World Bank, the United Nations socioeconomic agencies and the United Nations Conference on Trade and Development (UNCTAD), the Organisation for Economic Co-operation and Development (OECD), the World Trade Organization (WTO), and the G8. It ends by considering the future of global governance — indeed, whether it will have, and should have, a future at all.

An Intellectual Historical Tour

It is instructive to preface a discussion of modern global governance with a selective survey of how past economic liberals looked askance at the subject. The journey begins with the eighteenth- and nineteenth-century Scottish and English classical economists.

The classical economists, from David Hume and Adam Smith to John Stuart Mill and Alfred Marshall, represent a congress of economic liberalism and political realism. They looked forward to increasing international economic integration through more liberal economic policies and more porous borders. At the same time, they were perfectly happy with an international political system of sovereign nation-states. This is why they stuck to practical considerations of the nation and the national interest in their political economy. Smith's classic book was entitled *The Wealth of Nations*, not 'The Wealth of the World'. National governance, not global governance, was seen as the core mechanism in dealing with international economic issues. To them, globalisation did not presage the retreat of the state. On the contrary, national governments, acting independently, retained crucial functions in maximising the gains from, and minimising the risks of, opening to the world economy.

The centrepiece of classical liberalism's international political economy in the nineteenth century was the argument in favour of unilateral free trade. It fits hand in glove with the reality and logic of an international political system of sovereign nation-states. As initially set out by Smith, a policy of unilateral free trade is pursued in the national interest. Other states, also acting in their own interests, follow the pioneering example of one or a few by adopting free trade when the national benefits of such a policy become readily apparent. In the classical liberal conception, therefore, free trade is a policy pursued by national governments separately and independently, and spread by a process of competitive emulation between states. Its overall political context is manifestly one that works with the grain of national sovereignty.

The argument in favour of unilateral free trade in the nineteenth century was also bound up with the classical liberal aversion to the alternative policy of reciprocity, that is, with liberalising trade through intergovernmental nego-tiation. Reciprocity was rejected due to the cumbersome, time-consuming procedures and inherent politicisation of intergovernmental bargaining. It was also rejected, not least, for its prospect of mutually damaging, tit-for-tat retaliation when liberalisation became hostage to haggling over export con-cessions. Hence, the classical economists were sceptical of intergovernmental policy co-ordination precisely because it encouraged government failure at the international level.[1]

By the 1930s, in the midst of the Depression, even economic liberals changed tack. Lionel Robbins and Friedrich von Hayek were symptomatic of this turn away from national governance and toward world government. To them, it was the unfettered exercise of national sovereignty that provided governments with an open-ended invitation to pursue beggar-thy-neighbour policies, leading inexorably to system-breakdown. The solution, it seemed, lay in a new form of international federation, with a system of international authorities that would chain national sovereignty and prohibit national governments from engaging in illiberal actions inimical to international order. Only then could a stable, prosperous, and lasting international order be restored (Robbins 1937, Hayek 1944).

However, there was a rare dissenting voice who stayed true to the classical liberal view of international economic order that prevailed in the eighteenth and nineteenth centuries. The German economist Wilhelm Röpke (1959; see also Sally 1998, ch. 7) advocated what might be termed 'liberalism from below' as opposed to 'liberalism from above'. The latter relies on solutions at an international level to restore international order. In contrast, the former relies on governance at the national level, and is sceptical of the politicisation and bureaucracy associated with international organisations and mechanisms of intergovernmental policy co-ordination. Röpke was particularly scathing of what he saw as the false internationalism of interwar idealism, including the utopian blueprints for economic unions and federations advocated by Robbins, Hayek, and others. Unlike the latter, he did not see national sovereignty in international relations as the root cause of international disorder. Rather, the root cause was the centralisation of power, and the invasion of the economic sphere by politics *within* nation-states that spilled over into international friction. The solution did not lie in the will-o'-the-wisp of world government. Governments, he argued, would not relinquish the necessary amount of sovereignty to international authorities. Besides, the essential attachment to the *civitas* was and would remain at the national level. On the contrary, Röpke believed that international order could only be restored 'from within and beneath' in the reconstruction of sound political and economic order within separate nation-states. Hence his policy preferences, both for the interwar crisis and for the restoration of a liberal international economic order after 1945, were similar to those of preceding classical economists. They advocated unilateral, example-setting measures at the national level rather than concerted intergovernmental action. Like his predecessors, Röpke worked with the grain of national sovereignty rather than against it.

By 1945, the utopian dream of world government had almost evaporated. Its residue was a more modest belief in some form of international policy co-ordination, usually involving the establishment of new international organisations. These would co-exist with the continued exercise of national sovereignty. It is this bandwagon onto which most economic liberals climbed immediately after the last world war. Jacob Viner (1951) is a case in point. He saw no prospect of a return to pre-1914 conditions, given widespread government intervention in domestic and foreign economic affairs in the name of full employment and other social goals. Reciprocal international agreement, therefore, was the only way forward to gradually bring about freer trade and capital mobility. This broadly accounted for his approval of the Bretton Woods agreements and the Havana Charter, despite their many illiberal traits.[2]

The last word in this *Ideengeschichte* goes to Jan Tumlir, the Czech émigré who served as director of research at the General Agreement on Tariffs and Trade (GATT). Writing a generation after Röpke, Tumlir (1983; see also Sally 1998, pp. 162–166) pointed to the fatal flaw in Robbins' quest for international authorities to stem the tide of international economic disorder. To him, new international set-ups were more likely to be diplomatic authorities than apolitical enforcers of an international rule of law. In all probability, they would furnish an extra arena for playing out intergovernmental power struggles. This led Tumlir to be sceptical of intergovernmental agreements as the primary solution to international economic disorder. It led him, like Röpke, to place more emphasis on the domestic or intra-national legal and policy foundations of international economic order. Tumlir, in no doubt about the classical liberal provenance of his approach, came to regard proper constitutional observance within nation-states as crucial. A liberal international economic order then emerged as a by-product of a well-adjusted domestic order rather than as a direct product of intergovernmental agreements, let alone international federation.

Hence, from Hume and Smith to Tumlir, with a bit of a blip in the interwar period thanks to Hayek and Robbins, there was a consensus on liberalism from below. This approach continued to rely on national governance for international economic order, with a considerable — if not blanket — scepticism of international policy co-ordination. This prism can be useful for examining the contours of global governance today, in particular the landscape of present-day international organisations.

Global Governance Today: A Coup d'Oeil

International economic policy co-ordination, or what some see as embryonic global governance, encompasses the following forms: formal international agencies and intergovernmental mechanisms with representation on a planetary scale, or at least covering several regions of the world; bilateral and regional agencies and intergovernmental mechanisms; and, finally, informal arrangements between governments and private parties that facilitate the mutual adjustment of public policies on a bilateral, regional, or global scale. This chapter restricts itself to the first type of policy co-ordination and, more specifically, to the 'headline' intergovernmental mechanism — the G8 — and the leading international economic agencies — the IMF, the World Bank, the OECD, the WTO, and relevant agencies within the United Nations system, especially UNCTAD.

Two fundamental questions are germane to the G8 and the agencies under the microscope: What are their functions? How well do they perform these functions?

The International Monetary Fund and the World Bank

The IMF and the World Bank, often referred to as the 'Bretton Woods twins', share some common features. Although influenced and funded by member governments, they retain autonomy in initiating and implementing policy. Their main concern is with lending programmes, for which they have special sources of finance. They have significant advisory and monitoring activities in member countries. Last, but by no means least, they conduct substantial in-house applied research.

The original intention at the Bretton Woods Conference was to have a clear division of labour between the IMF and the World Bank. The former was to concentrate on short-term balance of payment problems, while the latter was supposed to channel long-term finance for development purposes. By the 1980s, neither agency had a clear *raison d'être* in terms of its founding objectives. The IMF no longer had to support a system of fixed but adjustable exchange rates, which had collapsed in 1971. The resurgence of private international capital flows — practically non-existent in 1944 — raised serious questions about the World Bank's central role in providing development finance. At the same time, the division of labour between the two agencies became increasingly blurred. In particular, the IMF, far from focussing narrowly on short-term macroeconomic policy problems, began to busy itself with long-term microeconomic policies and structural problems.

Perhaps the distinguishing mark of these Washington-based institutions is the power of their purse, that is, their concessionary lending programmes. Since the 1980s, this power has manifested itself through policy conditionality. The IMF's stabilisation packages and the World Bank's structural adjustment programmes have been contingent on the implementation of specific policies by borrowing countries. Commentators habitually mention policy conditionality in the same breath as the 'Washington Consensus', the paradigm of ideas in the IMF and the World Bank that, since the late 1970s, has placed conservative monetary and fiscal policies, coupled with internal and external liberalisation, high on the list of priorities.

Surely, the success or failure of the Bretton Woods twins, at least in the past two decades, must be judged at the altar of policy conditionality. This applies equally, or almost equally, to the regional development banks and bilateral aid agencies that have followed the World Bank and the IMF in applying conditionality to the disbursement of loans and grants. In the case of the Bretton Woods twins, there is little clear-cut success to report, and much failure.

Many studies show a poor correlation between the disbursement of conditional aid and actual sustained policy reform. Where successful and sustained policy reform has occurred, as in East Asia, East Europe, and some Latin American countries (especially Chile, Mexico, and Argentina), it has emerged primarily from below. Governments have pushed through reforms unilaterally in response to domestic and external conditions, frequently of crisis proportions. Conditional aid has had little to do with it. In particular, there is no discernible link between trade sector loans — an important element of most Structural Adjustment Loans — and sustained trade liberalisation. In the case of Chile, radical external liberalisation in the 1970s — the benchmark of modern Latin American policy reform — went ahead independently of the two Washington institutions.

Much more important than conditional aid has been the demonstration effect of seeing successful antecedent examples of external opening feeding through to higher growth, as in East Asia from the 1960s, and then Chile from the 1980s. In the words of David Landes (1998, p. 44), reforms were 'initiated from below and diffused by example'. At best, one can conclude that IMF and World Bank aid served as a 'good housekeeping seal of approval' to national reforms that would have gone ahead anyway (Haggard 1995, pp. 25–26; Edwards 1995, 124f).

The problem, however, lies with the vast majority of developing countries and countries in transition with partial and sputtering reforms, rather than comprehensive and sustained reforms. The weak reformers, especially in Africa, the Middle East, South Asia, and the former Soviet Union, have relied far more on conditional aid than the successful reformers have.

For most countries in the developing world, intractable domestic political problems have hindered bold unilateral reforms, leading governments to go cap in hand to the World Bank and the IMF in crisis situations. These two institutions then disburse aid, providing borrowers undertake specific reforms in the future. Then follows a ritual dance between the multilateral agencies and borrowing governments. Aid staves off the immediate crisis, thereby weakening the incentive to reform at home. Governments do not deliver promised reforms, given the lack of domestic political support for them. The World Bank and the IMF then hold up further planned tranches of aid, but eventually resume the flow, once again contingent on *ex post* reforms that usually fail to see the light of day. All too often, the end result is botched stop-go reform combined with a build-up of debt owed to aid agencies. The whole process severely undermines the credibility of governments' reform programmes in the eyes of investors.[3]

The World Bank and the IMF derive their prestige and influence over developing countries from their lending programmes. Hence, both agencies have huge institutional incentives to keep the developing world on a drip-feed of debt, although the evidence tends to show it does not work. Official aid is invariably infested with arbitrary politics — not only in national aid agencies but also in the multilateral agencies. Wherever and whenever the power of the purse is involved, arbitrary political decisions cannot be far behind, however vigorous the rhetoric of 'strict and objective' conditionality. Arguably, this is a case of global governance gone horribly wrong, which leads to legitimate calls for the abolition of national, regional, and multilateral aid agencies.

This is not to say that the Washington institutions have not played a constructive role in policy reform at all. On the contrary, they have been useful in two respects: policy dialogue and the dissemination of research. The ongoing and intensive exchange of information and ideas between World Bank and IMF staff on the one hand and national policymakers on the other has contributed to the intellectual climate in favour of policy reform across the developing world. IMF and World Bank research and publications have occasionally performed a similar function (Edwards 1995, pp. 130–131; Henderson 1998a, p. 117). Therefore, although there is a case for removing the power of the purse, i.e., lending, there might be a credible argument to retain a downsized, slimline World Bank and IMF that focus on policy dialogue and research. Such soft policy co-ordination may do some good and would be far less susceptible to government failure than hard policy co-ordination involving *ad hoc*, discretionary loan packages.

The United Nations Socioeconomic Agencies: The Case of UNCTAD

There are a number of UN agencies charged with 'economic development' functions, including the United Nations Development Programme (UNDP), the United Nations Industrial Development Organization (UNIDO), the Food and Agriculture Organization (FAO), and UNCTAD. The UNDP stands out with its considerable budget for project and programme aid in developing countries, backed by large numbers of operational staff in those countries. It is one of the conspicuous offenders in terms of UN bureaucracy and incompetence, and often accused of highly politicised, wasteful, and ineffectual field operations, particularly in Africa. The FAO's drawbacks are similar. UNIDO, after undergoing a forced slimming cure, is a relatively minor culprit, although it is difficult to divine a clear-cut function for it. All three should be candidates for abolition, starting with the UNDP.

UNCTAD also has very little to show for its 35 years of existence. Until recently, it promoted a development agenda that gave succour to profligate macroeconomic policies and *dirigiste* microeconomic policies, including rampant protectionism. In the old GATT, UNCTAD's contribution was to advocate special and differential treatment for developing country members. The latter insisted on sweeping exemptions from GATT rules, but at the same time sought market access concessions from developed countries. This was a classic case of developing countries shooting themselves in the foot. By marginalising themselves from GATT deliberations, developed countries had no incentive to offer market access where it mattered, especially in agriculture and textiles. Led by UNCTAD and the G77, the developing world retained self-destructive protectionist policies and squandered limited political capital on calls for a New International Economic Order (NIEO).

By the 1980s, a wave of unilateral liberalisation swept through the developing world. Many of the strong liberalisers began to play an active and constructive part in the Uruguay Round of the GATT. This trend continued in the WTO. An effective minority of developing countries ditched the baggage of special and differential treatment in favour of general rules and obligations guaranteeing market access. All this threatened to make UNCTAD completely irrelevant.

Since the mid 1990s, UNCTAD has promised substantial internal reform, especially under the leadership of its secretary general, Rubens Ricupero. It has belatedly moved in a pro-liberalisation direction, endorsing what many developing countries started doing a decade or two ago. Nevertheless, reform has been more rhetorical than substantive. The UNCTAD secretariat leaves much to be desired, as recruitment takes place according to Byzantine and frequently less than meritocratic UN procedures. In terms of quality, it compares badly with the WTO down the road in Geneva, and with the OECD and the research staffs in the IMF and the World Bank. Internally, the agency is divided between modernisers and anti-liberal dinosaurs with vestiges of NIEO ideology from the 1970s. Internal incoherence translates into bureaucratic muddling-through, with often contradictory policy positions. UNCTAD has been trying to build a common positive agenda for developing countries in the WTO, but without success. This is due in large part to the fact that the active and effective minority of developing countries in the WTO does not take UNCTAD seriously.[4]

There is a case for developing countries to have an OECD-like secretariat where government officials could get together for serious and fruitful discussions on different aspects of economic policy. However, even with the requisite political will and financial support, this can only take place with a professional, high-quality secretariat outside the UN system. UNCTAD, within the UN family, is otiose and fatally flawed. It should be scrapped.

The Organisation for Economic Co-operation and Development

The OECD is the intergovernmental agency *par excellence*. Unlike the IMF and the World Bank, the OECD secretariat has little autonomy, possess few powers of initiative, and does not administer lending programmes. Rather, it exists to service the collective discussions of national officials on a wide range of economic policy issues. The OECD's core process is multilateral surveillance, which allows member governments to scrutinise each other's policies regularly. A substantial output of applied research, again driven by what members feel they need, informs this process of regular review and commentary on public policies.

The OECD's particular advantage is that it brings together officials from different countries, and indeed from different government departments within the same country, to provide a transdepartmental perspective, as well as a cross-national one, on a gamut of macroeconomic and microeconomic policies. This is a unique vantage point from which to undertake multilateral policy surveillance. Sometimes, solid research and regular, intensive discussions have paved the way for concrete negotiations and agreements in other fora, especially in the GATT/WTO. Considerable OECD research and discussion preceded the Uruguay Round negotiations and agreements on agriculture, trade in services, and intellectual property. Most of the 'new issues' on the trade policy agenda, such as foreign direct investment, competition policy, and environmental and labour standards, have also received a thorough airing in the OECD.[5]

The OECD is not without its problems, exacerbated by poor leadership in the 1990s. Its major recent blunder was to attempt a full-blown negotiation on the Multilateral Agreement on Investment, which failed spectacularly (Henderson 1999b). This was a typical case of bureaucratic overstretch and hubris. The OECD is ill suited to house international negotiations, whereas it is reasonably well suited to its core task of policy surveillance through research and the regular exchange of information and ideas. In the future, it should restrict itself to the soft policy co-ordination it has performed not too badly in the past.

The World Trade Organization

In a world of incompetent, self-serving, and failed international organisations, the GATT and its successor, the WTO, stand out as resounding successes. There is one very good reason: The WTO has a reasonably clear and useful mandate — to negotiate and enforce rules on international trade (Irwin 1998, pp. 130–132).

Nearly all other major international agencies have diffuse and often mutually contradictory functions. Conspicuously, the IMF has expanded its sweep to cover microeconomic and structural issues for which it has little expertise or competence, and in which, as many would argue, it has no right to meddle. The World Bank, under James Wolfensohn's leadership, has lost its clear focus on growth as the chief means to reduce poverty and added a bewildering array of other catchy, vaguely defined, and difficult-to-achieve objectives. The thinking behind the so-called Comprehensive Development Framework is muddled, and its implementation threatens to scatter limited resources in too many directions at the same time.[6] As for UNCTAD, it is difficult to say what it does, apart from keeping its staff and delegates comfortably underemployed near the balmy waters of Lake Geneva.

The WTO has a constitutional *raison d'être* embodied in Articles I, II, and III. This is the reduction of barriers to the international exchange of goods and services on a non-discriminatory basis, informed by the principles of Most Favoured Nation (MFN) and national treatment. Admittedly, from the GATT's inception, and even with the WTO, governments have enjoyed plenty of built-in flexibility to resort to discriminatory protection.[7] Nevertheless, rules are the foundation stone of the WTO. These rules, as laid out in Articles I to III, are classically liberal in inspiration. They are simple, clear, and negatively defined — that is, they tell governments what not to do, namely engage in discriminatory protection, but otherwise leave governments free to do as they wish.[8]

Although they took the argument to utopian extremes, Robbins and Hayek were searching for a GATT-like solution to the international disorder of their day. Their international authorities were to issue negative ordinances, proscribing harmful actions by national governments, such as protection, but prescribing nothing. As Hayek admitted in his later work, the post-1945 international organisations failed largely because they undertook an increasing number of positive functions, or, in other words, *ad hoc* discretionary measures, instead of concentrating on negative ordinances. Such a trend only added extra layers of government failure to what was in any case on the rise within nation-states (Sally 2000b). This is precisely the malaise that plagues international agencies today, with the exception of the WTO.

To Tumlir, international rules such as the WTO's Most Favoured Nation clause are mechanisms to protect individual property rights against excessive government. By entering into international agreements, governments collectively tie their own hands, forswearing discriminatory intervention in property rights and resource allocation in specified policy domains. The goal is to enable national societies, in the name of freedom and prosperity, to adapt flexibly to external change, which can only take place via the spontaneous co-ordination of a well-functioning price mechanism, not via open-ended government intervention. In national jurisdictions, the rules of private law that govern property and contract provide a stable framework within which private agents interact according to freely forming prices. Non-discriminatory and negatively defined international rules are an additional bulwark of constancy and predictability to the rule base within nation-states: they are, as Tumlir puts it, 'a second line of domestic constitutional entrenchment' (Tumlir 1983, p. 72; 1980, p. 3).

Tumlir (1983, p. 400) holds that most economists, lawyers, and political scientists who advocate international policy co-ordination do not believe in rules. They prefer instead 'co-operation without rules'. They see policy co-ordination in terms of specific, *ad hoc* measures agreed upon in the public policy equivalent of private cartels. At one extreme, this leads to a seemingly unconditional acceptance of international action for its own sake. As Tumlir (1981, p. 179) says, 'international organisations, negotiations, agreements and functions seem to be favoured, wholesale and uncritically, more for their international character than for their substantive content'. This is international government failure gone mad; it has nothing to do with a rule-based international economic order.

Thus, the WTO comes closest to a classical liberal conception of how an international agency should behave, although, it must be said, the fit is far from perfect. Apart from the numerous departures from MFN and national treatment sanctioned by the WTO treaties, the negotiating process has a pre-programmed mercantilist logic: members make requests and offers to elicit export concessions from others, which leads to the economically nonsensical belief that exports are good and imports are bad. Not only does this divert attention from the fundamental economic truth that national gains from trade arise from import liberalisation, but it also hinders a first-best policy of unilateral liberalisation.

A more appropriate and constitutional way to look at the mutually reinforcing tracks of unilateral and multilateral liberalisation would be to pursue unilateral liberalisation on its own merits. A commitment to binding WTO rules would then be a means of locking in and bolstering measures undertaken at the national level. Hence, WTO rules, viewed from below, reinforce national rules protecting property and contracts, thereby enhancing the clarity, coherence, and credibility of national trade policy. Seen this way, they are indeed the second line of domestic constitutional entrenchment (Sally 1999).

With the metamorphosis of the GATT into the WTO, rules on market access go broader and deeper. They are now enforceable by a revamped dispute settlement mechanism with teeth and bite. This is the closest the world economy has come to an international rule of law, at least since 1914, but all is far from good news for votaries of free trade governed by negative ordinances. In particular, a number of Uruguay Round agreements impose new and burdensome regulations on developing countries that threaten to hinder, rather than promote, market access. The agreement on trade-related intellectual property rights is the chief villain. It sets a dangerous precedent for highly dubious calls to harmonise standards, according to developed country norms, in other areas, such as on labour, food safety, and the environment. If this trend continues, WTO agreements will not be worth the paper on which they are written. Rather than setting rules for market order, they will open the door to spiralling protection by rich countries trying to impose their arbitrarily defined standards on poor countries. This, then, would be a game of power, not of rules.

Finally, one secret to the WTO's success is that, like the OECD, it is an intergovernmental agency that serves the needs of member governments without enjoying the power of the purse to pursue its own policies, such as lending programmes. Just as the OECD is a forum for research and discussion, the WTO is a forum for intergovernmental negotiations on market access and rule enforcement. Bereft of vast funds to administer, it remains a relatively slimline international agency with a high-quality secretariat (Henderson 1998a, p. 103). It should stay that way.

The G8

G7/8 Summits have some justification in terms of a soft policy co-ordination role. There is nothing particularly bad, and perhaps some good, in getting leading policymakers around a table once in a while to discuss the great issues of the day. Almost inevitably, the debates end up being too brief and superficial. They compare badly to the more intensive and detailed policy surveillance and dialogue that takes place at the OECD, or even at the IMF and the World Bank.

Nevertheless, items on the G8 agenda may well send the requisite signals for follow-up, and more concrete policy discussions and initiatives. Some G7 initiatives have failed abysmally or been misguided, such as the attempt to co-ordinate macroeconomic policies in the late 1970s and the attempts at exchange rate co-ordination in the 1980s. Other initiatives may have some worth, for example in spurring multilateral trade negotiations. In recent years, G8 meetings have covered a widening range of domestic economic issues, such as education and labour markets, and an even wider range of non-economic issues. This trend may or may not be wise. However, it does weaken the G8's ability to focus on the core international economic issues for which such summitry was originally intended.

Whatever the merits of the G8 in terms of soft policy co-ordination, it stretches the imagination to ascribe to it a central role in global governance. Its role remains very modest, certainly in comparison to the WTO, OECD, the World Bank, and the IMF. Furthermore, it is difficult to see how governments can usefully strengthen the G8 mechanism to play a more important part in international policy co-ordination.

A Future for Global Governance?

International policy co-ordination is thus a curate's egg. There is some useful soft co-ordination through policy surveillance and dialogue, welcome hard co-ordination through WTO rules, and much counterproductive aid disbursement, sullied by arbitrary politics, bureaucracy, and incompetence. Enthusiasts of policy co-ordination are usually purblind to the latter phenomenon, while underestimating the utility of policy surveillance and dialogue and WTO rules. Fans of global governance, however, have more ambitious schemes in mind. Some of their ideas are discussed below.

Pop Internationalism, Globalisation, and Global Governance

Proposals for stronger global governance normally proceed from a distinctive view of globalisation. For many, the latter is a relatively recent phenomenon, powered by a technological revolution and accelerating at a wild pace. This technologically pre-programmed and seemingly unstoppable process, it is argued, is responsible for wrenching social dislocation within and between nation-states, especially in exacerbating inequalities between rich and poor. At the national level, governments are impotent in confronting this overwhelming external force. Their powers to tax and spend, particularly to protect welfare states, are seriously diminished. Thus, national governments are in headlong retreat, obsolescent in the face of global problems. The latter, so the argument goes, demand global solutions, which is where global governance enters the fray.[9]

Recent UNDP publications are prime examples of this global-problems–global-solutions thesis. In economic terminology, concerted global action is necessary to correct global market failures and provide global public goods. New forms of global governance, therefore, should supply vaguely defined public goods, such as sustainable development and global equity. One UNDP publication, for example, recommends a new global tripartism, bringing together representatives of governments, businesses, unions, and civil society to discuss global problems and take requisite action (Kaul, Grunberg, and Stern 1999).

There is a need for a searching, critical look at this diagnosis of globalisation and the cure of global governance. To begin with, conceived of as cross-border economic integration, globalisation is not a blindingly novel phenomenon. It dates from at least the early nineteenth century. True, modern transportation and communication technologies are accelerating the pace of globalisation in the late twentieth and early twenty first-centuries. However, technological change is itself historically grounded. It is by no means evident that the internet, air transport, satellite communications, and the containerisation of shipping, *inter alia*, produce effects that are wholly different and vastly greater than was the case with previous technological revolutions. (For a different perspective on the extent of globalisation, see Bordo, Eichengreen, and Irwin 1999.) Lastly, on a number of indicators, such as the ratio of trade and net capital flows to gross domestic product, the world today is not nearly as integrated as popular perception would have it, nor is it hugely more integrated than it was a century ago.

A misdiagnosis of globalisation, exaggerating its novelty and concrete effects, leads straight to the fallacious 'retreat of the state' thesis. Contrary to this pop internationalist perception, globalisation is not driven by the pre-programmed inevitability of technological progress, in the face of which national governments are supposedly powerless, or at least increasingly less effective. Rather, technological progress, and with it globalisation, depends crucially on policy choice at the national level.

Fundamentally, national policy choice determines the domestic competitive environment and how open or closed national economies are to the international economy. As was the case during the last high-water mark of globalisation, which occurred roughly during the period between 1870 and 1913, governments retain autonomy to perform their core economic policy functions — the protection of property and the enforcement of contracts, and the provision of other public goods — as well as autonomy in a gamut of other policy areas.

Perhaps most important of all, governments still set the national stance on international trade, foreign direct investment, portfolio capital flows, and cross-border migration. This, in turn, determines how integrated the national economy becomes with the global economy.

National policy choice, therefore, is the critical factor in dealing with the risks and opportunities of globalisation. Right through the nineteenth century, national governance co-existed with increasing international economic integration. This remains the case today. Hence, national governance is as important as ever. Global governance enthusiasts miss this essential point with their utterly false conclusion that 'new' globalisation demands global, instead of national, governance.[10]

Pop internationalist hype paints a distorted picture of the alleged intra-national effects of globalisation and, consequently, of the possibilities for national governance. There are false claims galore. One is that increasingly mobile multinational enterprises drive down environmental and labour standards everywhere. Another is that capital mobility and tax competition shrink national tax income and consequently squeeze welfare states. Both assertions are spurious: the evidence is simply not there (Organisation for Economic Co-operation and Development [OECD] 1998, pp. 73–75, 88–89, 106–109). The reality is quite different: governments retain wide leeway to set their own standards, for example on the environment and on conditions of work, and to set their own policies on taxation and expenditure.

Perhaps the most egregious claim is that globalisation leads to increasing inequality within and between countries. The 'trade and wages' debate has witnessed the spillage of much economic ink in examining the effects of North-South trade on income differentials in the developed world. On this score, most economists conclude that globalisation is not a major factor in widening income inequalities (OECD 1998, pp. 66–72).

More important from a development perspective is the charge that globalisation widens the chasm between rich and poor countries, that is, that it benefits already rich and newly rich societies while marginalising poverty-stricken societies. It is true that the gap between the richest and poorest countries has increased through the nineteenth century and through most of the twentieth century. Furthermore, the world economy today exhibits marked divergence in national economic performances, especially within the developing world. East Asia, Eastern Europe, and some Latin American countries are on very high or relatively high growth paths, but Africa, the Middle East, South Asia, and the former Soviet Union are left behind. How has this state of affairs come about?

Global governance enthusiasts would say that globalisation forces poor people in poor countries into more misery. This is not so. In reality, national policies are the central pivot in determining whether societies gain or miss out from globalisation. There is a wealth of evidence to show that countries with macroeconomic policies geared toward budget balance and price stability, good institutional infrastructure, and openness to the world economy have registered much higher growth in real incomes than those countries with profligate macroeconomic policies, weak institutions, and protectionism. In particular, countries with liberal trade policies have grown appreciably faster than those with protectionist policies (World Bank 1997; Sachs and Warner 1995).

The crucial point is that national policies, not global governance, have a primary influence on national economic performance. The divergence in national policies, particularly in national external policies, goes a long way to explain the divergence in economic performance. Put bluntly, poor countries remain poor not because of globalisation, but because profligate and protectionist national policies prevent private actors from taking advantage of globalisation. The very fact that there have been, and are, striking differences in national external policies, right through the last century and in the here-and-now, shows that national policy choice is real and substantial. To a very large extent, governments, even in the poorest developing countries, are free to choose. By arguing that globalisation is the problem rather than inappropriate national governance, the global governance camp gets cause and effect the wrong way round.

To recapitulate, a false diagnosis of globalisation leads to the false conclusion that national governance is in decline. This, in turn, points directly to a false cure of global governance. A key classical liberal insight, from Hume and Smith to Röpke and Tumlir, is that as far as public policies are concerned, dealing with globalisation is, first and last, a matter of national governance. In the nineteenth century, the classical economists thought of the subject exclusively in terms of national governance.[11] A century and more later, one should allow more room for a degree of soft and hard international policy co-ordination along the lines previously mentioned. Nevertheless, the importance of policy surveillance and dialogue, and even WTO rules, should not be exaggerated, let alone be thought of as ends in themselves. They should be seen as a means to the more important end of better national governance. From this perspective, policy co-ordination could serve as a helpful auxiliary to national governance. However, it should never be forgotten that the latter, not the former, is the fount and matrix of public policy.

Cross-border Externalities and Policy Co-ordination

It should be evident that ambitious claims for global governance rest on very shaky foundations. To be sure, the rationale for more modest international policy co-ordination stands on stronger ground where identifiable and significant cross-border externalities are involved, as might be the case with global warming. Here appropriately designed policy co-ordination might make a constructive contribution. However, the record of proliferating multilateral environmental agreements unfortunately indicates otherwise. The Montreal protocol is a case in point. Instead of relying on market-friendly mechanisms such as the 'polluter pays' principle based on an assignment of property rights, it favours quotas and trade sanctions. The implications of this are rather illiberal, particularly for the rule integrity of the WTO (Roessler 1998, p. 222). The last thing the world needs is a fresh crop of badly designed multilateral agreements and bureaucratically heavy international agencies that compromise the good work of the WTO.

Although there is a role for policy co-ordination where major cross-border externalities are involved, such externalities are rare. The overwhelming majority, including environmental externalities, are local and can be dealt with at national or sub-national levels. Even in cases where a cross-border situation calls out for concerted international action, intervention should only occur if requisite knowledge is at hand to deal with the problem, and if mechanisms are in place to minimise government failure. The presumption, therefore, should be in favour of thorough discussion and careful deliberation, taking great care to avoid precipitate action.[12]

Anti-liberalism, NGOs, and Global Governance

The final issue concerns a pervasive and sometimes profound anti-liberal disposition among advocates of global governance. As mentioned earlier, much policy co-ordination, beset by government failure and without adequate knowledge to deal with problems at hand, distorts market processes rather than improves them. It seems that those favouring ever more intergovernmental action and a more powerful role for international agencies are much exercised by perceived market failure, but oblivious to actual and potential international government failure. Moreover, those who wax lyrical about stronger global governance tend to view international political cartels, intervening vigorously in product and factor markets, as a means of arresting and reversing the two-decade-old trend of market-oriented policy reform across the world economy (Henderson 1998b, pp. 58–65, 111–112).

The alliance of global governance and anti-liberal sentiment, on markets in general and globalisation in particular, finds vocal support in many circles, and perhaps most noticeably within the UN family. Again, the UNDP, with its broadening flow of pro-global governance publications, should be singled out. The UNDP, like the World Bank, has an increasing attraction for 'civil society', as represented, apparently, by a plethora of non-governmental organisations (NGOs). The attraction dazzles so much that UNDP staff now advocate a form of global corporatism, bringing non-governmental organisations into formal decision-making mechanisms with governments, businesses and trade unions (Kaul, Grunberg, and Stern 1999).

This throws up a number of vexing problems. It is all very well to share information and engage in a more intensive dialogue with private parties, whether they be businesses, unions, or non-business NGOs. It is quite another matter to bring them into supranational or intergovernmental decision-making procedures. At the international level, governments — an increasing percentage of them now democratically elected — are the rightful claimants to domestic accountability. Just as businesses and unions represent partial interests and cannot claim 'democratic accountability' at home, neither can NGOs. The latter are quite out of order in claiming to speak on behalf of civil society, whatever that means. Governments and international agencies should forcefully reject such claims.

Finally, it is striking that the most influential NGOs — those that are well organised, well funded, and most vocal — are based in the developed world. They have a strong streak of anti-market, anti-globalisation sentiment. An emotive, unanalytical pop internationalism animates much of their policy thinking. If put into practice, it would harm consumers in the West and practically everybody else in the rest of the world. These organisations — most of them single-issue groups — do not 'represent' societies anywhere, least of all in the developing world.[13]

Conclusion

'Goodthink' on global governance is no substitute for good governance. Indeed, it diverts attention from good governance, and probably does harm by giving succour to anti-liberal constituencies and by promoting anti-liberal nostrums. The obverse of looking askance at global governance is to look favourably at the nineteenth-century model. One should embrace globalisation in the name of freedom and prosperity, and reap its gains through better national governance. Soft and hard policy co-ordination can provide a supporting cast of characters, but national governance is central to the plot and must play the leading role.

Notes

1 This argument relies on Sally (1998, pp. 54–60). On classical liberal arguments about unilateralism versus reciprocity, see Smith (1976 [1776], pp. 489–493), and Robbins (1958, p. 255).
2 See in particular 'Two Plans for International Monetary Stabilisation', 'The Bretton Woods Agreement', 'International Finance in the Post-War World', and 'Conflicts of Principle in Drafting a Trade Charter', all in Viner (1951).
3 For skeptical views of IMF and World Bank conditional lending, see Yeager (1998), Meltzer (1998), Calomiris (1998), and Vasquez (1998).
4 For a critical view of UNCTAD's record, although one that is perhaps slightly less skeptical and pessimistic than mine, see Henderson (1998a, pp. 110–111).
5 For a lucid coverage of the OECD and its works by the former head of its Department of Economics and Statistics, see Henderson (1993, pp. 11–35).
6 For an explanation of the Comprehensive Development Framework, see World Bank (1999, pp. 13–30).
7 On the post-war compromise between power and rules in the GATT, see Jacob Viner's superlative 'Conflicts of Principle in Drafting a Trade Charter,' in his *International Economics* (1951).
8 For a negative definition of rules, see Hayek (1960, p. 19).
9 This is a summary of an economically illiterate but popularly accepted view of globalisation. For such treatments that fall clearly into the pop internationalist or do-it-yourself-economics category, see Gray (1998), Soros (1998), and Martin and Schumann (1997). For a more economically literate treatment of the alleged distributional effects of globalisation, see Rodrik (1997).
10 For this view of globalisation, which emphasises historical continuity and national governance, see Sally (2000a) and Henderson (1998b, pp. 58–65, 111–121).
11 A handful of international agencies, such as the International Postal Union and the International Telegraph Union, were established in the nineteenth century. However, these were small-scale, technical, and apolitical creations, unlike the major international agencies set up in the twentieth century.
12 On knowledge problems and government failure in international policy co-ordination, see Sally (1998).
13 On NGOs, anti-liberal attitudes, and democratic accountability, see Henderson (1999a).

References

Bordo, Michael, Barry Eichengreen, and Douglas Irwin (1999), 'Is Globalization Today Really Different Than -Globalization a Hundred Years Ago?', National Bureau of Economic Research Working Paper No. 7195.

Calomiris, Charles (1998), 'The IMF's Imprudent Role As Lender of Last Resort', *Cato Journal*, Special Issue on Money and Capital Flows in a Global Economy, vol. 17, no. 3.

Edwards, Sebastian (1995), 'Comments', in Stephen Haggard, *Developing Countries and the Politics of Global Integration*, Brookings Institution, Washington DC.

Gray, John (1998), *False Dawn: The Delusions of Global Capitalism*, Granta Books, London.

Haggard, Stephen (1995), *Developing Countries and the Politics of Global Integration*, Brookings Institution, Washington DC.

Hayek, Friedrich A. von (1944), *The Road to Serfdom*, Routledge, London.

Hayek, Friedrich A. von (1960), *The Constitution of Liberty*, Routledge, London.

Henderson, David (1993), 'International Economic Co-operation Revisited', *Government and Opposition*, vol. 28, no. 1.

Henderson, David (1998a), 'International Agencies and Cross-Border Liberalisation: The WTO in Context', in Anne O. Krueger (ed.), *The WTO as an International Organisation*, World Trade Organisation, Geneva.

Henderson, David (1998b), *The Changing Fortunes of Economic Liberalism: Yesterday, Today and Tomorrow*, Institute of Economic Affairs, London.

Henderson, David (1999a), 'The Changing International Economic Order: Rival Visions for the Coming Millennium', *International Finance* vol. 2, no. 3.

Henderson, David (1999b), *The MAI Affair: A Story and Its Lessons*, Royal Institute of International Affairs, London.

Irwin, Douglas (1998), 'Comments on the Paper by David Henderson', in Anne O. Krueger (ed.), *The WTO as an International Organisation*, World Trade Organisation, Geneva.

Kaul, Inge, Isabelle Grunberg, and Marc Stern (eds.) (1999), *Global Public Goods: International Co-operation in the Twenty-first Century*, Oxford University Press, New York.

Landes, David S. (1998), *The Wealth and Poverty of Nations: Why Some Are So Rich and Others So Poor*, Norton, New York.

Martin, Hans-Peter, and Harald Schumann (1997), *The Global Trap: Globalisation and the Assault on Prosperity and Democracy*, Zed Books, New York.

Meltzer, Allan (1998), 'Asian Problems and the IMF', *Cato Journal*, Special Issue on Money and Capital Flows in a Global Economy, vol. 17, no. 3.

Organisation for Economic Co-operation and Development (1998), *Open Markets Matter: The Benefits of Trade and Investment Liberalisation*, Organisation for Economic Co-operation and Development, Paris.

Robbins, Lionel (1937), *Economic Planning and International Order*, Macmillan, London.

Robbins, Lionel (1958), *Robert Torrens and the Evolution of Classical Economics*, Macmillan, London.

Rodrik, Dani (1997), *Has Globalisation Gone Too Far?*, Institute for International Economics, Washington DC.

Roessler, Frieder (1998), 'Domestic Policy Objectives and the Multilateral Trade Order: Lessons from the Past', in Anne O. Krueger (ed.), *The WTO as an International Organisation*, World Trade Organisation, Geneva.

Röpke, Wilhelm(1959), *International Order and Economic Integration*, Reidel, Dordrecht.

Sachs, Jeffrey, and Andrew Warner (1995), 'Economic Reform and The Process of Global Integration', in William C. Brainard and George L. Perry (eds.), *Brookings Papers on Economic Activity*, vol. 1.

Sally, Razeen (1998), *Classical Liberalism and International Economic Order: Studies in Theory and Intellectual History*, Routledge, London, pp. 54–60.

Sally, Razeen (1999), 'National Trade Policy Reform, The WTO and the Millennium Round: The Case of Developing Countries and Countries in Transition', Paper prepared for the World Trade Organization seminar, Cato Center for Trade Policy Studies, Washington DC, 17 November.

Sally, Razeen (2000a), 'Globalisation and Policy Response: Three Perspectives', *Government and Opposition*, vol. 35, no. 2, pp. 239–253.

Sally, Razeen (2000b), 'Hayek and International Economic Order', *ORDO*, vol. 51.

Smith, Adam (1976 [1776]), *An Inquiry into the Nature and Causes of the Wealth of Nations*, Book IV, University of Chicago Press, Chicago.

Soros, George (1998), *The Crisis in Global Capitalism: Open Society Endangered*, BBS/Public Affairs, New York.

Tumlir, Jan (1980), 'National Sovereignty, Power, and Interest', *ORDO*, vol. 31.

Tumlir, Jan (1981), 'Evolution of the Concept of International Economic Order, 1914–1980', in Frances Cairncross (ed.), *Changing Perspectives of Economic Policy: Essays in Honour of Sir Alec Cairncross*, Methuen, London.

Tumlir, Jan (1983a), 'International Economic Order and Democratic Constitutionalism', *ORDO*, vol. 34.

Tumlir, Jan (1983b), 'Need for an Open Multilateral Trading System', *World Economy*, vol. 6, no. 4.

United Nations Development Programme (1999), *Human Development Report 1999*, United Nations, New York.

Vasquez, Ian (1998), 'Official Assistance, Economic Freedom, and Policy Change: Is Foreign Aid Like Champagne?', *Cato Journal*, vol. 18, no. 2.

Viner, Jacob (1951), *International Economics*, The Free Press, Glencoe, IL.

World Bank (1997), *World Development Report 1997: The State in a Changing World*, World Bank, Washington DC.

World Bank (1999), *World Development Report 1999/2000: Entering the 21st Century*, World Bank, Washington DC.

Yeager, Leland (1998), 'How to Avoid International Financial Crises', *Cato Journal*, Special Issue on Money and Capital Flows in a Global Economy, vol. 17, no. 3.

Part II
The Broad Agenda

6 The G7 and the Debt of the Poorest

BARBARA DLUHOSCH

The Task: Achieving Debt Sustainability

In 1996, the Highly Indebted Poor Countries (HIPC) initiative was launched to help resolve the problems of the poorest countries that faced considerable difficulties in servicing their external debt. The initiative aims at putting them in a situation to honour their obligations without rescheduling so that they may return to a sustainable debt path. At the G7 Summit in Cologne in June 1999, the leaders agreed to extend debt relief and programmes for sustaining development to help these countries get started without being drowned by the burden of repayment and interest rates. This extension was conditional on concluding adjustment programs supported by the International Monetary Fund (IMF) and the World Bank. However, there are considerable doubts about whether this G8 remedy will be effective. Trade might be a much better cure for the disease, as it does not suffer from the principal-agent problems suffered by the Cologne Debt Initiative.

The HIPC Initiative

Taken together, all developing countries had a nominal external debt of US$2095 billion in 1996. This corresponds to a net present value (NPV) (that is, interest and principal discounted at market rates) of US$1865 billion. The difference reflects the fact that interest rates on many of the loans to these countries are below market rates, if not free of any interest at all. In terms of NPV, the debt amounts to 36 percent of the gross national product (GNP) or 169 percent of the export earnings of the Less Developed Countries (LDCs) (World Bank 1999b).

Forty-one of these countries are currently classified as HIPCs according to the HIPC initiative. They consist of two sub-groups. The first comprises 32 countries that had a per capita GNP in 1993 of US$695 or less and had either a 1993 NPV debt-to-exports ratio higher than 220 percent or an NPV debt-to-GNP ratio higher than 80 percent. The second sub-group consists of nine countries that received (or are potentially eligible for) concessional rescheduling of debt from Paris Club[1] creditors (Boote and Thugge 1998). In 1996, highly indebted countries faced a total nominal debt of US$214 billion, which corresponds to US$167 billion in NPV terms, and an NPV debt-to-GNP ratio of 111 percent and an NPV debt-to-exports ratio of 446 percent.[2] Most of the HIPC debt is owed by sub-Saharan African countries (namely US$156 billion in nominal terms and US$120 billion in NPV, which corresponds to an NPV debt-to-GNP ratio of 120 percent and an NPV debt-to-exports ratio of 521 percent) (World Bank 1999b).

Since 1988, almost two thirds of the increase in debt of those 41 HIPC countries has been due to outstanding interest payments and principal repayments. From 1990 to 1994, net resource flows, including bilateral grants to HIPCs, amounted to approximately 8 percent of GNP. Nonetheless, these concessional flows were not considered to go far enough to allow for sustainability or a permanent exit from rescheduling for a reasonable period.[3]

Consequently, in 1996, the HIPC initiative aimed to provide procedures for debt relief thanks to loans from multilateral institutions such as the IMF and the World Bank, conditional on a process for qualifying that makes sure that reforms are under way. After three years, 67 percent of debt could be forgiven according to the Naples conditions.[4] The HIPC initiative allowed for a further reduction of debt (a debt forgiveness of up to 80 percent) after three more years of sustained reforms. This debt relief was subject to a two-stage process (conditional on reforms) and involved a rescheduling of payments. At the first stage, Paris Club creditors provide flow rescheduling according to the Naples terms and the debtor must establish a three-year record of good performance. After that time, if the country qualifies according to the IMF and Word Bank (the decision point) and requests additional support to facilitate sustainability, the country enters the second stage. At this stage, Paris Club creditors provide further concessional debt reduction and the country must establish a second three-year track record of good performance, after which it reaches the completion point. If the country qualifies, the creditors make a joint effort to provide sufficient assistance for debt sustainability and the Paris Club members reduce the debt up to 80 percent (Boote and Thugge 1998).

The sustainability indicators built into the HIPC initiative involve both the NPV debt-to-exports ratio and the debt-service-to-exports ratio. The target rates were defined on a case-by-case basis with a debt-to-exports ratio of between 200 percent and 250 percent in NPV and between 20 percent and 25 percent for the ratio of debt service to exports. For countries considered highly open according to their export-to-GNP ratio (namely, a ratio of at least 40 percent) and with strong efforts to generate fiscal revenue for servicing the debt (that is, a minimum threshold of 20 percent of GNP); the NPV debt-to-export target was set at below 200 percent and the NPV debt-to-exports ratio at 280 percent in NPV terms at the completion point (Boote and Thugge 1998).

So far, seven countries have benefited from the HIPC initiative (Bolivia, Uganda, Burkina Faso, Guyana, Mozambique, Côte d'Ivoire, and Mali). They received debt relief worth a total of US$3078 million in NPV terms, which relieved them from an estimated nominal debt service of US$6060 million. Bolivia received US$448 million and Uganda received US$347 million; US$115 million was approved for Burkina Faso, US$345 million for the Côte d'Ivoire, US$253 million for Guyana, US$128 million for Mali, and US$1442 million for Mozambique (all figures in NPV). Countries such as Myanmar, Liberia, and the Democratic Republic of Congo were not included because they lacked the political will to reform.

The G7 and the Cologne Debt Initiative

In addition to bilateral attempts to help these countries service their debt, in June 1999 the G7 leaders endorsed the Cologne Debt Initiative, which proposes further relief for highly indebted poor countries (see Appendix D). The Cologne Debt Initiative aims 'to reinforce the [HIPC] initiative so as to enhance the prospects for a robust and lasting exit for qualifying countries from recurrent debt problems'. It consists of five parts: conditionality or complementary measures, procedural suggestions, a reassessment of the criteria for potential eligibility, the volume of debt relief, and the financing of the package.

According to the Cologne Debt Initiative, debt relief should be conditional on major and continuing reforms in debtor countries. This would require strong links between debt relief, adjustments, policy reform, and measures explicitly directed at reducing poverty. In their pursuit of sustainability and poverty reduction, LDCs would be assisted by the International Financial Institutions (IFIs). Debt relief could be accelerated by shortening the second stage set out in the HIPC initiative, an option that would be available to debtor countries whose performance had improved. In effect, therefore, the completion point of the second stage could be reached sooner; the G7 leaders, in fact, suggested a floating completion point. In addition, the IFIs would provide interim relief so that countries that qualify under the HIPC initiative would receive debt relief even sooner, before debt reduction is implemented at the completion point. Moreover, debt reduction could be front loaded, so that most of the relief would be granted at the beginning. Last but not least, the criteria for potential eligibility would be reassessed and lowered. In particular, according to the Cologne Debt Initiative, the NPV debt-to-exports ratio should be reduced from 200 to 250 percent to a single target of 150 percent and the NPV debt-to-revenue ratio should be reduced from 280 percent to 250 percent. Furthermore, the criteria aimed at coping with problems of moral hazard should also be reduced. The export-to-GDP ratio should be reduced from 40 percent to 30 percent and the tax-revenue-to-GDP ratio should be reduced from 20 percent to 15 percent.

These measures are intended to ensure deeper, faster, and broader debt relief (in other words, relief accessible by more countries). They aim to reduce the debt of the poorest countries by US$71 billion in NPV in addition to the existing debt relief programs of another US$27 billion plus US$20 billion owed to the G7 countries under Official Development Assistance. The Cologne Debt Initiative would be financed by interest income and the interest on proceeds of the sale of up to 10 million ounces of the IMF's gold reserves. Multilateral development banks would contribute, supplemented by bilateral contributions to the HIPC Trust Fund, with an appropriate sharing of the burden. Other creditors would be encouraged to contribute to debt relief.

After the Cologne Summit, the IMF and World Bank (1999) submitted the modified HIPC initiative along these lines to the IMF Executive Board (1999) and the World Bank. They agreed to the basic suggestions. In particular, they supported reducing the NPV debt-to-exports ratio to 150 percent, reducing the NPV debt-to-fiscal-revenue ratio to 250 percent, and reducing the eligibility threshold for the openness of an economy to an exports-to-GDP ratio of 30 percent and a debt-service-to-exports ratio to 15 percent of GDP. (The statement issued by the Executive Board also reflects some dispute over what is the most important indicator in the analysis of debt service.) As the Executive Board points out, measures of debt relief would be supplemented by attempts at poverty reduction and there are a number of suggestions for speeding up reforms and the decision-making process, and for simplifying the implementation of the HIPC initiative, mostly as outlined by the G7 finance ministers (1999).

Sustainability Indicators: How Unpleasant Is the Debt Arithmetic?

How much of a burden is the debt for LDCs? The intertemporal budget constraint is a useful guide. From this perspective, today's primary deficits (that is, deficits less interest payments) require future primary surpluses. This fact is related to the calculation of the debt in present value (PV) terms. Compared to GNP, the numbers seem large. In 1995–97, a number of HIPCs reached a debt-to-GNP ratio of more than 200 percent (in PV): Angola's debt amounted to 244 percent of GNP, the Democratic Republic of Congo's to 215 percent; the Republic of Congo had a debt-to-GNP ratio of 248 percent, Guinea-Bissau of 258 percent, and Nicaragua of 268 percent. Sao Tome and Principe had a ratio of 375 percent (World Bank 1999b).

However, quite apart from the discounting issue, timing matters. What matters in particular is when the debt is to be repaid. Calculations of the debt-to-GNP ratio in NPV suggest that repayment is now due and that there are no further inflows. However, this contradicts relative endowments and the debt cycle. As long as trade does not equalise factor returns internationally, capital should flow north-south because LDCs' relative endowments of capital are comparatively small and investments should yield a relatively high return. Given fresh money, loan payments can be rescheduled. Hence, as far as sustainability is concerned, the amount of debt itself is a poor indicator. On a microeconomic scale, the decisive parameter is the rate of return on funded projects compared to interest payments; on a macroeconomic scale, the corresponding measure is the growth rate versus the interest rate.

In fact, most of the debt is due to principal repayments. The amount that is due to accumulated interest payments is comparatively small, because many of the loans have been granted at low or no interest rates. As a group, the HIPCs owe a concessional debt of almost 50 percent of their total debt. For some individual countries, it is as high as 90 percent; for example, in Mali, in 1997 it was 89 percent, Burundi 92.8 percent, and in Lao PDR 96.7 percent (World Bank 1999a). Because most of the loans are granted at low interest rates, interest payments amount to an average of approximately 6 percent of export earnings (see Table 6.1). From this perspective, the number of countries facing a severe debt crisis is considerably smaller than what the stock of debt suggest.

The question of the extent to which interest payments are a burden remains, however. The severity of the burden depends on how loans have been allocated (see Siebert 1989; Dluhosch, Freytag, and Krüger 1996). If funds are used for consumption rather than investment, cash flow is low and transfers are painful.

Projects such as famine relief, health measures, and basic infrastructure pay in a very indirect way. In addition, there is little fresh money that would allow loans to be rolled over. Generally speaking, net capital flows from developed countries to LDCs are small compared to flows among, for instance, industrial countries. Some interpret this relationship as proof of the inapplicability of relative endowments and rates of return; they maintain that growth would feed on itself thanks to increasing returns. However, the empirical proof of this interpretation is slim. There is convincing evidence that the East Asian miracle was caused by increased input and capital accumulation rather than by growth in total factor productivity (TFP) (Young 1992) and in a considerable number of countries the 'miracle' was built on government guaranties and subsidies. However, calculations also reveal that the lack of fresh capital is

Table 6.1 Key Indebtedness Ratios, 1995–1997
(US$ million and percent)

Country	Total EDT[a] (1997)	EDT/ EX[b]	PV[c]/ EX	EDT/ GNP[d]	PV/ GNP	TDS[e]/ EX	INT[f]/ EX
Bolivia	5248	401	252	73	46	32	14
Burkina Faso	1297	423	237	53	30	16	6
Côte d'Ivoire	15 609	423	305	191	138	30	11
Guyana	1610	245	143	274	159	17	6
Mali	2950	524	220	118	50	17	6
Mozambique	5990	1217	708	264	153	29	12
Uganda	3708	478	269	60	34	21	6
Average of 41 countries	–	349	272	126	98	15	6

a EDT: external debt
b EX: exports
c PV: net present value of external debt
d GNP: gross national product
e TDS: total debt service
f INT: interest payments

Source: World Bank 1999b.

due to risk, so that rates of return are much smaller than relative endowments suggest (Lucas 1990).

From the perspective of sustainability, in many cases the rate of return declines because of a lack of government will to reform rather than because of a lack of projects. Too frequently, additional money and the leeway it provides are either spent on arms or privatised instead of channelled into projects that offer a reasonable rate of return (even if calculation may be difficult). Expected rates of return for investors are reduced even further in cases where countries lack the willingness rather than the ability to pay. Nonetheless, the primary focus must be on the ratio of interest payments to the ability to sell and earn international exchange. Selling and exporting revenues are also a matter of macroeconomic performance, including non-distorted exchange rates.

One indicator of the vulnerability of debt sustainability is the amount of short-term debt in relation to total debt.[5] For the HIPCs as a group, the numbers are stable: the share of short-term debt totalled 18.1 percent of total debt in 1980, 15.2 percent in 1990, 17.2 percent in 1995, and 16.4 percent in 1997. Differences among countries exist, however. In the Democratic Republic of Congo, for instance, the share of short-term capital climbed from 7.2 percent in 1990 to 26.8 percent in 1997, in the Côte d'Ivoire from 7.7 percent to 26.9 percent in 1993 (with a slight reduction to 17 percent in 1997), in Equatorial Guinea from 5 percent in 1985 to 21.7 percent in 1997, in Liberia from 8.4 percent in 1985 to 32.1 percent in 1997, and in Sudan from 11.6 percent in 1980 to 37 percent in 1997 (World Bank 1999a). Yet, again the time structure of debt is not set externally but is a matter of the riskiness of investment, which in turn is, *inter alia*, a function of the country's macroeconomic policies as well as its microeconomic policies.

Achieving Sustainable Development Via Softening Budget Constraints

Even though the arithmetic of debt is unpleasant, debt relief may not be appropriate. Two types of arguments in favour of debt relief can be distinguished. The first is of the efficiency-enhancing type, the second is distributive in nature. The efficiency-enhancing argument comes in four variants. The first is the hypothesis that without debt relief LDCs will not achieve sustainable development. This argument relates to the development-push arguments of the 1940s and 1950s (Rosenstein-Rodan 1943; Hirschman 1958; Myrdal 1957; Nurkse 1958). According to these theories, industrialisation and, more generally, development depend on market size. As forward and backward linkages are missing, local markets are considered to be too small to sustain a business. Therefore, the economies of these countries can hardly start unless they receive help, in other words, unless they receive a development push. This argument has been recently elaborated by Murphy, Shleifer, and Vishny (1989). However, apart from the fact that businesses are not necessarily restricted to local markets (except where economic policy is protectionist), if the argument holds true aid should pay off. Put differently, there should be no need for debt relief. Some may consider that this has not yet happened because debt relief simply has not gone far enough to make an impact. At any rate, rather than requiring debt relief, this variant of the efficiency-enhancing argument calls for a careful selection of investment projects with the help of institutions that have local knowledge.

Internationally co-ordinated efforts might enhance efficiency insofar as they gather and bundle information and somehow pool the experience gained in economic development. In fact, there is an underlying fixed-cost argument: the costs of gathering information are largely fixed costs, which might be too high for an individual investor (see Krueger 1998, p. 1999). However, this is again a matter of market size, rather than of the cost-benefit calculation of an investor. Many individual investors can share in the costs. This in itself does not yet require international co-ordination; neither does it necessarily involve debt forgiveness. The argument that information would otherwise be poorer and that LDCs would be more inclined to give additional information if they had the prospect of debt relief applies to any fresh money, private sources included. There should be an incentive to provide such information no matter who the recipient, if information and the additional loans pay off.

The second variant of the efficiency-enhancing argument is the scapegoat argument. Because policy reform involves costs, particularly for those with vested interests, internal opposition to reforms might be lessened by turning to an international institution or agreement. The classic example is the attempt to curb inflation if the formation of expectations is backward looking (because otherwise policy reform is not credible). In sub-Saharan countries, for example, monetary policy is often tied to other currencies, so policy reform of institutions and fiscal policy is a major issue to which this argument might apply. Fiscal restraint and institutional reform cause a temporary retardation in economic growth. Overcoming the opposition to institutional reforms may be the strongest argument in favour of international co-ordination, much stronger than any argument based on market failure in capital markets or incomplete markets. With reference to World Bank lending, Gavin and Rodrik (1995, p. 331) therefore remark 'this suggests that, much more than its lending operations per se, the Bank's role as policy advisor and institution builder has been the key to its impact on economic development'. As in business consulting, the contribution to development is not necessarily superior knowledge but the opportunity to have somebody from the outside who can be held responsible, thus lowering internal protest and political disputes. Otherwise, policymakers might not carry out reforms in order to avoid the risk of being thrown out of office. Multilateral attempts might have the additional advantage over bilateral ones of reducing dissent. Generally speaking, policy reforms are supposed to gain credibility with the help of internationally co-ordinated efforts. However, more important than the prospect of debt relief is the bestowal of a reputation of success, since debt relief does not *per se* deliver successful economic reforms nor an income stream.

The third variant is the problem of achieving co-ordination on debt relief (see Sachs [forthcoming]). Without an internationally co-ordinated effort, debt relief might not come about. This applies if there is a considerable share of bilateral debt (rather than multilateral debt), which might create a free-rider problem as each creditor waits for another to make a concession. This is where the G7 can play a role by providing a forum where numbers are both sufficiently small to reach an agreement and sufficiently large to make an impact. International co-ordination might be one means to solve a prisoner's dilemma and create a better equilibrium.[6] Still, it requires that there are potential co-operative gains to be reaped by debt relief.

The fourth variant of the efficiency-enhancing argument proposes possible gains from co-operation due to externalities, even if classic development-push arguments do not apply (Krueger 1998). However, in contrast to the debt crisis of the 1980s and the Asian crisis of the 1990s, the systemic risk involved seems to be low. Indeed, providing debt relief is a signal that may increase systemic risk rather than reduce it. One could argue exactly the opposite of the externality argument, namely that debt relief itself generates an externality because it creates incentives for a misallocation of resources.[7] In fact, principal-agent problems can make for some unpleasant arithmetic. This can be seen in the discussion about the IMF's role in the recent Asian crisis, which was caused largely by the expectation of private investors of a bail-out. A related position argues that debt relief mitigates the concern of potential investors that after they have invested their money and are thus captured, they must contribute to government revenues by way of increased taxes to service the outstanding debt, which diminishes expected rates of return. This is the bail-out argument. Debt relief creates a problem of moral hazard but does not address the problem properly. Rather, it perpetuates any current dependence on aid and lays the foundation for the next round of debt relief. Therefore, debt relief suffers from a credibility problem. It aims at a development push for LDCs, but it only works if the international community would commit to a 'no debt-relief rule' in the future.[8] Granting debt relief gives the wrong signal, making the commitment not credible. Thus, the game goes on. To achieve a better equilibrium via co-ordination, one must prove that the G7 or any other informal or formal international institution can evaluate risks better than private investors can. There are occasions for which this may hold true, such as infrastructure projects and health care (Sachs 1999). However, as already mentioned, specific projects should be selected carefully with the help of institutions that have local knowledge.

With regard to the distributional type of argument, such as the one described by John Rawls (1971), some states are born into an environment that is less conducive to economic growth than the one that exists in other parts of the world (Sachs 1999). There can be no doubt that difficult environmental circumstances, poor health conditions, difficult climate, famines, and so on contribute to the malaise. Nonetheless, debt relief might be the wrong tack.

The G7's Contribution to Sustainable Development: Trade Instead of Aid

There is one variant of the externality argument that is more convincing. Higher growth rates in LDCs are associated with positive (pecuniary) externalities insofar as the scarce resources are used more efficiently.[9] Although LDC growth might hurt workers in developed countries by way of Stolper-Samuelson and Rybczynski effects,[10] on the whole their growth involves a dividend for developed countries as well. Therefore, developed countries should have an economic interest in the enhanced growth of LDCs. Again, because the benefits are widespread, an economically efficient equilibrium may not come about if efforts are uncoordinated: each country or its citizens have a small stake in the dividend (which is not yet visible). Hence, one could argue that unless these interests are co-ordinated and bundled, the chances of realising this dividend are at best low. Such a dividend calls for a removal of barriers to trade, including inappropriate exchange rate arrangements that distort international trade flows.

The trade argument has two sides. With regard to LDCs, trade liberalisation implies removing barriers to trade and capital flows. In fact, the claim for trade liberalisation goes much further than trade policy in the narrow sense of the term. Unrealistic exchange rate policies, import licences, and, more generally, the barriers to import that are common in LDCs reduce exports as they deter imports. The latter applies to import substitution policies of various sorts as well as the protection of industries that compete with imports (Krueger 1997, 1998). Therefore, policy reform in these areas must be included in any attempt to promote trade. Consequently, openness indicators should be given more weight instead of less (as suggested by the G7 and in the IMF and World Bank report).

As to the second side of the trade argument, the G7 could make a co-ordinated effort in trade liberalisation, particularly in sensitive areas such as agriculture.[11] Clearly, there is a role for the G7 in economic development because trade liberalisation has positive public repercussions. Notably, it meets the criterion of non-rivalry.[12] In particular, trade liberalisation in goods with low skill content lowers barriers for development. Otherwise LDCs must get a foothold in markets that require more advanced technology and more human skills, which is much more difficult to achieve.[13] As with so many cases, the work starts at home. To protect the very industries and markets that could make a good start is inconsistent with the claim to further economic development in lagging countries. In trying to remedy side effects such as retarded development in LDCs, governments often resort to more intervention and protection, including financial aid and its principal-agent problems.

One of the major problems for LDCs is the implementation of market-friendly institutions and the elimination of corruption and conflict. The problem of governance is more easily detected than remedied. Trying to promote market-friendly institutions using tied aid has its limits. Trade-propelled growth is one means to overcome the opposition against reform, because it transforms relative returns of rent-seeking actvities versus market activities in favour of market activities. It destabilises collusion, promotes competition, and encourages a more efficient use of scarce resources. Hence, 'it is probable that trade policy changes have a higher rate of return to LDCs than most other feasible policy changes' (Krueger 1990, p. 101).[14]

Notes

1   The Paris Club is an informal group of creditors that have met regularly in Paris since 1956 to negotiate debt restructuring and rescheduling with debtor nations that are facing debt-servicing difficulties.
2   Data are taken from the World Bank Debtor Reporting System and World Bank Staff estimates for 1999.
3   See for instance Gerster (1998).
4   At the 1994 G7 Summit in Naples, the Naples conditions replaced the London terms, which were introduced in 1991 to grant up to 50 percent of debt relief. The London terms in turn replaced the Toronto terms introduced in 1988 with a level of concessionality of up to one third (see Boothe and Thugge 1998).

International Monetary Fund and World Bank (1999), 'Modifications to the Heavily Indebted Poor Countries (HIPC) Initiative', <www.imf.org/external/np/hipc/modify/hipc.htm> (September 2000).

Krueger, Anne O. (1990), 'Trade Policy as an Input to Development', in *Perspectives on Trade and Development*, Harvester Wheatsheaf, New York.

Krueger, Anne O. (1997), 'Trade Policy and Economic Development: How Do We Learn?' *American Economic Review*, vol. 87, pp. 1–22.

Krueger, Anne O. (1998), 'Whither the World Bank and the IMF?', *Journal of Economic Literature*, vol. 36, pp. 1983–2020.

Larosière, Jacques de (1985), 'Interrelationships between Protectionism and the Debt Crisis', *Aussenwirtschaft*, vol. 40, pp. 219–228.

Lucas, Robert E. (1990), 'Why Doesn't Capital Flow from Rich to Poor Countries?', *American Economic Review*, vol. 80 (Papers and Proceedings).

Murphy, Kevin M., Andrei Shleifer, and Robert W. Vishny (1989), 'Industrialization and the Big Push', *Journal of Political Economy*, vol. 97, pp. 1003–1026.

Myrdal, Gunnar (1957), *Economic Theory and Underdeveloped Regions*, Duckworth, London.

Nurkse, Ragnar (1958), *Problems of Capital Formation in Underdeveloped Countries*, Blackwell, Oxford.

Rawls, John (1971), *A Theory of Justice*, Harvard University Press, Cambridge, MA.

Rodrik, Dani (1997), 'Trade Policy and Economic Performance in Sub-Saharan Africa', Study commissioned by the Swedish Ministry of Economic Affairs <www.ksg.harvard.edu/rodrik/papers.html> (September 2000).

Rosenstein-Rodan, Paul (1943), 'Problems of Industrialization in Eastern and South-Eastern Europe', *Economic Journal*, vol. 53, pp. 202–211.

Sachs, Jeffrey (1999), 'Helping the World's Poorest', *Economist*, 14 August, pp. 17–20.

Sachs, Jeffrey (forthcoming), 'Do We Need a Lender of Last Resort?' Graham Lecture, Princeton International Finance Series.

Sachs, Jeffrey, and Andrew Warner (1995), 'Economic Reform and the Process of Global Integration', *Brookings Papers on Economic Activity*, vol. 1, no. 95.

Shleifer, Andrei, and Robert W. Vishny (1993), 'Corruption', *Quarterly Journal of Economics*, vol. 108, pp. 599–617.

Siebert, Horst (1989), 'The Half and the Full Debt Cycle', *Weltwirtschaftliches Archiv*, vol. 125, pp. 217–229.

World Bank (1999a), *Global Development Finance 1999*, Washington DC, <www.worldbank.org/prospects/gdf99> (September 2000).

World Bank (1999b), HIPC Debt Tables in Global Development Finance 1999, Washington DC, <www.worldbank.org/hipc/about/debt-table/debt-table.html> (September 2000).

Young, Alwyn (1992), 'A Tale of Two Cities: Factor Accumulation and Technical Change in Hong Kong and Singapore', *NBER Macroeconomics Annual*, MIT Press, Cambridge, MA.

7 Modern Concert Diplomacy: The Contact Group and the G7/8 in Crisis Management

CHRISTOPH SCHWEGMANN

Introduction

The decades since World War II have been marked by an intensive process of institutionalising the international political system. One significant result has been the establishment of international organisations such as the United Nations (UN), the European Union (EU), and the North Atlantic Treaty Organization (NATO). A second result has been the formation of dozens of international regimes on such important issues as nonproliferation, disarmament, and climate change. Together, these international organisations and regimes constitute the co-operative framework for a rule-governed management of international conflict.

Over the past 25 years, however, there has been a parallel development to such rule-guided processes. In 1975, seven powers decided to address issues of common concern collectively through policy co-ordination outside formal international organisations. This decision by the greatest industrial powers, that is, the G7 — the United States, Canada, Japan, Britain, Germany, France, and Italy — was later recognised as the establishment of an international concert similar to the European Concert of Powers in the nineteenth century (Kirton 1989, 1993, 1997, 1999; Dewitt and Kirton 1983, Lewis 1992, Wallace 1984). However, even though the G7 and, with the addition of Russia, the G8 are prominent, they are not the only modern international concerts in world politics. There are also the Contact Group for Namibia (1977–1982) and the Contact Group for Bosnia and Kosovo (1995–1999). The existence of such groups supports the hypothesis that modern concerts arise periodically to guide the efforts of the international community represented in international organisations. However, despite the occasional suggestion (Odom 1995), this hypothesis has never been seriously explored by scholars of international relations. It deserves a careful, comprehensive, conceptual, and empirical analysis, now, after the unexpected military conflict in the Balkans and Kosovo as the twentieth century ended, and the presence of a still precarious peace in those regions as the twenty-first century begins.

This chapter conducts such an analysis. It examines the concept of modern concert diplomacy and its impact in recent regional crisis management. To do so, it first develops the concept by contrasting it with other concepts of multilateral co-operation, especially international regimes and international organisations. Second, the chapter assesses the role played by modern concert diplomacy in contemporary international relations in an examination of a critical case study of great power diplomacy in Bosnia-Herzegovina and Kosovo within the framework of the Contact Group and the G7/8. In so doing, it contributes to a deeper understanding of their role in ending the hostilities among the ethnic parties and in shaping the post-war order in that region. The chapter concludes with a look at the future tasks and roles of concert diplomacy in general, and the G7/8 in particular, in managing violent international crises.

This analysis argues that concerts are institutions that rely on few informal rules and mainly serve to co-ordinate policy, in contrast with international regimes and organisations that are explicitly established for a rule-guided management of international relations. Its exploration of the two critical cases confirms that the G7/8 and the Contact Group share the same underlying logic. Both demonstrate the use and effectiveness of modern concert diplomacy for high-security crisis management. More specifically, both concerts served as lightly institutionalised arenas for policy co-ordination among an exclusive group of powerful states that aimed to lead the international community. Their reference to international principles, rules, and norms further confirmed this intention, and helped to give their efforts legitimacy in the outside community of states.

Within the concert, the role of the EU also gave lesser states a substantive constraining role. Although the Contact Group and the G7/8 were both born of crisis, the willingness of their great-power founders to transfer subsequent activities in order to establish international order shows how concerts reinforce, rather than replace, the existing organisational array (cf. Kirton 1993). In future crises, great power management under the guidance of the G8 rather than a contact group flag could enhance the impression of legitimacy and place a regional crisis into a broader global context. It could also create the unwanted impression that the G8 feels responsible for crisis management all over the world in ways that meets neither the G8's capacities nor its intentions. Such a move should thus be approached with caution.

Modern Concert Diplomacy

The Concept of 'Concert': The Quest for a Theory

An interest in institutions has dominated international relations theory over the past few decades (see Katzenstein, Keohane, and Krasner 1998). However, very few scholars have focussed their attention on the concept of concert diplomacy, and those who have done so have not pointed to the conceptual robustness or the empirical or policy relevance of the concert approach to global governance in the modern age (Kupchan and Kupchan 1991, Jervis 1985). Instead, the bulk of the theoretical work focuses on co-operation in international regimes (e.g., Keohane 1982, Krasner 1983, Young 1982, Kohler-Koch 1989, Mueller 1993) and international organisations (e.g., Archer 1992, Rittberger 1994). A broad consensus has emerged that international regimes are best conceived of as 'sets of implicit or explicit principles, norms, rules, and decision-making procedures around which actors' expectations converge in a given area of international relations' (Krasner 1982, p. 186). In so doing they constitute 'negotiated orders' (Young 1983, p. 99). Taking a wide definition of regimes, one could argue that the G7 is part of a global regime for finance and trade, while the Bosnian Contact Group is an informal part of a European security regime. Such an extensive understanding of regimes, however, does not take the different roots of these institutions into account and therefore does not generate a productive application of regime analysis.

International (governmental) organisations, as distinct from regimes, are entities with a purpose. They are bureaucratic organisations, with explicit rules and specific assignments of rules to individuals and groups, which are deliberately created and designed by states. In external relations they can be actors in international politics (see Keohane 1989, p. 3).

Nonetheless, the work of some scholars represents a notable exception to the general focus on international regimes and organisations, and is a useful first step in developing and applying the concert concept to international relations in the modern period. Elrod (1976), Jervis (1985), and Kupchan and Kupchan (1991) stress the importance of the old Concert of Europe for early institution building in international relations or value it as an early security regime (Jervis 1983). Yet, only Kirton (e.g., 1989) and Wallace (1984) recognise the existence of modern concert diplomacy, identify the G7/8 as its leading empirical expression, and argue that the G7/8 is best understood as a modern international concert. In particular, Kirton (1989) analyses the specific functions of modern concerts. However, despite an early suggestion that other entities such as the Namibian Contact Group fall into this category (Dewitt and Kirton 1983), Kirton has not yet expanded his analysis beyond the case of the G7/8. Wallace (1984) analyses the appropriateness of political summitry for collective crisis management, but he does not distinguish between summitry within international organisations (e.g., Council of the European Community, North Atlantic Council) and summitry outside of them (e.g., G7).

Other recent instances of modern concert diplomacy, such as the Contact Group for Namibia (Karns 1987) and the Contact Group for Bosnia and Herzegovina (Boudevaix 1997), are the focus of suggestive studies that demonstrate the impact of both contact groups on crisis management in each particular case. These studies, however, are not written from a theoretical perspective, and remain rather descriptive.

This overview of the state of research on modern concert diplomacy indicates that there is a clear need for a definition of modern concert diplomacy as the foundation for a fresh theoretical elaboration, broad empirical application, and careful assessment of its role in international politics. Using Elrod's definition (1976, p. 162) as a point of departure, a concert can be defined as 'the great powers meeting together at times of international crisis to maintain peace and to develop European solutions to European problems'. This definition remains valid, if one substitutes 'specific' for 'European', for both old and modern forms of concerts. However, an analysis of modern concerts must take into account the current structure of the international system, which differs from that of the nineteenth century in several respects. Three modern features are most relevant for understanding contemporary concert diplomacy, because they all constitute restrictions on rational state options. These three new structural features are the growing interdependence between states in the international system, the density of institutionalised relations between states, and the recognition that direct war between nuclear powers is no longer an option for governments in the nuclear age. Thus, the difference between old and modern concerts and between modern concerts and regimes must be explored in more detail.

International regimes and organisations are institutions in international politics. The same was true for the nineteenth-century concert. At the Congress of Vienna in 1815, the concert powers took the opportunity to standardise and codify the rules of diplomatic practice and pronounce on other problems in the international system (Archer 1992, p. 7). In the years between 1815 and 1854, the concert worked as a 'conceptual norm among the great powers of the proper and permissible aims and methods of international politics' (Elrod 1976, p. 163). In the twentieth century, however, this function of setting norms and rules for the old concert of power has been transferred to international organisations and the regimes they embed and implement. Most of these rules are now part of the UN Charter (e.g., sovereignty) and of international law in general or have become conventions in diplomatic practice (e.g., reciprocity). Moreover, additional rules and norms are created by international organisations and regimes and not by concerts, especially as the latter only operate from time to time. Hence, it should be difficult to find institutional characteristics in modern concerts. As Keohane (1989, p. 3) points out, an institution is commonly believed to exist if a set of implicit or explicit rules that constrain activities, shape expectations, and prescribe roles can be identified.

In analysing the G7/8 or the Contact Group, one can identify some core general principles, norms, and rules that both constituted the basis for the classic concerts and now serve the specific functions of modern concerts. The underlying common core principle of concert diplomacy is the agreement among a group of great powers that an international crisis is jeopardising international order and that system stability can only be re-established by concert diplomacy, that is, by collective leadership over other states (see Elrod 1976, p. 162; Jervis 1983, p. 179).

Norms that 'are standards of behavior defined in terms of rights and obligations' (Krasner 1982, p. 186) are less easy to identify than are principles. Moreover, due to the informality of concerts, it is difficult in concert analysis to distinguish the convertibility of principles into norms and the implementation of norms into specific rules. As a general norm or rule of concert diplomacy, one can identify the will to act with a sense of solidarity in all questions of a general interest (Elrod 1976, p. 164). This norm or rule demands comprehensive deliberations and negotiations and makes conference diplomacy a common decision-making procedure for acting in concert. A second norm or rule is that the concert powers must respect one another's legitimate rights, as no great power and concert member can be humiliated. 'They must not be challenged either in their vital interests or in their prestige and honor' (Elrod 1976, p. 166). The third norm or rule of concert diplomacy, and one that is particularly relevant for the role of the Contact Group and the G7/8 in Bosnia and Kosovo, is that territorial changes in a region where a concert is established are subject to the collective sanction of the great powers. This means, in the words of Elrod (1976, p. 165), 'The great powers acting in concert determined the acceptable and appropriate limits of change'.

The characteristic procedures of concerts are, in addition to the periodic conference diplomacy noted above, the appearance of the members as a group (the Contact Group, the G7/8) with common positions, expressed in common declarations toward the public. Another key feature is the rule of unanimity and consent in decision making. This visibility is a quality that concerts share with international organisations, although not all such organisations share the consensus procedure, in formality or practice.

Although both modern concerts and regimes can be structured by principles, norms, rules and procedures, there is a crucial difference. In contrast to regular regimes, the typical characteristic of concerts is the explicit noncodification of rules and procedures. Consequently, further institutional development into an international organisation is not an aim of the concert parties.[1] Concerts and regimes share a functional approach to the treatment of the problems they are dealing with (see Müller 1993, p. 30). However, modern concerts are responding to a demand for co-ordination, not regulation. Therefore, *ad hoc* diplomacy remains an important instrument in concert diplomacy. It enables the states to react quickly to a deficit of co-ordination among the great powers. Through concert diplomacy, states hope to increase their flexibility by not accepting wider limitations in their scope of action due to a set of rules, especially as encoded in formal, intergovernmentally agreed treaties or charters. In a nutshell, a concert is an institution that is not meant to be one.

A conception of a modern concert emerges from Elrod's definition of concerts and this argument contends that concerts are institutions. A modern concert is an institution with few, mainly implicit, principles, norms, rules, and procedures and is formed by great powers in the event of international crisis with the aim of re-establishing security and stability by policy co-ordination among the concert powers.

This definition of a concert as a group of great powers implies that the number of participants is restricted. The criterion for membership is power, mainly expressed in terms of military and economic strength. Thus, for the world of international trade and finance and for European-centred international security, one can identify a core group of powers that feel a sense of systemic responsibility and thus feel themselves to be in charge when crises occur. These states are the United States, Britain, and France. These powers — all permanent members of the UN Security Council — constitute the core around which other powerful states such Germany, Russia, Italy, Japan, and Canada unite. The composition of a specific concert will depend on the particular crisis and the power structure among interested parties. In particular, the recent discussions about including China into the G8 (to create the G9) shows that there is a tendency to include states in a concert if they are regarded as key actors in a certain issue area or geographic region (see Chapter 11). Nonetheless, the concert parties must not focus their attention only on great powers. Instead, they must realise that the environment in which modern concerts function is characterised (albeit with regional differences) by complex interdependence and by a dense net of institutionalised relations. Thus, concert powers must consider that many external powers and even actors such as the European Commission can affect concert formation and functioning. Bargaining for access to a concert, on a bilateral or multilateral track, especially by medium powers and strong regional powers, is predictable. Small states and representatives of international organisations are likely to refer to agreed rights and obligations in the treaties and charters of the organisations to which concert great power members belong in order to gain some influence on concert activities.

The Contact Group and the G7/8 in Bosnia and Kosovo

The Genesis of the Contact Group

Embedded in the definition of modern concerts is the fact that such concerts arise in the event of an international crisis. The identification of such a crisis generates the demand for the concert in the view of the great powers. Therefore, the establishment of a concert is not automatic. It depends on specific circumstances. In particular, for a concert to emerge, three conditions must be met: 1) all relevant great powers must agree in their analysis that a crisis occurred, 2) other institutions such as international organisations must not be able to manage the crisis on their own in a way that the great powers regard as satisfactory, 3) the great powers must share the conviction that they can re-establish stability by acting in concert together.

In 1975, the G7 process was started by the governments of the United States, Britain, Canada, Japan, France, Germany, and Italy. Canada followed as a formal member in 1976. The group was created because diplomats recognised that the security and economies of their countries were affected by international developments on which they had little influence (e.g., the 1973 oil crisis and embargo that became an instrument in the 1990–91 Middle East war). Observing that existing international institutions had little leverage in dealing with this crisis, these officials concluded that global leadership by the most powerful economies would enhance the ability of the organisations to manage the crisis (Putnam and Bayne 1987, p. 26; Bayne 2000).

The creation of the Bosnian Contact Group followed a similar logic. The 'Yugoslavian war of dissolution' (Gow 1997) in Bosnia-Herzegovina and

Croatia followed an institutional crisis of the Socialist Federal Republic of Yugoslavia (FRY). This crisis culminated in the declaration of sovereignty of Croatia, Slovenia, and the Macedonian Republic in 1991 and of Bosnia-Herzegovina in 1992. The European Community (EC), although mainly concerned at the time with the reunification of Germany and the negotiation of the Maastricht Treaty, tried to preserve the Yugoslavian state by mediating between the parties. In 1991, a common conference with the United Nations (later called the International Conference on Former Yugoslavia [ICFY]) took place with the aim of preventing the escalation of violence between Serbs, Croats, and Bosnian Muslims. In the years between 1992 and 1994, neither negotiations by the negotiation team of the UN and EC, nor an economic embargo against Serbia and Montenegro could stop the violence. Moreover, several United Nations Security Council (UNSC) declarations and the deployment of the UN Protection Force (UNPROFOR) proved unable to end the war. As a result, the horrors of ethnic cleansing and the massacres of civilians grew.[2]

The crisis had direct effects on the countries in the region, such as the transition states of Romania and Bulgaria. They suffered severe losses in their gross national product (GNP) due to the international embargo against Serbia. In addition, EU states such as Germany and Italy and Yugoslavia's neighbour Austria were forced to care for an estimated half a million refugees. The pan-European dimensions of the problem thus soon became clear.

The initiative to form a contact group came from EU negotiator David Owen. He, among others, realised that the negotiations within the UN-based ICFY in Geneva had decisively failed. Owen had a positive first-hand experience with the Contact Group for Namibia when he was British foreign minister, and consequently thought that substantial progress could be made only if the Europeans involved the United States and Russia in the management of the Balkans. The European states would have to offer a diplomatic framework for policy co-ordination that was acceptable to the U.S. and Russia. The Contact Group was thus not the result of new attitudes among the great powers of Britain, France, and Germany, as smaller European states often claimed (see de Wijk 1998, p. 175). Instead, there was no other choice than to renationalise the European approach if the EU as a whole wanted to safeguard its interests (see Owen 1996, p. 368).

Before 1994, the United States was remarkably absent from the Yugoslavian stage. In February 1994, Russia demonstrated its influence on the Bosnian Serbs by persuading them to withdraw their heavy weapons from the Sarajevo mountains. Then, in March 1994, U.S. diplomats (supported by German colleagues) gained their first success in Bosnian crisis management, when they convinced the Bosnian Croats and Muslims to create a confederation. Russia and the United States, in diplomatic partnership with the ICFY, worked out a compromise for the Krajina region at Zagreb (the so-called Z-4 Group). This solution, however, was eventually not accepted by the conflicting parties (Cohen 1995, p. 310; Tindemans *et al.* 1996, p. 47).

Due to this diplomatic offensive by the United States, the ICFY became increasingly irrelevant, as the belligerents began to think they could gain more through direct negotiations with the Americans. Although the U.S. was very interested in having a common approach with the Europeans, it did not want to deal with all 12 governments or with the EU troika. For the United States, the most relevant partners were the UNSC Permanent Five (P5) members France and Britain, as well as Germany. Dealing with the EU would not serve the needs of the U.S., given that the EU presidency was held by Greece, which followed a conflicting policy on Yugoslavia (Owen 1996, p. 365).

Therefore, two main forces created the Contact Group. The first was the refusal of the American government to co-operate with Owen and UN negotiator Thorwald Stoltenberg within the framework of the ICFY. The second was the conviction of some major European diplomats that the solution required close co-operation among the main European powers, the U.S., and the Russian Federation. Consequently, the U.S., Russia, France, Britain, and Germany, encouraged by Owen, established a policy-making group at an experts' level, in which representatives of the five powers participated. This followed the official appearance of the Contact Group on the European stage at its first meeting at the ministers' level on 26 April 1994 in London.

As expected, the composition of the Contact Group was heavily criticised by those left on the outside. Nonetheless, as with its G7 membership in 1975, Italy was the only state that managed to enter the Contact Group for Bosnia at a later phase. It entered the Contact Group as the holder of the EU presidency in the first half of 1996, and proved reluctant to leave when its term of office was over.[3] Eventually, Italy managed to stay in the Contact Group by exerting enormous pressure on the U.S. Among other things, it threatened to forbid the deployment of new U.S. Stealth bombers on NATO air bases in Italy (Bildt 1999, p. 101).

Of most interest in the relations between the great powers and international institutions was the tension between the European great powers of France, Britain, Germany, and Italy and the smaller members of the European Union. In regard to the G7/8, the influence of the European Union has been well analysed (Putnam and Bayne 1987, p. 152ff; Ullrich and Donnelly 1998).

Here it was clear that high politics remained a domain of the national states, although decisions became more transparent due to the efficient functioning of information systems within the EU. The observations of the Contact Group provide a similar portrait.

In contrast to the diplomats from the concert powers of the U.S., Russia, France, Britain, Germany, and Italy (since 1996), representatives of the European Commission and the European presidency (which had to report to the other EU countries) had only observer status in the Contact Group. As in the case of the G7/8, the formal reason for this partial EU involvement was the existence of European treaties, especially the Common European Foreign and Security Policy in Title V of the Treaty of European Union (see Chapter 8).

While the Contact Group's member states regarded themselves as (at least formally) equal, there were different perceptions concerning the representation of the European Commission and the European presidency. On the one hand, there was a certain scepticism on the part of the Commission (Directorate General 1A) as to whether it was within the Commission's competence to demand an active role in the Contact Group. On the other hand, the European Contact Group member states did not like to be reminded to take European positions into consideration. The influence of the European presidency, therefore, varied across the states holding that position. Contact Group member states used their position as EU president to gain additional authority in the Contact Group, while they were less willing to accept the authority of the EU presidency when it was controlled by smaller and non–Contact Group member nations. This parallels the early stages of EU involvement in G7 Summits. Consequently, the observations of the European Community involvement at G7 Summits by Putnam and Bayne (1987, p. 153) remain valid for the European Union's role within the Contact Group: 'The larger Community members retained a good deal of flexibility. They could act with the weight of the Community behind them if they so wished. But in practice they almost always spoke as independent powers...'. The countries holding the EU presidency operated as freely as the others and seldom assumed the role of spokesperson for the European Union, although the EU presidency constantly reported via the EU's communication system to other EU member states.

The non-European Contact Group members, namely the U.S. and Russia, treated the EU presence as an intra-European issue and accepted the presence of the European Commission and the EU presidency without difficulty. For them it was important that EU participation did not complicate or jeopardise the deliberations within the Contact Group. During the negotiations at Dayton and Rambouillet, EU special envoys Carl Bildt and Wolfgang Petritsch gained a more prominent role while representing the European Contact Group states in the negotiation team with their Russian and U.S. colleagues (Vitaly Churkin–Richard Holbrooke and Boris Mayorski–Christopher Hill). This arrangement had its origin in pragmatic U.S. considerations. It was by no means an expression of a European wish for common representation (see Neville-Jones 1996, p. 48).

Occasionally, members of other international organisations and special experts were invited to take part in discussions at all Contact Group levels. The special envoys of the EU or UN, or representatives of the Organization for Security and Co-operation in Europe (OSCE), were the most prominent. This procedure again demonstrates that the Contact Group took a problem-solving approach. It finds a parallel in the G7/8 Summits where external states and organisations are invited for discussion on specific issues of common concern (Kirton 1999, p. 47). At least in the case of Bosnia, such expanded meetings with the Contact Group were considered important by external participants. As Robert Frowick, head of the OSCE Mission in Bosnia-Herzegovina, concluded: 'Also, the leaders of many of these organizations [United Nations High Commissioner for Refugees, International Police Task Force, International Committee of the Red Cross, Council of Europe, etc.] met frequently at Contact Group meetings, Peace Implementation Council sessions, international seminars, and other gatherings. For my part, the Contact Group meetings have always been of greatest relevance to OSCE activities per se' (Frowick 1997, p. 3).

The Contact Group in Crisis Management

The management of the crisis in Bosnia-Herzegovina saw three phases of Contact Group involvement: the negotiations on the Contact Group Plan in the summer of 1994 until the summer of 1995, the Dayton process from the summer of 1995 until the winter of 1995, and the peace implementation phase in the winter of 1995/96. In the Kosovo crisis, the Contact Group was mainly involved first during the Holbrooke-Milosevic agreement in the summer and autumn of 1998 and then during the Rambouillet process of February and March 1999. For this analysis of concert diplomacy, the establishment of the peace implementation in Bosnia and the Rambouillet process require detailed analysis. They both deal with the interface between the two concerts active in the crisis — the Contact Group and the G7/8 itself. With the creation of the plan to implement peace in Bosnia, the Contact Group secured the support of the G7 (among other international institutions) for the reconstruction of the country. In contrast, the failure of the Rambouillet process led to direct G8 involvement in regional crisis management.

An assessment of the Contact Group's role in crisis management in Bosnia shows both the limits as well as the potential of concert diplomacy. The latter first became apparent when the concert powers presented the Contact Group Plan in May 1994. Similar to former peace plans by EU and UN negotiators, the plan was presented as one widely supported by the international community. It included incentives in case of acceptance and threats in case of rejection. It was not negotiable in principle. In addition, the plan constituted an obvious step toward a realistic approach, by accepting for the first time that territorial gains would be kept by the Serbs.[4]

To promote the acceptance of the Contact Group Plan, member states tried to assert pressure on the warring parties. According to their real or perceived influence, Russia attempted to convince the Serbs in Belgrade and Pale, the U.S. pressured on the Bosnian Muslims and the Germans negotiated with the Croats. Diplomats from the United Kingdom and France and the co-chairmen of the Yugoslavia Conference shuttled between the camps to gain support for the Contact Group's peace package (Cohen 1995, p. 312).

The peace plan eventually failed because of opposition from the Bosnian Serbs, who were not willing to relinquish a great part of their territorial gains (in May 1994 they occupied approximately 72 percent of Bosnia-Herzegovina). However, the effort showed that concert diplomacy by the Contact Group could help to co-ordinate the efforts of the great powers and unite the activities of the international organisations behind the leadership of the Contact Group.

The limits of concert diplomacy became visible between autumn 1994 and summer 1995, when the Contact Group states could not agree on measures to force the Bosnian Serbs to participate seriously in peace negotiations. The question was whether NATO should launch an air campaign to bring the Serbs to the negotiating table and whether it would be helpful to lift the arms embargo for Muslim and Croatian forces. Four opposing positions in the Contact Group were identifiable. First, the United States was promoting a 'lift and strike' strategy. Second, France and Britain were threatening to withdraw their ground forces if the U.S. undertook unilateral actions. Third, Russia held air strikes to be unreasonable and considered evacuating its UN contingent in the event of U.S. air attacks. Fourth, Germany, while generally supporting the American position, was in favour of lifting the arms embargo, but tried to prevent a UNPROFOR withdrawal (Owen 1995, pp. 376, 383). The question of air strikes was also a question of status. For Russia in particular, the rule of solidarity and mutual respect among the powers was at stake.

Eventually, dramatic changes on the battlefield in favour of Croat and Muslim forces was necessary to bring about a new consensus in the Contact Group. This consensus about the post-war regime in the former Yugoslavia and the new stalemate between the warring parties constituted the basis for the Dayton peace conference.

The Dayton Accords and Bosnia Peace Implementation

The negotiations at Wright-Patterson Air Base in Dayton, Ohio, in November 1995 brought about a peace settlement for Bosnia-Herzegovina. The format for the peace talks, arranged by the U.S., was characterised by a sharing of work among the delegations, although the U.S. delegation led by Richard Holbrooke had considerably more staff present. The negotiations themselves can be summed up as an example of how power games among the Contact Group allies could be played without eventually having led to a lowest common denominator agreement. Despite the diverse views among the concert powers, the negotiations brought about a substantive agreement over the post-war order.[5]

Considering the complexity of the conflict, it remains difficult to judge whether the Contact Group's unity was decisive in securing ratification of the General Framework Agreement. The Contact Group definitely supported the negotiations. The developments on the battlefield, the strong U.S. involvement, and the use of military pressure by the international community had signalled to all warring parties that they could not hope for more territorial gains if the war continued. The General Framework Agreement itself, with its civil and military chapters, was nevertheless a result of the co-ordination of great power positions in the Contact Group. The Contact Group met each morning and whenever necessary for deliberations to find consent on a common strategy for the negotiations with the parties. This made it impossible for Serbs, Croats, and Muslims to play Contact Group powers off against each other (see Bildt 1999, ch. 9).

The effectiveness of this concert is even better demonstrated by the interaction of national and multinational actors in the peace implementation phase. The organisation of the peace implementation was arranged in the annexes of the General Framework Agreement. According to the agreement (Annex 1-A), the military mission had to be controlled independently by NATO, which held control over the Implementation Force (IFOR, later the Stabilization Force [SFOR]). Both IFOR and SFOR were led by Supreme Headquarters, Allied Powers Europe (SHAPE). Responsibility for civil-military co-operation resided in the Civil Military Co-operation section of NATO. NATO therefore had full control over its co-operation with civil agencies.

Like IFOR/SFOR, the OSCE mission was headed by the U.S. According to the General Framework Agreement, OSCE's task was subdivided into three sections: the election committee for preparing, running, and monitoring elections; the human rights section; and the section on arms control and confidence-building measures. The mission of the United Nations was executed by two sub-organisations, the United Nations High Commissioner for Refugees (UNHCR) and the United Nations Mission in Bosnia and Herzegovina (UNMIBH). The latter, according to Annex 11 of the General Framework Agreement, held control over the International Police Task Force, the civil affairs division, and the mine-sweeping program (see Office of the High Representative [OHR] 1995b).

Financial help for the reconstruction of industry and infrastructure was provided by the World Bank, the International Monetary Fund, the European Bank for Reconstruction and Development, and, to a large extent, by the European Union and single donor countries.

The steering committee of the Peace Implementation Council and the subordinate High Representative played a special role in organising the implementation of the peace process. Both bodies were established at the London Peace Implementation Conference, as agreed upon in Dayton by the Contact Group states. They should be considered the successors to the Geneva Conference of the EU and the UN.

The Peace Implementation Council consists of representatives of all states, international organisations, and agencies present at the London Conference. At the time the Council was established, France was chair of the G7, so it was the first to co-ordinate its activities. A steering committee chaired by the High Representative was established to meet monthly and to maintain close contacts with the OSCE and the UN (but notably not with NATO). The steering committee included representatives from all G8 countries — France, Germany, Britain, the United States, Canada, Japan, Italy, and Russia — plus representatives from the EU presidency, the European Commission, and the Organisation of Islamic Countries (OHR 1995a). Since 1996, the steering committee has met about twice a year at the ministerial level. A peace implementation conference with all parties concerned takes place every year in December.

The Office of the High Representative, first held by EU negotiator Carl Bildt, had to fulfil a complex task of co-ordination between governmental and nongovernmental civil missions, even though it had no authority over them.

For instance, the High Representative chaired the Joint Civilian Commission, in which political representatives of the parties to the conflict, the commander of IFOR/SFOR and representatives of several civilian organisations were present.

Thus, the organisation of the peace implementation process clearly illustrates the possibilities available to the Contact Group to design and establish a useful institutional mix for all kinds of tasks related to the goal of peace implementation. The concert powers collectively defined competencies and responsibilities, created additional institutions if necessary, and agreed to watch over the state of the peace implementation process. At the same time, the specific interests of the Contact Group states were safeguarded by the typical distribution of tasks and roles: the three European states — France, Germany, and Britain — used the economic and political power of the EU. The U.S. secured its influence thanks to its leading role within NATO. Russia's role remained marginal because of its lack of economic strength, and was restrained to a rather symbolic contribution to IFOR/SFOR, where it held the deputy command. However, due to its close co-operation with the West, Russia was thought to gain at least some influence on the design of the NATO mission, especially regarding the constraints of the operation. Furthermore, all Contact Group member states used their influence on the OSCE, whose head of mission was an American (Robert Frowick). On the UN Security Council members of the Contact Group worked together in drafting the relevant UN resolutions to back the decisions of the Contact Group.

The Kosovo Crisis and Rambouillet Process

If the Dayton process yielded a successful outcome, Rambouillet produced a failure. The aim of the Rambouillet conference, which took place from 6 to 23 February 1999, in the same place where the first G7 Summit was held, was to stop the violation of human rights and to restore Albanian autonomy in Kosovo. Its purpose was also to prevent Western governments from intervening with NATO air strikes, as NATO threatened to issue activation orders for both limited air strikes and a phased air campaign. Since the Contact Group initiated the Rambouillet process, one must ask whether it had contributed to this failure, or whether the circumstances did not allow for a successful outcome for these negotiations.

As indicated above, there was a stalemate between the forces on the ground in Bosnia at the time of the Dayton negotiations. During the Rambouillet negotiations, by contrast, Yugoslavian forces had just entered a further phase of their so-called 'Operation Horseshoe' to expel the Albanian population from the region. This operation had started after the OSCE-led Kosovo Verification Mission (KVM) to observe the withdrawal of Serb armed forces had failed in the winter of 1998/99. This mission had been the core substantive feature of the Holbrooke-Milosevic agreement of October 1998. In spring 1999, the Kosovo Liberation Army (KLA) remained a weak force, although it was still growing. It was only lightly armed and unable to protect Albanian villages. Since Milosevic did not expect NATO to intervene in favour of the Kosovar Albanians, he had no reason to negotiate and did not appear personally at the Château Rambouillet. The Albanian delegation, dominated by radical KLA leaders, did not have much interest in making concessions either. Considering their weakness on the battlefield, they were more interested in a NATO military intervention, which would have served as unintentional air support, than in signing an agreement that left many of their desires unfulfilled. In contrast to the conference at Dayton, at Rambouillet, policies were made elsewhere.[6]

Despite the fact that there was less chance of forging an agreement in Rambouillet, it is noteworthy that it was not just the negotiations that appeared to be difficult. Relations among the Contact Group delegations were tense as well. Dayton had been dominated by the U.S. delegation, so there was consensus among the Europeans in the Contact Group that the Kosovo negotiations should be led by the Europeans and should therefore take place in Europe. However, a European leadership role appeared to be difficult to play when four European states were competing for it. Germany, which had been promoting the idea of such a conference since October 1998, and which held the presidency of the Council of the European Union, tried to take the lead in the diplomatic process. Yet it was quickly outmanoeuvred by France and Britain. These two governments had already met before the Contact Group ministerial meeting of 29 January 1999 and agreed (together with Washington) to hold the conference at Château Rambouillet near Paris and to have Hubert Vedrine and Robin Cook act as co-chairmen of the conference.[7] A third proposal from this meeting suggested that the foreign ministers of France and Britain take part in the negotiations, together with Christopher Hill and the Russian Boris Mayorski. According to a German media report, German foreign minister Joseph Fischer had to intervene three times to obtain the appointment of the Austrian EU special envoy Wolfgang Petritsch as a third negotiator for all Europeans, instead of Cook and Vedrine. Fischer also secured an informal EU foreign ministers' lunch to discuss a common approach.

While the Dayton negotiations were characterised by a division of the Contact Group into three, the situation in Rambouillet was even more complex. Although the negotiating team of Hill-Mayorski-Petritsch worked very well together, the unity of the Contact Group was not as tight as it had been in 1995. The reason lay in games of relative power being played among single Contact Group states. For instance, although Mayorski co-operated effectively within his competence, he had been ordered by Moscow not to negotiate on the security annex of the agreement.[8] Therefore, the Rambouillet process did not fail because of any particularly difficult details of the NATO mission. Indeed, the Contact Group did not even address the issue of the mission itself. Rather, when the draft of the security annex (Annex B) was presented to the FRY/Serb delegation, Mayorski had to declare that the Contact Group did not support this proposal since Russia did not agree to it. Thus, the FRY/Serb delegation could later declare it had not seen a Contact Group draft concerning NATO involvement, although they well knew what the document contained.

By the time European Contact Group members convened, France and Britain had already met to discuss common positions. In this way, the Europeans gave up on considering an OSCE force, which would have been acceptable for Russia. They agreed instead on a NATO-led operation. Only Italy, whose view remained isolated, remained committed to an OSCE mission.

In mid February 1999, when there was no substantial progress in sight, the U.S. delegation began bilateral talks with the Yugoslavian government. Secretary of State Madeleine Albright telephoned President Milosevic.[9] On 16 February, Hill decided to fly to Belgrade with Cook and Vedrine to seek a 'last chance' settlement. Neither Germany as EU presidency, nor Italy, nor Wolfgang Petritsch as the EU negotiator were informed of this. German and European attempts to secure the support of at least Petritsch failed. Mayorski, also uninformed, even considered leaving Rambouillet and moving into the Russian embassy.

In a news conference, the negotiators downplayed this episode. Petritsch stated: 'Let me just add that we are working as a team, basically. But of course ... there might be situations where some of us have bilateral chores to fulfil, so this is nothing extraordinary. The centre of the negotiations is here in Rambouillet ..., but in many ways it is necessary that things will be done also some place else if we speak of some aspects of this ... we consider it not as a breach of anything' (Contact Group 1999).

Despite these games of relative power within the Contact Group, there were some substantial outcomes from the group's deliberations. Against the background of the massacre at Racak on 15 January 1999 — where 45 Albanian civilians were killed by FRY armed forces — and the breakdown of the cease-fire and the full resumption of hostilities in January, the Contact Group stated at its meeting on 29 January that the situation in Kosovo remained a threat to peace and security in the region, and one that raised the prospect of a humanitarian catastrophe. This action was encouraged by announcements by the secretary-generals of NATO and the UN, Javier Solana and Kofi Annan respectively, whose statements contained a similar content (North Atlantic Treaty Organisation [NATO] 1999a; United Nations 1999). The ministers 'called on both sides to end the cycle of violence and to commit themselves to a process of negotiation leading to a political settlement'.

To that end, the Contact Group:

- considered that the proposals drafted by the negotiators contained the elements for a substantial autonomy for Kosovo and asked the negotiators to refine them further to serve as the framework for an agreement between the parties;
- recognised that the work done by the negotiators had identified the limited number of points that required final negotiation between the parties;
- agreed to summon representatives from the Federal Yugoslav and Serbian governments and representatives of the Kosovar Albanians to Rambouillet by 6 February, under the co-chairmanship of Vedrine and Cook, to begin negotiations with the direct involvement of the Contact Group. The Contact Group recognised the legitimate rights of other communities within Kosovo. In the context of these negotiations, it would work to ensure their interests were fully reflected in a settlement;
- agreed that the participants should work to conclude negotiations within seven days. The negotiators would then report to Contact Group ministers who would assess whether the progress made justified a further period of less than one week to bring the negotiations to a successful conclusion (OHR 1999a).

Additionally, the Contact Group insisted that the parties accept that the basis for a fair settlement must include the following principles set out by the Contact Group:

- The necessity of an immediate end to the violence and a respect for the cease-fire;
- A peaceful solution through dialogue;
- An interim agreement, that is, a mechanism for a final settlement after an interim period of three years;
- No unilateral change of interim status;
- Territorial integrity of the FRY and neighbouring countries;
- Protection of the rights of the members of all national communities (preservation of identity, language, and education; special protection for their religious institutions);

- Free and fair elections in Kosovo (municipal and throughout Kosovo) under the supervision of the OSCE;
- No prosecution for crimes related to the Kosovo conflict (with the exception of crimes against humanity, war crimes, and other serious violations of international law);
- Amnesty and release of political prisoners;
- International involvement and full co-operation by the parties on implementation (Weller 1999).

On 23 February 1999, the final day of the Rambouillet talks, the Contact Group member states agreed on the 'Interim Agreement for Peace and Self-Government in Kosovo'.[10] The agreement set out comprehensive and detailed rules for the future distribution of powers between Kosovar Albanians and Serbs and for the constitutional system, including democracy-building and confidence-building measures. Despite national differences, the members of the Contact Group held together, an achievement that was articulated in the co-chairmen's conclusions to the Rambouillet accord on 23 February: 'These have been complex and difficult negotiations, as we expected. The important efforts of the parties and the unstinting commitment of our negotiators Ambassadors Hill, Petritsch and Mayorsky [*sic*], have led to a consensus on substantial autonomy for Kosovo, including on mechanisms for free and fair elections to democratic institutions, for the governance of Kosovo, for the protection of human rights and the rights of members of national communities; and for the establishment of a fair judicial system' (OHR 1999b). However, the Rambouillet accord was not signed at the Château. The Contact Group had to agree to host a follow-up conference to cover all aspects of implementation on 15 March (OHR 1999b).

Also, the Serb delegation did not contribute constructively to the discussions at Rambouillet. Indeed, the opposite was true. Instead of discussing several aspects of implementation as suggested by the Contact Group, the FRY/Serb delegation presented a counter-draft in order to reopen the topic of a political settlement, including non-negotiable principles. The counter-draft was a radical amendment of the interim agreement, including the correction or deletion of points Serbia had agreed to earlier (such as the whole civilian mission including substantive parts of the OSCE Mission). Even the word 'peace' in the title 'Agreement for Peace and Self-Government' was deleted. As Marc Weller (1999, p. 235), writes, 'In effect, the draft would have introduced a regime of what external observers have described as an institutionalized system of apartheid in Kosovo'.

Under these circumstances, further negotiations made no sense. It was decided to declare the draft of 23 February ready for signature on 18 March

1999. Mayorski refused to attend the formal meeting at which the Kosovar Albanian delegation signed the agreement. According to Weller (1999, p. 235), 'There was even an attempt to prevent the European Union negotiator from witnessing the signature. This attempt was overruled by the government representing the Presidency of the European Union [Germany]'. For the first time an overt conflict in the Contact Group was visible.

The following day, the last attempt to engage the FRY/Serb delegation in substantive discussions proved fruitless. The co-chairmen then issued the following statement:

1. The Rambouillet accords are the only peaceful solution to the Kosovo problem.
2. In Paris, the Kosovo delegation seized this opportunity and, by their signature, have committed themselves to the accords as a whole.
3. Far from seizing this opportunity, the Yugoslav delegation has tried to unravel the Rambouillet accords.
4. Therefore, after consultation with our partners in the Contact Group (Germany, Italy, the Russian Federation, the United States, the European Union, the Chairman in Office of the OSCE), we consider there is no purpose in extending the talks any further. The negotiations are adjourned. The talks will not resume unless the Serbs express their acceptance of the accords.
5. We will immediately engage in consultations with our partners and allies to be ready to act. We will be in contact with the Secretary General of NATO. We ask the Chairman in Office of the OSCE to take all appropriate measures for the safety of the KVM. The Contact Group will remain seized of the issue.
6. We solemnly warn the authorities in Belgrade against any military offensive on the ground and any impediment to the freedom of movement and of action of the KVM, which would contravene their commitments. Such violations would have the gravest consequences (Weller 1999).

On 22 March, a negotiator team led again by Holbrooke travelled to Belgrade for one last attempt to persuade the FRY/Serb government to cease military operations in Kosovo and to sign the Rambouillet accord. Again no progress was made. Instead the Yugoslavian parliament officially rejected the interim agreement the following day. Holbrooke then returned to Brussels to brief the North Atlantic Council on the discussions in Belgrade. His information convinced NATO that Milosevic would not change his mind. NATO then authorised the commencement of military operations against the FRY (NATO 1999b).

When it became obvious that the interests within the Contact Group were too diverse, the price of preserving the unity of the Contact Group was deemed to have become too high. The Western members of the Contact Group thought that NATO air strikes against the FRY would serve their interests better than maintaining Contact Group co-operation with the Russian Federation. After the start of the military operation, the Contact Group did not officially meet again. An unofficial meeting was held during the NATO operation on 7 April 1999 in Brussels, but it did not result in a statement.

G8 Involvement

During and after the NATO campaign, Contact Group functions were transferred to the G8 framework. There were several reasons for the transfer. Russia had cut off co-operation with NATO countries in several fora, such as the NATO–Russia Council; it was not yet willing to return to the negotiating table, where its concerns about NATO air strikes, without a UN Security Council resolution, had been overtly rejected. The annual G8 Summit was about to take place in Cologne in June, which presented a good opportunity to put the Russian government back on stage, with Viktor Chernomyrdin as one of the peace mediators (along with the Finnish president Martti Ahtisaari and Strobe Talbott from the U.S.). Also, it meant upgrading the negotiations to the level of heads of state and government from the ministers' level. In addition, since the deliberations would include questions of reconstruction and peace-building, it made sense to have the participation of Canada (then a nonpermanent member of the UN Security Council) and especially Japan as potential donor countries. Furthermore, as described before, the G7/8 was already involved in the Bosnian peace-implementation process. Therefore, there was a certain tradition of G8 involvement.[11]

Nonetheless, the mediation role during the Kosovo War was a new task for the G8, because in Bosnia it had not obtained any role in crisis management and the crisis was not part of the formal Summit agenda between 1991 and 1996 (see Hajnal 1999, ch. 6). Only after the peace implementation process had started did the issue appear on the Summit agenda, although not in a prominent position. At the Lyon Summit (29 June 1996), the G8 took several decisions with reference to the peace implementation conferences, which had incorporated the G8 in the institutional set-up of the process. The decisions concerned elections and institutions, the International War Crimes Tribunal, reconstruction, the refugee problem and the rule of law, and regional and security issues. It also expressed the G8's commitment to the peace process and support for all institutions involved (G8 1996). At the following Summits in Denver and Birmingham, the developments on the territory of the FRY had been part of G8 deliberations (G8 1997, 1998). However, similar to the Contact Group during the time between 1996 and summer 1998 the G8 was fulfilling a mere supervisory function over the peace building efforts. The G8 leaders expressed their commitment to the peace agreement and warned all parties against hindering the peace process. The 1998 Birmingham declaration also expressed its concern about the developments in Kosovo and urged the parties to find political solutions. However, at no time were the G8 statements as detailed and as comprehensive as corresponding Contact Group statements (OHR 1998a, 1998b). This confirms the impression that the heads of governments used the summits to promote the peace process, but were not willing to actively involve the G8 system in crisis management. They left this task to the Contact Group which was especially invented for it.

Hence it was natural that the G8 efforts to secure peace for Kosovo were in practice a continuation of Contact Group activities with more actors involved. After the Ahtisaari/Chernomyrdin efforts gave some hope for reaching an agreement with President Milosevic, the foreign ministers of the G8 met on 6 May 1999. They reached agreement on most aspects of peace implementation. During the preparation of the Cologne Summit, the G8 states had additional gatherings at the political directors' and ministers' levels. These talks led to the announcement of the 'general principles on the civilian aspects of the implementation of an interim peace settlement', adopted by the G8 foreign ministers in Cologne (10 June 1999). These followed the blueprint of the Bosnian peace implementation as designed by the Contact Group. Moreover, the foreign ministers prepared a draft version of a UN Security Council resolution to back the peace implementation process in Kosovo.

In this process, the Russian delegation behaved as co-operatively and constructively as it always had before the Contact Group broke apart. However, as discussed above, a basic principle of concert diplomacy declares that states are restricted to discussing issues that belong to a certain range of topics acceptable to all members of the group and on which consensus can be reached. The question of a NATO presence in Serbia, as included in the Military Annex of the Rambouillet accord, did not fall into that category, because Russia refused to negotiate about it. When NATO had also ignored Russian resistance to air strikes without a prior resolution, the Western members of the Contact Group destroyed the foundations of the group. Nonetheless, the fact that a new basis for negotiations was found so quickly illustrates the robustness of the relationship between Russia and its Western partners. It also shows that Russia had realistically assessed its impact on the Balkan question. After the Western alliance ignored the UN Security Council, Russia knew that it had to co-operate in order to gain at least some influence on the peace agreement. Therefore, it was easy for the Russian government to agree to the G8 as a forum for negotiations, and one that could serve as a high-profile stage to demonstrate Russia's important role in shaping a post-war order for Kosovo.

Nevertheless, the G8 Summit itself was no more than a formal upgrading of the Contact Group to the level of heads of state and government. Kosovo did not take as much room in the Cologne leaders' deliberations as the media coverage suggested. The G8 Statement on Regional Issues, for instance, treated the Kosovo issue just as one among others, including Cyprus, the Middle East, Nigeria, and Kashmir (see Appendix C). As is usual for G7/8 statements, the final Communiqué of 20 June 1999 dealt with a wide range of issues and did not refer again to Kosovo. Instead, issues such as international trade, the world economy, the debt initiative, social security, and nonproliferation formed the core of this declaration.

The Summit suggests that the G7/8 is not willing to become engaged in crisis management at the level of the leaders. The treatment of Kosovo peace implementation by G8 foreign ministers, however, was a natural way out of the dilemma that arose when the Contact Group was discredited as an arena for negotiation in the view of the Russian government. The G8 negotiations took place at the ministerial level and therefore were not distinct from Contact Group meetings. Even the participation of the EU remained the same. It was just the discreet presence of Canada and Japan that made the difference.

One should also note the links between the G8 Summit and the Stability Pact for South Eastern Europe, announced at Cologne on 10 June 1999. This pact — the outcome of a German initiative — had gained the full support of the European Union at its summit in Cologne. The EU was prepared to take a leading role in organising the Stability Pact (see Cologne European Council 1999). Although this conference of states and international organisations was directly connected to the G8 foreign ministers meeting, Japan and Canada did not participate. They were, however, included among the 'facilitating' actors, which suggests that it was the former Contact Group formation of states that had led the peace implementation process in Kosovo and not all G8 member states together. The Stability Pact is another example of the co-ordination capability of the Contact Group states, because it describes exact roles for all important states, including the U.S. and the Russian Federation, and for international organisations such as the UN, NATO, the OSCE, EU, international finance institutions, and the OECD. As with the Bosnian experience, co-operation with Japan and Canada remained crucial for financing the Stability Pact. Canada is also an important member of NATO. Nevertheless, for the

European members of the Contact Group and the United States, there is little incentive and no reason to involve these states in European crisis management.

Conclusion

This analysis demonstrates that the G7/8 and the Contact Group share the same logic. They are both excellent cases of the use and effectiveness of modern concert diplomacy for high-security crisis management. Both concerts served as lightly institutionalised arenas for policy co-ordination among an exclusive group of powerful states. In contrast to other occasions when great powers meet to co-ordinate their behaviour, the G7/8 and the Contact Group met officially and were visible entities. This characteristic distinguishes G7/8 and Contact Group negotiations from great power deliberations in the preliminary stages of North Atlantic Council or UN Security Council meetings. In concerts such as the Contact Group and the G7/8, the great powers behave as different entities because they aim to take the lead in the international community of states. This intention is also expressed in their reference to international principles, rules, and norms.

This claim gives excluded states and international organisations the possibility of exerting pressure on the member states. The fact, however, that the legitimacy of neither the G7/8 nor the Contact Group was successfully challenged not only mirrors international power relations. It also demonstrates that the 'governance' of this group of states is widely accepted. In the case of the Contact Group, this acceptance flowed from the recognition of a sphere of influence for its member states, on the part of such states as China. The question of legitimacy was not raised before the Contact Group itself split up into the Western (NATO) states and Russia.

Moreover, the participation of the EU in both institutions illustrates that at least France, Britain, Germany, and Italy no longer act entirely as sovereign states. Due to the European treaties, all EU member states have substantial leverage to control G7/8 and Contact Group activities beyond the economic realm.

As concerts, both institutions were born of crises. They came into being because international organisations were not able to deal with a crisis in a way that satisfied the interests of a group of great powers. However, in Bosnia and Kosovo the peace implementation process is now operated by established international organisations and newly created institutions. This development shows that acting in concert is not the first choice of the great powers as an institutional means through which to perform all functions. Rather, at times of global interdependence and for broader burden sharing, they rely ever more on smaller states. Concert diplomacy can thus be seen as a supplement to a multilateral approach in international politics, and as a tool to preserve and improve the effectiveness of international organisations by providing flexibility to its most powerful members. Hence, there is no conflict between concert diplomacy and multilateralism within international organisations. Both are features of international institutions in their own right. Organisations and concerts might serve the same end, but they are invented for different purposes. International organisations such as the UN were established for the rule-guided management of conflicts and to foster co-operation among states. Modern concerts such as the G8 and the Contact Group help to co-ordinate policies of great powers that already co-operate in many ways and arenas.

The question that must be posed after this assessment of Contact Group and G8 relations is whether the great powers will preserve the formal distinction between the two concerts in any future crisis that generates a similar need for great power co-ordination. As distinct from the Contact Group label, sailing under the G8 flag could enhance the impression of legitimacy and could place a regional crisis into a broader global context. This, however, would give the unwanted impression that the G8 feels responsible for crisis management all over the world, an impression that meets neither the G8's capacities, nor its intentions.

Notes

1   The Birmingham and the Cologne Summits of the G7/8 (1998 and 1999 respectively) have confirmed that the head of states want to preserve the informal character of the meetings.
2   For a comprehensive analysis of the war in Kosovo, see Calic (1996), Cohen (1995), Gow (1997), and Giersch (1998).
3   In the case of Italy joining the G7, it was the other way round. The U.S. and the European states wanted to include Italy, but used its EC presidency as an argument to justify the exclusion of the European Community (Garavoglia 1984, p. 6).
4   Cohen (1995) cites the U.S. diplomat Charles Redmann, who confirms that he 'admitted that the map left ethnically cleansed areas under Serbian control, but explained that the contact group had found it necessary to "jump over the moral bridge in the interests of wider peace"'
5   For a detailed analysis of the Dayton talks, see Gow (1997), Neville-Jones (1996), Holbrooke (1998), and Bildt (1999).

6   U.S. Ambassador Christopher Hill, who was already on Holbrooke's team at Dayton, considered the Rambouillet negotiations to be even more difficult than those at Dayton (Contact Group 1999).

7   Germany was in favour of a conference at Petersberg near Bonn, while Austria suggested Vienna (*Die Zeit* 1999).

8   '... if there were active discussion on military aspects ... I can assure you that we [the Russian Government] were not taking part in those discussions' (Contact Group 1999).

9   The negotiating team complained that visits by ministers merely served national interests and disturbed the negotiations (*Die Zeit* 1999).

10   A full text version of the Interim Agreement for Peace and Self-government in Kosovo can be found at <bicc.uni-bonn.de/coop/fiv/suedost/rambouillet.html> (September 2000).

11   In the past, it was even observed that an *ad hoc* meeting of G8 foreign ministers (to discuss Indian and Pakistani nuclear tests) in London on 12 June 1998 had been transformed into a Contact Group meeting. This meeting also included Canada and Japan — presumably, however, due to the vagaries of timing (Hajnal 1999, p. 39).

References

Archer, Clive (1992), *International Organizations*, second edition, Routledge, New York.

Bayne, Nicholas (2000), *Hanging in There: The G7/G8 Summit in Maturity and Renewal*, Ashgate, Aldershot.

Bildt, Carl (1999), *Peace Journey: The Struggle for Peace in Bosnia*, Weidenfeld and Nicholson, London.

Boudevaix, Francine (1997), *Une Diplomatie informelle pour l'Europe*, Le Groupe de Contact Bosnie, Paris.

Calic, Janine-Marie (1996), *Krieg und Frieden in Bosnien-Hercegovina*, second edition, Suhrkamp, Frankfurt.

Cohen, Lenard J. (1995), *Broken Bonds: Yugoslavia's Disintegration and Balkan Politics in Transition*, second edition, Westview Press, Boulder, CO.

Cologne European Council (1999), 'Conclusions of the Presidency', 3–4 June, Cologne, <www.europarl.eu.int/dg7/summits/en/kol2.htm> (September 2000).

Contact Group (1999), 'Press Briefing by the Contact Group Negotiators', Rambouillet, 18 December, <www.diplomatie.fr/actual/evenements/ramb28.gb.html> (September 2000).

Dewitt, David, and John Kirton (1983), *Canada as a Principal Power: A Study in Foreign Policy and International Relations*, John Wiley, Toronto.

Die Zeit (1999), 'Wie Deutschland in den Krieg geriet', no. 20, 12 May.

Elrod, Richard (1976), 'The Concert of Europe: A Fresh Look at an International System', *World Politics*, January, pp. 159–174.

Frowick, Robert (1997), 'Concept of Mutually Reinforcing Institutions: Lessons Learned in Bosnia and Herzegovina', Paper presented at the Organization for Security and Co-operation in Europe Seminar on Co-Operation among International Organizations and Institutions: Experience in Bosnia and Herzegovina, Portoroz, Slovenia, 30 September.

G8 (1996), 'Lyon Summit: Decisions Concerning Bosnia and Herzegovina', 29 June, Lyon, <www.ohr.int/docu/d960629a.htm> (September 2000).

G8 (1997), 'Denver Summit of the Eight: Statement on Bosnia and Herzegovina', 22 June, Denver, <www.ohr.int/docu/d970622a.htm> (September 2000).

G8 (1998), 'Birmingham Summit of the Eight: Statements on FRY/Kosovo and Bosnia and Herzegovina', 17 May, Birmingham, <www.orh.int/docu/d980517a.htm> (September 2000).

Garavoglia, Guido (1984), 'From Rambouillet to Williamsburg: A Historical Assessment', in Cesare Merlini (ed.), *Economic Summits and Western Decision-Making*, St. Martin's Press, London, pp. 1–42.

Giersch, Carsten (1998), *Konfliktregulierung in Jugoslawien 1991–1995, Die Rolle von OSZE, EU, UNO und NATO*, Nomos, Baden-Baden.

Gow, James (1997), *Triumph of the Lack of Will: International Diplomacy and the Yugoslav War*, Hurst &Company, London.

Hajnal, Peter (1999), *The G7/G8 System: Evolution, Role, and Documentation*, Ashgate, Aldershot.

Holbrooke, Richard (1998), *To End a War*, Random House, New York.

Jervis, Robert (1983) 'Security Regimes', in Stephen D. Krasner (ed.), *International Regimes*, Cornell University Press, Ithaca, NY, pp. 173–194.

Jervis, Robert (1985), 'From Balance to Concert: A Study of International Security Co-operation', *World Politics*, October, pp. 58–79. (Also in Kenneth Oye [ed.], *Co-operation Under Anarchy*, Princeton, New Haven, 1986.)

Karns, Margaret P. (1987), 'Ad Hoc Multilateral Diplomacy: The United States, The Contact Group, and Namibia', *International Organization*, vol. 41, no. 1, pp. 93–123.

Katzenstein, Peter, Robert Keohane, and Stephen Krasner (1998), 'International Organization and the Study of World Politics', *International Organization*, vol. 52, no. 4, pp. 645–685.

Keohane, Robert O. (1982), 'The Demand for International Regimes', *International Organization*, vol. 36, no. 2.

Keohane, Robert O. (1989), *International Institutions and State Power: Essays in International Relations Theory*, Westview Press, Boulder, CO.

Kirton, John (1989), 'The Seven-Power Summit as an International Concert', Paper presented at the International Studies Association Annual meeting, April, London.

120 *Guiding Global Order*

Kirton, John (1993), 'The Seven Power Summit as a New Security Institution', in David Dewitt, John Kirton, and David Haglund (eds.), *Building a New Global Order: Emerging Trends in International Security*, Oxford University Press, Toronto, pp. 335–357.

Kirton, John (1997), 'Le rôle du G7 dans le couple intègration regionale-securité globale', *Études Internationales*, vol. 28, pp. 255–270.

Kirton, John (1999), 'Explaining G8 Effectiveness', in Michael Hodges, John Kirton, and Joseph Daniels (eds.), *The G8's Role in the New Millennium*, Ashgate, Aldershot, pp. 45–68.

Kohler-Koch, Beate (1989), 'Zur Empirie und Theorie internationaler Regime', in Beate Kohler-Koch (ed.), *Regime in den Internationalen Beziehungen*, Nomos, Baden-Baden, pp. 17–85.

Krasner, Stephen D. (1982) 'Structural Causes and Regime Consequences: Regimes as Intervening Variables', *International Organization*, vol. 36, no. 2.

Krasner, Stephen D. (ed.) (1983), *International Regimes*, Cornell University Press, Ithaca.

Kupchan, Charles, and Clifford Kupchan (1991), 'Concerts, Collective Security, and the Future of Europe', *International Security*, vol. 16, pp. 114–161.

Lewis, Flora (1991), 'The "G7½" Directorate', *Foreign Policy*, vol. 85, pp. 25–40.

Müller, Harald (1993), *Die Chance der Kooperation. Regime in den internationalen Beziehungen*, Wissenschaftliche Buchgesellschaft, Darmstadt.

Neville-Jones, Pauline (1996), 'Dayton, IFOR, and Alliance Relations in Bosnia', *Survival*, vol. 38, no. 4, pp. 45–65.

North Atlantic Treaty Organization [NATO] (1999a), 'Press Statement' (011), 28 January, < www.nato.int/docu/pr/1999/p99-011e.htm> (September 2000).

North Atlantic Treaty Organization [NATO] (1999b), Press Statement (040), 23 March, <www.nato.int/docu/pr/1999/p99-040e.htm> (September 2000).

Odom, William (1995), 'How to Create a True World Order', *Orbis*, vol. 39, no. 2, pp. 155–172.

Office of the High Representative [OHR] (1995a), 'Conclusions of the Peace Implementation Conference Held at Lancaster House', 8–9 December, <www.ohr.int/docu/d951208a.htm> (September 2000).

Office of the High Representative [OHR] (1995b), 'The General Framework Agreement for Bosnia and Herzegovina', 14 December, <www.ohr.int/gfa/gfa-home.htm> (September 2000).

Office of the High Representative [OHR] (1998a), 'Contact Group: Statement on Kosovo', 25 March, Bonn, <www.ohr.int/docu/d980325b.htm> (September 2000).

Office of the High Representative [OHR] (1998b), 'Contact Group: Statement', 29 April, Rome, <www.ohr.int/docu/d980429a.htm> (September 2000).

Office of the High Representative [OHR] (1999a), 'Conclusions', London, 29 January, <www.ohr.int/docu/d990129a.htm> (September 2000).

Office of the High Representative [OHR] (1999b), 'Rambouillet Accords: Co-Chairmen's Conclusions', Rambouillet, 23 February, <www.ohr.int/docu/d990223a.htm> (September 2000).

Owen, David (1995), *Balkan Odyssey*, Victor Golancz, London.

Putnam, Robert, and Nicholas Bayne (1987), *Hanging Together: Cooperation and Conflict in the Seven-Power Summits*, revised edition, Harvard University Press, Cambridge, MA.

Rittberger, Volker (1994), *Internationale Organisationen*, Leske u. Budrich, Opladen.

Tindemans, Leo, *et al.* (1996), *Unfinished Peace: Report of the International Commission on the Balkans*, Aspen Institute, Berlin; Carnegie Endowment, Washington DC.

Ullrich, Heidi, and Alan Donnelly (1998), 'The Group of Eight and the European Union: The Evolving Partnership', *G8 Governance*, no. 5.

United Nations 1999, 'Statement by the Secretary-General Kofi Annan', Press Release SG/SM/6878, Brussels, 28 January.

Wallace, William (1984), 'Political Issues at the Summits: A New Concert of Powers', in Cesare Merlini (ed.), *Economic Summits and Western Decision-making*, St. Martin's Press, London.

Weller, Marc (1999), 'The Rambouillet Conference on Kosovo', *International Affairs*, vol. 75, no. 2, pp. 221–251.

Wijk, Rob de (1998), 'De Contactgroep: een Europese Veiligheidsraad?', *Internationale Spectator*, April.

Young, Oran R. (1983), 'Regime Dynamics: The Rise and Fall of International Regimes', in Stephen Krasner (ed.), *International Regimes*, Cornell University Press, Ithaca, NY, pp. 93–114.

8 The G7/8 and the European Union

KLEMENS FISCHER

Introduction

Since 1975, the group of the world's seven most important industrial nations has met annually at the level of the leaders, with Russia invited to take part as a full member in a new, enlarged G8 in 1998. Many existing analyses of the G7/8 Summit have emphasised how each member is equally free to combine with any other to produce a genuine form of concert governance or collective management (Kirton 1999, pp. 45–69; Bayne 2000). Yet within this G7 and now G8 there has always existed, at least geographically, an American bloc, a European bloc, and an Asian bloc (with Russia now joining Japan as a member of the latter).[1] Within the European bloc, only 4 of the 15 member states of the European Union (EU) are full members of the G7/8, even though the EU itself has participated in the annual summit since 1977.

This membership arrangement has given rise to complex relationships between the EU and the G7/8, and made the roles played by Germany, France, Italy, and Britain complicated because of their dual membership in both institutions. Over the past decade and a half, scholars and analysts of the G7/8 and the EU have devoted too little attention to these two critical topics, although a few have offered widely varying views about the nature of these relationships, the way issues are resolved, and the impact of these relationships on the European members and the EU and G7/8 themselves (Lamy 1998, Hainsworth 1990, Ostry 1990, de Silguay 1997). Moreover, even fewer have done so in the recent years since Russia became a member of the G8, and since the EU reached a new stage in its development with the advent of European Monetary Union (EMU) and the Euro (Bergsten *et al.* 1997, Ullrich and Donnelly 1998).

To explore the dynamics of these relationships, particularly the possible areas of conflict for the European members of the G7/8 due to their simultaneous membership in the EU and the G7/8, it is necessary to conduct two forms of analysis. The first is a classic legal-institutionalist approach that identifies the basic differences between international organisations and supranational organisations; this approach examines in some detail the internal structure and competencies of the EU and assesses the formal relationship between the two institutions.

This analysis serves as a foundation for a second, behaviourally based analysis of how Germany balanced its two roles as host of both the EU and the G7/8 in the first half of 1999, and how the agenda and conclusion of the two institutions at their 1999 summits meshed for the two organisations and for their four common country member states, especially in the two critical issue areas of the environment and international trade.

The analysis concludes that there is no formal or legal connection between the EU, as a supranational institution, and the G7/8, as an informal or quasi-intergovernmental one. Thus the parallel membership of Germany, France, Italy, and Britain in both does not cause difficulties as long as these countries respect their legal obligations of membership in the EU. However, there is a strong behavioural connection, as both bodies at summit level deal with very similar agendas. Germany, as the 1999 host of both bodies, mounted a very successful performance as honest broker; however, it remains unclear whether all four European members managed their common agenda in each body with similar success. The 1999 EU Summit placed more stress on rapid action on core environmental issues, but less on ambitious multilateral trade action, although there was no evidence that the commitments made by the four EU members at the G7/8 differed from their EU positions. Nonetheless, improved intra-EU co-ordination in the lead-up to the to the G7/8 meetings and a stronger presence for the EU itself in the G7/8 meetings would have value, above all in maximising the transparency and expertise of both bodies.

Traditional International Organisations and Supranational Organisations

International Organisations

International organisations can be defined as formal institutional structures that transcend national boundaries and are created by multilateral agreements among nation-states or among international bodies. Their purpose is to foster international co-operation in areas such as security, law, economic policy, social policy, and diplomacy (see Shaw 1997, p. 890ff; Köck and Fischer 1997, p. 57; Evans and Newnham 1998, p. 270). International organisations are of two basic types: the public variety known as intergovernmental organisations

(IGOs), such as the United Nations, the North Atlantic Treaty Organisation (NATO); the North American Free Trade Agreement (NAFTA), and the private variety, known as non-governmental organisations (NGOs), such as the International Red Cross and Amnesty International. Within this group of international organisations one can distinguish between those of universal character, such as the United Nations, and those of regional character, such as NAFTA.

In IGOs, members retain ultimate authority and the organisation is only a means for co-operative action. IGOs have six common characteristics (Köck and Fischer p. 60; Evans and Newnham, p. 270):

- Formal treaties that establish the organisation (thus an organisation's competence is initially limited to the specifics of the establishing convention);
- Voluntary membership;
- Permanent organisation;
- A constitutional structure;
- Common interests of the members; and
- A (consultative) conference.

As others have observed (Hodges 1999, pp. 69–74), the G7/8 does not fulfil the requirements of an intergovernmental international organisation. It can be seen as a quasi-international organisation or, more accurately, as an informal group. That classification does not reduce the great importance or influence of the G7/8 in world policy. However, it is important from a legal point of view.

Supranational Organisations

Supranational organisations are also IGOs. They therefore share the common characteristics identified above. Supranationality refers to laws or institutions that exercise authority above the state. Supranationalism refers to decision-making bodies that supersede or override the sovereign authority of the individual states that constitute the relevant organisation. The power and authority of supranational organisations are not confined to one but embrace many spheres. Usually, the transfer of authority from the state is voluntarily limited and specific.

The five main characteristic features of supranational organisations are as follows (Köck and Fischer 1997, p. 63; Evans and Newnham 1998, p. 524; Ipsen 1990, p. 72):

- The organisation can bind members by decisions taken by the majority;

- An independent organ not subject to the members' directives can have binding authority over the organisation;
- The organisation has the authority to pass legal acts that apply directly to member states;
- Those legal acts can affect individuals directly;
- The organisation has an obligatory jurisdiction in case of conflict between the member states, between the organs of the organisation, and between the organs and individuals.

Traditional international organisations are defined by the principle of co-operation and by the sovereignty of the member states. Supranational organisations, in contrast, are defined by the transfer of power and authority from the member states to the organisation.

The clearest example of a supranational organisation is the EU. It clearly fulfils all the requirements of such an institution.[2] The EU, as shown below, has a common political structure authorised to take decisions by majority voting within prescribed areas for the member states. It is thus important to examine those particular policy areas in which this feature of supranationality most strongly applies.

The European Union: Structure and Fields of Competence

Structure

The European Union is based on three pillars — the supranational community pillar and two intergovernmental pillars (the common foreign and security policy is one pillar and the other is co-operation in the fields of justice and home affairs — see Figure 8.1). The three pillars share the same institutions.[3] However, these institutions play different roles in each of them.

The EU's institutional framework does not reflect the principle of separation of powers (Glöckler *et al.* 1998, p. 32). The executive and the legislative power are shared by the so-called 'institutional triangle' consisting of the European Parliament, the Council of Ministers, and the European Commission. Many of the duties resulting from these powers are shared among the different institutions in a manner that renders it impossible to describe any one of them as sole legislator or sole executive (Craig and Búrca 1998, p. 49). Only the judicial power, entrusted to the European Court of Justice, is separate from the other two authorities.

There are five principal institutions identified in Article 7 of the Treaty Establishing the European Community (TEC) that are entrusted with carrying out the tasks of the European Community. These are the Council of Ministers, the European Commission, the European Parliament, the Court of Auditors, and the European Court of Justice.

The balance of power within the institutions and the competencies of those institutions are set out in the TEC. The Commission ensures that the provisions of the TEC and related measures taken by the institutions are applied. It formulates recommendations and delivers opinions on matters dealt within the TEC, and has its own power of decision and can shape the measures taken by the Council and the European Parliament; it also exercises the powers conferred on it by the Council for implementing the rules laid down by the latter.[4] The Council co-ordinates the general economic policies of the member states, has the power to take decisions, and confers on the Commission, in acts adopted by the Council, powers for implementing the rules laid down by the Council.[5] The Council and the Commission are responsible for ensuring the consistency of the external activities of the EU. Together, they oversee the implementation of the external policies, each in accordance with its respective powers.[6] The European Parliament can adopt resolutions calling on the Commission and the Council to develop or modify existing policies or introduce new ones;[7] it also participates with the Council in decision making[8] and

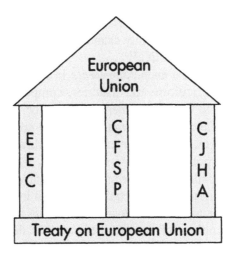

EEC: European Economic Commission
CFSP: Common Foreign and Security Policy
CJHA: Co-operation in the Areas of Justice
and Home Affairs

Figure 8.1   The European Union

exercises control in the EU policy cycle.[9] The external representation of the EU lies in the hands of the Council,[10] in particular with regard to agreements between the European Community and one or more states or international organisations.

The Competencies

European integration is meant to create an ever closer union among the peoples of Europe, through a process in which decisions are taken as openly as possible and as closely as possible to the citizens. The EU in particular strives for consistency among its activities as a whole in the context of its external relations, security, economic, and development policies. The area of competencies of the Community and the member states is laid down in the TEC. The principle of subsidiarity[11] sets another limit to the competencies of the Community. Subsidiarity is the principle that decisions should be taken at the lowest level consistent with effective action within a political system (Bainbridge and Teasdale 1995, p. 430). The Community thus acts within the limits of the powers and objectives conferred upon it by the TEC. In areas outside its competence, the Community takes action, in accordance with the principle of subsidiarity, only if the objectives of the proposed action cannot be sufficiently achieved by the member states and can therefore, by reason of the scale or effects of the proposed action, be better achieved by the Community. Any action taken by the Community cannot go beyond what is necessary to achieve the objectives of the TEC.[12]

The Community has the main competence in such fields as customs and commercial policy, agriculture and fisheries, competition, single market, currency, transport, and the environment. The member states have the main competence in such fields as state organisation and administration, culture, education, development, telecommunications, structural policy, and foreign, security, and defence policy.

The effect of the main competence of the Community can be clearly shown in the case of the environment. All legal acts — both intra-EU and extra-EU — concerning environmental matters are dealt with at the Community level. The environmental policy of the member states is determined either by regulations or by directives. In case of directives, the member states must implement the legal act at the national level.

In the area of commercial policy the question of competence must be examined more closely than in other policy areas. The main competence resides in the Community. However, member states are responsible for their own commercial policy as long as their actions do not interfere with the Community's Common Commercial Policy (CCP), which has two basic objectives. On the one hand, the EU aims to promote an open multilateral trading system; on the other hand, it aims to defend EU interests in relations with trading partners (Glöckler *et al.* 1998). The CCP covers the EU's relation to the European Free Trade Association (EFTA), to the African, Caribbean, and Pacific countries, to the Most Favoured Nation (MFN) principle in accordance with World Trade Organization (WTO) rules, and to the WTO itself.

The Formal Relationship between the G7/8 and the European Union

In order to understand whether the EU itself has a direct, formal relationship with the G7/8, one only has to examine the list of the full members of the G7/8. Only four member states of the EU are members of that group, not the EU itself. This means that there is no official representation of the EU in the G7/8. As the G7/8 is not, legally speaking, an international organisation such as the WTO, the relationship is not covered by the requirements of the CCP. In consequence, there is no formal relationship between the EU and the G7/8.

The Internal EU Relationship to the G7/8

In the case of formal relations between the EU and international organisations, the procedure laid down in Article 300 of the TEC applies. The Commission makes recommendations to the Council, which authorises the Commission to open the necessary negotiations. The Commission conducts these negotiations in consultation with special committees appointed by the Council to assist it in this task, within the framework of such directives as the Council may issue to it.

In the case of the G7/8, Article 300 of the TEC does not apply because the G7/8 is not an international organisation; moreover, the EU itself is not a member of the group. Therefore, there is no reason for the Council to work out directives for the Commission because there is no mandate for the Council to do so.

The question remains whether the four member states of the EU that are in the G7/8 are bound to co-ordinate their position within the G7/8 with the other member states of the European Union or with the EU itself. The prevailing opinion is that there is no reason for co-ordination if the position of the relevant states does not interfere with co-ordinated EU positions or policies, or if the relevant states do not bind the EU in any way with their respective positions within the G7/8.

The European Commission had maintained that it must participate in the meetings of the ministers of finance of the G7. This is necessary, in the Commission's view, because of the requirements of the TEC, in particular Title IX on Common Commercial Policy, and because of questions concerning the Euro and related EU policy. The Council decided that the Commission should not be permanently involved, but should participate only if its respective competence would be affected. Not only did the Council decide against the official participation of the Commission, but the United States also came to the same conclusion. The U.S. holds that the G7/8 is an informal group so there is no need to invite the European Commission.

Nevertheless, since 1977 the president of the European Commission has participated in the annual summits of the G7/8.[13] The formal and legal arguments against the participation of the Commission may be justified. However, given the current emphasis on openness and transparency, it is worth reconsidering this particular judgement. The European Commission's participation could be warranted on the basis of mutual interest. First, it is in the interest of the members of the G7/8 because of the character and function of the Commission as a brain trust, and because of the important role played by the Commission within the EU's policy cycle. If the Commission were involved directly in the meetings of the G7/8, it could react more directly and immediately on results, such as by preparing proposals for legal acts of the Community to implement G7/8 commitments. Second, it would be in the interest of the EU itself and of those member states of the EU who are not members of the G7/8. The information from and about the G7/8 that they receive would be more transparent and perhaps more neutral.

In addition, the influence of the EU as a whole in world trade and the extensive interdependence among it and other G8 members in the trade sphere also point to the advantages of more formal participation by the EU in the G7/8 (see Figure 8.2).

The Position of Germany as EU and G7/8 Chair in the First Half of 1999

Because there is no formal or legal connection between the EU as a supranational institution and the G7/8 as an informal or quasi-intergovernmental one, the parallel membership of Germany, France, Italy, and Britain in both bodies causes no difficulties as long as these countries respect their legal obligations of membership in the European Union. However, because at the summit level both bodies deal with a very similar agenda, and the same European countries are often called on to take leadership roles in both institutions, there is a strong behavioural connection that can bring complex challenges for the diplomacy of the common big four European member states.

These challenges faced Germany in the first six months in 1999 when it was asked to perform, balance, and integrate three roles simultaneously. First, Germany was a member state of the EU. Second, at the time it held the Presidency of the EU. Third, it was host of the G7/8 Summit in late June in Cologne, where it had also hosted the European Council Summit a few weeks earlier. This multifaceted challenge meant much work for Germany, particularly in displaying its diplomatic instincts in a way that balanced all three roles and allowed it and each of the summits and their institutions to succeed.

Holding the Presidency of the EU allowed Germany to chair all Council meetings and to host the European Council. The Presidency must co-ordinate the position of the Union on each of the many issues it faces, and thus must

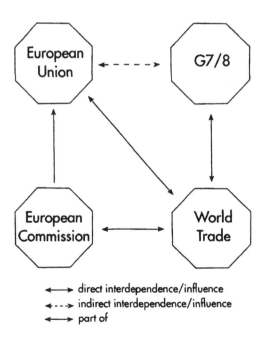

Figure 8.2   Influence and Interdependence in World Trade

play the role of an 'honest broker'. This role is difficult because there is assumed to be no national position of the Presidency during the period in which it occupies the chair. Moreover, the collapse of the whole European Commission in March 1999 produced unexpected problems for the Presidency. The search for a new president of the Commission proved to be successful. However, the transition left Germany with the burden of hosting another European Council Summit in Berlin from 24 to 25 March 1999. Moreover, it was one with an overburdened agenda.

Formally, Germany's position as host of the G7/8 meeting did not interfere with its holding the Presidency within the EU. Nevertheless, it did mean, on the one hand, a double organisational burden (for Germany) and, on the other hand, it meant Germany had to play the role of honest broker for a second time. In the end, Germany fulfilled both roles extraordinarily effectively. It proved to be a very accomplished host and an equally accomplished honest broker.

The Positions of the European Union and the Outcome of the G7/8 Summit in Cologne

In order to determine whether there is influence or interdependence between the European Union and the G7/8, it is useful to compare the outcomes of the two institutions' June 1999 Summits — the European Council from 3 to 4 June 1999 and the G7/8 Summit from 18 to 20 June 1999.

Following their Cologne meeting, and as recorded in the Conclusions of the Presidency, the Cologne European Council (1999) adopted positions on the following topics:
- Growth, employment, competitiveness, and sustainable development (European Employment Pact; broad guidelines for economic policies; tax policy; a single market for financial services; improvements in functioning of the international financial system; indebtedness of the poorest countries; climate policy, environment, and sustainable development);
- Further development of the EU (in the areas of freedom, security, and justice; EU Charter of Fundamental Rights; human rights; operation of the institutions; intergovernmental conference on institutional questions; Common European security and defence policy; enlargement process);
- External relations (western Balkans; Stability Pact for South-eastern Europe; common strategy on Russia; other common strategies [Ukraine, Transatlantic relations, European-Japanese relations, Middle East,

Euro-Mediterranean Partnership, European Union-Latin American Summit, northern dimension, Transcaucasian Summit, East Timor, Macao]); and
• The World Trade Organization.

As seen in the G8 Communiqué at Köln 1999 (see Appendix B), the G8 Summit adopted nine positions. A comparison of its communiqué's positions with those of the Cologne European Council reveals they are very similar (see Table 8.1).

It is clear that there is little difference in the agenda on broad areas and specific issues dealt with by both bodies. Although this chapter is not the

Table 8.1 Topics Discussed at the 1999 Cologne European Summit and G7/8 Summit

European Council Agenda	G7/8 Summit Agenda
• Growth, employment, competitiveness, and sustainable development	• Getting the world economy on track for sustained growth • Designing policies for more employment • Investing in people • Strengthening social safeguards • Redoubling efforts to protect the environment
• Further development of the EU	• No comparable item on the agenda
• External relations	• Deepening the development partnership; • Launching the Köln Debt Initiative; • Tackling global changes
• World Trade Organization	• Building a world trading system that works for everyone
• No comparable item on the agenda	• Promoting nonproliferation, arms control, and disarmament

place for a detailed comparison of all issue areas, it is useful to examine more closely the actual content of the positions adopted by each body in two critical issue areas — the natural environment and international trade — in order to see if the actual commitments made display the same degree of similarity in their content, detail, and ambition.

Environment

Paragraphs 29 to 32 of the Conclusions of the Presidency of the European Council (Cologne European Council 1999) deal with environmental issues under the title 'Climate Policy, Environment, and Sustainable Development'. Here the European Council emphasises the EU's desire to fulfil the commitments undertaken in Kyoto to reduce greenhouse gas emissions and to press vigorously for speedy ratification of the Kyoto protocol under the action plan adopted in Buenos Aires. The European Council views the ratification and implementation of the Kyoto protocol as an important milestone, but it also stresses the urgent necessity of further measures, especially in industrialised countries. The Council attaches much importance to the development of joint and co-ordinated policies and measures at the Community level to supplement the efforts of the member states, and encourages all relevant sectors to contribute within the framework of an overall climate protection strategy. Climate policy is the most important example of the Council's commitment, founded on the Treaty of Amsterdam,[14] to incorporate the requirements of the environment and sustainable development into other Community policies. It sees a special need for action in determining the prerequisites for less emission-intensive and more environmentally friendly transport systems, with regard to increased unhindered consumption and further development of renewable energy sources. The Council also considers it necessary to develop an appropriate framework for energy taxation and, under Economic and Financial Questions, calls for an early decision on this matter.

The G8 Communiqué dealt with the environment in paragraphs 31 to 33 (see Appendix B). The G8 pledged to step up its efforts to build a coherent and environmentally responsive framework of multilateral agreements and institutions to underscore its commitment to sustainable development. The G8 agreed to continue to support the multilateral development banks in making environmental considerations an integral part of their activities and to do likewise when providing its own support. In particular, the members promised to work within the Organisation for Economic Co-operation and Development (OECD) toward common environmental guidelines for export finance agencies. The

G7/8 considered climate change an extremely serious threat to sustainable development and pledged therefore to work toward timely progress in implementing the Buenos Aires Plan of Action with a view to early entry into force of the Kyoto protocol. To this end, the G7/8 members committed themselves to develop and implement domestic measures including those under the United Nations Framework Convention on Climate Change. They welcomed the efforts of the developing countries, particularly the intention announced by some of them in Buenos Aires, to undertake further commitments to abate their greenhouse gas emissions.

The wording of the commitments on the environment in both the Conclusions of the Presidency and the G8 Communiqué is quite similar. The Conclusions stress climate change, in particular the ratification process of the Kyoto protocol. Both documents consider climate change to be an extremely serious matter and urge action, especially an early start on enforcing the Kyoto protocol.[15] The Conclusions refer to another important topic of environmental policy, namely sustainable development. Here the EU wants to incorporate the requirements of the environment and sustainability into other Community policies. The Communiqué states very clearly that there must be an environmentally responsive framework committed to sustainability. The EU goes further in the environment section of the Conclusions when it considers the necessity of a framework for energy taxation and more environmentally friendly transport systems.

The fact that the European Union, unlike the G8, can base its commitments on a legal foundation, including one with supranational elements, reveals a significant difference between the Conclusions and the Communiqué on the topic of the environment. The Conclusions thus go further than the G8 Communiqué. Moreover, they are more detailed. These differing legal bases mean that European Council and Commission must develop the EU's policies. They can therefore indirectly bind the member states that are not members of the G8. The Conclusions of the Presidency bind all EU member states, whether they are a member of G7/8 or not. If EU member states act on the international scene in another role — for example, as member of the G7/8 — they cannot go further than the limits set by the European Council.

World Trade Organization

Paragraphs 99 to 102 of the Conclusions of the Presidency (Cologne European Council 1999) deal with the WTO. Here, the European Council attaches great importance to strengthening the multilateral trading system. It emphasises that a further multilateral liberalisation of trade is the best way of meeting the challenges posed by swift and far-reaching economic change and increasing globalisation. The European Council strongly advocates the launch of a new comprehensive round of negotiations in the WTO framework at the third WTO Ministerial Conference in Seattle at the end of 1999. That round should begin in the year 2000 and if possible should be concluded within three years. A range of topics, including labour standards, environment, development, and transparency, should be negotiated in order to achieve substantial and balanced results for the benefit of all WTO members. The European Council, with an eye to the opportunities for growth afforded by trade, considers a closer integration of the developing countries into world trade to be essential. It is therefore prepared to offer those countries improved market access. The European Council welcomes the accession of other states to the WTO. It endorses the efforts made by China and Russia to date to achieve WTO accession, and urges the Council and the Commission to support early accession by China on the basis of a fair balance of interests and to encourage Russia's endeavours to adapt to the requirements of WTO accession.

The G8 Communiqué deals with the WTO in paragraphs 8 to 11 and 31 (see Appendix B). Here the G8 members renew their strong support for the WTO and their commitment to an open trade and investment environment. They call on all nations to resist protectionist pressures and to open their markets further. The G8 members agree that environmental considerations should be taken into account in the upcoming round of WTO negotiations. This round should include a clarification of the relationship between multilateral environmental agreements and key environmental principles on the one hand and WTO rules on the other. They encourage those states not yet members of the WTO to accept its principles and join it. The G8 will seek a more effective way within the WTO to address the relationship between trade and the environment and to promote sustainable development and social and economic welfare world-wide. The G8 member states encourage all members of the WTO to make proposals for progress in areas where developing countries and, in particular, the Least of the Less Developed Countries (LLDCs) can make solid and substantial gains. All countries should contribute to the new round and benefit from it. The G8 reaffirms its commitment to the LLDCs on improved market access. The G8 members urge greater co-operation and policy coherence among international financial, economic, labour, and environmental organisations, and conclude that the consequences of developments in biotechnology must be dealt with at national and international levels in all the appropriate fora.

In the area of trade, neither the wording nor the contents of the Conclusions of the Presidency and the G8 Communiqué coincide to a substantial degree. The EU supports the multilateral trading system and urges more liberalisation. It considers the closer integration of developing countries as important. Nevertheless, the statements of the European Council on the WTO are not very detailed. The timetables and targets mentioned in the Conclusions must be seen as more political declarations of intent than as concrete commitments. Indeed, they are cautious and reserved. In sharp contrast stands the section on the WTO in the Communiqué. The G7/8 goes into much more detail, at times in aggressive ways, when calling on all nations to resist protectionist pressures. The G7/8 also urges more liberalisation, in wording that is more open and direct. Furthermore, the G7/8 wishes to include environmental issues in the round of WTO negotiations. Biotechnology is dealt with, whereas this subject is not even mentioned in the entire Conclusions of the Presidency. Evidently, the members of the G7/8 feel free to demonstrate their will to guide the WTO negotiations and reveal that they consider themselves the key players in that organisation. Again, one can identify an example of political declarations of intent. The G7/8 'urges' and 'wishes' but does not set out action that would require legal implementation. This gives it more flexibility than the EU.

Conclusion

This analysis demonstrates that there is no formal or legal connection between the European Union and the G7/8. Whereas the EU is a supranational organisation, the G7/8 is an informal group of sovereign nation-states. The parallel membership of four member states in the EU and in the G7/8 does not cause problems as long as the states fulfil their obligations resulting from their membership in the EU. Nevertheless, it is evident that there are behavioural links between both bodies. An examination of the 1999 Conclusions of the European Council and of the G8 Communiqué from the Cologne Summit reveals that both meetings dealt with very similar agendas. The question of whether the four member states of the EU could successfully negotiate in the G8 and could manage similar conclusions at the G8 Summit compared to the European Council cannot yet be answered definitively. The similar results and even the wording indicate that the four EU member states yield a strong influence in the G7/8. The EU stresses environmental issues more than the G8, but is more cautious in dealing with WTO questions. In retrospect, the more reserved Conclusions of the European Council on the

WTO negotiations in Seattle have proven to be more realistic than the more ambitious calls of the G8. Most important, a comparison of both documents reveals no evidence that the four EU member states agreed at the G8 Summit to commitments in a way that would differ from EU positions. The limits of the G7/8 Summit have been set — indirectly — at the European Council as far as direct competencies of the EU are concerned. The four EU member states felt bound and were bound to the positions for legal reasons.

Nevertheless, the question of whether there is a need for further intra-EU co-ordination in the run-up to G7/8 meetings should not only be considered from a legal point of view. The same is true for the presence of the European Commission in the G7/8 meetings. If both the European Union and the G7/8 want to have maximum transparency and expertise, the current relationship should be reconsidered. Here the goal should be to identify and implement the best arrangement for both the EU and the G7/8. Both the EU and the G7/8 play an eminent role in world policy. People all over the world watch what these bodies do. In order to have clear and effective outcomes, all partners involved should participate in decisive meetings. For the G7/8, it would be interesting to have the European Commission on board in order to use its professional knowledge. Whether there should be closer co-operation between the EU and the G7/8 is a very delicate political decision, but on an informal level it would help to co-ordinate the activities of both bodies in affairs they have in common. Still, whether they should enlarge or deepen is a crucial question for both. Enlargement as such cannot be the solution, but the use of all intellectual and professional resources must be established in order for the EU and the G7/8 to be able to face the challenges of the twenty-first century.

Notes

1   The American bloc consists of the United States of America and Canada; the European bloc comprises Germany, France, the United Kingdom, and Italy; and the Asian bloc contains Japan and Russia.

2   Those five characteristics all apply to the EU: the decisions made by the Council of Ministers have binding authority over the members; the European Commission constitutes an independent body with authority over the EU; the Council's regulations apply, as do the Commission's decisions; and legal conflicts between constituent states and organs are handled by the European Court of Justice.

3   Article 3 Paragraph 1 of the Treaty Establishing the European Community (TEC) states that the EU shall be served by a single institutional framework that will ensure the consistency and continuity of the activities carried out in order to attain its objectives while respecting and building upon the *'acquis communautaire'*.

4   See Article 211 of the TEC.
5   See Article 202 of the TEC.
6   See Article 3 Paragraph 2 of the TEC.
7   See Article 192 Paragraph 2 of the TEC on the decision preparation role.
8   See Article 192 Paragraph 1 of the TEC on the co-legislator role.
9   See Article 193 of the TEC.
10   See Article 300 of the TEC.
11   See the Treaty on European Union from 7 February 1992 (referred to as the Maastricht Treaty).
12   See Article 5 of the TEC.
13   This does not enlarge the respective group to a group of nine because of the president of the European Commission participates as an observer.
14   The revision of the Treaty on European Union dated 2 October 1997 is known as the Amsterdam Treaty.
15   It is not the task of this article to scrutinise whether the EU or the G7/8 are working on this topic in Realpolitik or not.

References

Bainbridge, T., and A. Teasdale (1995), *Penguin Companion to the European Union*, Penguin, London.

Bayne, N. (2000), *Hanging in There: The G7 and G8 Summit in Maturity and Renewal*, Ashgate, Aldershot.

Bergsten, F., et al. (1997), 'G7: Going, Going...', *International Economy*, vol. 11, no. 4.

Cologne European Council (1999), Presidency Conclusions, Document 150/99 (Presse 0), 3 to 4 June, <ue.eu.int/en/Info/eurocouncil/index.htm> (September 2000).

Craig, P., and Gráinne de Búrca (1998), *EU Law: Text, Cases, and Materials*, second edition, Oxford University Press, Oxford.

Evans, G., and J. Newnham (1998), *Dictionary of International Relations*, Penguin Books, London.

Glöckler, G., L. Junius, G. Scappucci, S. Usherwood, and J. Vassallo (1998), *Guide to EU Policies*, Blackstone Press Limited, London.

Hainsworth, Susan (1990), 'Coming of Age: The European Community and the Economic Summit', Country Study No. 7, Centre for International Studies, University of Toronto, Toronto, <www.library.utoronto.ca/g7/scholar/hainsworth1990/bisfor.htm> (September 2000).

Hodges, M. (1999), 'The G8 and the New Political Economy', in M. Hodges, J. Kirton, and J. Daniels (eds.), *The G8's Role in the New Millennium*, Ashgate, Aldershot, pp. 69-73.

Ipsen, K. (1990), *Völkerrecht*, third edition, Beck, Munich.

Kirton, J. (1999), 'Explaining G8 Effectiveness', in M. Hodges, J. Kirton, and J. Daniels (eds.), *The G8's Role in the New Millennium*, Ashgate, Aldershot. pp. 45-68.

Köck, H. F., and Fischer, P. (1997), *Internationale Organisationen*, third edition, Linde Verlag Vienna.

Lamy, Pascal (1988), 'The Economic Summit and the European Community', Bissell Paper No. 4, Centre for International Studies, University of Toronto, Toronto, <www.library.utoronto.ca/g7/scholar/lamy1988/lamtext4.htm> (September 2000).

Ostry, Sylvia (1990), 'Canada, Europe, and the Economic Summits', Paper presented at the All-European Canadian Studies Conference, The Hague, 24–27 October, <www.library.utoronto.ca/g7/scholar/ostry1990/ost1.htm> (September 2000).

Shaw, M. N. (1997), *International Law*, fourth edition, Cambridge University Press, Cambridge.

Silguay, Y.-T. de (1997), The Impact of the Creation of the Euro on Financial Markets and the International Monetary System, Address to the Institute of International Finance, Washington, DC, 29 April 29.

Ullrich, H., and A. Donnelly (1998), 'The Group of Eight and the European Union: The Evolving Partnership', *G7 Governance*, vol. 5, <www.library.utoronto.ca/g7/governance/gov5> (September 2000).

Part III
The New Directions in Global Governance

9 The G20: Representativeness, Effectiveness, and Leadership in Global Governance

JOHN J. KIRTON[1]

Introduction

One of the most persistent criticisms of the G7 since its inception in 1975 has been the way in which this exclusive club of the world's most powerful major industrial democracies has served as an unrepresentative, and thus illegitimate and ineffective, subset of the global community it seeks to lead (Commission on Global Governance 1995, ul Haq 1994, Jayawardena 1989, Smyser 1993, Brzezinski 1996, Bergsten 1998, *Economist* 1998, Hajnal 1999, Hodges 1999). These criticisms, flowing from both the policy and scholarly communities, have been countered by an equally insistent argument that the effectiveness of the G7 as a source of badly needed leadership for the full global community depends critically on the very small size, highly selective membership, and common values of the forum (Kirton 1993, Bayne 2000). The debate between these competing schools has recently become all the more intense, as the G7, despite its continuing shortcomings, has become an important contributor to global governance, and thus one that countries seek to enter. Indeed, the longstanding debate between G7 membership 'expansionists' and 'minimalists' has now entered a new phase. Expansionists have steadily added new candidates to their list of the actors worthy of inclusion. Some minimalists have accepted the 1998 expansion of the G7 into a new G8 with Russia as a member, recommended other candidates for at least partial inclusion, or argued that a revival of G8 effectiveness requires an expansion of membership as the new world of the twenty-first century dawns (Kirton 1999a; Cutter, Spero, and Tyson 2000).

For its first quarter century, the G7 itself responded to the classic logic of the minimalists, by barely expanding beyond the original six countries (France, the United States, Britain, Germany, Japan, Italy) and Canada, which had been promised a place from the start. This minimalism has been maintained in the

143

face of repeated pleas, from the very inception of the G7, from a broad range of countries, led by the Netherlands, Belgium, and Australia, that repeatedly sought inclusion in this highly restricted plurilateral club. Indeed, only Canada, the European Union (EU), and Russia succeeded in securing admission in 1976, 1977, and 1998 respectively. An equally vigorous and variegated group of claimants has directed their energies, with considerably more success, at securing admission to the many G7-incubated forums, at the official and ministerial level, established to deal with the pressing political security and transnational-global issues of the day (Hajnal 1999). Yet in the domain of finance, where the claims for inclusion have been particularly intense, the G7 has long remained hermetically sealed at all levels. It was only in 1986 at the Tokyo Summit that Italy and Canada, long-time members, were admitted to the Group of Five finance ministers, which continued to meet for a time 'at five' members as well as 'at seven'. Even with Russia's admittance to the newly named 'Summit of the Eight' in 1997 and permanently to the leaders-level G8 institution itself in 1998, the G7 has continued to meet on its own to deal with macroeconomic and finance issues.

Given this dominance of minimalism during the G7's first quarter century, it was all the more surprising that the closing years of the twentieth century brought an outburst of new G7-centred and sponsored institutions at the ministerial and official levels in the field of finance. The process of expansion began, most broadly, at the meeting of the leaders of Asia-Pacific Economic Cooperation (APEC) forum in Vancouver in November 1997. Here U.S. president Bill Clinton pioneered a short-lived Group of 22 (G22) to discuss the unfolding Asian financial crisis and ways to strengthen the international financial system in response. The process continued in the spring of 1999 when the G7 created a new body, the Financial Stability Forum (FSF), first made up of the G7 states but soon with four new members added. The FSF was to confront the challenge of dealing with issues once considered technical but now viewed as having greater political consequence and relevance to the broader world.

By far the most ambitious attempt to move from the G7 to a broader forum for global financial governance came with the creation of the G20 in September 1999, in accordance with the commitment made by G7 leaders at their Cologne Summit in June of that year. As with the G7 itself at the moment of its creation, the formal mandate of this new political level forum centred on financial matters but also embraced the full economic domain. The members of the G7 collectively contained a predominant share of the world's economic capabilities. Moreover, in sharp contrast to the many issue-specific bodies incubated in the G7, which had regularly arisen since the G7's start, the G20 quickly generated claims that it would soon supersede the G7/8 itself. Indeed, no less an authoritative, well-positioned participant than Ernst Weltke, President of the Bundesbank, declared at the time of the G20's first ministerial meeting that the organisation could replace the G7 or at least take over its leading global role (Porter 2000).

Is the G20 in fact a major, step-level jump into a more genuinely global governance of the international financial and economic system in the crisis-prone globalised system of the twenty-first century? Or is it yet another of the proliferating array of informal, consultative bodies struggling to find a significant role in a world where established institutions, while increasingly under assault, still hold a predominant place? The sceptics can readily point to the G20's origins as a transitory response to the 1997–99 Asian-turned-global financial crisis, to its origins as an effort to institutionalise and thus contain U.S. institution-creating unilateralism in a way that reflected and reinforced G7 dominance, and to the restricted novelty of its agenda and actions during the G20's first year. Yet the visionaries can counter with several credible claims. The G7 itself was founded amidst financial crisis grounded in inexorable linkages to a full range of other issues. The G7 was also created by forward-looking finance ministers from outside the United States who wished to continue their informal meetings when they became leaders. Moreover, the crisis-ridden world of the early twenty-first century, much like in the early 1970s, needs a new centre to combine the capabilities and address the vulnerabilities of a fresh set of leading countries to cope with the new agenda and system that has arisen.

This chapter argues that it is the visionary conception that is likely to prevail, particularly if the G20's founding custodians successfully steer it in a direction that gives it the authority of the leaders themselves and the full breadth, novelty, and ambition of the agenda they demand. For the G20's origins, early operation and prospects are well accounted for by an expanded version of the realist and liberal-institutionalist concepts combined in the concert model of G7/8 governance (Kirton 1989, 1993, 1999a). This model explains why particular institutions prevail and others fail as effective centres of global governance. More specifically, the G20 is destined, at a minimum, to remain important as a way of reinforcing the leadership and legitimacy of the G7/8 by ensuring that the latter's initiatives are understood, accepted, 'bought into', and thus implemented by a broad group of consequential countries. But it also, reciprocally, will do so by ensuring that the G7/8 itself performs its leadership role with a full sensitivity to the perspectives, positions, and domestic political priorities and politics of this broad group. The G20, more than its leading institutional competitor, the International Monetary and Financial Committee (IMFC) recently created by the International Monetary Fund (IMF), has the flexibility, and the lateral and vertical linkages, to emerge as the leading centre of legitimisation, sensitisation, and timely, well-targeted action in the emerging international system. Moreover, the G20's current seminal custodians, led by Canada's minister of finance Paul Martin, are constructing and implementing the vision required to endow the G20 with the political authority and broad, innovative, ambitious agenda and accomplishment to render it effective as a broadly representative leadership forum.

To develop this analysis, this chapter first examines the existing embryonic literature on the fledgling G20, argues that its origin, operation, and prospects are well accounted for by the concert model, and explores the ways in which the logical international institutional 'trilemma' of representativeness, effectiveness, and leadership faced by the G20, along with other such institutions, can be resolved in the G20 architecture. It next discusses the origins of the G20 in the emergence of the New Arrangements to Borrow (NAB), the G22, the FSF, the Cologne Summit 'GX', and the G20 itself. Then, it analyses the initial year of the G20's operation, from the deputies meeting in November 1999 through the December 1999 Berlin ministerial, the March 2000 deputies review session. the Washington meetings of the IMF and the International Bank for Reconstruction and Development (IBRD), the G7 and the IMFC in April 2000, and planning for the October 2000 Montreal ministerial of the G20. Finally, the chapter looks ahead at prospective approaches and architecture for the October 2000 and post-October G20, and draws conclusions as to the group's future importance and role.

The G20 and the 'Trilemma' of Global Governance

To date, the most complete, theoretically grounded analysis of the origins, early operation, and future prospects of the G20 comes from Tony Porter (2000). He argues that the concept of legitimacy, as opposed to standard realist, liberal-institutionalist and Gramscian explanations, is critical to accounting for the creation of both the G20 and the FSF. In Porter's analysis, although realist theories may account for U.S. leadership in creating the earlier G22, the subsequent G20 cannot be seen as a direct benefit to the U.S. alone or to its G7 colleagues, especially in relation to the non-G7 powers that had their relative power enhanced by membership and that apparently made no bargaining concessions to secure admission. Similarly liberal-institutionalist approaches may account for the G20's role in reducing transaction costs, creating economies of scale in learning, reducing uncertainty, and enhancing monitoring in the wake of the 1997–99 financial crisis and for the use of the G7 as a regime 'nest'. However, the absence of rational bargaining among G7 or full G20 members, the absence of concessions from non-G7 members to secure membership, and the momentary crisis-induced weakness of developing country members at the time of their admission constitute important departures from liberal-institutionalist claims.

Gramscian approaches fare even less well. Despite its capitalist-friendly appearance, the G20 increased the autonomy of member states relative to the business community, saw business groups play no consequential role in the group's formation or operation, and emphasised two key ideas — private-sector burden sharing and slow capital account liberalisation with selective capital controls — that were antithetical to the interests of the wealthy classes. While the G20's efforts to minimise the frequency and severity of financial crisis and instability are indeed in the interests of wealthy and the broad mass of newer investors, these interests are shared by all citizens in the crisis countries and the international community as well. A superior explanation thus flows from the dynamics of legitimacy — the way the FSF and G20 provided technical and political legitimacy on economic, technical, and democratic levels.

Porter's account properly points to the crucial role of crisis, in particular the second shock (Kirton 1989) of the 1997–99 global financial crisis that delegitimised the prevailing institutions (the IMF, the G10,[2] the Basle Committee on Banking Supervision, and even the G7 on its own) and prompted a call for a new, more broadly representative forum that shifted the prevailing pre-crisis neoliberal doctrine to a more socially sensitive approach to globalisation. Yet, a more detailed examination of the evolution and early operation of the G20 suggests a more robust role for realist and liberal-institutionalist interpretations than Porter presents. The initiative to create the G22 was more a personal initiative of President Bill Clinton than a U.S. state interest (Krasner 1978). Yet, it gave the U.S. government, along with its fellow members of the G7 concert, a shared interest in creating a regularised, institutionalised forum with a permanent, fixed membership and proper reporting relationship to the G7 and the other established international institutions in which it was nested. Even with the apparent decade-long 'Goldilocks' economy and the 1997–99 crisis-driven resurgence in relative U.S. power against G7 countries other than Britain and Canada, the G20, as

148 Guiding Global Order

with the G7 itself in 1975, mobilised systemically predominant capabilities to combat a now much more global threat and one that a post-hegemonic U.S. could no longer combat alone, as the September 1998 Long-Term Capital Management (LTCM) crisis revealed (Kirton 2000).

Most importantly, in an intensely globalised world, the equalisation of intervulnerability (Keohane and Nye 1989), more than capability, required the involvement in an expanded regime of those countries able to contribute resources to the G7 in the face of systemic threats, or, as importantly, able to infect it directly through vulnerabilities within their national systems. Unlike the members of the earlier Organization of Petroleum Exporting Countries (OPEC), the Group of 77, the Consumer-Producer dialogue, the Cancun 'global negotiations' groups, or the 1989 G15, the G20's outer, non-G7 ring of middle powers thus mattered in multidimensional power terms. They mattered both for the reinforcing capabilities and the destructive vulnerabilities they brought in a tightly wired world. Indeed, the global geographic extent, contagious speed, and domestic destructiveness of the new globalisation, dramatically displayed by the 1997–99 global financial crisis, required a far greater predominance of capabilities than before, as well as far more states inside the core, to lead in implementing the domestic measures to prevent such systemically and socially destructive crises from arising.

Furthermore, unlike the divided world of the cold war era, the international community now possessed enough democratic polities — or those moving toward more democratic forms of governance — around the globe. This made it possible to create a permanent institutionalised association for effective global governance based on shared domestic values. It was from this democratic or proto-democratic stratum that the G20's outer members were drawn and from its democratic values that its common purpose was forged.

Beneath the unified appearance it presented to the outside world, the G20 was marked by significant bargaining over fundamental issues in its creation and early operation. The most profound issue was the overall architectural question of whether the G20 or the rival IMFC would emerge as the effective political centre of economic governance in the new era. A second was the question of membership, with different G7 members having distinctive preferences, and each enjoying some success as it sought to reinforce its national advantage in the new institution and bring into being its preferred approach to world order. And the third issue, as shown by the debate over the new principles of private-sector participation and controlled capital account liberalisation, was the way that the initial division between G7 and non-G7 members, showed signs of yielding to a reciprocal flow of influence and to fluid coalitions of G20 members that crossed the divide from the G7 to the non-G7 members.

In short, in the post–cold-war, post-crisis, intensely globalised world of the early twenty-first century, an expanded form of the concert equality model that explains the emergence, operation, and effectiveness of the G7/8 accounts to a high degree for the creation, early activity, and probable impact of the G20 as well. Still in its initial years, the new G20 forum has defined by predominance without, equality within, multifaceted intervulnerability rendered visible by a second shock, the common purpose of embryonic democratic governance, and the fluid pattern of making internal coalitions, in which any member could combine with any other on the basis of interest and distinctive national values. It was the embryonic reservoir of common purpose, the role of coalitional fluidity in knitting together the large collection of members beyond the confines of a K-group (Snidal 1989), and the G20's resistance to further expansion that showed that the principle of constricted participation remained relevant. Indeed, it was only the character of political control by popularly elected leaders that was absent. Yet, even here, there were early signs of forces at work to bring this feature into effect.

A second analysis of the G20, that offered by Pierre Marc Johnson in Chapter 13, 'Creating Sustainable Global Governance', rests implicitly on the core elements of this expanded concert model and points to the major missing ingredient of political control. Johnson views the G20 as a 'promising organisation that could play a significant role in global governance'. In his view, its promise rests on its combination of the 19 countries plus the EU, the European Central Bank (ECB), the IMF, and the World Bank. It further rests on the G20's predominant concentration of 87 percent of the world's gross domestic product (GDP) (and 65 percent of its population), the special strength and influence that come from its operation by economics and finance ministers, its comprehensive and flexible agenda, and its first chair's focus on an expansive agenda that includes poverty reduction and other measures to ensure that the benefits of globalisation are widely shared.

Johnson thus sees the G20 as a body able to play a significant role in fostering a new north-south bargain that would restart a new round of negotiations on multilateral trade liberalisation, bring together trade, environment, and development issues, and design and foster a new system of global governance. He concludes by asking the 'highest authorities' in the G8 and G20 to integrate a broad array of trade, financial, environmental, and social issues to secure a new coherence in global governance for the twenty-first century.

The application of the concert model to the new system of pervasive, penetrative intervulnerability and expanding domestic-level democratic governance thus does much to account for the creation, early operation and potential path of the G20. However, its emergence as an effective centre of global governance ultimately depends on its success in meeting and resolving the contradictions among three central performance criteria for international institutions that serve as the underlying causes of the legitimacy they secure.

The first component of this international institutional 'trilemma' is representativeness — or the number and balance of various dimensions of the actors included in the forum. As Table 9.1 shows, the G20 currently contains more than double the number of countries, and two more multilateral institutions, than the G8 does. Non-G7 and G8 countries predominate. There is a rough balance between developed and developing countries, and Organisation for Economic Co-operation and Development (OECD) and non-OECD members. G20 members come from all geographic regions, with a particularly robust representation from Asia, and from all of the world's major geopolitically relevant civilisations. Relative to its IMFC rival, the G20 can be open to criticism only on the grounds that it underrepresents Africa, traditional western European middle powers, and the francophone world. Moreover, the participation of the IMF and the World Bank gives the G20 a claim to at least a second-hand representation of the universal membership of the global community, over the broad and expanding array of finance, development, and many related international and domestic issues these Bretton Woods institutions now govern. However, as with the G7 and G8, the unique presence among regional organisations of the EU and ECB constitutes an imbalance that privileges developed and European countries rather than the broad array of emerging, smaller, developing, and least developed countries from most other regions of the world. More broadly, the G20 has not been created with an architecture, nor has it yet devised a process, for incorporating civil society representatives, even in the classic form that international institutions such as the OECD or the International Labour Organization have long had.

The second component is that of effectiveness, defined as the ability to reach and implement timely, well-tailored collective agreements to solve and ideally prevent the crises and problems of the day. There is a clear tradeoff between representativeness and effectiveness. Additional members in themselves compromise the capacity for effective action, for the reasons specified in liberal-institutionalist theory. Yet, the G20 has minimised the additional transaction costs created by its larger membership in several ways.

Table 9.1 Financial Forums and Their Membership

	G5 (1975)	G7 (1975)	G10ᵃ (1962)	G8 (1997)	G22 (1997)	G20ᵇ (1999)	IMFCᶜ (1999)	G33 (1999)
Canada		x	x	x	x	x	x	x
France	x	x	x	x	x	x	x	x
Germany	x	x	x	x	x	x	x	x
Italy		x	x	x	x	x	x	x
Japan	x	x	x	x	x	x	x	x
Russia				x	x	x	x	x
United Kingdom	x	x	x	x	x	x	x	x
United States	x	x	x	x	x	x	x	x
Algeria							x	
Argentina					x	x	x	x
Australia					x	x	x	x
Belgium			x				x	x
Brazil					x	x	x	x
Chile								x
China					x	x	x	x
Côte d'Ivoire								x
Denmark							x	
Egypt								x
Gabon							x	
Hong Kong SAR					x			x
India					x	x	x	x
Indonesia					x			x
Korea					x	x		x
Malaysia					x			x
Mexico					x	x	x	x
Morocco								x
Netherlands			x				x	x
Poland					x			x
Saudi Arabia						x	x	x
Singapore					x			x
South Africa					x	x	x	x
Spain								x
Sweden			x					x
Switzerland			x				x	x
Thailand					x		x	x
Turkey						x		x
United Arab Emirates							x	

a. Observers: Bank for International Settlements (BIS), European Commission (EC), the International Monetary Fund (IMF), and the Organisation for Economic Co-operation and Development (OECD).

b. Includes two institutional representatives (European Union and IMF/World Bank).

c. International Monetary and Financial Committee (IMFC), formerly the Interim Committee, established in October 1974.

The additional non-G8 member states contain many that have been involved in other G7-centric regimes in various fields. Moreover, the additional international institutions — the IMF and IBRD — have been in close association with the G7/8 in recent years at the levels of the leaders and lower. The costs in transactions, transparency, and monitoring thus ought to be sustainable, especially if an early emphasis can be placed on open, informal dialogue, and on those non-divisive agenda items where there is a very broad and deep reservoir of at least latent consensus among the members.

To be sure, the inclusion of different kinds of actors — ministers of national governments and international civil servants heading international and regional organisations — has compounded the obstacles to effective collective decision making. At the same time, the participation of these officials has enhanced the prospects of compliance and effective implementation, given the capacity of the non-state bodies and the second-hand inclusion of other countries through the international institutions (Kokotsis 1999; and Kokotsis and Daniels 1999). The G20 faces the initial task of ensuring genuine representativeness among its existing members through open and meaningful dialogue on core finance items that command considerable consensus; nonetheless, its emergence as an effective centre of global governance will depend on its ability to move into actual decision making on more difficult issues, if only in response to crises where other charter-bound, bureaucratically constrained international organisations prove too slow.

The third component of the trilemma is leadership, best seen as the task of producing new directions in process and principle for the broader international community as part of crisis response, crisis prevention, or proactive reform of the global order. These directions are those on which outside actors can coalesce, for leadership requires followership. Here there is a tradeoff between effectiveness and leadership, as the task of reaching and implementing decisions on issues at the heart of the institution's competence and acknowledged role in the international institutional division of labour may be compromised should the institution embrace a broader array of subjects and interrelate them in ways that offer a political redefinition rather than one at the technical level. Moreover, there is also a tradeoff between representativeness and leadership, as institutions with a large number of diverse forms of members find it more difficult to arrive at consensus in identifying far-reaching new directions for global order.

The challenge for the G20 is to resolve these tradeoffs within this trilemma, in ways that are at least as, if not more, successful than either the pre-existing G7/8 at its core or the competing IMFC. Failure to do so would confine the

G20 to being primarily a second-tier body for the legitimisation of G7/8 deliberations, direction setting, and decisions, or would restrict the task of shaping a new global order to the leadership of the IMFC and the confines of an IMF charter and institutional culture grounded in the world of 1944.

The Origins of the G20

The G20 emerged most directly from efforts during the 1990s to broaden the traditional G7 and G10 centres of international financial governance and to include actors with additional and rapidly growing capability, in order to help stem the deepening and broadening intervulnerability that a rapidly globalising system brought. The process began in the aftermath of the December 1994 Mexican peso crisis with the emergence of the NAB. It continued with the creation of the G22 and FSF, bred by the 1997–99 global financial crisis. It culminated with the establishment of the G20 itself. Throughout the process, there has been a recurrent effort to combat the intervulnerability highlighted and accentuated by crisis, to institutionalise and constrain unilateral U.S.-centred leadership, and to combat regional solutions in favour of a new approach to global governance tailored to the demands of a new era.

The New Arrangements to Borrow

The origins of the G20, and the larger process of broadening the G7 network of consultation to include major developing countries or emerging markets in the domain of finance, date from the mid 1990s and the first financial crisis of that decade. The creation of the G7-dominated NAB was prompted by the Mexican peso crisis and the G7's call, at the 1995 Halifax Summit, to the G10 to double the monies available to the IMF under the General Arrangements to Borrow (GAB) (Bergsten and Henning 1996). The IMF Executive Board approved the NAB on 27 January 1997. Its approval entered into force on 17 November 1998. The NAB, whose secretary is housed at the IMF, is similar to the longstanding GAB, but brings to bear more funds and additional contributors. Both the NAB and GAB were used during the 1997–99 crisis. The fact that the NAB had more money and more flexibility than the GAB proved essential in the successful containment of the crisis.

Of the 25 members of the NAB, those with the lowest contribution of 340 million Special Drawing Rights (SDRs) are the Hong Kong Monetary Authority, Finland, Korea, Malaysia, Singapore, and Thailand. Canada, the lowest ranked G7 member in the NAB, has 1396 SDRs while the U.S., the top-ranked G7 member, has 6712.

The G22, November 1997

A further step toward expanding the G7 concert and the older G10 in the finance domain came with the formation of the G22, created at the personal initiative of President Bill Clinton at the November 1997 APEC leaders' meeting in Vancouver. The group's activities over the subsequent year centred on reports on particular aspects of the international financial architecture. The G22's activities proved instrumental in the creation of the new G20, as a successor body more closely integrated with the work of the established International Financial Institutions. The experience with the G22 and parallel G33 had highlighted the need for a 'regular international consultative forum with a broader membership than the G-7' and one integrated into the governance structures of the IMF or World Bank (Canada 1999a).

When Clinton proposed the formation of the G22, it was just as the Asian financial crisis had engulfed Thailand and Indonesia and was about to infect South Korea. There was thus general support among G7 countries to follow such leadership. The subsequent South Korean crisis in December appeared to justify this instinct (Kirton 2000). Yet as liberal-institutionalist theory would predict, there was also widespread concern, within the U.S. Treasury and among other G7 members, about to whom the new body would report, what its mandate and membership would be, and how its work would relate to that of the other established international institutions with longstanding mandates and analytic and implementing capacity. These concerns led to initiatives to create a more institutionalised and permanent body, initially known as GX, that would have a defined role vis-à-vis the established institutions and the new forums then being negotiated, such as the IMFC.

The Financial Stability Forum, February 1999

A subsequent step toward a crisis-driven broadening of G7 governance in finance came in Bonn on 22 February 1999, when the G7 finance ministers created the Financial Stability Forum (Porter 2000). The FSF was based on a formula composed by German central bank governor Hans Tietmeyer. Its purpose is to 'promote information exchange and co-ordination among the national authorities, international institutions and international regulatory or experts' groupings with responsibilities for questions of international financial stability' (Financial Stability Forum [FSF] 1999). Its initial membership consisted of representatives from the finance ministries and central banks and leading supervisors of each of the G7 countries, along with the chairs of the international supervisory organisations and representatives of international financial institutions.

The FSF first met at the IMF in Washington on 14 April 1999. At the Cologne Summit in June 1999, G7 leaders decided to expand the group beyond G7 member countries to include the systemically important emerging economies. Thus Hong Kong, Singapore, Australia, and the Netherlands were added as participants for the FSF's subsequent meeting in Paris on 15 September 1999.

The G20

The new G20 forum of finance ministers and central bank governors was created by the Cologne G7 Summit on 18 June as part of the birth of a trilogy of new international institutions. In their communiqué (G7 1999a) the G7 leaders first disavowed the need for new institutions and affirmed the central role of the IMF and World Bank. Then, they welcomed:

- the establishment of the new Financial Stability Forum to enhance international co-operation and co-ordination in the area of financial market supervision and regulation;
- the strengthening and reform of the governance structures of the International Financial Institutions (IFIs), by *inter alia* giving permanent standing to the IMF's Interim Committee as the 'International Financial and Monetary Committee' [*sic*] and by further improving IMF surveillance and programs; and
- the commitment to work together with the IMF and the World Bank to establish an informal mechanism for dialogue among systemically important countries, within the framework of the Bretton Woods institutional system.

The G20, chaired for its first two years by Canadian finance minister Paul Martin, was formally created at the meeting of the G7 finance ministers on 25 September 1999. It was established as 'a new mechanism for informal dialogue in the framework of the Bretton Woods institutional system, to broaden the dialogue on key economic and financial policy issues among systemically significant economies and promote cooperation to achieve stable and sustainable world economic growth that benefits all' (G7 1999b). At its first meeting in Berlin in December 1999, the G7 finance ministers were to invite 'counterparts from a number of systemically important countries from regions around the world to launch this new group', as well as representatives of the EU, IMF, and World Bank.

As outlined by Martin, the G20's mandate is to 'promote discussion and study and review policy issues among industrialized countries and emerging markets with a view to promoting international financial stability' (Kirton 1999b). Its initial 19 country members consisted of the G7 plus Argentina, Australia, Brazil, China, India, Mexico, Russia, Saudi Arabia, South Africa, South Korea, and Turkey. Canada would host the second meeting in 2000. The chair would rotate among participants after two-year terms, with the initial chairs being chosen from among the G7 countries.

The Origins of the G20

The G20 was in the first instance a U.S.-led initiative, in accordance with classic realist models of benign hegemony in international regime formation and American leadership in G7 co-operation (Keohane 1984, Cohn 2000, Putnam and Bayne 1987). As with the creation of the earlier G22, the process of forming the G20 was one in which the U.S. effectively initiated the proposal, created the momentum, set the agenda, and had a leading but by no means complete role in choosing the members.

In doing so, the U.S. was inspired by several forces. Larry Summers, first as U.S. Deputy Secretary and then as full Treasury Secretary after Robert Rubin's resignation following the Cologne Summit, along with some Treasury officials sought to create a compact group of systemically significant countries that would take what was agreed by the G7 and legitimise it internationally. In the wake of the 1997–99 global financial crisis and the strong congressional, specialist, and public criticism that the IMF received in response, including calls for its abolition or a dramatic narrowing of its a mandate, the U.S. Treasury came to view the IMF, with its large powerful staff, as a technocratic body that as a result resisted U.S. proposals for rapid, U.S.-conceived but badly needed reform. The Treasury team tended to regard the IMF Interim Committee as a forum where the agenda was already set by IMF staff, with all issues already resolved by prior consultation and ministers thus relegated to the minor role of delivering prepared statements. In creating the G20, the U.S. players in part sought to escape such institutionalised constraints.

Yet U.S. frustration and leadership did not alone account for the creation of the G20 or predominantly determine the shape of the body that emerged. For the G20, from its conception as the GX to its September birth, was the product of distinctive perspectives and approaches among G7 members and an ensuing process of bargaining and genuine mutual adjustment. The Canadians were used to channelling U.S. impulses into constructive, collective, and institutionalised directions, and had their own vision of how best to reform the international financial system, dating from the G7 Summit they had hosted at Halifax in 1995. Thus, the Canadians were from an early stage very supportive. They pushed the proposal forward enthusiastically, and sought to have their own finance minister appointed as the first chair of the new group.

Apart from the advantages brought by procuring the prominence and prerogatives of chair, the Canadians were propelled by several factors. At the APEC leaders meeting in Vancouver, where the G22 was born, the Canadians had shared the concerns of their U.S. Treasury counterparts about how the G22 would fit in with the broader array of existing and newer institutions already at work. As skilled and dedicated shapers of international institutions, they had asked about the reporting mechanism for the G22 and from where it would derive its mandate and legitimacy, as well as how much credibility it would have given that its membership and operations were so clearly defined by what could be ever-changeable political preferences in Washington. They had thus sought to transform the G22 into a successor body that would be less subject to Washington politics, and thus have greater stability, added value, effectiveness, and credibility.

The British, the Germans, and the Japanese joined the Americans and the Canadians in being the most enthusiastic advocates among the G7 for the creation of the new group. Britain, however, although supportive, was concerned that the G20 not diminish in practice the prominence of the new IMFC, of which Britain's finance minister Gordon Brown was the first chair. This helped lead to an early British emphasis on a narrowly focused agenda for the G20.

The French, supported by the Italians, resisted the creation of the G20. They feared that it would undermine the authority of the IMF, then headed by their compatriot Michel Camdessus, and the IMFC they preferred as the central new forum. France eventually acquiesced in the formation of the G20 but still pushed for the creation of a new council of ministers at the heart of the IMF. To secure such a forum, they wished to turn the Interim Committee into a council.

Throughout 1999, the French continued to push for the Interim Committee to be further strengthened and given more powers and profile. For example, they sought ministerial working groups of the IMFC to deal with specific issues such as transparency. Under this concept, five to six ministers would meet two to four times per year and report back to the full IMFC on options. This could be done, on issues such as the development and implementation of standards, for decisions needed at the ministerial level. As 1999 ended, the acceptance of these proposals remained possible, although they had not yet been officially endorsed.

As with the G7 itself in 1975, the G20 was thus partly the result of a Franco-American accommodation, with the remaining G7 members lined up somewhat predictably on each side. These coalitions played into the selection of Paul Martin as the first chair. Most G7 members could see that the new body would look too much like a U.S. creature if, as with the G22 and Willard Group, the U.S. treasury secretary chaired it or if the first meeting was held in the U.S. Thus the U.S. canvassed other G7 countries for their candidates for a chair. Some suggested Gordon Brown, chair of the IMF's Interim Committee. This was a body that the G7 ministers said they were not in competition with and whose legitimacy as a consultative, advisory, and potential decision-making committee of the IMF they did not want to detract from.

At the same time, the creation of the G20 was the result of an epistemically grounded converging view among G7 members and some outsiders on the need for a balanced and representative institution at the ministerial level that remained small enough to foster an open dialogue on global economic and financial issues and thereby generate consensus on major outstanding issues. The 1998–89 work of the G22 and the two G33 'officials' seminars, when juxtaposed against the cascading global financial crisis that was devastating emerging markets at that time, suggested to many the need for a more potent and effective forum. It further suggested that such a forum's work be focussed on reducing vulnerability to crisis by creating appropriate exchange rate arrangements, liability management, and international codes and standards, as it became increasingly clear to many inside and outside the G7 that weakness in those areas had created and compounded the crisis.

The Selection of the Membership

The selection of the members for the new group was again initially led by the U.S., although to a lesser extent than with the G22 two years before. The G7 Communiqué had specified the G20 would consist of those that were a 'systemically important country', or a 'key emerging market'. Members were further expected to have a different viewpoint than that of the most industrialised countries and serve as representatives of the various geographic regions.

The most obvious candidate was China. Regarding the others, there was much discussion about membership. Some lists excluded Australia, Korea,

Turkey, and Saudi Arabia. In the case of Saudi Arabia, its provision of ample funding proved decisive in the end. In the case of Turkey, the overall strategy of linking it more firmly to the West, of which G20 membership was one important component, proved persuasive. Here the calculation was that a move was needed, given the precarious probability of EU membership for Turkey, and that a G20 association would help further lock in Turkey to the 'West' and deepen the democratic tradition in the country. Its inclusion paved the way for significant new IMF financial support for Turkey.

There were many questions initially about Indonesia as a suitable candidate for G20 membership. Despite its acknowledged capability, even with a crisis-devastated economy, in the categories of GDP and population, it was a country rife with corruption, seen as being in danger of falling apart. But it could thus be viewed as requiring further incentives for democratisation — in the form of prospective future G20 membership for demonstrated performance in the move toward democracy. In the end, one of two initially unfilled country positions was reserved for Indonesia. Its membership would be awarded once its stable democratic transition was completed and current G7 concerns about its political and human rights abuses were addressed.

Other Asian countries also claimed a place. Malaysia's claim was rejected, in part due to its imposition of capital controls, its broad attack on globalisation during the 1997–99 financial crisis, its attachment to Asian values and the regional Asian Monetary Fund (AMF), and its recent treatment of its well-regarded finance minister and the lack of respect for the rule of law revealed by this treatment.

Another Asian claimant was Thailand. Its case received considerable sympathy from Canada, which had provided Thailand with exceptional financial support during the crisis in the spring of 1998 (Kirton 2000). Some G7 members felt that Thailand's inclusion was warranted by its size and its rejection of currency controls during and after the crisis, and by the need the for presence of another Asian country, especially a member of the Association of South-East Asian Nations (ASEAN), to reduce the Eurocentricity of the prospective G20 and old centres of governance such as the G10. In the end, however, capability as well as democratic governance and neoliberal economic policy mattered. Thailand was left out because it was too small.

A victory for the European members of the G7 came with the admission of the EU and the ECB — the only regional organisations admitted to the G20 club. The EU's existing place in the regime nest of the G7 and its defensive positionalist determination made it difficult to deny its claim. This was despite U.S. impatience, evident here and in the initial discussions at the IMF over the future reform of quota share arrangements, with the apparent Eurocentricity of so many economic governance arrangements as the emerging, Asia-Pacific–centred global economy of the twenty-first century dawned.

After the EU was allowed in, the U.S. drew the line, insisting on no more Europeans. The Europeans had wanted the EU's Council of Ministers to participate, as they do at the G7. The Dutch, Belgians, and Spaniards pressed their claim, as they did with the G7 in 1975 and subsequently. The U.S. refused. With this success in the G20, the U.S. then turned to the task of reducing the weight of the Europeans in the IMF and its Executive Board by reconfiguring the quotas to reflect the new weight of developing countries. This move came at the expense of France, Britain, and Italy, and favoured Japan, Korea, and China, as well as Germany.

The Institutional Design

The G20 was designed as a deliberative body rather than a decisional one, but a forum tailored to encourage the 'formation of consensus on international issues' (Canada 1999a). Moreover, it was one with a policy focus, given its mandate to promote international financial stability. Most importantly, while its G7-specified subject area was the domain of finance, and while early analysts have seen it in this frame (Porter 2000), its first chair, Paul Martin, suggested a very comprehensive and ambitious mission for the new body, whose substantive core represented a major revision of the neoliberal orthodoxy with which other institutions were so strongly associated. Martin, who took a strong personal interest in designing and developing the new forum, and brought to this task a strategic vision, announced at the outset that the G20 would 'focus on translating the benefits of globalization into higher incomes and better opportunities everywhere', including working people around the world (Beattle 1999). The distributional and broad political ideals were clear, as the stable and sustainable world growth the new forum was to foster was to benefit all.

Furthermore, Martin saw the G20 concentrating on longer term policy rather than immediate issues. Overall, he envisaged a flexible and comprehensive mandate. Indeed, skilfully employing the prerogatives of chair, he declared at the outset: 'There is virtually no major aspect of the global economy or international financial system that will be outside of the group's purview' (Canada 1999b). Across both time and policy space, then, the G20 was conceived from the start to be major source of political-level strategic leadership, rather than a technically oriented, limited, issue-specific forum. This ambitious concept was enriched with a more specific expression eight months later when Martin stated:

'It has a mandate to explore virtually every area of international finance and the potential to deal with some of the most visible and troubling aspects of today's integrated world economy — including the devastating effects of financial crises, the growing gap between rich and poor, and a system of governance that has not kept pace with the sweeping changes taking place in the global economy' (Canada 2000b). Indeed, as the first G20 ministerial hosted in Canada approached, Martin declared that the time had come for the G20 to 'tackle the broader problems associated with globalization'.

The G20's relationship with other bodies also suggested a robust role for the new institution. It would operate within the framework of the Bretton Woods institutions, involve their representatives (including the chairs of the Interim and Development Committees) and the EU fully in its substantive discussions, in order to ensure that its work was 'well integrated'. It would 'help co-ordinate the activities of other international groups and organizations, such as the Financial Stability Forum', 'facilitate deliberations' in the IMFC, and potentially develop 'common positions on complex issues ... to expedite decisionmaking in other fora' (Canada 1999a).

Its potential importance was further suggested by its institutional characteristics. These included the firm control of the chair by the G7, a two-year rotational cycle for the chair, the linking of its meetings to those of the G7 meetings at the start of each year, the presence of a deputies process to prepare for and support the meetings, the ability to call on the resources of the IMF, World Bank, and outside experts, and the ability to 'form working parties to examine and make recommendations on issues related to its mandate' (Kirton 1999b).

Martin's early emphasis showed the major effort under way to have the new institution develop into a very influential forum. The Canadians initially considered the possibility of holding the second ministerial meeting in Toronto in June 2000, a mere six months after the first, despite fears that this could detract from the lead-up to the G7 finance ministers meeting and G7/8 Summit in Japan in July. The Canadians hoped that the timing and location would better enable the new group, whose conclusions could be recorded in a Chair's Statement, to influence the G7/8 meeting itself.

One Canadian concern at the outset was to have an inclusive, regionally balanced forum replete with differing perspectives, and thus avoid having the body re-create and become victim to traditional divisions, including those on a geographically regional or older north-south divide. Canada preferred to keep the group focussed on sharing experiences and open discussion, rather than on the statement of hard, often inherited positions. Its instinct thus differed from the views of some, such as another newly included finance minister, who saw the G20 as an excellent opportunity for the 'South' to press its issues against the 'North'.

Although there was some scepticism about this potentially G7-dominated body, the non-G7 members took it seriously and gave it a good chance to succeed. In this, they were led by the largest and most difficult country — non-democratic China. China proved ready to join the new group, in part due to the G7's and Martin's desire to use it to promote better supervisory and self regulation-arrangements. Moreover, China's sheer weight, given this attitude, was important in ensuring that the G20 could become a form for meaningful reciprocal influence across the G7/non-G7 divide, as it was clear that China would deal from a position of strength in the new G20.

There were, however, questions as to whether China alone could make this fledgling group much more than a G7-led legitimisation club. Some saw the G20 as part of the crisis-bred 'G7-isation' of the world, with the G20 born to make G7 initiatives palatable to the wider world by securing a broader consensus for G7-generated ideas. In this view, the G20's 11 non-G7 member states were destined to affect issues merely at the margin, to be informed of G7 initiatives, and to be given some semblance of participation. Here, the G20 underscored the fact that the G7 did not want to leave the reform of the international financial system to the IMF or the World Bank, where developing countries had an institutionalised, longstanding role and the capacity of a large and well-equipped secretariat to call upon. A more optimistic projection arose from China's reluctance to occupy a position merely as a full member of other developing country groupings. Its position could thus help prevent the G20 from becoming a new north-south dialogue, or a collection of small, dependent, neoliberal countries echoing the views of a U.S.-led, unified G7.

The G20 in Operation

Vancouver, November 1999

The first phase of the G20's actual operation came with the initial preparatory meeting of its deputies in Vancouver, Canada, in November 1999. This meeting was designed to determine the rules of the game, for ministerial adjustment and approval the following month in Berlin, and to have the new body sustain, rationalise, legitimate, and globalise what was neglected in the G7.

There was general agreement on several basic points. The G20 should focus on an efficient exchange of ideas on the key issues of finance, build consensus on these ideas, and demonstrate leadership by example. The group's finance ministers and central bankers would deal with selected economic issues and not broader ones, as the G7 did. There would be one ministerial meeting per year and two deputies meetings. The World Bank and the IMF would provide input for the G20's work. The emphasis was on that fact that the G20 was not a decision-making forum, would work on a confidential basis, and would have no secretariat and no working groups.

Beyond these basics, however, there was a substantial difference of opinion on what the substantive agenda, and by implication the ambition, of the G20 should be. The IMF led one tendency, arguing that in order to add value to a system already replete with institutions, the G20 should focus on difficult issues where the IMF's own Executive Board had not been able to agree. These were such issues as capital account liberalisation, orderly and well-sequenced liberalisation, private-sector involvement, and Contingent Credit Line (CCL) reform. Such an agenda would ensure the body was used and would eliminate any excuse for it to avoid hard decisions.

The alternative position, led by Canada, secured consensus from the group. This was to start somewhat gently, by focussing on central issues where there already was a substantial measure of existing, emerging, or prospective agreement from all those within the group. This set included some complex and controversial issues, such as appropriate exchange rate regimes and private-sector involvement. The Canadians were particularly firm on their preferred approach, arguing it was needed to build momentum for, and comfort and confidence in, the new body.

Session two of the deputies session, taking place in the afternoon, took up the issues of exchange rates, capital account, and financial-sector debt management. Little new ground was broken, relative to earlier discussions at bodies such as the G7, the IMF Executive Board, and the OECD.

Session three dealt with the role of the international community. The IMF argued that the CCL should be examined by the G20, with a view to securing a G7-G20 agreement on its reform. Similar processes were recommended for collective action clauses for modifying bonds (where a joint public-private sector working group was suggested) and on debt standstill. These ideas were not adopted.

Although nothing controversial or radical emerged from the deputies meetings, there were a number of important procedural decisions taken. These discussions would serve as the agenda for the ministers in Berlin. At that meeting, there would be no communiqué and therefore no drafting session; there would only be a relatively informal chairman's concluding statement. And, in accordance with the call of the Canadian chair, the G20 ministers would start with the issues on which there was some reasonable prospect of securing an effective consensus.

Berlin, December 2000

Thus the topics, issues, and documentation for Berlin were taken almost entirely from the experience of other international institutions. Once again, the IMF-led coalition asked the G20 to deal with issues where there was no consensus in the Executive Board, the IMFC, or the international community, and the Canadians countered that the G20 should start with the issues on which there was minimum agreement in order to build momentum. In a display of effective policy leadership, the Canadians, with the support of Germany and the U.S., drove the process in favour of this latter approach. It was one, notably, that was antithetical to any earlier notion that the G20 would be a forum for the rapid legitimisation of U.S.-bred new ideas for IMF and international financial system reform. In keeping with Canadian desires, the G20's agenda thus focussed on exchange rate arrangements, financial-sector regulation, and supervision and prudential liability management. These were, in Martin's judgement, 'all areas of architectural reform in which national governments working collectively have become increasingly prepared to take the steps required to reduce vulnerabilities to crises' (Canada 2000a).

In a display of broadly shared intellectual and technical leadership, the documentation for the Berlin meeting was prepared by the Canadians and Germans, and only to a lesser extent the U.S. The meeting, which was designed to be informal, would issue a one-page chairman's statement and serve as a round table, to 'get to know you', set the rules of the game, and identify the purpose of the group.

The G20 ministerial started in the evening and proceeded for the following full day. It dealt with standard broad topics and featured an open floor. Martin encouraged ministers to chime in, ask questions, and share their point of view. In its discussions of macroeconomic forces and prospects, the discussions tended to be thematic, focussing on areas where the global economy as a whole was vulnerable, rather than on the situation in or performance of individual countries.

There was some reading of prepared statements from emerging countries. But most participants on the whole were happy with the informal discussion, even if it repeated the dialogue at other forums. The ministerial thus featured free-flowing discussion, as the Canadian chair had hoped, even if the conclusions were familiar. The fact that the meeting was held in Europe made it more difficult for the European members to speak as anything other than good Europeans with a single European voice. This fact reinforced the reluctance of some non-European members to add more European claimants to the club.

The G20 ended by creating no working groups or requesting any work from other international institutions. More contentious issues, as raised in a public call by Larry Summers for reform of the IMF on the eve of the meeting, were discussed a little as part of the dialogue on 'vulnerabilities' in the international system. But the Summers proposal was by no means the central focus, and most discussion of it took place in the corridors. It was clear that the U.S. would not enjoy disproportionate influence in setting the G20 agenda.

The meeting did show some signs of the challenges involved, and registered some small successes in, bridging the potential north-south or established-versus-emerging economy divide. On issues such as codes, an 'Anglo-Saxon'/ German project, Canada and the U.S. saw the Turks and others as agreeing to their preferred approach, as these others sat in the room and seemed to agree, in contrast to the hesitancy they had expressed in the IMFC and IMF Executive Board.

The developing countries, however, saw the dynamics in a somewhat different light. They viewed the meeting as a way to learn and to exchange views rather than as a negotiation out of which decisions would come. They continued to insist that more work needed to be done on major issues. They thus set clear limits to any co-optation and buy-in for the G7-led program.

The G20 ministerial in itself did not immediately and clearly change any minds on the part of resistant emerging economies about the issues of transparency, codes, and governance, which the three English-speaking countries (the U.S., UK, and Canada) regarded as the core bases of the new international financial architecture. Following the meeting, China and Brazil continued to express deep concerns about IMF programs and, along with Mexico and Argentina, about strong conditions imposed from an external source. Arrayed against them still stood the three 'Anglo' countries, Germany, and to a lesser extent Japan. They wanted clear codes adopted by all countries.

Yet there were concrete signs of initial institutional effectiveness. Most notably, all G20 countries agreed to ask the IMF and the World Bank to examine how their national financial rules measure up to international standards and how those rules might be strengthened. With appropriate follow-up this could indeed represent 'an important breakthrough in the establishment of generally accepted principles of global governance' (Canada 2000b).

Hong Kong, March 2000

The G20 deputies met again in Hong Kong in March to review the results of the Berlin ministerial and to begin preparations for the next ministerial, to be held in Montreal on 24–25 October 2000. The deputies met just prior to the meeting of the IMFC deputies preparing for the IMF-World Bank spring ministerial, with its first ever IMFC meeting, in mid-April 2000. The G20 deputies proved to be pleased with the results of Berlin. Their consensus led the Canadians to adopt a more ambitious approach to their meeting in Montreal.

Washington, April 2000

Canadian ambitions were further fuelled by the experience of the G20's major competitor organisation, the IMFC, at the latter's inaugural outing in Washington in April. The IMFC meeting did show several promising signs that it would develop as an effective forum. Under the decisive leadership of Gordon Brown, the IMFC moved through an ambitious agenda, including controversial items such as Highly Indebted Poor Country (HIPC) debt relief (for which Uganda, with its recent purchase of a prime ministerial Gulfstream jet, stood as the test case). The discussion was sufficiently spontaneous that the ministerial discussions produced several meaningful changes in the draft Communiqué prepared by the deputies and IMF officials. Perhaps the most consequential point was the placement of a strong statement on the continuing and central role of the IMF at the front of the Communiqué. This was in direct response to the thousands of protesters who had assembled on the streets of Washington in an effort to draw attention to the IMF's alleged defects and to prevent the IMFC meeting from taking place at all, which had been the goal of some. The changes in the Communiqué were supervised by Brown himself, with other ministers, but none of the regular officials, allowed in the drafting room.

At the same time, there were few signs that the IMFC would develop the momentum required to surpass the G20 as the central forum for broader global governance. The IMFC agenda was largely confined to traditionally finance-centred subjects. It failed to solve the impasse over HIPC created by the Ugandan case. The meeting chaired by Brown was fairly stilted, with many members making prepared remarks. In the view of some, he tended to be very directional and end discussion prematurely. Due to the demonstrators, a few consequential figures, notably France's new finance minister Laurent Fabius, failed to make it to the meeting, leaving France to be represented by its more experienced central bank governor Jean-Claude Trichet.

Conclusion: The Future G20

As it moved beyond its first-year anniversary, the G20 showed signs that it could well develop as the effective, broad centre of governance for the global community for the twenty-first century. The G20 included the systemically important countries of the future, as had the G7 before the Mexico meltdown of 20 December 1994 ended the twentieth century in the finance field. Moreover, although the membership of the two competing bodies — the G20 and IMFC — substantially overlapped, there were important differences. The 24-member IMFC contained, as country members, Belgium, Denmark, the Netherlands, Switzerland, Algeria, the United Arab Emirates, Gabon, and Thailand. It was a collection that was modest in its aggregate gross national product or other capabilities, and heavily weighted toward Europe, the Middle East and Africa, as befitting the IMF's origins in 1944 and adjustment in the wake of the 1973 oil shocks. The G20, in contrast, contained Korea and Turkey. This gave it an advantage not only in collective predominance within the system, constricted participation and reduced transaction costs, but also in average weight (equality among members within the group), geographic balance, and strategic location. Given current and projected growth rates, such as Korea's 9 percent growth in 1999, it was clear that the G20 would be the weightier institution by far five to ten years hence.

There was, moreover, a difference in the formula of representation. The IMFC's constituency model gave it the advantage in global representation, if indirectly, whereas the G20 led in the freedom for the major emerging economies to act as individual actors, rather than representing the consensus views of the constituency below. At the IMFC, Turkey was cast in with a constituency represented by a continental European middle power. Brazil, Argentina, and Mexico each represented several other Latin American countries. The G20 detached these countries from these other influences. Together with the more constricted participation, this made the G20 a forum for more flexible and free-wheeling discussion and consensus formation than the IMFC.

The venerable, charter-created, and -bound IMFC did wield two additional advantages. One came in the sphere of formal legitimacy. As part of the IMF's organisation, the IMFC was accountable to the whole world and could draw on the IMF's extensive organisational resources. The G20, by contrast, was accountable to itself and informally to its G7 parent, and mobilised the national resources of its chair and members for the effective implementation of its consensus. Secondly, with Gordon Brown as chair of the IMFC, and Horst Kohler as the new Managing Director of the IMF, it was unlikely that their respective institutions would defer easily to the G20's leadership on the vast agenda they shared.

In other respects, the two major contending bodies were largely equal. In both, the effort to secure acceptance for the new codes and practices of transparency and surveillance showed a clear case of the G7 at work, with the G20 and IMFC serving as legitimating bodies as the G22 had before. Yet, as more difficult issues emerged, the flexibility, smaller size, and individual country freedom of the G20 suggested that this body would be able to provide a more timely and balanced result.

The prospects for the G20 depend on the ability of its current custodians to realise the ambitious goals they are actively contemplating. Those prospects also depend on the G20's chair finding the winning answers to a series of complex questions, and thus minimise the tradeoffs in the underlying representativeness/effectiveness/leadership trilemma that the new institution faces.

One challenge is the G20's ability to supersede older consultative groups, such as the G10, while resisting any temptation to add any of its Eurocentric members to a globally balanced G20 that already contains the four European G7 members and the EU. The *pro forma* nature of the G10 meeting in Washington in April 2000 suggests that the G10 could easily be terminated, its agenda folded into that of the G20, and its European members such as Switzerland left outside or represented through innovative arrangements through the EU.

A second challenge is to maintain the still-constricted size, global reach, geographic balance, and weight of the G20 by adding new members very selectively. Canada, still in the chair, for example, retains some sympathy for adding Thailand. It has similar sympathy for its bilateral free-trade partner and G20 claimant Chile, whose case is strengthened by the presence of Argentina and Brazil in the group. Yet, any additions of these or other members raise broader questions about the overall architecture of global governance.

Part of the architectural issue is the addition of other regional international institutions alongside the EU as members, in the context of a new global-governance arrangement. Such an approach would constitute a compact means for adding new voices, giving the G20 much more extensive, even near universal representation, while further diluting the remaining Eurocentricity of the group.

A further challenge, already accepted by Paul Martin (Canada 2000b), is to increase representativeness downward, by finding a formula for effective civil society participation. This process could begin with having the chair, or the G20 collectively, meet with civil society organisations in a separate forum on the eve of the October meeting in Montreal. Canada's experience in hosting APEC, with its Business Forum, could provide some useful experience in this respect. Such a move would stand in contrast to the IMFC, where civil society representatives in Washington in April were left entirely on the outside.

It remains to be seen how and when the G20 might move to meet at the leaders level (see Chapter 13). Doing so would give the G20 a decisive advantage over the IMFC, given the unlikelihood of that body ever involving heads of government and state in any council arrangement. It would also give the G20 all the advantages that political control brings. The G20 could respond to some of the same dynamics that led G5 ministers meeting in the Library Group since 1973 to help foster the birth of the G7 itself, when some of their finance minister participants became leaders themselves. It would be possible for this graduation of the G20 to take place rapidly, beginning perhaps with a call from the ministers in October for leaders to hold a 'Summit of the Twenty'.[3]

Such a summit would require an agenda, ambition, and achievement worthy of leaders, who already live in a summit-crowded world. It must be an agenda much broader than the finance and related economic domain, and one with a novelty and magnitude worthy of leaders' time and appropriate for the potential founding of a new institutionalised leaders forum. The issue of the overall coherence in global governance constitutes such a focus. Here, G20 leaders could address the question of what the architecture should be for coherent global governance in the twenty-first century. This would include coherence in the international and financial institutions, ways to make a co-ordinated assault on poverty reduction, and, as Paul Martin has recognised, the need to reform the IMF and World Bank together with, and in ways that would enable them to co-operate better with, the agencies of the United Nations and the World Trade Organization (Canada 2000a). It would embrace ways to forge a meaningful and balanced trade-environment regime, perhaps through the birth of a new world environmental organisation; it would answer the need for new global governance institutions to cope with the information technology revolution and competition policy in a globalised market. It would continue the program begun by Canada at the last G7 Summit it hosted, in Halifax in 1995. It would also move the world beyond the 'accountants' views of coherence — the wasteful duplication arising from the IMF and World Bank performing the same functions — to embrace the larger questions of whether the world needs new institutions to meet the many new challenges that the twenty-first century brings.

Notes

1   The author thanks Tony Porter and numerous officials in G20 member governments and international organisations for their assistance in providing information, insights, and comments on an earlier draft of this chapter. The information and interpretation contained herein remain the sole responsibility of the author.
2   The G10 is made up of the G7 finance ministers plus others (see Table 9.1).
3   Central to the G7 system of global governance is its character as a leaders-driven, top-down forum, in which subordinate ministerial and official bodies come after or remain subordinate to the leaders' forum itself (Bayne 2000). The G20, in contrast, was born at the ministerial and hence political level, but as a mid-level institution able to expand both upward and downward. Moreover, the G20, unlike some G7-incubated bodies, was created as a laterally broad institution from the start.

References

Bayne, Nicholas (2000), *Hanging in There: The G7 and G8 Summit in Maturity and Renewal*, Ashgate, Aldershot.
Beattle, Alan (1999), 'New Forum to Supplement G7 Work', *Financial Times*, 27 September, p. 5.
Beauchesne, Eric (1999), 'Martin Warns against Complacency', *Montreal Gazette*, 26 September, p. A9.
Bergsten, Fred (1998), 'The New Agenda with China', *International Economic Policy Briefs*, vol. 98, no. 2, pp. 1–2.
Bergsten, Fred, and Randall Henning (1996), *Global Economic Leadership and the Group of Seven*, Institute for International Economics, Washington DC.
Brzezinski, Zbigniev (1996), 'Let's Add to the G-7', *New York Times*, 25 June, p. A11.
Canada (2000a), 'Statement by the Honourable Paul Martin, Minister of Finance for Canada, to the Institute for International Economics', Washington DC, 14 April, <www.fin.gc.ca/newse00/00-031e.html> (September 2000).

Canada (2000b), 'Speech to the House of Commons Standing Committee on Foreign Affairs and International Trade: The Honourable Paul Martin', Department of Finance, Ottawa, 18 May, <www.fin.gc.ca/newse00/00-041e.html> (September 2000).

Canada (1999a), 'New G-20 Forum: Backgrounder', Department of Finance, Ottawa, <www.library.utoronto.ca/g7/g20/g20backgrounder.htm> (September 2000).

Canada (1999b), 'Finance Minister Paul Martin Chosen as Inaugural Chairperson of New Group of Twenty', Press Release 99-080, Department of Finance, 25 September, <www.fin.gc.ca/newse99/99-080e.html> (September 2000).

Cohn, Theodore (2000), *Global Political Economy: Theory and Practice*, Longman, New York.

Commission on Global Governance (1995), *Our Global Neighbourhood: The Report of the Commission on Global Governance*, Oxford University Press, New York.

Cutter, W. B., J. Spero, and L. D. Tyson (2000), 'New World, New Deal: A Democratic Approach to Globalization', *Foreign Affairs*, vol. 79, no. 2, pp. 80–98.

Economist (1998), 'Welcome to China, Mr. Clinton', vol. 347, no. 8074, p. 17.

Financial Stability Forum (1999), 'First Meeting of the Financial Stability Forum', Press Release, 6 April, <www.fsforum.org/Press/P19990406.html> (September 2000).

G7 (1999a), 'G7 Statement', Cologne, 18 June, <www.library.utoronto.ca/g7/summit/1999koln/g7statement_june18.htm> (September 2000).

G7 (1999b), 'Statement of G-7 Finance Ministers and Central Bank Governors', 25 September, Washington DC, <www.library.utoronto.ca/g7/finance/fm992509state.htm> (September 2000).

Hajnal, Peter (1999), *The G7/G8 System: Evolution, Role, and Documentation*, Ashgate, Aldershot.

Hodges, Michael (1999), 'The G8 and the New Political Economy', in Michael Hodges, John Kirton, and Joseph Daniels (eds.), *The G8's Role in the New Millennium*, Ashgate, Aldershot, pp. 69–74.

Jayawardena, L. (1989), 'World Economic Summits: The Role of Representative Groups in the Governance of the World Economy', *Journal of the Society for International Development*, vol. 4, pp. 17–20.

Keohane, Robert (1984), *After Hegemony: Cooperation and Discord in the World Political Economy*, Princeton University Press), Princeton.

Keohane, Robert, and Joseph Nye (1989), *Power and Interdependence*, second edition, Scott, Foresman, Glenview, IL.

Kirton, John (1989), 'The Seven Power Summit as an International Concert,' Paper presented at the International Studies Association Annual Meeting, London, April.

Kirton, John (1993), 'The Seven Power Summit and the New Security Agenda', in D. Dewitt, D. Haglund, and J. Kirton (eds.), *Building a New Global Order: Emerging Trends in International Security*, Oxford University Press, Toronto.

Kirton, John (1999a), 'Explaining G8 Effectiveness', in Michael Hodges, John Kirton, and Joseph Daniels (eds.), *The G8's Role in the New Millennium*, Ashgate, Aldershot, pp. 45–68.

Kirton, John (1999b), 'What Is the G20?', <www.library.utoronto.ca/g7/g20/g20whatisit.html> (September 2000).

Kirton, John (2000), 'The Dynamics of G7 Leadership in Crisis Response and System Reconstruction', in Karl Kaiser, John Kirton, and Joseph Daniels (eds.), *Shaping a New International Financial System: Challenges of Governance in a Globalizing World*, Ashgate, Aldershot, pp. 65–94.

Kokotsis, Eleanore (1999), *Keeping International Commitments: Compliance, Credibility, and the G7, 1988–1995*, Garland Publishing, New York.

Kokotsis, Eleanore, and Joseph Daniels (1999), 'G8 Summits and Compliance', in Michael Hodges, John Kirton, and Joseph Daniels (eds.), *The G8's Role in the New Millennium*, Ashgate, Aldershot, pp. 75–94.

Krasner, S. (1978), *Defending the National Interest: Raw Materials Investments and U.S. Foreign Policy*, Princeton University Press, Princeton.

Porter, Tony (2000), 'The G-7, the Financial Stability Forum, the G-20, and the Politics of International Financial Regulation', Paper prepared for the International Studies Association Annual Meeting, Los Angeles, California, 15 March.

Putnam, Robert, and Nicholas Bayne (1987), *Hanging Together: Co-operation and Conflict in the Seven-Power Summits*, second edition, Sage Publications, London.

Smyser, W. R. (1993), 'Goodbye, G-7', *Washington Quarterly*, vol. 16, no. 1, pp. 15–28.

Snidal, D. (1989), 'The Limits of Hegemonic Stability Theory', *International Organization*, vol. 39, no. 4, pp. 579–614.

ul Haq. M. (1994), 'The Bretton Woods Institutions and Global Governance', in Peter Kenen (ed.), *Managing the World Economy*, Institute for International Economics, Washington DC, pp. 409–418.

10 International Macroeconomic Policy Co-operation in the Era of the Euro

MARTIN J. G. THEURINGER

Introduction

International macroeconomic policy co-operation has always been a major focus at G7 Summits as well as at meetings of finance ministers and central bank governors. The Cologne Summit of 1999 was no exception. Particularly in Germany, the limits, scopes, and dangers of policy co-ordination were hotly debated 'on the road to Cologne' for two basic reasons. First, target zones were included in the discussion about the reform of the international financial architecture. While in earlier times, German policymakers fiercely opposed such major reforms of the international monetary system, this time it was a German finance minister who pressed for a stronger co-ordination of G7 macroeconomic policies.

Second, the Cologne Summit was the first meeting of heads of government to take place after the third stage of the European Monetary Union (EMU) had begun: the Euro had been introduced and the European Central Bank (ECB) had started its operations. Hence, a German monetary and exchange rate policy no longer exists. An important question is how this change affects the G7 process of policy co-operation and whether these changes are in the German interest. Such 'international effects' of the Euro are not yet fully understood; some have suggested that the introduction of the EMU could lead to a new era of international economic policy co-operation (Commission of the European Communities 1990, 1997), while others, in particular in Germany, fear that the G7 framework could help to undermine the ECB's independence and *de facto* lead to a weakened Euro.

This chapter argues that the EMU will make it more difficult for policymakers to commit to internationally agreed-upon policy adjustments. This should not — at least not from a German perspective — be regarded as a major problem. The chapter has three main parts: the first section gives a brief overview of the theoretical rationale and political reality of G7 policy co-operation and co-ordination. The second section describes the German perspective on such co-operation. The third section discusses the implications of the EMU with respect to policy making within the G7 framework, followed by a conclusion.

Policy Co-ordination and Policy Co-operation within the G7 Framework

Probably the most crucial lesson that policymakers had to learn after the 1971 breakdown of the Bretton Woods system has been that even in a flexible exchange-rate system, countries cannot act independently of one another. Policy measures in the U.S. spill over and feed back to Germany and other G7 countries and vice versa. If policymakers neglect macroeconomic interdependence, the overall outcome will not be Pareto-optimal: each country could do better if policymakers were able to internalise the externalities that arise from national stabilisation policies.

This insight has been formalised in the game-theoretic literature on policy co-operation (see Canzoneri and Henderson 1991). In the standard symmetrical two-country model, the policymaker in each country faces a tradeoff influenced by foreign policy. Transmission may either be positive (the locomotive scenario) or negative (the 'beggar my neighbour' scenario).[1] Policymakers have two options available: they can either co-operate or they can not co-operate. In the former, the policymakers maximise a weighted average of both their countries' individual welfare functions. In the latter, they 'play Nash', that is, they neglect any existing interdependence by taking the other policymakers' policies as given. The lesson of the standard model is twofold: First, in the absence of uncertainty, the co-operative solution strictly dominates the non-cooperative (Nash) solution.[2] Second, in order to achieve an efficient outcome, policymakers must commit to a co-operative solution, that is, they must make explicit bargains about setting policy instruments.[3] Hence, the game-theoretic literature recommends explicit policy co-ordination as an adequate response to the problem of economic interdependence.

G7 governments did not, however, pay much attention to the recommendation of the game-theoretic literature.[4] In fact, efforts of policy co-ordination — clearly defined, mutual commitments to alter macroeconomic policies — have been hard to find since the G7 first met in Rambouillet in 1975.

The most ambitious efforts to co-ordinate demand policies were the 1977 London and the 1978 Bonn Summits. At Bonn, Germany and Japan committed to undertake expansionary fiscal policies, using the locomotive theory. Although the results of this summit are frequently criticised as having added to domestic inflationary pressures in Germany (Reszat 1994), they are widely disregarded as an example of 'true' policy co-ordination, that is, an adjustment of policies that would not have taken place in the absence of any co-ordination (see, for example, Kenen 1989, p.17; Garavoglia and Padoan 1994).

The second half of the 1980s saw considerable but failed efforts by the G7 to co-ordinate explicit fiscal and monetary policies. As it is widely perceived today (see, for example, De Grauwe 1996, p. 139; Baltensperger 1999, p. 466f), the demand for co-ordination arose from the mix of an expansionary U.S. fiscal policy during President Ronald Reagan's first term of office (1981–84), a rather restrictive fiscal policy in the other industrialised countries, and contractionary monetary policies in the aftermath of the second oil-price shock. Again based on the locomotive theory, it was argued that the surplus countries Germany and Japan should pursue an expansionary monetary and fiscal policy. However, despite intense U.S. pressure, Germany refrained from participating in any far-reaching co-ordination of demand management (Kitterer 1999, p. 199).

That same period also witnessed considerable attempts to co-ordinate monetary policies through exchange rate targeting. The Plaza Agreement in 1985 marked the beginning of a period of intensive exchange rate management, which culminated in the Louvre accord of 22 February 1987, to 'foster stability of exchange rates around current levels' (Funabashi 1988). However, co-ordination of exchange rate policies relied predominantly on co-ordinated sterilised interventions in foreign exchange markets, rather than co-ordinated interest-rate cuts or foreign exchange interventions that would affect the monetary base (Weber 1996). In other words, the major industrialised countries were not willing to subordinate monetary policies to the goal of external stability.

Overall, instead of explicitly co-ordinating their policies, the G7 governments relied on loose forms of policy co-operation to address the problem of macroeconomic interdependence. Since 1975, G7 policy co-operation has consisted mainly of information exchange, policy consultation, and, to a very limited extent, mutual policy adjustments. The efficiency of this approach is hard to evaluate. On the one hand, empirical research suggests that the bulk of the potential benefits of policy co-operation results precisely from this type of policy co-operation.[5] On the other hand, the relatively loose approach of the G7 did not prevent the governments of the major industrialised countries from frequently neglecting the international repercussions of their policy actions (Corden 1994, p. 229f).

A number of economists have therefore expressed concerns about the current system of relatively loose and flexible G7 policy co-operation and have developed a number of proposals to address the lack of policy co-ordination. The most prominent is the proposal to establish target zones for the G7 countries' real effective exchange rates. According to the standard proposal, which dates back to John Williamson in 1985, G7 governments should keep market rates within reference range of up to 15 percent on each side. The target zones should be adjusted regularly and — if necessary — supported by adjustments in monetary policy. More ambitious target-zone proposals involve co-ordinated management of global demand, as well as the inclusion of fiscal policies in the co-ordination scheme (Williamson and Miller 1987, Bergsten and Henning 1996).

The German Consensus View on International Policy Co-ordination and Co-operation

Calls for activist policy co-ordination as well as exchange rate target zones have usually met with strong resistance in Germany.[6] The German position on international macroeconomic policy co-operation is characterised by a broad consensus among German economists as well as policymakers. The two keys of this consensus are first to support such flexible and loose forms of policy co-operation as information exchanges, and second to oppose international commitments on monetary or fiscal policy that may present a danger for price stability.[7]

German academics overwhelmingly oppose the idea of explicit international policy co-ordination. Two reasons are of particular importance: first, it is doubted whether enough information is given to implement the advice derived from the game-theoretical models. Because they consider the available knowledge to be too limited to fine-tune the economy, most German economists reject demand management, whether in the national context or in that of the G7 (see, for example, Sachverständigenrat 1987/88, para. 329ff). In fact, it can be shown that the problem of uncertainty is much more pronounced when stabilisation policy is internationally co-ordinated; the existing empirical models already differ in the sign of transmission effects (Bryant *et al.* 1989) and may cause policy co-ordination to be counterproductive, if agreements are made on the basis of the 'wrong' model (Frankel and Rockett 1988).

The second reason that many German economists oppose international policy co-ordination is that they have developed a deep distrust of the efficiency of collective decision-making processes. Roland Vaubel (1983), for example, has argued that international policy co-ordination would allow policymakers to build cartels against the private sector. Isolated inflationary policy would be punished by international financial markets in the form of increased risk premiums, increased capital export, and a depreciated currency. A surprise joint monetary expansion would, however, remove these constraints and hence benefit more inflationary outcomes. As with cartels, policy co-ordination would lead to higher prices (in this case, the price of holding money) and a reduced output (that is, real money balances).

Others have argued that co-ordination would make it easier for policymakers to delay policy actions they ought to be taking regardless of international considerations. This would be so because policy co-ordination would impose peer pressure on stability-oriented countries to expand rather than forcing less stability oriented countries to undertake politically difficult adjustments (Scheide and Sinn 1989); also, unfinished or unsettled reforms could be used strategically in international negotiations (Klodt 1999, p. 17). Overall, the presumption is that policy co-ordination would weaken macroeconomic discipline by mixing responsibilities, thus undermining monetary stability.

Uncertainty about political bargains, as well as distrust of their efficiency, leads most German economists to oppose the various target-zone proposals fiercely. The Sachverständigenrat (Council of Economic Experts) (1986/87, para. 245ff; 1995/96, para. 420ff) argues that available exchange rate models do not provide reliable guidance for calculating equilibrium exchange rates and that the negotiation of exchange rate targets would reflect political compromises rather than economic rationality. The true equilibrium exchange rates would therefore lie outside the target zones. Others have rejected the notion of target zones and more ambitious rule-based co-ordination schemes on the basis of assignments: if budgetary policy is inflexible and countries have divergent inflation preferences, national stability as well as global stability can only be maintained if monetary policy aims for the goal of domestic price stability.[8]

German policymakers' attitude toward G7 macroeconomic policy co-operation was for the most part characterised by consensus among the finance ministry and the Bundesbank on those two basic principles of support for loose forms of policy co-operation and scepticism about international commitments that may restrain Germany's ability to maintain price stability at home.[9] However, the co-ordination of the German position at G7 meetings was not without tension. In particular, potential conflicts arose out of the sensitive balance of powers among the two German players in the global co-operation game.

German independence made the Bundesbank a very powerful player at G7 meetings: it could participate in international agreements on monetary policy but was independent enough to resist pressure to accept deals that would have undesirable consequences for domestic monetary stability. However, Germany's independence was limited with respect to exchange rate policy: the federal government had the authority to commit the Bundesbank to an international agreement on currency stabilisation and hence *de facto* to remove its monetary autonomy.

The German finance minister, however, was unable to make binding commitments at G7 Summits. In general, the German political system leaves little room for internationally agreed compromises on fiscal policy.[10] Hence, if the finance minister wanted to participate in the process of international policy co-ordination, negotiations had to focus on exchange rates. This led to potential conflicts: the finance minister preferred exchange rate targeting as the main focus of G7 policy co-ordination, while the Bundesbank distrusted it for fear it would limit its independence.

It is worth noting the German policymakers were, by and large, able to solve their co-ordination problem harmoniously. G7 policy co-operation was indeed strongly centred on exchange rate targeting, but the Bundesbank never lost control over its instruments. The German governments were frequently tempted to use the G7 process as a backdoor for political influence over domestic monetary policy (Henning 1994, p. 348f), but resisted the temptation. This was partly because of the broad consensus that prevailed in Germany with respect to policy co-operation and partly because of broad public support for the Bundesbank's independence, which would have made it politically dangerous for any German politician to undermine its autonomy (Michaelis 1994, p. 96). According to Henning (1994), it was the strong position of the Bundesbank in particular that prevented firm international commitments on exchange rates from being made among the G7 governments in the 1980s.

European Monetary Union, Macroeconomic Policy Co-ordination, and Exchange Rate Stabilisation

Since the start of the third stage of the European Monetary Union, a German monetary and exchange rate policy no longer exists. The currencies of the 11 participating countries have been irrevocably fixed and the single currency, the Euro, was introduced on 1 January 1999. The control of European monetary policy was transferred from the Bundesbank to the ECB. Consequently, at G7 meetings the once influential governor of the Bundesbank has been replaced by the governor of the European Central Bank. An important but frequently neglected question is whether these changes will lead to major changes in the G7 process of policy co-operation and if so, whether these changes run counter to German interests.[11]

Will the EMU Bring a New Era of International Policy Co-ordination?

The European Commission (Commission of European Communities 1990,1997) was the first to speculate that the EMU would lead to a new era of policy co-ordination. It held this position for two reasons. First, because of the unification of European monetary and exchange rate policies, the EMU would effectively reduce the number of players involved in the co-ordination game, which would make it easier to negotiate and enforce international commitments with respect to monetary policy. Second, the EMU would reduce the asymmetry between the U.S. and Europe by transforming small to medium-sized economies into a single large economic bloc. The U.S. would therefore be unable to pursue macroeconomic policies of benign neglect and would have more interest in policy co-ordination; moreover, because of increased interdependence, the gains from policy co-ordination (and hence the costs of non-coordinated policies) would increase.

Both arguments are unconvincing. With respect to the first, although the EMU reduces the number of central banks that participate at the G7 Summits from seven to four, before the EMU existed, the central banks from France and Italy were not able to make commitments at G7 meetings anyway, because the assignment rules of the European Monetary System (EMS) dictated that the Bundesbank set the inflation rate for the region as a whole, while the central banks of the remaining EMS countries adjusted their interest rates to stabilise their nominal Deutschmark exchange rates. Hence, the EMU basically did not unify European monetary and exchange rate policy, but rather replaced the Bundesbank with the ECB, which represents the interests of not only Germany, Italy, and France, but also Finland, Austria, Ireland, and the Benelux countries (Belgium, Luxembourg and the Netherlands), none of which are members of the G7. Hence, instead of reducing the number of players, G7 consultations on monetary matters will become more complicated, not less.

With respect to the second argument, the EMU may well reduce the costs of non-cooperative transatlantic policy making. The ECB faces a different short-term tradeoff of inflation versus employment than the Bundesbank faced when it was responsible for the conduct of European monetary policy. The

ECB's tradeoff should be less steep because output and inflation are less affected by exchange rate swings in Euroland as a whole than in Germany alone.[12] In comparison to the Bundesbank, the ECB should therefore have less incentive to use the exchange rate to stabilise output or reduce inflation. Put differently, a non-cooperative solution in the policy game between the U.S. Federal Reserve and the ECB is more efficient than the non-cooperative solution in the U.S. Federal Reserve–Bundesbank game. Hence, the EMU reduces the danger that G7 countries will engage in depreciation or appreciation races as described in the beggar-my-neighbour scenario of the game-theoretical literature on policy co-ordination.

It is, moreover, sensible to assume that the ECB will refrain from participating in locomotive-type co-ordination agreements that stimulate world aggregate demand. The Maastricht Treaty obliges the ECB to give priority to the goal of internal price stability. In particular in the early years of the EMU, the ECB will likely be concerned with proving its ability to maintain domestic stability. Co-ordinated demand stimulation may, however, run counter to this effort (Rogoff 1985); because co-ordinated monetary expansion makes it possible for participating countries to inflate at lower costs (in the short run), wage setters may internalise this incentive and raise their inflationary expectations. Put differently, policy co-ordination schemes based on the locomotive theory imply risks for the reputation of the central bank. In case of a global recession, the 'young' ECB must therefore stick to non-coordinated policy making (Issing and Winkler 1999).

Finally, the ECB has even less incentive to participate in exchange rate co-ordination programs than the Bundesbank had before. As argued above, swings in the dollar-Euro exchange rate affect inflation and output in Euroland less than dollar-Deutschmark swings affected inflation and output in Germany.[13] Compared to the Bundesbank, the ECB should therefore have less interest in stabilising exchange rates, because it is easier to maintain stability at home in the light of fluctuations of exchange rates. In addition, as is explained below, the ECB is independent only in its pursuit of domestic, but not (fully) in the conduct of external monetary policy. It may perceive exchange-rate policy co-ordination as an implicit threat to its independence and hence oppose it.

EMU and Exchange Rate Management: A Threat to the Independence of the ECB?

Particularly in Germany, fears are widespread that the European Commission's Ecofin Council could force the ECB to participate in exchange-rate co-ordination schemes. Events on the road to the Cologne Summit showed that these fears are not groundless: the Lafontaine-Strauss-Kahn initiative in January 1999 to establish target zones for the dollar-Euro rate has been interpreted by most German observers as an effort to use monetary or exchange-rate policy for direct employment effects (see, for example, Ohr 1999, Reimann 1999). Although the initiative failed, fears still persist that in future the Council may undermine the ECB's independence by committing it to an internationally agreed exchange-rate target (see, for example, Müller and Straubhaar 1999).

The basic problem is that the Maastricht Treaty divides the responsibility for external monetary policy between the ECB and the Ecofin Council, as had been the case in Germany. The ECB is free to operate in the foreign-exchange market, but the Council can in principle commit the bank to defend an exchange-rate peg. However, in contrast to Germany, where no formal law ruled the division of labour between the Bundesbank and the federal government, the Maastricht Treaty is relatively specific and puts strong constraints on the Council in exploiting its competencies.

Those constraints are particularly strong if the Council concludes a formal exchange-rate agreement, that is, a fixed-rate system of the Bretton Woods type or a formal target-zone system (with public announcement of the reference zones as well as a commitment of monetary policy to defend the zone). For this case, Article 109(1) of the Treaty requires that the Council must act unanimously, which would currently require consensus among the finance ministers of 11 countries. After extending the monetary union to those countries not included at the beginning and eventually to new entrants in the EU, there would have to be unanimity among 15, 20, or even 25 members (Henning 1997, p. 36). This heavy requirement would rule out any resurrection of a global fixed or quasi-fixed exchange rate system for the foreseeable future (Gros 1998, p. 349).

The constraints are less binding with respect to relatively loose forms of exchange-rate co-operation such as the Plaza or Louvre agreements. According to Article 109(2) of the Maastricht Treaty, the Council has the authority to formulate 'general orientations' for exchange-rate policy in relation to currencies outside the European Community by acting on a qualified majority recommended by the European Commission and after consulting the ECB.

At first glance, Article 109(2) seems to offer a loophole that may create conflicts among the Council and the ECB with respect to exchange-rate policy. Currently, general orientations could be established by building a coalition among the finance ministers of five countries: Germany, France, Italy, Spain, and Portugal (Müller and Straubhaar 1999), which all face severe unemployment problems and hence could be encouraged to seek creative ways to extract more expansionary monetary policies from the ECB. Moreover, given the constrained ability to co-ordinate fiscal policies (reinforced by the Growth and Stability Pact) and the unwillingness of the ECB to participate in monetary co-ordination strategies (due to concerns about its reputation), exchange-rate stabilisation will remain the main focus of G7 co-operation. There may be incentives for the EMU finance ministers to make use of the guideline clause to prevent being reduced to passive participation in global policy co-ordination.

On second glance, however, fears surrounding Article 109(2) are exaggerated. First, the Council cannot commit the ECB to use monetary policy to pursue exchange-rate targets. The treaty is widely understood to refer to informal currency agreements similar to the Louvre agreement (Kenen 1995, p. 122), which involved only sterilised interventions. Moreover, Article 109(2), Sentence 2, requires that the 'general orientations shall be without prejudice to the primary objective of the ESCB [European System of Central Banks] to maintain price stability'. This gives the ECB the right to reject orientations if interventions would conflict with internal monetary stability.

Second, despite possible constraints, the European Central Bank exerts great *de facto* influence for two reasons: ECB dissent, if made public, would effectively undermine any attempt to influence target rates because exchange-rate targets would lack credibility (Henning 1998,p. 41). Second, experiences with sterilised foreign-exchange market interventions suggest that they are quite ineffective (see, for example, Weber 1996). This will make it possible for the ECB to claim that it is trying hard but that it is unsuccessful in influencing the exchange rate. Hence, exchange-rate policy co-operation presents a relatively small risk to the ECB's independence (Currie 1998, De Grauwe 1998, Gros 1998).

Conclusion

This chapter has argued that the European Monetary Union will not lead to a change in regime with respect to G7 macroeconomic policy. Macroeconomic interdependence will continue to be addressed predominantly in informal ways, such as with regard to information exchange or mutual consultation. Policy co-ordination will take place only occasionally, in exceptional circumstances, and will likely remain focussed on exchange-rate management. In contrast to widespread fears in Germany, the Council will not be able to misuse this form of policy co-operation to undermine the independence of the ECB.

Nevertheless, some risk remains, in particular because it is questionable whether conflicts between the Council and the ECB over exchange rate policy will be solved as smoothly as they were previously with the German finance ministry and the Bundesbank. In order to remove potential conflicts, the ambiguities of Article 109(2) of the Maastricht Treaty must be clarified. This would require that the Council would define precisely the circumstances under which the general orientation clause will be invoked.[14]

A major advantage of a more precise assignment of responsibilities with respect to external monetary policy would be to give the ECB more leeway to act on the exchange-rate front. Without further clarification of Article 109(2), G7 exchange-rate co-operation will always fuel speculation with respect to the ECB's independence. This again might induce the ECB to oppose efforts to co-ordinate exchange-rate policies even in circumstances when such a strategy could contribute to more global stability without incurring risks for monetary stability within Euroland.

Notes

1   If a transmission is positive, a policy measure in country A improves the tradeoff in country B. If a transmission is negative, a policy measure in country A makes it more difficult for the policymaker in country B to reach the target.

2   In the beggar-my-neighbour scenario, stabilisation policy is too active from a global perspective, while in the locomotive scenario, policymakers use their instruments too passively.

3   If a commitment device is not available, no co-operative solution can be reached as each country's policymaker has an incentive to cheat.

4   According to Corden (1994, p. 229), there is 'a mountain of theory, but only a molehill of results'.

5   See Bryant (1995, p. 40f) for a concise overview of this literature. The assumption, which underlies the non-cooperative solution in basic game-theoretic models, is that policy co-operation as information exchange prevents policymakers from behaving in a myopic and insulated manner.

6   Former German finance minister Oskar Lafontaine's *target-zone initiative* in January 1999 (Lafontaine and Strauss-Kahn 1999) represents an exception.

7   The German preference for low inflation is usually traced back to historical experiences: Germans were traumatised by two episodes of hyperinflation in the first half of the twentieth century, experienced the costs of imported inflation from the U.S. in the second half of the 1960s, and have enjoyed the benefits of monetary stability and autonomy since the breakdown of the Bretton Woods system.

8   See Sachverständigenrat (1987/88, para 340) and, for a detailed theoretical analysis of the assignment problem, Landmann (1991).

9   For these 'consensus views', see Pöhl (1987) and Tietmeyer (1988).

10 The inflexibility of German fiscal policy stems mainly from the country's federal structure. Decisions about public finance frequently require the approval of the Bundesrat (if they affect Länder affairs), which makes the acceptability and feasibility of any internationally agreed strategy uncertain even if the majorities in both houses do not differ. Moreover, because of highly independent state and local governments, the weight of the federal government in fiscal policy making is rather limited (Reszat 1994).

11 Three theoretical papers have considered the impact of the EMU on policy co-operation: Giavazzi and Ghironi (1997) analysed strategic interactions among policymakers in the transition to EMU; Eichengreen and Ghironi (1997) compared U.S.-European policy interactions under the rules of the EMS and EMU; and Martin (1997) has analysed how the size of the EMU zone determines the exchange rate policy of the ECB.

12 In other words, the ECB faces the tradeoff of a large country, while the Bundesbank conducted monetary policy from the point of view of a medium-sized country. This analysis differs from Eichengreen and Ghironi (1997) who — incorrectly — assume that the Bundesbank (under the EMS) and the ECB (under EMU) face the same tradeoff because they both make monetary policy for all Europe.

13 This point is frequently made in the literature (see, for example, Kenen 1995, Alogoskoufis and Portes 1997, Henning 1998), although it is based on different reasoning. It is frequently spelled out that the ECB would adopt a position of benign neglect toward the exchange rate similar to the U.S. Federal Reserve, because Euroland is much more closed than the individual countries participating in the EMU. However, the ECB has a European-wide perspective, while the Bundesbank had a German perspective, when formulating monetary policy in Europe.

14 The European Council took the first step toward clarification in Luxembourg on 12–13 December 1997. The Council announced it would use Article 109(2) only in 'exceptional circumstances' such as 'clear misalignments' and 'that these general orientations should always respect the independence of the ESCB and be consistent with the primary objective of the ESCB to maintain price stability'. It is, however, unclear how binding the commitment of the Council is and how the term 'misalignment' is to be understood.

References

Alogoskoufis, George, and Richard Portes (1991), 'The Euro, the Dollar, and the International Monetary System', in Paul R. Masson *et al.* (eds.), *EMU and the International Monetary System*, International Monetary Fund, Washington DC, pp. 58–78.

Baltensperger, Ernst (1999), 'Monetary Policy under Conditions of Increasing Integration', in Deutsche Bundesbank, *Fifty Years of the Deutsche Mark*, Oxford University Press, Oxford, pp. 439–524.

Bergsten, Fred C., and Randall C. Henning (1996), *Global Economic Leadership and the Group of Seven*, Institute for International Economics, Washington DC.

Bryant, Ralph C. (1995), *International Coordination of National Stabilization Policies*, Brookings Institution, Washington DC.

Bryant, Ralph C., *et al.* (eds.) (1989), *Macroeconomic Policies in an Interdependent World*, Brookings Institution, Centre for Economic Policy Research, and International Monetary Fund, Washington DC.

Canzoneri, Matthew B., and Dale W. Henderson (1991), *Monetary Policy in Interdependent Economies: A Game-Theoretic Approach*, MIT Press, Cambridge, MA.

Commission of European Communities, Directorate-General for Economic and Financial Affairs (1990), *One Market, One Money: An Evaluation of the Potential Benefits and Costs of Forming an Economic and Monetary Union*, Office for Official Publications of the European Communities, Luxembourg.

Commission of European Communities (1997), 'External Aspects of Economic and Monetary Union', *Euro Papers*, no. 1, European Commission, Brussels, <europa.eu.int/comm/economy_finance/document/europap/eup01en.htm> (September 2000).

Corden, Max (1994), *Economic Policy, Exchange Rates, and the International System*, University of Chicago Press, Chicago.

Currie, David (1998), 'Will the Euro Work?', Research Report Number P526, Economist Intelligence Unit, London.

De Grauwe, Paul (1996), *International Money: Postwar Trends and Theories*, second edition, Oxford University Press, Oxford.

De Grauwe, Paul (1998), 'The Design of the European Central Bank', in Hans-Hermann Francke Eberhart Ketzel, and Hans-Helmut Kotz (eds.), *Europäische Währungsunion: von der Konzeption zur Gestaltung*, Duncker und Humblot (Kredit und Kapital), Berlin, vol. 14, pp. 295–316.

Eichengreen, Barry, and Fabio Ghironi (1997), 'How Will Transatlantic Policy Interaction Change with the Advent of EMU?', Discussion Paper No. 1643, Centre for Economic Policy Research, London.

Frankel, Jeffrey A., and Katharine E. Rockett (1989), 'International Macroeconomic Policy Coordination When Policymakers Do Not Agree on the True Model', *American Economic Review*, vol. 78, no. 3, pp. 318–340.

Funabashi, Yoichi (1988), *Managing the Dollar: From the Plaza to the Louvre*, Institute for International Economics, Washington DC.

Garavoglia, Guido and Pier Carlo Padoan (1994), 'The G-7 Agenda: Old and New Issues', *International Spectator*, vol. 29, no. 2, <www.library.utoronto.ca/g7/scholar/garavoglia1994/index.html> (September 2000).

Giavazzi, Francesco, and Fabio Ghironi (1997), Out in the Sunshine? Outsiders, Insiders, and the United States in 1998, Discussion Paper No. 1547, Centre for Economic Policy Research, London.

Gros, Daniel (1998), Delivering Price Stability in EMU: The European System of Central Banks, Hans-Hermann Francke, Eberhart Ketzel, and Hans-Helmut Kotz (eds.), *Europäische Währungsunion: von der Konzeption zur Gestaltung*, Duncker und Humblot (Kredit und Kapital), Berlin, vol. 14, pp. 341–364.

Henning, C. Randall (1994), *Currencies and Politics in the United States, Germany, and Japan*, Institute for International Economics, Washington DC.

Henning, C. Randall (1997), *Cooperating with Europe's Monetary Union*, Policy Analysis in International Economics Series, no. 49, Institute for International Economics, Washington DC.

Issing, Otmar, and Bernhard Winkler (1999), 'On the Credibility of Co-ordination', in Otto G. Mayer and Hans-Eckart Scharrer (eds.), *Transatlantic Relations in a Global Economy*, Nomos, Baden-Baden, pp. 95–99.

Kenen, Peter B. (1989), *Exchange Rates and Policy Coordination*, Manchester University Press, Manchester.

Kenen, Peter B. (1995), *Economic and Monetary Union in Europe: Moving Beyond Maastricht*, Cambridge University Press, Cambridge.

Kenen, Peter B. (1999), 'EMU and Transatlantic Economic Relations', in Otto G. Mayer and Hans-Eckart Scharrer (eds.), *Transatlantic Relations in a Global Economy*, Nomos, Baden-Baden, pp. 77–94.

Kitterer, Wolfgang (1999), 'Public Finance and the Central Bank', in Deutsche Bundesbank (ed.): *Fifty Years of the Deutsche Mark*, Oxford University Press, Oxford, pp. 165–218.

Klodt, Henning (1999), *Internationale Politikkoordination: Leitlinien für den globalen Wirtschaftspolitiker*, Discussion Paper No. 343, Kiel Institute of World Economics, Kiel.

Lafontaine, Oskar, and Dominique Strauss-Kahn (1999), 'Europa-sozial und stark', in *Die Zeit*, 14 January, p.17.

Landmann, Oliver (1991), Alternative Währungsordnungen im Lichte des Zuordnungsproblems, in Jürgen Siebke (ed.), *Monetäre Konfliktfelder der Weltwirtschaft*, Duncker and Humblot, Berlin.

Martin, Philippe (1997), The Exchange Rate Policy of the EURO: A Matter of Size?, Working Paper 97-06, Centre d'études prospectives et d'informations internationales, Paris, <www.cepii.fr/ANGLAIS/DOCW9706.HTM> (September 2000).

Michaelis, Jochen (1994), 'DM-Exchange Rate Policymaking', in Hans-Eckart Scharrer (ed.): *Economic and Monetary Policy Cooperation*, Nomos, Baden-Baden, pp. 75–100.

Müller, Henrik, and Thomas Straubhaar (1999), 'Das trojanische Pferd der Währungsunion: Dem Euro droht die Politisierung durch die Hintertür des Außenwerts', *Frankfurter Allgemeine Zeitung*, 5 June, no. 127, p.15.

Ohr, Renate (1999), 'Gefährliche Therapie: Eine Schwankungsbremse durch Zielzonen bringt mehr Schaden als Nutzen', *Rheinischer Merkur*, Bonn, 19 February.

Pöhl, Karl Otto (1987): 'You Can't Robotize Policymaking', *International Economy*, vol. 1, no. 6, pp. 20–26.

Reimann, Winfried (1999), 'Fixkurs-Nostalgie', *Börsen-Zeitung*, 24 February.

Reszat, Beate (1994), 'Germany's Role in International Macroeconomic Policy Co-operation', in Hans-Eckart Scharrer (ed.), *Economic and Monetary Policy Cooperation*, Nomos, Baden-Baden, pp. 47–74.

Rogoff, Kenneth (1985), 'Can International Policy Co-ordination Be Counterproductive?', *Journal of International Economics*, vol. 18, no. 3/4, pp. 199–217.

Sachverständigenrat zur Begutachtung der gesamtwirtschaftlichen Entwicklung [Council of Economic Experts] (1986/87), *Weiter auf Wachstumskurs, Jahresgutachten 1986/87*, Kohlhammer, Stuttgart.

Sachverständigenrat zur Begutachtung der gesamtwirtschaftlichen Entwicklung [Council of Economic Experts] (1987/88), *Vorrang für die Wachstumspolitik*, Metzger-Poeschel, Stuttgart.

Sachverständigenrat zur Begutachtung der gesamtwirtschaftlichen Entwicklung [Council of Economic Experts] (1995/96), *Im Standortwettbewerb*, Metzger-Poeschel, Stuttgart.

Scheide, Jochen, and Stefan Sinn (1989): 'How Strong is the Case for International Coordination?', in J. A. Dorn and W. A. Niskanen (eds.), *Dollars, Deficits, and Trade*, Kluwer Academic Publishers, Boston, pp. 397–422.

Tietmeyer, Hans (1989), 'Anmerkungen zu den neuen internationalen Kooperationsbemühungen seit der Plaza-Verabredung 1985', in Bub Norbert (ed.), *Geldwertsicherung und Wirtschaftsstabilität: Festschrift für Helmut Schlesinger*, Knapp, Frankfurt, pp. 479-497.

Vaubel, Roland (1983), 'Coordination or Competition Among National Macroeconomic Policies?', in Fritz, Machlup, Gerhard Fels, and H. Muller-Groeling (eds.), *Reflections on a Troubled World Economy: Essays in Honour of Herbert Giersch*, St. Martin's Press, London.

Weber, Axel A. (1996), 'Foreign Exchange Intervention and International Policy Co-ordination: Comparing the G3 and EMS experience', in Matthew B. Canzoneri, Wilfred J. Ethier, and Vittorio Grilli (eds.), *The New Transatlantic Economy*, Cambridge University Press, New York, pp. 54–113.

Williamson, John (1985), *The Exchange Rate System*, Policy Analyses in International Economics Series, vol. 5, Institute for International Economics, Washington DC.

Williamson, John, and Miller, Marcus M. (1987), *Targets and Indicators: A Blueprint for the International Coordination of Economic Policies*, Policy Analyses in International Economics Series, vol. 22, Institute for International Economics, Washington DC.

11 The G7/8 and China: Toward a Closer Association

JOHN J. KIRTON[1]

Introduction

On 13 February 2000, Japanese prime minister Keizo Obuchi, host of the 2000 G7/8 Summit, en route to Bangkok for a meeting of the United Nations Conference on Trade and Development (UNCTAD), called for China to become more closely associated with the work of the G7/8 system. He declared: 'China is a major power in Asia and therefore I would like to have China's voice reflected in the Summit'.[2] His call followed by four months that of his predecessor as G7/8 host, German chancellor Gerhard Schroeder, who, in Tokyo on 2 November 1999 on his way to China, called more boldly for China to 'attend', become 'involved in discussions' at and become a 'part of' the G8 Summit in the future (Suk 1999). Just over a year earlier, speaking on 17 May 1998 at the conclusion of that year's Summit, host Tony Blair of Britain had noted that in their final session of the Summit the leaders had 'paid particular tribute in the discussion we had this morning to the work that China has done in the aftermath of the Asian economic crisis and to its very strong commitment to financial stability' (G7 1998). China's emerging relevance to and association with the G7/8 was further underscored, at the ministerial level, by its inclusion in the new G22 that President Bill Clinton had launched at the Asia-Pacific Economic Cooperation (APEC) leaders' meeting in November 1997, by China's membership in the new G20 that the G7 finance ministers created in September 1999, and by Hong Kong's involvement in the new Financial Stability Forum (FSF) the G7 created and expanded in 1999.

These developments make it clear that China has at long last acquired strong and comprehensive relevance as a potential partner of the major industrial democracies as they work through the G7 and G8 to offer global governance to an unstable world. Moreover, the actual advances in China's association with the G7 reflect an emerging consensus that after two decades of reform, opening, and rapid growth, China, whatever its current problems, has acquired increasing influence on the prospects for peace and development of the Asian region and the world as a whole, and that it is ready to play a more responsible role. Yet, at the same time, the G7's association with China remains largely confined to the financial domain, at the ministerial level, and in forums where other non-G7 members have been added to the inner core. Furthermore, Prime Minister Obuchi's limited overture was subsequently met with an emphasis, from Japan and others, that any move toward actual involvement in the 21–23 July 2000 Kyushu-Okinawa Summit would require a consensus among all G8 partners and a request from China itself. The growing momentum toward a recognition and limited realisation of the need for greater China-G7/8 association seemed to be accompanied by great uncertainty and continuing deep-seated reservations about the process, path, pace, and purpose of the association.

Such uncertainty and reluctance in the real world of diplomacy has long existed in the analytical world of the academy, where the extensive literature on China's relevance to the G7/8 and vice versa has featured a vigorous debate. Here one school of thought treats China as an outside object, warranting no institutionalised association with the G7 (Bayne 1995, Sachs 1998, Kirton 1999). A second school of thought views China as a worthy associate of the G7/8, although one lacking at present, and perhaps for some time, a legitimate claim for full membership (Whyman 1995, Hodges 1999). A third school of thought regards China, at present and for a considerable period of time before, as a legitimate member of some or all of the G7/8 system (Jayawardena 1989, Smyser 1993, ul Haq 1994, Commission on Global Governance 1995, Brzezinski 1996, Bergsten 1998, *Economist* 1998). This debate has featured not only major disagreement on the basic issue but also limited analytic advance and a complete lack of attention to many of the core underlying issues. These are the particular forms such an association should take: the rationale and ultimate objective underlying such an association and, above all, the process of moving toward the *status quo* of a continuing G7 and a new, still somewhat fragile G8 (following Russia's full inclusion in 1998), into a system in which China, without or with others, has a comfortable and meaningful place.

This chapter addresses these underlying and timely analytic and policy issues. It considers the rationale and the forms that such a singular, enhanced association might take and the steps required to forge a closer link in the near future. To be sure, any major move toward full membership must await China's demonstrable domestic acceptance of the foundational democratic political values that all G8 members share. Yet, China's current clear commitment toward marketisation and external liberalisation, its existing advances in political and social openness, and the very weakness and instability it is experiencing, in part as a result of implementing these economic measures, puts it in a similar position to the USSR/Russia with which the G7 developed a privileged dialogue from 1991 to 1993. Moreover, China has the potential to be a source of strength as well as vulnerability in reinforcing the precarious stability that has now returned to the international financial system, and in forwarding the recently interrupted move toward a genuinely global system of open finance. A similar logic of capability and vulnerability at a time of systemic and domestic instability applies in the political and security domain, where the G7/8's central character as a concert form of global governance enhances China's claim.[3] China's current role in the G20, alongside such countries as Argentina, Turkey, and South Korea, is an insufficient recognition of its weight in the world, but also a suitable incubator to socialise it into the role of an effective collaborator at a higher level.

The G7/8 Summits in Okinawa, Japan, in July 2000 offered an auspicious occasion for taking the first step toward forging an enhanced association. It is a process that, whether begun before or after Okinawa, should include India along with China, embrace economic as well as political issues, and involve the leaders, but carry no presumption of permanence or inevitable progression toward full membership. A pre-Summit dinner dialogue between China and India and the G7/8 leaders, taking place on site the evening before the opening of the G7 and the G8 Summits, is the ideal place to start.

To develop this analysis and argument, this chapter first reviews the debate over how far and by what formula China should become associated with a G7/8 that expanded in 1998 to embrace Russia as an almost full partner. It then examines the altered attitude toward China of the G7 leaders, ministers, and officials as they moved from their initial 1975 and longstanding treatment of China as an absent irrelevance, then in 1989 to their consideration of it as an adversary to be punished, to their recent approach premised on China's role as a useful and, in some respects, essential associate. It next explores the part China played in the Asian-turned-global financial crisis of 1997–99 and in the effort to reconstruct the international financial architecture that came in the wake of that crisis. It continues with a review of China's role as a highly relevant, responsible, and leading power and G7 associate in the new G22, G20, and (through Hong Kong) the FSF. It concludes by specifying how the G7/8 should best move to associate China with it in the near term.

The Debate over China's Relationship to the G7: Object, Associate, or Member

The issue of China's proper relationship with, or even prospective place in, the G7/8 has been a recurrent part of the debate over reform of the Summit process launched at the end of the European cold war. Amidst the rich array of opinions featured in this debate, three broad schools of thought about China have dominated. The first treats China as an outside object, neither worthy of greater inclusion, nor bringing valuable assets into the G7/8. The second considers China to be a valuable associate, with more formalised links to the G7/8 offering net advantages to both. The third judges China to be a legitimate member, particularly after the admission of Russia, of some if not all of the G7/8 institutions.

Outside Object

If China is considered to be an outside object, it warrants no institutionalised association with the G7. In 1999, the core position was that China lacked the full set of qualities required for membership in this exclusive club: 'Today's often touted prospective entrants — China, India, Indonesia, Brazil — will only be admitted if and when, in the still distant future, they become enduring market-oriented, democratic major powers, and thus acquire the fully systemic perspective, sense of responsibility and capacity to contribute to global order which flows from these attributes' (Kirton 1999, p. 48).

British diplomat and academic Nicholas Bayne (1995), shares this attitude, although for reasons rooted directly in the functioning of the G7/8 rather than the qualities of China itself. He writes: 'large populous countries, like China, India, Mexico and Brazil, deserve more weight as they open up their large internal markets ... [but] ... present G7 membership provides the best opportunity for exerting reciprocal pressure between the highly developed countries of Europe, North America and Japan, which would be lost if the composition were changed'.

Even those who believe the G7/8 Summit itself needs new members, for reasons of representativeness and legitimacy, do not necessarily privilege or even include China in their list of prospective associates. For example, American scholar Jeffrey Sachs (1998) has argued for the G8 to expand into a G16. Although he considers the developing countries of Brazil, India, South Korea, South Africa, and Nigeria (at the time still democratic), Chile, and Costa Rica, he does not specify China as a desirable new entrant.

It is noteworthy that those who treat China as an outside object consider it to be a member of a large class of prospective associates, with Brazil and India the most frequent colleagues or surrogates. By this calculus, those who find the G7/8 grounded in a particular value or deficient in a certain aspect could well favour others on the list. If one privileges the G7/8's democratic character, the core value reflected in the seminal statement of the group's *raison d'être* issued at its first Summit in Rambouillet, France, in November 1975, India would make the obvious candidate. A desire for greater geographic representativeness would point to Brazil (given the presence of existing member Japan to represent Asia).

Worthy Associate

The second school of thought views China as a worthy associate of the G7/8, although one lacking at present, and perhaps for some time, a legitimate claim for full membership. British scholar Michael Hodges (1999, p. 71) has argued that 'China is a major player, not only in the regional context of the 1997–98 Asian crisis, but also in the world economy as a whole'. He concludes that 'it may be useful to extend formalised links between the G7 or G8 and China, given the growing importance of China to the global economy.'

A more developed analysis in the same direction comes from American analyst William Whyman (1995). He treats China not only in the context of other candidates, but also of Russia in the years just prior to its admission into the new G8. Whyman begins by noting the need to give 'large emerging economies such as China, India and Brazil' a voice in the major international economic regimes 'or their support for an open, multilateral economic system and their domestic economic liberalization cannot be assured' (p. 151). The new constellation of power and the new global challenges further underscore a claim. He continues: 'if the G-7 follows a path that refocuses on guiding the international economic system, there is a logic to including the emerging giants of the twenty-first century such as China, India, Brazil, and maybe even Indonesia, Nigeria or a unified Korea' (p. 157). He concludes, however, that in the short to medium term, such a prospect is unlikely, and that limited moves toward greater association should be sought.

Legitimate Member

The third school of thought regards China, at present, as a legitimate member of some or all of the G7/8 system of institutions. This approach begins with the longstanding criticism of the G7/8 as lacking legitimacy or effectiveness because it excludes such robust and rising powers as China (Commission on Global Governance 1995, ul Haq 1994, Jayawardena 1989). The case, argued by those who want either to expand the G7 or replace it with a more representative institution as the centre of global economic governance, rests on several major claims. The world's 10 largest and most rapidly growing economies based on purchasing power include China, India, Brazil, and Russia, with Mexico, Indonesia, and the Republic of Korea not far behind; these countries have much of the world's population, and without them the G7 accords low priority to the development issues that preoccupy most of the world. Expanded membership would thus make the G7 or its replacement more representative and effective.

One of the earliest calls for China to be given full membership made a more comprehensive claim. Writing in 1993, American analyst W. R. Smyser argued, presciently, that the G7 should focus on devising 'new international financial and monetary arrangements that can handle the potential crises that might arise and that one can already foresee,' that should be given full membership in 1994, and that '[a]s soon as possible after that, and subject to political developments in Beijing, the People's Republic of China [PRC] should also be invited to the summit meetings.' He continued: 'The PRC now has one of the world's fastest growing private sectors, a considerable trade surplus, and the potential for explosive advances in modern industry. It has the world's largest population, and it must join the global economic and political system to help that system function effectively. No summit can carry out any decisions that it may make if the PRC does not agree to them. Once the PRC joins, the summit will be the G-9, and it will again be the central coordinating mechanism of the world' (pp. 26–27). Notably, however, given his conception of the Summit's central purpose, Smyser felt that Russia and the PRC should be excluded from the G7 monetary and financial forum, which would be reserved for those who hold 'the financial balance of the world'.

These calls were echoed, in a less singularly China-focused fashion, soon after. Immediately prior to the Lyon 1996 Summit, American scholar and former official Zbigniev Brzezinski (1996) called for the creation of a G11. He argued that the G7 'membership is no longer representative of power or of principle and it needs to be expanded. Russia ... cannot now be excluded ... China, India and Brazil are as entitled to participation as Russia and in some respects much more so'.

By 1998, American analyst Fred Bergsten, just before President Clinton's June 1998 visit to China, argued the converse of the Smyser proposition. Bergsten cited the World Bank's estimate of China as the world's third largest economy and its 'increasingly central role in the world economy'. He thus judged it 'should shortly begin participating in the "finance G-7"' of ministers and central bank governors. However, its continued failure to democratise, Bergsten concluded, rendered its participation in the Summit itself premature. Sharing this view was the editorial staff of the British magazine the *Economist* (1998), which in 1998 declared China to be 'an island of stability, perhaps a new economic leader in the region, worthy of a seat at the G7's top financial table' (p. 17).

The Asian financial crisis led others to look with favour on full membership for China in the G8 itself. Canadian scholar Peter Hajnal, writing in 1999, suggested that, despite its 'lack of commitment to democracy and human rights,' China is a 'plausible future candidate' for the Summit itself, by virtue of its position as 'a potentially major economic power', the only United Nations Security Council (UNSC) Permanent Five member not in the new G8, and with an economy by many indicators that surpasses Russia's (p. 30).

Others sought to admit China by modifying the G7/8 system more broadly. Canadian analyst and former sherpa Sylvia Ostry has outlined an expanded G8 with three concentric circles. Here an inner G3 of the U.S., Japan, and Germany for leadership and crisis management, is joined by a middle ring of the current G7/8 with the possible addition of China for geopolitical, security, and global issues, and an outer circle of representative major regional powers such as Brazil, India, Australia, South Africa, and a more democratic Nigeria (Hajnal 1999, pp. 29–30). Alternatively, the case for admitting China through the contraction of G7 membership has been offered by one of Canada's leading economic journalists, David Crane (1997). He suggests that the 1997–99 financial crisis created the case for a new G5, composed of the U.S., Germany, Japan, Russia, and China alone. Most recently, a group of high-placed foreign policy officials in the Clinton administration and on the Al Gore presidential campaign team have joined the call for China to be included in the G8 (Cutter, Spero, and Tyson 2000).[4]

The debate over China's proper relationship with the G7/8 thus features disagreement on two major dimensions. The first is China's suitability as a member, given its domestic and international economic, political, social, demographic, and geographic behaviour, character, and capabilities, in absolute as well as relative terms, in a transforming international system. The second is the impact of Chinese membership on the G7/8 itself, in both positive and negative ways. Much less attention has been given to several other crucial issues: the treatment the G7 and the institutions it controls has actually accorded China during the past decade; China's desire for closer association; the effect of greater G7/8 association and membership in adjusting China's behaviour, definition of interests, and sense of identity; why the particular combination of China's vulnerabilities and G7/8 capabilities may provide the basis for a claim; the impact of greater Chinese association on the other major claimants in the world; and the G7's need for China in order to maintain the concerted power of the G7/8 over the global system and an effective equality of power among its members within.

Especially when judged against the volume and variety of the analysis in the debate over Summit reform and the place of China within it, it is also noteworthy how little intellectual effort has been devoted to devising reasons and formulae for China to become more associated with the G7/8 system, in ways that fall short of full membership. This lacuna is especially unfortunate, given the major interrelated issues that require careful consideration for such an advance to occur. These include the specific formula that will maximise the benefits and minimise the costs for China's enhanced participation (for China, the G7/8 itself, and outsiders); the impact that China's enhanced association would have on other potential associates, including fellow regional Asian and APEC partners such as South Korea and India; and whether such association can be reversed, held at a particular level indefinitely, or, following the Russian, European Union, Canadian, and Italian cases before it, only serve as a prelude to ever more full membership.

The G7/8 Treatment of China, 1975–99: From Adversary to Associate

The intellectual movement by outside analysts toward contemplating a closer formal association of the PRC with the G7/8, fuelled in part by the challenges of the international financial system in the 1990s, has been matched by the changing treatment accorded to China by G7/8 leaders, ministers, and officials themselves. This progression has seen China move from an irrelevant absence in the period from 1975 to the late 1980s to a targeted adversary in 1989 and the following few years, and to a potential associate in the 1990s. It has culminated in the public proposals by the G7/8 host leaders in 1999 and 2000.

From Irrelevant Absence to Targeted Adversary

During the G7's first decade China was publicly absent as a direct object of attention. It was relevant largely as a matter of geopolitical context and private concern. China formed part of the adversarial environment the G7 faced as it increasingly dealt with a host of largely geopolitical issues. These focussed on global arms control, such as nuclear proliferation, the missile technology control regime, and intermediate nuclear forces, and on regional security issues, such as the Indo-Chinese refugees, Kampuchea, and stability on the Korean peninsula. Although China was a direct calculation in the closed discussions among leaders and ministers, it was deemed neither sufficiently relevant nor sufficiently within the domain of potential public suasion or verbal deterrence to be worthy of direct mention in the G7's various communiqués.

This changed in 1987 when the Chairman's Summary on Political Issues at the Venice Summit included the passage: 'In Asia, we agreed that particular attention should be paid to the efforts for economic reform undertaken by China' (Hajnal 1989, p. 352). For the first time China had become an object of direct, public G7 attention, an implicit if highly tentative associate, an object of economic rather than political interest, and one whose domestic as opposed to external policies were of note.

It is useful to compare this initial treatment of China with that accorded the Soviet Union the same year. The G7 at Venice declared: 'We are following with close interest recent developments in the internal and external policies of the Soviet Union. It is our hope that they will prove to be of great significance for the improvement of political, economic and security relations between the countries of East and West. At the same time, profound differences persist; each of us must remain vigilantly alert in responding to all aspects of Soviet policy' (Hajnal 1989, p. 345). It is noteworthy that the G7 recognised perestroika in both Russia and China with an equal, early sense of significance, but directed at China none of the suspicion visited upon Russia.

The following year saw a decisive reversal in the G7's attitude toward China, prompted by the Tiananmen incident. The 1989 Paris Summit of the Arche, which received the letter from Mikhail Gorbachev that ultimately led to Russia's inclusion in the new G8, issued a special 'Declaration on China' that condemned China's violent repression in defiance of human rights. Here Canadian prime minister Brian Mulroney combined with host President François Mitterrand, against the resistance of Japan and the United States, to achieve an endorsement of high-level sanctions aimed at China, including the suspension of bilateral ministerial contacts, the arms trade, and World Bank loans. With the Paris Summit celebrating the 200th anniversary of the political birth of the Franco-American concept of human rights, the Declaration on China highlighted democracy and human rights as the core shared property of G7 members and China's attachment to antithetical values. Moreover, armed with this referent, the G7 signalled its concern over Hong Kong.

However, even with this emphasis on democracy, the 1989 Summit did include the hope that the interruption of Tiananmen would soon be past, and that the economic reform noted the previous year would be accompanied by its political equivalent. The G7 leaders declared: 'We look to the Chinese authorities to create conditions which will avoid their isolation and provide for a return to cooperation based upon the resumption of movement towards political and economic reform, and openness' (Hajnal 1989, p. 408).

The Move Toward A Potential Associate

This same emphasis, led again by Mitterrand and Mulroney over the resistance of the U.S. and Japan, arose at Houston in 1990. Despite a relaxation of its members' sanctions, the G7 continued to express collective concern, in part to exert a deterrent effect on future PRC action. However, they did acknowledge some positive developments in China, and moved to support new lending that would contribute to the reform of the Chinese economy in the environmental field. Moreover, it was the environmental issue that brought China for the first time into the core Economic Declaration, and did so as one of a group of G7 associates. Indeed, it rendered China an object of G7 praise. The G7 stated: 'We applaud the announcement in London by some major developing countries, including India and China, that they intend to review their position on adherence to the Montreal Protocol and its amendments' (Hajnal 1991, p. 22). Even in the immediate aftermath of Tiananmen, China had become an ecological associate.

At London in 1991, China was dealt with only in the Chairman's Summary. But it now attracted a full paragraph and again was the object of applause. The G7 stated: 'We welcome China's cooperation with the international coalition in opposing Iraqi aggression and over other regional issues'. It approved the continuation of a process, already underway, of rebuilding contacts with China and concluded that, 'Unconditional extension of Most Favoured Nation status to China by the US would contribute to there goals' (G7 1991). The G7 had thus come to see China as a responsible associate in global security matters and, in classic G7 fashion, was willing to link this to favourable treatment on economic issues such as trade.

In 1992 at Munich, China again received G7 approval, this time for China's acceptance of major international arms control regimes. A paragraph in the Chairman's Statement described China's recent developments toward economic reform as 'encouraging', but also called for 'greater efforts toward political reform', and asked for 'considerable further improvement' in human rights

(G7 1992). It welcomed China's accession to the Nonproliferation Treaty and application of the Missile Technology Control regime. It further expressed the hope that China would play 'a more constructive role in the international sphere'.

Although China was absent from the G7 statements at Tokyo 1993 and Naples 1994, it returned as a subject of attention and approval at Halifax in 1995. A 'China paragraph' in the Political Declaration welcomed 'China's growing participation in international and regional fora dealing with political, economic and security issues' (G7 1995). Noting that each member would pursue its dialogue with China 'in the interests of a more stable and prosperous world,' it looked forward to a smooth 1997 transition in Hong Kong 'with the object of maintaining its economic prosperity and social stability'. A subsequent paragraph called on the parties to a territorial dispute in the South China Sea to resolve their differences peacefully, in accordance with international norms.

By Lyon 1996, the G7's treatment of China focussed exclusively on arms control. Here the G7 welcomed China for joining with other G7 members and affiliate Russia in signing two treaties establishing nuclear weapons free zones in the South Pacific (with France, Russia, Britain, and the U.S.) and in Africa (with the U.S., France, and Britain, but notably not G7 affiliate Russia).

The 1997–99 Advance

Denver 1997 marked a major advance in the attention the G8 accorded China. Surrounded by Russia's robust participation in the Denver 'Summit of the Eight', the imminent transition in Hong Kong (taking place a mere two weeks after the Summit), and the visibility of the U.S.-China relationship in the U.S., the Denver Declaration dealt with China in two ways. First, it welcomed 'the recent agreement among Russia, Kazakstan, Kyrgystan, Tajikistan, and China on reduction of military forces along their borders' and declared it to be 'an important contribution to the region's security.' Second, and most importantly, it dealt at length with Hong Kong. Here, amidst the attention devoted to the maintenance of Hong Kong's political freedoms its the post-transition period, the G8 placed equal emphasis on the economic dimension. Noting the G8's 'durable interests in this financial and economic center', it called for the preservation of stability, prosperity, and an independent monetary and economic system. It noted that Hong Kong's fundamental freedoms and the rule of law were the essential underpinnings for Hong Kong's future economic success.

Behind this articulated agreement among the G8 lay a deeper consensus about China's relationship with the G7, at the moment of Russia's major step toward full admission. There were media reports that the Japanese, angry that the U.S. had invited Russia's President Boris Yeltsin essentially as a full participant, were asking why China was not invited (Erlanger 1997). Yet no one in the host U.S. government, or any other G7 government, had considered including China in the G7 (Kirton 1997). There was an underlying if largely unarticulated conviction that China did not play by the rules of the game of democracy and free trade, to a degree unlikely to be changed by the APEC logic of ameliorating its attitudes and action through inclusion and the socialising effects of personal bonding among leaders in an informal setting. Equally, however, no one in the U.S. government argued that there was a need to create a *de facto* G8, with Russia included, in order to counter a now powerful Chinese threat.

This consensus remained firm despite the acute debate raging in the United States about American policy toward China. This debate pitted the business community against those from the liberal-left who were concerned about human rights issues such as Tibet. The geopolitical right also saw China as the emerging threat. The U.S. and Japan tacitly endorsed a gentle version of this view. Responding directly to the Chinese missiles fired at Taiwan the previous year, they issued new defence guidelines allowing military co-operation in the extended maritime reaches off Japan (Fry, Kirton, and Kurosawa 1998). The Chinese strongly opposed this move, viewing the extension of Japanese support for U.S. military operations as aimed directly at them. Such an atmosphere heightened the conflict between the G7's historic role as the moral centre for rendering judgements about the practices of non-democratic regimes, including the PRC, and the latter's desire to play to the individual commercial self-interest of G7 members.

In preparation for Denver, the U.S., seeking a Congressional renewal of authority to trade with China on the basis of Most Favoured Nation (MFN), proposed that the G7 issue a strong statement on Hong Kong. This proposal was supported by Britain. Canada and other G7 members were cautious. However, all came to agree that the Denver Summit should issue an extensive statement of support for democratic freedom in Hong Kong. In the lead-up to Denver, the PRC learned that the draft G7 Communiqué included a passage on Hong Kong. In keeping with their general aversion to having the G7 develop a view on China, the Chinese protested strongly. Yet, none of the G7 suggested altering the proposed passage in response.

At Denver, there was much private discussion among the leaders about China's intentions for Hong Kong, as well as an extensive treatment by the foreign ministers. The positions of the G7 members were consistent with those publicly seen in the earlier co-sponsorship of the United Nations resolution on human rights in Geneva and subsequently in the G7 members' decision to send representatives to attend the installation of the new legislature in Hong Kong (a ceremony that ultimately only the Americans and British boycotted). The U.S. and the British pushed to have the G7 issue a strong statement of support for the preservation of democratic freedoms in Hong Kong. The Japanese, while quite concerned about the PRC take-over, were reserved. Canadian prime minister Jean Chrétien's and Foreign Minister Lloyd Axworthy's interventions were consistent with Canada's very strong policy of engaging China and their attitude that no country would outflank Canada as a friend of China in the region. Despite these cautions, they fully shared the general anxiety about PRC behaviour and the conviction that a clear statement of concern was required. They stressed the importance of holding free elections for a new legislature within a year, a commitment they felt had been successfully recorded in the concluding Communiqué. The leaders agreed to co-ordinate their positions on the hand-over. The extensive Communiqué statement on China employed language that the U.S. had been using for months and emerged unchanged from the draft of a week prior to the Summit.

The second area that concerned China was trade. At the spring 1997 news conference in Europe announcing the enlargement of the North Atlantic Treaty Organization (NATO) and Russia's participation in the Denver Summit of the Eight, U.S. secretary of state Madeleine Albright and deputy secretary of the treasury Larry Summers had indicated that the U.S. looked forward to Russia joining the World Trade Organization (WTO) on 'commercially acceptable' terms. The Denver Communiqué, in contrast, noted: 'We support the goal of early Russian accession to the WTO on the basis of conditions generally applicable to newly acceding members' (G7 1997a). The apparent softening raised the question of whether Russia might be a precursor for an early and special arrangement for the PRC to enter the WTO. However, there was no G7 support for such a relaxation. The Communiqué of the G7, meeting alone without Russia, affirmed this strict condition. It read: 'We attach a high priority to expanding the membership of the WTO, on the basis of commitments to adhere to WTO rules and to provide commercially meaningful market access' (G7 1997b). In the case of China, the U.S., in particular, with a major trade deficit with China, insisted that it accede to the WTO only when it had fulfilled all the normal conditions. Canada's position was similar, although it was prepared to support early access once China met basic conditions for financial services liberalisation and access for agricultural products.

Such issues highlighted the need for the G7 to remain an exclusive forum of like-minded members with advanced economic credentials and understandings to perform the essential task of stabilising the world economy at a time of incipient crisis. Yet, the onset of the Asian financial crisis in the weeks following Denver began to change G7 attitudes. The autumn 1997 visit to Washington of Jiang Zemin, and his November 1997 post-APEC tour of Canada took place largely on the terms demanded by the PRC. They represented an act of normalisation after the strained U.S.-China relationship since Tiananmen and a reinforcement of the strengthening Canada-China relationship of the Chrétien years.

The shift in attitude was evident at Birmingham in 1998. Here, host Tony Blair noted in his concluding press conference that the G7 'paid particular tribute in the discussion we had this morning to the work that China has done in the aftermath of the Asian economic crisis and to its very strong commitment to financial stability' (G7 1998). Indeed, it was only the late timing of the discussion that prevented the tribute from being encoded in the Communiqué itself (Bayne 1998).

At Cologne in 1999, the focus on debt relief and Kosovo and the end of the 1997–99 financial crisis left little room for attention to China. Yet China's performance during these difficult two years had left a lasting legacy. The G7 at Cologne decided to expand the membership of the new FSF, and to create a new, broader group (then termed the GX) of systemically important countries. The new members included Hong Kong in the FSF and China itself in the GX.

By the time of the Cologne Summit then, the G7/8 had come a long way from its historic absence of direct interest in China, and the Tiananmen-bred treatment of China as an adversarial repressive regime. The G7's initial, pre-Tiananmen interest in China in the domestic economic domain had expanded to embrace a full array of economic, political, and global subjects on the domestic, regional, and international planes. Moreover, the 1997–99 financial crisis had brought China to a position where it was applauded by the G8 for its constructive role and made a core associate in the new fora created by the G7 to build a new international financial architecture in the wake of the crisis.

The Schroeder and Obuchi Overtures

It was thus not surprising that 1999 G7/8 host, German chancellor Gerhard Schroeder, visiting Tokyo on November 2, 1999, en route to China, publicly declared his support for a further step. At a news conference with then Japanese Prime Minister Keizo Obuchi at the Japan National Press Club, Schroeder called for China to 'attend', become 'involved in discussions' at, and become a 'part of' the G8 Summit in the future. Noting the size and importance of China, he argued: 'In the 21st century, it will certainly be meaningful to involve

China in discussions on controlling and preventing regional conflicts and promoting international co-operation' (Suk 1999). In response, Japan — host of the 2000 Summit — sounded a cautious note, asking publicly whether 'a membership expansion would enable us to maintain effective policy coordination' and 'whether China wishes to join.' The same day, China publicly urged the G8 to listen more to Beijing and other developing countries, pointed out that China is the largest developing country and expressed the hope that the G8 could narrow the gap between developed and developing countries, while also promoting global stability and balanced development.

This bold plea for a major Chinese involvement on the part of the outgoing host was followed by a far more consequential, if more limited overture by Obuchi. On February 13, 2000, he stated: 'China is a major power in Asia and therefore I would like to have China's voice reflected in the Summit'. He quickly added, however, 'While taking into account what China wants to do, we would like to consult each member of the G8' about China's involvement.

To the casual observer, there was much to suggest that this condition-laden call was of little immediate significance. It was publicly uttered en route to a conference of UNCTAD, which is dominated by developing countries and where China loomed large, particularly as a country that had just agreed to join the WTO. A Japan seeking to reinvigorate the process of multilateral trade liberalisation, following the stillborn start of the Millennium Round at Seattle in November 1999, had good reason to hold out the prospect of such a reward to the liberalising, WTO-legitimising, less developed China. Domestically, Obuchi was struggling to survive to host the Summit by keeping together his divided coalition government. A key part of the three-party coalition was the New Komeito party, whose leader, Takenori Kanzaki, had called for China to participate as an observer at the G8 Summit during his visit with China's vice-president Hu Jintao in Beijing in November. Within the G7, it was widely assumed that the U.S., unhappy with China's human rights record, would veto any Chinese involvement, thus allowing Obuchi to gain credit in Asia for sponsoring a fellow Asian country while leaving the G8 intact and the U.S. to take the blame. Should the U.S. prove unreliable, it was assumed that Britain, a few years after the Hong Kong transition, would be reluctant.

Externally, vis-à-vis China itself, it was further judged that Beijing, while welcoming an invitation, would not want to overtly solicit one and thus leave Obuchi an easy way out. Bilaterally, the uneasy Chinese-Japanese relationship was one in which China was uncomfortable with Japan speaking for Asia at such global gatherings as the G8, and for possessing through membership a status that China lacked. But it was equally uneasy with a process in which Japan served as its sponsor into and mentor within the G8 club. Moreover, China, aware of the process and the reasons by which Russia had joined the G8, was reluctant to follow a similar path for fear that this would convey the impression that its own economic weakness was forcing it to become a supplicant to join a 'Western' capitalist club. Finally, the status-sensitive Chinese looked with disdain on the prospective half measures proposed — holding a post-Summit meeting with the G8, joined by other Asian countries. Perhaps China preferred to hold out for full membership all at once.

There was a substantial ambivalence within Japan and its leadership about whether the time was ripe for it to take an assertive foreign-policy role of the sort that a serious initiative to secure China's G8 membership would entail. Historically, Japan had previously sponsored Australia (in 1979) and Indonesia (in 1993) as Asian candidates for G7 inclusion, giving Japan a record of trying to 'Asianise' the annual gathering, but an equally strong track record of enjoying very little success.

Yet, there were good grounds for believing that more than regional diplomatic politeness might be at work. Within Japan, the urgings of Obuchi's coalition partner were reinforced by an Okinawan government spokesman, who said his government would push Tokyo to invite China as an observer. Kanzaki's call in Beijing was made the same month as Schroeder's appeal, suggesting that a momentum might be at work embracing the outgoing and incoming host. Obuchi, in an effort to realise his stated desire to have Okinawa focus on Asian issues, had been unusually diligent in travelling to other countries in the region to solicit their views on what the Okinawa Summit should discuss. He and members of his government travelled to India and Pakistan, among others, and he was to meet the leaders of the Association of South-East Asian Nations (ASEAN) on the margins of the UNCTAD conference to solicit their views. Japan had also invited China's Zhu Rongji to visit Japan before the Summit. An economically struggling and modestly armed Japan had a strong interest in managing its economic and security relationship with neighbouring China and good reason to believe, given Japan's own experience within the Summit, that G8 inclusion could be an effective way of constraining and socialising China in the ways that Japan wished. Moreover, Prime Minister Obuchi, with his direct experience as foreign minister, was among those who wished to and who could lead Japan into a more ambitious foreign policy role, beginning with using the Okinawa Summit to showcase Japan's recently battered regional leadership and promote Asian interests on the world stage. Securing China's inclusion would be a bold stroke.

It was for these reasons that Obuchi had in fact decided at an early stage to include China in his Summit. His plan was to invite the leader of China, along with the leaders of India, South Korea, and one other Asian country to come for a post-Summit meeting with the G8, following the formula the G7 had employed with Russia from 1991 onward as well as with the heads of major international organisations in selected years. At least some of the prospective Asian participants offered Obuchi a positive response.

In the ensuing week, the response to the Obuchi initiative from Japan's G8 partners and China suggested that there might be more momentum to the process than the usual G7 minuet of each member trying to stop expansion while not being singled out as the one who said no. The United States, thought to be the most opposed as a consequence of China's human rights record, and facing a difficult Congressional vote on acceptance of China's new WTO membership, showed a surprising initial openness. U.S. ambassador to Japan Thomas Foley told Kanzaki that the U.S. would not oppose China's participation, but added that Japan should consult with the other G8 members. Thomas Pickering, U.S. Under-secretary of State for Political Affairs, indicated to the Nihon Keizai Shimbun that Washington could accept China as an observer at this year's Summit and understood the opportunity the Summit offered to meet with Asian nations including China. But he added that an official expansion of the G8 framework was a different issue. It was left for State Department spokesman James Rubin to say that the U.S. would consider any proposal, not yet issued, by the Japanese hosts for China to attend as an observer. He noted that Asian issues would certainly be discussed as part of the Summit, and that a full half of the existing G8 members — the U.S., Japan, Canada, and Russia — bordered the Pacific Ocean.[5] Deputy secretary of state Strobe Talbot, after meeting with Obuchi on 16 February, kept the prospect alive, saying: 'We believe this summit has a significance beyond the confines of the G8,' and that it would be a good opportunity to show the importance of globalisation, especially on the economic front.

Among other consequential G8 partners, the Germans under Chancellor Schroeder were known to be sympathetic to China's inclusion. The British government was thought to be sympathetic only if India were invited as well.[6] The Canadians, while watchful of Washington's reaction, could be assumed to be ultimately favourable, given Prime Minister Chrétien's longstanding desire not to let Canada be outflanked as a friend of China. Yet, Canada also had serious reservations, based on a desire to maintain the integrity and effectiveness of a G7/8 club that was central to its foreign policy, and a defensive positionalist instinct not to dilute the selective status that membership in the club brought them. It remained uncertain how the Russians would respond to this *de facto* dilution of their recently hard-won status, especially when granted to their longstanding rival in Asia at a time of Chinese growth and relative Russian decline. Across the G7, officials also expressed reservations that the inclusion of China could complicate consensus building, as China's singular rigid approach to many issues would make the group more heterogeneous, would foster divisions among members, and would risk repeating the mistake of including Russia, with the embarrassment and lack of concrete results that move had brought.

Within Japan there were similar divisions, with those from the prime minister's office and foreign ministry offering a different emphasis. Immediately after the Obuchi overture, foreign minister Yohei Kono cautiously noted that Japan had not yet made a decision and had not yet sounded out China on the issue. He added that the issue had not arisen in discussions among G8 members, including the sherpas, and that it was important to listen carefully to the opinions of other countries if the issue came up at future sherpa gatherings. The following day chief cabinet secretary Mikio Aoki said a decision could be made only after Japan had surveyed the opinions of other G8 members and that 'the most important' thing was to find out what China thought. Yet, he continued that Japan had been informally sounding out other countries and that if G8 participants and China agreed, then Obuchi would surely take a positive attitude toward the plan. He also indicated that Obuchi might meet Chinese premier Zhu Rongji prior to the Summit if China did not attend as an observer. Akitaka Saiki, Deputy Press Secretary to Obuchi, also said Japan would sound out China's views. By Friday, 18 February foreign ministry deputy spokesman Chikahito Harada said Japan had started discussing with G8 partners whether to invite China, and that it needed to seek 'the consensus of full consultation' from the G8 before officially making a proposal to China. Senior ministry officials said sherpas had started considering the issue. They and the G8 had to decide whether China would be a guest or full member, whether its presence would hinder discussion of political issues that could include human rights, and how China would react if, like Russia, it was excluded from the Summit's macroeconomic discussions. Yet they noted that even if China was not invited 'the G8 nations agree on the need to "link" China and the G8, given the country's increasing economic and political role in the international community'.

The Chinese reaction also showed some signs of forward movement. To be sure, the Chinese had not responded to Japan's invitation to Zhu Rongji to visit Japan before the Summit. Chinese foreign ministry spokesman Zhu

Bangzao on 15 February repeated the standard Chinese line that the G8 could play a bigger role in North-South co-operation, that China hoped the G8 would play an even more active role in enhancing international co-operation, promoting stability and economic development, and narrowing the gap between the North and the South, that China had always advocated wide representation for consultation, co-ordination, and decision making on global issues, and that 'the G8 should listen to other countries opinions, especially those from the developing countries'. Yet he added that China, already having had contact with the G8, attached importance to the G8's role. Two days later Bangzao said China had yet to be consulted through diplomatic channels. Chinese officials said Beijing would be happy to be invited to join the G8 forum but had not decided whether it would actively pursue a role within the club. Meanwhile China began to evaluate the risks and rewards of participation more intensively, weighing whether gaining a voice in the club of most powerful nations would be offset by involvement in a forum dominated by U.S. and its allies, with the attendant risk of compromising Beijing's distinctive foreign policy.

Amidst this flurry of public comment and diplomatic positioning, consideration of the Obuchi overture revolved around several considerations. The first concerned relative capability. There was a general acknowledgement that China had an important voice in its own right and deserved some form of inclusion on this account (*Financial Times* 2000). At the same time, Obuchi's rationale rested on China being, in more limited fashion, the 'major power in Asia,' rather than a major power globally or one whose internal characteristics (including market economy and democratic polity) made it a candidate for full-scale participation or permanent membership.

A second consideration married relative capability with institutional status. This began with the argument that now that Russia had been admitted, it was difficult to deny China's claim especially on the grounds of economic capability but also because of its political capability. A similar logic led some, given Russia's record at the Summit, to argue, conversely, that in the interests of the proper functioning of the institution and its absorptive capacity following Russia's recent admission, China should be kept out.

A third calculus married relative capability with the internal characteristics of the members and the institutional characteristics of the institution. This logic underscored the call for democratic India to join China, but to cap the group at 10 to maintain the 'K-group' advantages of constricted participation in the club (Snidal 1985). The G10 formula and its logic offered a way to deal with the inevitable outburst of claims should China move to inclusion, with the costs to regional partners such as South Korea, and with the longstanding desire of some to create a much more representative G30 (Camdessus 2000).

From this flowed the view that the G7 was an institution with a different purpose and effect than the rival United Nations (UN) with the Security Council at its core. Should the G8 have a similar 'talk shop' purpose, China's inclusion in the G8 would either duplicate or detract from the work of the UN. Yet, if the G8 had the distinctive purpose and effect of letting other major powers effectively influence an otherwise unconstrained pre-eminent United States, then the call for China's inclusion added value for the other members of the G8, and for the group as a whole.

This emphasis on the autonomous institutional power of the G7/8 as a distinctive type of international institution led to the second half of the Prime Minister Obuchi's plan — the move from whether the G8 members would welcome China's association, however tentative, to whether China itself wished to be involved. For beneath the tactical issue of who — China or the G8 — should go first in formally asking for a closer association lay China's substantive reasoning of whether it could affirm its distinctive foreign policy purposes and values in the G8, at the cost of the inevitable adjustments it would be induced to make. Here the recent Russian experience with Kosovo and to a much lesser extent Chechnya and the 1998 financial crisis suggested such adjustment effects were real (Kirton 2000).

The process of acting thus again depended on a particular combination of the relative capability of the members and the institutional characteristics of the G7/8 forum. The apparent G7/8 institutional norm of host leaders having the prerogative to invite one-off visitors clearly had its limits. As the French experience in 1989 and 1996 showed, and the Japanese experience in 1993 also revealed, all hosts are not created equal. As a host, second-ranked Japan remained more dependent than co-founder France on the acquiescence of the U.S. to secure some realisation of its initiatives.[7]

China's Role in the Global Financial Crisis of 1997–99

An important cause of the Obuchi initiative and of the G7/8's rapidly developing view of China as a worthy associate was the role China played in the response to the global financial crisis of 1997–99 and in the subsequent task of reforming the international financial system. Throughout the Asian and global financial crisis of 1997–99, China approached the challenge of both crisis response and system reform with clear, consistent, and distinctive positions. These positions often aligned with those of China's Asian neighbours and placed China at odds with the emphasis of the G7. Yet, from an early stage, China's positions were shared by some G7 members, including those from beyond Asia. As the crisis progressed, adjustments in the initial G7 consensus, in response to a changing reality, narrowed the still substantial policy gap. By the end, there was sufficient convergence and partial overlap that a closer and fruitful dialogue between the G7 and China could be envisaged.

As the Asian financial crisis opened, China faced the global economy from a position of relative strength. Unlike Japan and South Korea at a comparable stage of their economic development, China had an outward-looking policy grounded in considerable inward and outward foreign direct investment. And unlike Russia in the previous decade, China began in a state of economic strain at worst, accompanied by some considerable economic assets, and not in a state of economic collapse. Those assets included a major trade surplus, both overall and with the United States in particular, and the world's second largest store (after Japan) of convertible foreign exchange reserves. It was thus understandable that China sought to play a larger role in regional and global affairs, and that the crisis offered it an opportunity to do so.

Crisis Response

From the start of the crisis, China was active in the mobilisation of resources, beyond those of the International Monetary Fund (IMF) from its regular mechanisms, to deploy in support packages for the beleaguered Asian economies. It participated in the support package for Thailand and in the plan for Indonesia.

China's main contribution came, as the G7 at Birmingham recognised, in not devaluing its currency to keep pace with and retain its competitive position vis-à-vis its many Asian neighbours who were devaluing theirs. The threat of a Chinese devaluation may not have been particularly strong. Apart from Hong Kong, the crisis placed little strain on the Chinese economy. Nor was it in China's interest to devalue. There was little pressure on its export account, which continued its large surplus due to the relatively rising currency and soaring demand from the U.S., and the willingness of the latter to serve as a 'spender of last resort.' There was a general recognition that China's currency was locked to the U.S. dollar, and that any devaluation could have led to a massive loss of confidence in and flight of capital from China itself. Closer to home, China's export markets, beginning with Japan, were afflicted by a lack of domestic demand, rather than any currency-related price elasticity relating to the goods China wished to sell. Indeed, on a trade-weighted basis, its currency suffered no net appreciation of any harmful proportion. Moreover, capital inflows to China continued at a solid, if declining rate, and at one well in excess of that enjoyed by its crisis-afflicted neighbours. Any fear of devaluation thus did not reflect the trade and debt structure of the Chinese economy.

Throughout the crisis, China proclaimed at every opportunity that it would not devalue its currency. Its finance minister, vice-minister and central bank governor constantly argued at the IMF annual meeting, Interim Committee, Development Committee, and G24 meetings that China's refusal to devalue was its way of giving a guarantee to the international community and maintaining stability in the region. Their emphasis on this argument may have been enhanced by their sensitivity to those private-sector analysts who suggested, when the crisis broke, that its real origins lay in China's 1995–96 devaluation, and the attendant message that China favoured external adjustment rather than domestic reform of its own state-owned enterprises.

A second clear and consistent position was China's very early and very strong advocacy of substantial, low-conditionality funding packages for the afflicted Asian economies. China argued vehemently that the support package for Thailand should be larger, be offered earlier, have more front-end loaded disbursement, and come with lower conditionality (including none regarding banking reform and corruption) than the one offered by the IMF. It was a position that, in retrospect, appeared to some in the G7 to have considerable merit.

On the Indonesian package, from the outset China vocally opposed the rigidity of the IMF program, arguing that it went too far with fiscal compression. China's early advocacy of fiscal flexibility placed it in alliance with Japan, which was the leader in this coalition, and with Canada, which began to argue the case for stimulus and social sensitivity at an early stage. The Japanese push, aided by Canada and China, succeeded over time in changing IMF policy in this regard.

In these and subsequent cases, the Chinese rarely departed from a narrow conception of the IMF's role. They wished to allow national authorities in afflicted Asian economies to determine what was best for their own economies. In their view, the IMF should merely prepare analysis, offer options, describe costs and benefits, and allow the affected country to decide what to do, rather than prescribe a particular path.

China's sense of solidarity with its Asian neighbours was further demonstrated in its willingness to contribute to the support packages and its restraint in criticising other Asian partners. Consistent with its belief in the

'Asian way', and perhaps its fear of reciprocal criticism, its views were highly nuanced, balanced, and extremely sensitive in regard to political advice. It was indeed a major proponent of the Asian way, highlighting the particular circumstances and uniqueness of the East Asian societies, and thus the social, political, and cultural context of any adjustment program.

System Reconstruction

China also had a clear approach to international financial system reform. First, China argued internationally for regional responsiveness and responsibility in response to the crisis, rather than a reliance on the multilateral mechanisms of the IMF. Secondly, it was attracted, if not vocally, to the concept of a new Asian Monetary Fund (AMF), pioneered by the Japanese in the summer and autumn of 1997, as a substitute for the IMF (Kiuchi 2000). Thirdly, China very strongly opposed letting hedge funds have the freedom to move capital in and out of countries in ways that could destroy small economies. This was a position that received the strong support of most of its neighbours in the region. And fourthly, in contrast to the new orthodoxy in favour of flexible exchange rates as a shock absorber, China tended to favour as an international regime the fixed exchange rates backed by currency intervention that it enjoyed at home.

China's approach began with a sense of Asian solidarity. It played a very active role in the debate over the Japanese proposal for an AMF, initially offered as a stand-alone facility. Here China favoured a middle way, calling for complementary parallel instruments and mechanisms more sensitive to Asian values. Hong Kong was one of the earliest economies to provide the inter-bank swap arrangements among central banks that were the precursor to any AMF. Indeed, a major portion of the resources made available by other emerging Asian economies was through such provision of liquidity to central banks, with the Hong Kong contribution totalling several billion dollars.

China's support for a greater regional role was seen from the start of the crisis in its support for the 'Manila Framework' — the other strand of the now emerging Asian financial network. The framework was designed to bring together Asian finance ministers and central bankers. Here the Japanese proposed a formal mechanism, while the ASEAN countries preferred a less formal approach. China again sought a middle way, calling for a greater degree of co-operation and a framework that spelled out Asian values.

A similar positioning appeared in regard to the Asian Development Bank (ADB) — another large area where Asian countries were attempting greater regional co-operation. In the second version of their proposed AMF, the Japanese had suggested that the ADB could serve as the secretariat for the new entity. The U.S., Europeans, and Canadians continued to resist (as they had the initial proposal for a stand-alone facility). China supported developing regional co-operation but never voiced support for a separate institution, or declared that they wanted to undermine the IMF and World Bank.

On the broader issues of the new architecture, China often took a multitrack approach, in recognition of its responsibilities for the very different societies in Hong Kong and in mainland China. This duality was evident in China's position on transparency in the financial sector, corporate governance, accounting, and banking standards.

Yet, there were several areas where China stood in less restrained opposition to the position of the G7. On the codes of conduct proposed by the British, Canadians, Germans and, to some extent, the Americans, China was cautious. It was the most conservative country regarding the transparency of markets, the public sector, and central banks. Here it was one of the most virulent opponents, arguing that such transparency would cause not stability but greater volatility. On this issue, its divergence with the G7 widened, as Japan's initial 1997 support for discretion and confidentiality was replaced by a strong emphasis on full and fast publication.

China also opposed the G7 on the Codes of Good Practice for Social Policy. This was a project pioneered by Britain, Canada, the U.S., and Australia, and one that the World Bank began work on. China was the country most strongly opposed. Although Japan had reservations about the project, it was prepared to give support.

A further area of divergence was fiscal transparency and the Codes of Good Practice on Fiscal Policy. This was a favourite of Canada and Britain, where the IMF had started to develop a code. China stood in consistent opposition. In late 1997 and early 1998, China questioned the validity and value of the whole exercise. It subsequently stressed the voluntary nature of the code.

Despite these divergences, there were several areas where China was closer to the G7 consensus. China favoured lending into arrears, as did most G7 members. China, along with most G7 members, did not see moral hazard as the major problem that Germany did.

China was also very constructive regarding hedge funds, a subject of particular passion. It was very vocal about how at the margins highly leveraged banking, insurance, and securities firms and hedge funds could very quickly destabilise countries that were otherwise doing well. It thus called for greater international financial regulation. China was joined here by Japan, Malaysia, and other Asian countries. The U.S., Britain, Canada, and Europe remained much less concerned.

China's views reflected a broader, longstanding analysis of the causes and impact of the Asian crisis. Along with some Asian countries, China saw the virulence of the Asian crisis arising from the behaviour of foreign institutions and how they leveraged their portfolios by pouring billions into emerging markets and then pulling these funds out at the first sign of trouble. It regarded such herd behaviour, as in Indonesia, as socially destabilising, causing massive poverty, unemployment, civil unrest, domestic strife, family breakdown, and independence movements. Such results defied China's ideal of a 'social market economy', a concept that gives equal weight to economic development and social stability. Chinese leaders thus judged IMF programs primarily according to their impact on social stability and resisted IMF involvement in issues of corporate governance, securities commissions, risk management in financial markets, social practices, and political problems such as corruption.

Despite their still deeply grounded and substantially divergent positions, China thus played an increasingly vocal, active, engaged, and influential role in crisis response and system reconstruction. In the great debate between Asian regionalism led by Japan and Malaysia and Bretton Woods–based multilateralism, China often took a middle position in its public statements. On important issues, it shared a position similar to that of Japan, Canada, and many other G7 members. Moreover, it came to see itself as a large country and economy, an economic linchpin of Asia alongside Japan, and a responsible international citizen. It thus wished to, and felt it ought to, be involved in all relevant forums.

The Move toward Meaningful Association: From G22 to Financial Stability Forum and G20

This shifting role of China led to concrete moves by G7 leaders to bring China into a closer institutionalised relationship with the G7. Spawned initially by China's new financial power, and hastened by its responsible role in the 1997–99 Asian and global financial crisis, such a movement has centred on, and thus far been confined to, an association in the field of finance at the level of finance ministers and central bank governors.

The Early Associations

The move toward China's institutionalised association with G7-dominated finance forums began in the late 1990s with the New Arrangements to Borrow (NAB). The NAB arose from the December 1994 Mexican peso crisis and the ensuring Halifax G7 call to the G10 to double the monies available to the IMF under the General Arrangements to Borrow (GAB) (Bergsten and Henning 1996). Both the GAB and the new NAB were used during the 1997–99 crisis. The NAB's greater funding and flexibility proved essential in containing the crisis.

The Hong Kong Monetary Authority, one of the 25 members of the NAB, contributed 340 million Special Drawing Rights (SDRs). This puts it on a par with Finland, Korea, Malaysia, Singapore, and Thailand at the lowest level of contribution. By way of comparison, Canada, the lowest-ranked G7 member in the NAB, has a contribution of 1396 SDRs. The U.S., the top-ranked G7 member, contributed 6712.

A further step came with the formation of the G22, created at the initiative of President Clinton at the November 1997 APEC leaders' meeting in Vancouver. China participated as a member in the group's preparation of reports on aspects of the financial architecture. The activities of the G22 led to the creation of the new G20, as a successor body more closely integrated with the work of the established international financial institutions (Canada 1999).

The next step came in the spring of 1999 with the creation by the G7 finance ministers in Bonn on 22 February of the new Financial Stability Forum (1999). The FSF first met at the IMF in Washington on 14 April 1999. At the Cologne Summit in June of that year, G7 leaders decided to expand the FSF beyond G7 member countries to include the 'systemically important emerging economies'. Thus Hong Kong, Singapore, Australia, and the Netherlands were added as participants for the FSF's subsequent meeting in Paris on 15 September 1999.

The G20

China's most recent advance came with its inclusion as a founding member of the new G20 forum of finance ministers and central bank governors created at that same meeting in Paris. The G20 was designed as 'a new mechanism for informal dialogue in the framework of the Bretton Woods institutional system, to broaden the dialogue on key economic and financial policy issues among systemically significant economies and promote cooperation to achieve stable and sustainable world economic growth that benefits all' (G7 1999). Its initial 18 country members consisted, in addition to the G7, of Argentina, Australia,

Brazil, China, India, Mexico, Russia, Saudi Arabia, South Africa, South Korea, and Turkey.

Through the inclusion of China, the G7 recognised China as a 'systemically important country', a 'key emerging market' with a different viewpoint than that of the most industrialised countries, and a representative of the Asian region. It shared the former status with 10 other countries (including G8 member Russia), and the latter with fellow Asian region countries Australia, India, and South Korea. The pattern of membership thus constituted a recognition that in this financial forum, China was in the same class as Russia, and in one above that of Indonesia and Malaysia in terms primarily of power, but secondarily in political and economic performance and policy as well.

In diplomatic terms, China clearly had pride of place in this new institution. There was never any serious consideration of excluding it from the group. China was seen to rank above Argentina, Mexico, Korea, and Turkey, and as a country that might some day overtake Canada and Italy. While there was much discussion about membership, no one's list excluded China. In contrast, some lists excluded Australia, Korea, Turkey, and Saudi Arabia (although the latter's provision of ample funding proved decisive in the end).

The functions of the group suggested an even broader relevance for China. To be sure, the G20 was a deliberative rather than decisional body, but one designed to encourage 'the formation of consensus' on international issues' (Canada 1999). However, it was a body with a focus on policy, a mandate to promote international financial stability, a concentration on longer term policy issues rather than immediate ones, but a body where, in Canadian chair Paul Martin's words, 'There is virtually no major aspect of the global economy or international financial system that will be outside of the group's purview' (Beauchesne 1999).

China proved ready to join the new group, in part due to the G7's and Martin's desire to use it to promote better supervisory and self-regulation arrangements. It was clear that China would deal from a position of strength. It should quickly emerge as one of the most influential members, and advocate of a distinctive approach, within the club. With US$150 billion in foreign exchange reserves, second only to Japan in the world, it came with a position of domestic strength. That strength also gave it a particular perspective on managing the international financial system, generating a bias in favour of fixed exchange rates backed by currency intervention. An open question for G7 members, however, was whether in the area of trade in financial services, such as banking and insurance, China would be ready to recognise the need for a process of international participation on a fair basis over time, rather than one which sequestered the best part of its growing domestic market for domestic firms.

There are, however, legitimate questions as to whether this new involvement on the part of China in this fledgling group constitutes a sufficient degree and form of institutionalised association with the G7. One doubt stems from the view of some who see the G20 as part of the 'G7-isation' of the world. A second doubt arises from the known difficulties of China being positioned merely as a full member of other developing country groupings — in this case, the 11 emerging economies (minus the one Australian exception) that join with the G7 to constitute the G20. Although China is a full member of the IMF's Interim Committee and Development Committee, it is only an observer at the exclusively developing country clubs of the G24 meetings and (outside the Bretton Woods system) at the G77. This mutually beneficial arrangement arises from the fact that China does not want to be fully linked to such groups, given that it sees itself as large enough to constitute a group unto itself. In addition, such groups are reluctant to have China as a full member for fear that its exceptional size would lead it to dominate.

Conclusion: The Formula for Forging the Link

There are thus good grounds for moving to forge an enhanced institutionalised association of China with the G7/8, including involvement at the leaders level, and as early as the Japanese-hosted Okinawa Summit on 21–23 July 2000. In practice, although the Russian case should not be the only relevant referent, the G7/8 attitude is heavily based on its recent experience with Russia. This includes the issues of why the G7 had such a powerful interest in Russia, and whether the process and fact of Russia's admission have lessened the criteria of the domestic democratic and market character and the internal and external performance of a member in the larger interest of socialising difficult but powerful countries. It extends to whether the inclusion of Russia has thus far yielded as much, or more, than its early enthusiasts and ultimate deciders envisaged. Here the maintenance of a foundational form of democracy during the great challenge of the 17 August 1998 financial crisis and the Cologne Summit experience over Kosovo and subsequently with Chechnya suggest there is at least a minimal level of evidence to proceed. Yet, it is equally important to take a more forward-looking approach, and one more firmly focussed on the specificity of China.

From the perspective of the G7/8, the rationale for rapidly forging a closer link with China begins, as it did with Russia, with the collective strategic interest in the complete integration of China into the global system, with the full and balanced set of rights and obligations that accompany that status. The key question is whether China, even under its current leadership, has a political culture, ideological legacy, and distinctive national values that would allow it to contribute meaningfully to the development of a G7/8 consensus on core issues such as the reform of international institutions. From the perspective of China, the question is whether it wishes to move from its current position midway between the developing countries and the G7/8, and absorb the adjustments in its approach on several issues that such a movement toward greater association would require. There are grounds for considerable caution on both counts.

However, the record of the past decade offers several conclusions that provide a rationale, set a pace and path, and define a degree and form of advance, for forging the link. First, China's record during the 1997–99 financial crisis shows there are sufficient convergence and compatibility of interest between China and G7 members to make a further step toward institutionalised association potentially desirable and workable. Second, given the exceptional position of China and the need to maintain the G7/8's core asset of constricted participation, China, along with only India, should be accorded this incremental upgrade.[8] Third, such an upgrade should be limited, and be far less than full membership, in recognition of the core democratic character of the existing G7 club and the need to maintain a democratisation incentive vis-à-vis countries within and without. Fourth, such an association should not create a configuration limited to either the economic or the political domain, or indeed to a singular or selected aspect of the G7's agenda. For during the past decade, the G7 has cumulatively recognised China's multidimensional relevance. Moreover, from the inception of the G7 its unique strength has been its ability to link political and economic dimensions to the mutual support of objectives in each domain. And the objectives of both the G7 and China during the international financial crisis and system reconstruction were based on linking both domains, if with distinctive end states in mind. This factor of multidimensional relevance and linkage suggests an association that mobilises the unique ability of leaders to embrace, link, and trade off considerations from all domains.

The first step consists of further associating China with the G7's functional bodies, at the ministerial level and below, in domains where China is relevant but relatively uninvolved. Such a step has several precedents, both in the creation by the G7 of regimes initially confined to G7 members and expanded over time to include outside countries of greatest relevance. As the involvement of Ukraine at the 1995 Winnipeg ministerial conference suggests, it is also possible, even at the ministerial level, to select a single country for such association, and to do so in ways that do not create a presumption or dynamic of recurrent and permanent participation.

On the assumption that the G20 will serve in the near future as an adequate forum for dialogue on the core financial issues, the focus should be on G7/8 forums where China is most likely to make an issue-specific contribution. One such body is the annual G7/8 meeting of environment ministers, for it is here that China, along with Russia before it, has both the strongest claim on the grounds of issue structure capability and internal and systemic vulnerability (Keohane and Nye 1989). Of particular interest, given China's role in global and regional security, is associating China with the G8 foreign ministers forum. This could best take the form of a joint meeting on the margins of the G8 foreign ministers meeting at their regular gathering in the immediate lead-up to the annual leaders Summit.

A second component is an association at the level of the leaders. This would allow a full array of issues to be considered, at the discretion of each party to the dialogue. It would allow large, initially intellectual and cognitive linkages and tradeoffs to be made. It would reap the full advantage of the Summit's role as a deliberative institution. And it would better signify the enhanced status China deserves in the international community. The central objectives of the G7/8 would be to secure a first-hand understanding of the future intentions of China's leadership in the reform process and to encourage them to move from a regional to a stronger global perspective and sense of responsibility. The first Summit of the new millennium, held in Asia, would have provided an appropriate symbolic occasion for such a step. The presence of China and democratic India alongside it would have reinforced the objective of the Japanese host in having a genuinely Asian, as opposed to more broadly Asia-Pacific, focus for the Okinawa Summit.

Any move to association at the leaders level should go well beyond the existing inclusion of China on the pre-Summit tour of regional colleagues mounted by Prime Minister Obuchi. It should go beyond a meeting in Japan on the eve of the 2000 Summit between the Chinese leader and the Japanese prime minister as Summit host, along the lines of the honour Japan accorded to Indonesia's president Suharto when Japan hosted its last G7 summit in 1993. After all, even if, as in 1993, the Japanese prime minister were accompanied by any G7 colleagues who wished to participate (as President Clinton did in 1993), such a limited link would have little use. The difficult bilateral relationship between Japan and China would make for a strained encounter, and one too focussed on regional concerns rather than global ones. All G8 leaders need to learn directly, in a plurilateral setting (rather than a bilateral one where the Chinese leadership can play them off against each other) what Chinese domestic and foreign intentions are. Moreover, as the G7/8 is a forum with fully fluid coalitional patterns any agreements or understandings, however informal, that might result, would far more likely flow if the full G7/8 membership were there.

The preferred formula is thus to hold a formal meeting between China's leader and the G7/8 as a collective, on the eve of the opening of the G7 and G8 Summit. As with the dinner dialogue between the G7 leaders and the 15 developing country leaders that French president Mitterrand invited to Paris on the eve of the opening of the Summit in July 1989, such a format would enable an exchange of views on a full array of subjects, with a timing that would enable both G7 leaders and G8 leaders to take maximum account of China's positions and perspectives in their own deliberations in the following days. It would represent such a sufficiently large advance that it could make it easier for China's leadership to accept such an invitation. And should the experiment not show promise, it could easily be abandoned in favour of another path in subsequent years, as the 1989 precedent shows.

Such a step could well appear to be cautious, in contrast to the bold November 1999 vision aroused by Chancellor Schroeder of making China a full Summit member in one large, complete, and irreversible move. A similar contrast arose in the wake of U.S. president George Bush's public musings at Munich in 1992 that Russia should be admitted as a full member of the G8 club. But caution is in order, especially as the G7 and G8 remain fully preoccupied with absorbing a Russia whose challenges may well provide enough work for another decade, and given that China's internal and external intentions remain in considerable doubt. Yet, the lesson of Russia underscores the advantages of advancing the hitherto very tentative association with China, both to mobilise China's very real strengths and to address at an early stage its vulnerabilities before the costs they could create compound.

Notes

1   This is a revised and updated version of 'The G7 and China in the Management of the International Financial System,' a paper prepared for an International Think Tank Forum on 'China in the 21st Century and the World,' sponsored by the China Development Institute, the China International Center for Economic and Technical Exchange, and the National Institute for Research Advancement of Japan, in Shenzen, China, 11–12 November 1999. Valuable research assistance in the preparation of this chapter was provided by Gina Stephens, Natalie Armstrong, Ivan Savic, Diana Juricevic, Paul Jacobelli, and other members of the G8 Research Group.

2   Obuchi continued: 'While taking into account what China wants to do, we would like to consult each member of the G8' about China's involvement. Some news agencies such as Jiji Press translated the initial quote as: 'I would like to find a way to reflect China's say in the Summit as it is a major country in Asia'. Unless otherwise indicated, direct quotes such as this come from various newswire sources reporting the same event.

3   On the concert model and the G7/8 as a modern international concert, see Kirton (1993).

4   In contrast, candidate George W. Bush's proposals for G8 reform were limited to a call on 29 September 2000 for existing G8 energy ministers to meet annually.

5   Rubin specifically stated: 'It is really up to the Japanese to comment publicly on this idea ... we would consider any proposals carefully'.

6   While not representing the British government, on 15 February an editorial in the *Financial Times* (2000) concluded: 'If G8 meetings are valuable for informal debates, then there is no reason why China should not be included. But if it is it would be churlish not to invite India along, as the world's most populous democracy. A G10 should be the limit. If there were any more, it would cease to be a fireside chat at all.'

7   In 1989, France succeeded, overcoming U.S. resistance, in inviting 15 host-selected developing countries to a pre-Summit dinner with the G7 leaders. In 1996, France secured a post-Summit lunch of the G8 leaders with the heads of the International Monetary Fund, World Bank, WTO, and UN. In 1993, Japan secured only a pre-Summit meeting with itself and Indonesia that U.S. president Clinton attended.

8   The addition of India arises from the need to maintain an affirmation of the core democratic character of the G7/8 as a modern concert, as well as a need to provide an incentive for others to follow. This attribute trumps that of foreign-policy responsibility, and thus the argument of those who would conclude that including India would constitute a *de facto* reward for the bad behaviour of its nuclear explosions at the time of Birmingham 1998. Clinton's visit to India early in 2000 in practice eroded the force of this argument in any event. Given China's preferred position to stand between the G7 and the developing world while neither losing its constituency in the latter nor claiming to represent it, the Indian accompaniment could ease its introduction into the club.

References

Bayne, Nicholas (1995), 'The G7 Summit and the Reform of Global Institutions,' *Government and Opposition*, vol. 30 (Autumn), p. 497.

Bayne, Nicholas (1998), Jobs, Crime and Money: Challenges for the G8 Summit in 1998, <www.library.utoronto.ca/g7/evaluations/1998birmingham/impression/index.html> (September 2000).

Beauchesne, Eric (1999), 'Martin Warns against Complacency', *Montreal Gazette*, 26 September, p. A9.

Bergsten, Fred (1998), 'The New Agenda with China', *International Economic Policy Briefs*, vol. 98, no. 2, pp. 1–2.

Bergsten, Fred, and Randall Henning (1996), *Global Economic Leadership and the Group of Seven*, Institute for International Economics, Washington DC.

Brzezinski, Zbigniev (1996), 'Let's Add to the G-7', *New York Times*, 25 June, p. A11.

Camdessus, Michel (2000), 'Development and Poverty Reduction: A Multilateral Approach,' Address at the Tenth United Nations Conference on Trade and Development, Bangkok, 13 February.

Canada (1999), 'New G-20 Forum: Backgrounder', Department of Finance, Ottawa, <www.library.utoronto.ca/g7/g20/g20backgrounder.htm> (September 2000).

Commission on Global Governance (1995), *Our Global Neighbourhood: The Report of the Commission on Global Governance*, Oxford University Press, New York.

Crane, David (1997), 'Asia Crisis Brings Global Powershift', *Toronto Star*, 30 November, p. D2.

Cutter, W. B., J. Spero, and L. D. Tyson (2000), 'New World, New Deal: A Democratic Approach to Globalization', *Foreign Affairs*, vol. 79, pp. 80–98.

Economist (1998), 'Welcome to China, Mr. Clinton', vol. 347, no. 8074, p. 17.

Erlanger, Steven (1997), 'Russia Sits with Big 8, Party Crasher No More,' *New York Times*, 22 June.

Financial Stability Forum (1999), 'First Meeting of the Financial Stability Forum,' *Press Release*, 6 April, <www.fsforum.org/Press/P19990406.html> (September 2000).

Financial Times (2000), 'Chinese Chequers,' 15 February.

Fry, Michael, John Kirton, and Mitsuru Kurosawa (eds.) (1998), *The North Pacific Triangle: The United States, Japan, and Canada at Century's End*, University of Toronto Press, Toronto.

G7 (1991), 'Chairman's [British Foreign Secretary Douglas Hurd] Statement', London, 16 July, <www.library.utoronto.ca/g7/summit/1991london/chairman.html> (September 2000).

G7 (1992), 'Chairman's [German Foreign Minister Klaus Kinkel] Statement', Munich, 7 July, <www.library.utoronto.ca/g7/summit/1992munich/chairman.html> (September 2000).

G7 (1995), 'Chairman's Statement, Halifax', 17 June, <www.library.utoronto.ca/g7/summit/1995halifax/chairman.html> (September 2000).

G7 (1997a), 'Communiqué', Denver, 22 June, <www.library.utoronto.ca/g7/summit/1997denver/g8final.htm> (September 2000).

G7 (1997b), 'Confronting Global Economic and Financial Challenges: Denver Summit Statement by Seven', 21 June, Denver, <www.library.utoronto.ca/g7/summit/1997denver/confront.htm> (September 2000).

G7 (1998), 'Transcript "A" of the Press Conference Given by Prime Minister, Mr. Tony Blair', Birmingham, 17 May, <www.library.utoronto.ca/g7/summit/1998birmingham/blaira.html> (September 2000).

G7 (1999), 'Statement of G-7 Finance Ministers and Central Bank Governors', 25 September, Washington DC, <www.g7.utoronto.ca/g7/finance/fm992509state.htm> (September 2000).

222 *Guiding Global Order*

Hajnal, Peter (1989), *The Seven-Power Summit: Documents from the Summits of Industrialized Countries, 1975–1989*, Kraus International Publications, Millwood, NY.

Hajnal, Peter (1991), *The Seven-Power Summit: Documents from the Summits of Industrialized Countries: Supplement: Documents from the 1990 Summit*, Kraus International Publications, Millwood, NY.

Hajnal, Peter (1999), *The G7/G8 System: Evolution, Role, and Documentation*, Ashgate, Aldershot.

Hodges, Michael (1999), 'The G8 and the New Political Economy,' in Michael Hodges, John Kirton, and Joseph Daniels (eds.), *The G8's Role in the New Millennium*, Ashgate, Aldershot, pp. 69–74.

Jayawardena, L. (1989), 'World Economic Summits: The Role of Representative Groups in the Governance of the World Economy', *Journal of the Society for International Development*, vol. 4, pp. 17–20.

Keohane, Robert, and Joseph Nye (1989), *Power and Interdependence*, second edition, Scott, Foresman, Glenview, IL.

Kirton, John (1993), 'The Seven Power Summit and the New Security Agenda,' in D. Dewitt, D. Haglund, and J. Kirton (eds.), *Building a New Global Order: Emerging Trends in International Security*, Oxford University Press, Toronto.

Kirton, John (1997), 'Canada, the G7, and the Denver Summit of the Eight: Implications for Asia and Taiwan,' *Canadian Studies* 3 (1998).

Kirton, John (1999), 'Explaining G8 Effectiveness,' in Michael Hodges, John Kirton, and Joseph Daniels (eds.), *The G8's Role in the New Millennium*, Ashgate, Aldershot, pp. 45–68.

Kirton, John (2000), 'The Dynamics of G7 Leadership in Crisis Response and System Reconstruction,' in Karl Kaiser, John Kirton and Joseph Daniels (eds.), *Shaping a New International Financial System: Challenges of Governance in a Globalizing World*, Ashgate, Aldershot, pp. 65–94.

Kiuchi, Takashi (2000), 'The Asian Crisis and its Implications', in Karl Kaiser, John Kirton, and Joseph Daniels (eds.), *Shaping a New International Financial System: Challenges of Governance in a Globalizing World*, Ashgate, Aldershot, pp. 37–46.

Sachs, Jeffrey (1998), 'Global Capitalism — Making it Work,' *Economist*, vol. 348, no. 8085, pp. 23–25.

Smyser, W. R. (1993), 'Goodbye, G-7', *Washington Quarterly*, vol. 16, no. 1, pp. 15–28.

Snidal, D. (1989), 'The Limits of Hegemonic Stability Theory', *International Organization*, vol. 39, no. 4, pp. 579–614.

Suk, Sarah (1999), 'Schroeder Hopes China Will Join G-8, Learn from Japan,' *Kyodo*, Tokyo, 2 November.

ul Haq, M. (1994), 'The Bretton Woods Institutions and Global Governance', in Peter Kenen (ed.), *Managing the World Economy*, Institute for International Economics, Washington DC, pp. 409–418.

Whyman, William (1995), 'We Can't Go On Meeting Like This: Revitalizing the G-7 Process', *Washington Quarterly*, vol. 18, no. 3, pp. 139–165.

12 Corporate Governance: International Perspectives

DONALD J. S. BREAN

Introduction

This chapter presents a brief overview of modern corporate governance — the concept, the complexities, and the challenges for policy. The primary purpose of the chapter, which involves a perspective that extends beyond most general treatments of the topic, is to address the *international* dimension of corporate governance. As industry becomes increasingly international, questions of how business is governed — involving the laws and conventions that shape and constrain business behaviour — become increasingly complex. While each nation's commercial and contract law remains a sovereign prerogative, business ownership that spans international borders becomes subject to the laws of various countries. The result is legal overlap and potential conflict in the ways that nations deal with multinational enterprise.

The discussion for the most part is concerned with relatively large business — nationally influential corporations and multinational enterprises. Such firms are especially forceful in determining the strength and direction of the private sector. Correspondingly, it is a matter of economic, social, and political importance to understand how — in whose interest — such firms are governed.

Who Manages the Managers?

Industrial societies are organised around corporations. A corporation is an autonomous legal entity owned by shareholders with limited liability. The control of corporate affairs, that is, running the business, can become separate from ownership, especially when ownership is represented by shares dispersed widely throughout the country and, indeed, around the world. Separation of ownership and control gives rise to potential conflict of interest wherein those closest to the wheels of industry, the managers, make decisions — concerning, for example, real investment, risk, and the structure of finance — that may be at odds with the preferences and welfare of the owners.

If ownership and control are not separate, such as with family-owned business or closely held firms, the conflict of interest is absent or small. Significant problems can arise, however, when ownership is held by a large number of shareholders, each with relatively few shares. That particular focus — involving typically large, publicly traded corporations — and the legal and institutional means to make the interests of owners and managers congruent offer the most pertinent perspectives on corporate governance.

Issues of corporate governance arise whenever two conditions are present. First, as mentioned, there is the potential conflict of interest or *agency problem* involving parties within the sphere of the corporate organisation. Second, the *transaction costs* of addressing agency problems through contracts are such that they cannot be effectively dealt with through explicit contracts.

The agency problem adds substantial complexity to the economic theory of the firm. Conflicts of interest, especially their exploitation and consequences, are difficult to depict in a formal way. How, for example, does one know whether managers manage effectively and responsibly?[1] The conventional theory of the firm tends to be blasé if not naive with respect to such questions. That theory rests on the idea that the nebulous 'firm' makes decisions in light of inputs and outputs and technology in pursuit of maximum profit that belongs to the 'owners'. In fact, however, these corporate decisions are in the hands of people with strong personal interests such as their own well-being and security, and thus tends to create a setting for compromise and sometimes even corruption.

Managers are entrusted with corporate assets — property, buildings, machines, patents, trade marks, all the makings of a going concern — along with the potential to develop and expand these assets. Managers are assigned responsibility to make investment and production decisions in the best interests of the shareholders. Shareholders generally believe that their best interests are maintained when the value of their firm is maximised.

The theory of corporate governance places great stress on the concept of 'incomplete contracts'. The point of reference — a complete contract — would take account of all possible future circumstances, specifying the agent's (the manager's) actions and corresponding reward in each conceivable case that could unfold. In the real world of complex uncertainty, however, such complete spanning of future events is impossible. As a result, in practical terms, contracts involve substantial trust. Management is trusted to be knowledgeable, committed, honest, and competent to deal with the affairs of the corporation as time and unknown circumstances unfold.

At first glance, the question of the extent to which self-serving managers may exploit the shareholders may seem simply to be a 'distributional' issue; it may perhaps be a violation of justice, but it is not a matter of serious economic concern. That, unfortunately, is not correct. The economic consequence of weakness in corporate governance is too little investment, and often investment in the wrong things. This means a misallocation of resources, erosion of efficiency, and loss of output. The economy at large suffers.

If management expropriates shareholders' invested funds or behaves in any way whatsoever to reduce the efficiency with which those funds are used, the corporation is less productive and less profitable than it would otherwise be. Moreover, the mere prospect of management acting in other than the shareholders' best interest, with shareholders unable to limit such behaviour, means that less equity capital will flow to the industrial system. The expected return that shareholders require for corporate investment will be higher than it would otherwise be — compensation for the threat of confiscation — and this too chokes off investment.

The corporate governance issue, and the aim of institutional development to strengthen governance, is to ensure that management's interests are aligned with those of the shareholders. The focus on shareholders' interests is especially pertinent when held in contrast to the substantially greater security enjoyed by other suppliers of capital, either financial or human, to industry. Long-term bondholders, for example, are assigned priority claim on corporate earnings. They also insist on protective covenants to constrain management decisions that could otherwise increase the risk of debt and reduce its value. Short-term suppliers of debt, such as banks and trade creditors, generally have collateral-based recourse to real property, all the while insisting on regular accounts of the firm's overall credit position. Labour, of course, is protected by employment law, unions, or only slightly less formal associations. Labour's responsibilities and rewards are unambiguously defined in contracts.

Above all, in contrast to shareholders, the firm's bondholders, creditors, and labour have the option of a relatively quick and low-cost exit from the firm. Shareholders, however, commit large amounts of financial capital to industry on terms that are without specific contract, time expiry, or defined reward. Such vague terms create the risk of opportunistic behaviour on the part of management.

Two Systems: The Insider Model and The Outsider Model

Two fundamentally different systems for exercising corporate governance can be distinguished. The two systems are sometimes labelled the 'market model' — reliant on the controlling influence of markets, typically associated with the United States and Britain — and the more institutionally dominated 'bank model' as found in continental Europe and Japan.

Since the market model depends on external forces to exert influence on corporate behaviour, it is aptly termed the 'outsider' model. On the other hand, the bank model — which entails direct control by one or more large financial institutions — is often dubbed the 'insider' model.

The following discussion uses this outsider/insider terminology. It is important to recognise that the respective models of corporate governance both involve a broadly defined setting of institutions, laws, and social attitudes toward industry as well as specific firm-level arrangements for governance. The latter arrangements are reflected *inter alia* in governing boards and the structure of finance.

The Outsider Model of Corporate Governance

Distinguishing features of the outsider model of corporate governance include:
- Dispersed equity holdings. Many shareholders, each with a relatively small ownership claim on the company.
- Shareholders' interests, paramount in company and securities law.
- Well-developed capital markets, which are the *sine qua non* of the outsider model. Share prices are assumed to be efficiently determined.

The outsider model reflects an advanced stage of the separation of corporate ownership and control. Although shareholders collectively own the firm, the wide dispersion of shares and the relatively small holding of each individual shareholder tend to minimise the influence of individual shareholders in corporate affairs. The individual shareholder is likely to be uninformed if not outright indifferent to the operational concerns of the corporation.

In this setting, corporate management wields effective control of the firm's assets. Management has substantial incentive, sometimes referred to as *moral hazard*, to make decisions in its own self-interest. Well-known examples include managerial perquisites such as personal use of company assets — real estate, cars, company planes, personal staff, etc. Less obvious action (or inaction) by management to the detriment of shareholders includes corporate empire building, emphasis on expansion as opposed to profitability, excessively risky investments, and reluctance to pursue operational efficiencies including, if necessary, the replacement of management.

The outsider model of corporate governance is a system of laws, regulations, and, above all, market forces that constrain corporate management from acting in ways that are economically inefficient and costly to shareholders.

A legal and regulatory structure that defines and protects the rights of shareholders is central to the outsider model. Most importantly, shareholders are entitled to vote on company policy either directly or through proxy. Shareholders' rights must be reinforced by timely, objective, and accurate information to allow investors to stay abreast of the corporate activities and to make informed decisions. Disclosure laws, accounting and auditing standards, securities regulatioñs, shareholder records, and tax-filing requirements are facets of the system that ensures the proper flow of relevant information to existing and potential shareholders.

The collective interest of the dispersed equity ownership is entrusted to the board of directors. Indeed, much of the analysis of the merits — or otherwise — of the outsider model of corporate governance focusses on the role and effectiveness of the board in exercising its responsibility for oversight. In principle, shareholders ought to elect the members of the board who in turn select senior management. The common practice, however, is for the board to be selected by the shareholders from a slate approved by the top management.

A responsible, well-run, and effective board has certain fiduciary duties, including:
- evaluating the performance of the senior management;
- linking senior executive compensation to clear performance criteria;
- reviewing and evaluating strategic and operating plans.

Such responsibility demands commitment to board duties. To ensure such commitment,
- each board member should have significant stock ownership;
- directors ought to be compensated with stock;
- the board should consist of no more than three insiders;
- board members should be elected annually;
- there should be no interlocking directorships;
- receipt of fees from the company should result in a member's disqualification.

The outsider model of corporate governance puts great store in the efficacy, the efficiency, and the justice of markets. Vigilant and dispassionate forces of markets are required to control management effectively and to channel management's effort to the best interests of shareholders. In other words, markets identify and reward good management; markets also identify and

punish poor management. The good or the bad effort of management is assumed
to be measurable in the firm's stock price.

Supporting Markets

The outsider model is made operational through specific markets. Three
markets are especially relevant: the market for managers, the market for
corporate control, and the product market.

The *market for managers* is economic Darwinism. Winning managers
survive and thrive. Losers are dismissed. The market is the judge and the
enforcer. When one reads that the chief executive officer of a company has
been sacked by the board, one sees the market for managers in action. On the
positive side, effective managers are recognised, rewarded, and retained.

This process, if effective, ought to ensure that managers are kept on their
toes. However, while the economic logic seems sound, the implications for
corporate governance are ambiguous. The concept of a market for managers
does not distinguish between poor performance due to the principal/agent
problem — for which corrective action involves getting the incentives right
— as opposed to managerial incompetence, which tends to be redressed through
search and discovery of competent managers with some inevitable dismissals
in the process. As far as corporate governance is concerned, attention is more
usefully directed to the proper design of managerial incentives for performance
rather than to the necessary but negative function of smoking out the
incompetent. The subject of incentives is discussed below.

The *market for corporate control* rests on the idea that if the board of
directors is not representative of the shareholders' interests, or if management
is *not* responsive to the board's oversight, then the corporate mission, that is,
to maximise the shareholders' value, is frustrated. Indications that something
is amiss include operational inefficiency and failure to grow. The watchful
eyes of outsiders see stagnant results as opportunity — opportunity to acquire
under-valued assets, to purge the business of its inefficiencies, and to reap the
eventual gain. This, of course, characterised the turbulent times of the 1980s
and early 1990s with its corporate raiders, hostile take-overs, and leveraged
buyouts.

Consideration of the market for corporate control moves the discussion
into the realm of corporate finance. Financial markets are crucial. Raiders
look for undervalued assets where the root cause of the depressed value is
inept or unimaginative management. When forgone potential in share price
is detected, a raider reckons that a restructured company — management is

dispensable — along with restructured finances will unleash that potential. The initial problems are identified and the raider's calculation of potential gains is made in light of signals (prices) from the financial market. By borrowing against the value potential that has been identified, the raider draws new finances from that same market.

The mere threat of such aggressive action ought to be enough to keep management firmly focussed on the task of maximising shareholder value. The question is whether it works. The answer would seem to lie in the aftermath of hostile take-overs, the test being whether the value of target firms can be observed to increase following the announcement of the firm being taken over or at least being hotly pursued. Indeed, the evidence is quite clear that target firms do increase in value. Target shareholders on average capture substantial gains from tender offers. However, the bidding firms on average capture no gains, which is somewhat ironic inasmuch as the bidders are the instigators. Regardless, the increased market valuation of the target firm offers evidence in support of the view of an effective market for corporate control.[2]

Finally, in this summary of the outsider or market-based model of corporate governance, there is the relentless influence of the *product* market. In a variant of the better mousetrap theory, one should think of a mousetrap industry with several producing firms. If the management of one firm, Droppings, Inc., becomes lax and produces traps that fail to spring, then Droppings' traps will not sell well in the product market. The firm's share price will drop, leaving the firm a target for take-over. This is simply the mechanics of product competition. Competitive product markets force suppliers to manage quality and costs in order to survive. The role of the product market in corporate governance is to check products continuously. Managerial failure to produce at acceptable quality and cost will trigger corrective and value-restoring action. Investment flows to firms with promising products; investment is withdrawn from the losers.

The outsider model of corporate governance, along with the supporting concepts of the market for managers, the market for corporate control, and the product markets, outlines the institutional structure for the modern capitalist system, especially the part represented by large corporations with widely held equity ownership. To round off this overview, and in anticipation of the discussion of the insider model that follows, it is useful to point to an emerging pattern in corporate shareholding that in some respects contradicts the crucial premise of 'widely held' ownership: namely, the concentrated share holdings of large financial institutions such as pension funds, insurance companies, trusts, and, of course, mutual funds.

The premise of dispersed share ownership has come to imply indifferent, uninformed, and inactive ownership. However, the modern evolution of very large financial institutions with enormous holdings of corporate equities challenges the validity of the assumption of shareholder indifference. In today's major financial institutions, share acquisitions are assessed and managed by knowledgeable, informed professionals. To the extent that professional fund managers share essentially the same information and tend to be like-minded in their investment strategies, the market response to internal corporate developments — as institutions move in or out of the equities market — is likely to be stronger and more rapid than in earlier days. Moreover, institutional managers are becoming more activist and willing to approach management directly on matters of corporate strategy and performance. While closer and more informed relationships between institutional shareholders and corporate management may in fact strengthen corporate governance, the structure of the outsider model shows signs of evolving into something more akin to the insider model to which we now turn.

The Insider Model of Corporate Governance

Throughout much of the world, corporate ownership and control are not separate to the degree that one observes in the United States and the United Kingdom. Indeed, in most countries, ownership and control tend to be tightly paired and closely held by identifiable and cohesive groups of 'insiders' who maintain longer term stable relationships with the company. Insider groups are relatively small, their members are generally known to each other, and they typically have a substantial connection to the firm other than as passive suppliers of capital. With respect to corporate governance and 'managing the mangers', the insider groups in this model of proximity tend to communicate effectively in the process of monitoring the corporate strategy, operations, finances, and performance. As a result, the agency problem that characterises the outsider system is much less important.

The insider model of corporate governance is usually associated with continental Europe and Japan. Among these countries, however, there is substantial variation on the theme. Germany, for example, illustrates the classic bank-centred system. On the other hand, Japan's *keiretsu*, which is discussed at length later, involves a tight matrix of producers and suppliers with substantial industrial connections.

In the German tradition, each industrial firm has a 'house bank' with responsibility for most financial transactions of the company. The relationship between bank and company generally entails a high degree of confidentiality in financial matters, which often extends to secrecy on strategic and operational concerns as well. This institutionalised confidentiality runs counter to the philosophy of outsider regimes that require extensive public disclosure.

A powerful bank, in its role as central financier, supplants the function of financial markets. In Germany, the dominant role of banks in the corporate governance of non-financial industry has likely inhibited the development of capital markets that are a crucial element of the securities-based, disintermediated, outsider model. This is generally reflected in the patterns of equity ownership in countries of the 'outsider' as opposed to the 'insider' countries. For instance, whereas stock market capitalisation is almost two times the gross domestic product (GDP) in the United States and the United Kingdom, the comparable capitalisation-to-GDP multiples are 1.3 for Canada, 1 for Japan, and France, 0.7 for Germany, and 0.6 for Italy.

A distinct feature of the German system of corporate administration is the dual structure of a *supervisory board* and a *management board*. Public and private limited companies with more than 2000 employees are required to establish a supervisory board.[3] With half of its seats allocated to labour, the supervisory board has specific responsibilities for corporate governance including the power to appoint, monitor, and dismiss members of the management board. While the supervisory board is not directly involved in management, it nevertheless has a legal mandate to review investment plans (with power to veto investment projects) and to oversee information sent to shareholders.

Non-labour members of the supervisory board are elected by shareholders. In view of the substantial voting power vested in the firm's house bank, the elected members of supervisory boards often are *de facto* bank appointments. The views of such board members are likely to reflect the interest of banks over the interests of the other (e.g., minority) shareholders. A recent case illustrates the point:

Philip Holzmann, the German construction group saved from insolvency by a government-backed rescue effort, was at the centre of a storm over shareholder rights. In a move that is likely to intensify the debate about corporate governance in Germany and increase pressure to reform the system of close ties between companies and their bank creditors, Holzmann's small shareholders demanded compensation for losses that they suffered in Holzmann's financial restructuring. The small shareholders contend that both Holzmann's chief executive and the supervisory board, which includes membership from Deutsche Bank management, could have acted sooner to stem the company's losses. Moreover, the small shareholders assert that they were entitled to earlier and more detailed information about the financial problems of the group. The distress of Holzmann's angry shareholders points up the inherent weakness in corporate governance owing to interlocking boards and close ties between banks and the companies to whom they lend.

The insider model suffers considerable difficulty in identifying and pursuing goals. In attempting to reconcile the diverse interests of many stakeholders, a company can end up dealing with a conflicting array of performance objectives. In contrast, despite its seeming heartlessness, the outsider model provides the operational advantage of an unambiguous performance criterion — maximum shareholder value.

While Germany illustrates a classic version of the insider model of corporate governance centred on a company's house bank, other countries have systems of ownership/finance/governance with distinct insider characteristics. France, for example, has transformed several large industries from state-owned status to more or less privately owned companies that remain subject to state influence through laws and regulatory approval processes that constrain the firms, especially with respect to industrial decisions that affect employment and employee relations. Moreover, France lacks large domestic institutional investors — to be house banks *à la* Germany or to provide substantial capital for restructuring as in the U.S. and UK — and thus France's transitional form of governance involves inter-company holdings, where related firms keep an eye on each other, and shareholder agreements that formalise industries' responsibilities to their shareholders.

Sweden presents another interesting example of the transition and institutional development in corporate governance. In Sweden, the industrial ownership structure and governance practices of listed companies reflect elements of both the outsider and the insider systems. Swedish financial markets are highly liquid and are supported by a market-oriented legal framework of company law, securities regulations, and disclosure practices. Institutional investors have substantially increased their role in recent years; direct private ownership has dropped from about 70 percent of the market value in the mid 1960s to less than 20 percent today. Approximately one third of the market value is held by foreign investors. However, despite these distinct evolutionary features of a market-based outsider system, the owners of Swedish companies have generally been able to maintain and exercise considerable influence over corporate affairs. This is partly due to the role of intermediary investment companies. These investment companies are themselves listed joint-stock companies that serve as financial intermediaries with minority investments in a few companies that they actively monitor. The informed involvement and professional skill of the managers of these investment companies provide a crucial surveillance function. The ownership function in Sweden is upheld by a system of multiple voting rights that reinforces and concentrates the role of active owners. According to a recent review, the largest owner controlled on average 46 percent of the voting rights of the largest Swedish corporations (Nestor and Thompson 1999). The five largest owners controlled 72 percent of the votes. Sweden's regulations regarding voting rights, coupled with strong protection of minority shareholders, reflect the emphasis that the authorities have placed on enabling active ownership to be established in Swedish corporations.

The Swedish case is especially useful for illustrating the evolution of institutional and market structures that accommodate — or, in some respects, drive — the emergence of new modes of corporate governance. Being relatively small but with various highly successful domestic industries, Sweden's systems of finance and governance are changing internally as its companies focus more on external opportunities. For example, in 1987 ASEA AB of Sweden merged with BBC Brown Boveri Ltd. of Switzerland to form the industrial giant ABB. With ABB stock listed on major stock markets around the world, the requirements for disclosure and to some extent shareholder rights are determined by regulations established in, for example, New York and London. Once a Swedish company has met the most stringent requirements abroad, wherever they may be, the height of the bar is automatically raised in Sweden.

In summary, the industrial history and the level of institutional development in a particular country substantially shapes the insider model of corporate governance in countries where such a model predominates. Nevertheless, as industries grow and forge industrial or financial links abroad, a set of external industrial and institutional forces — most generally under the rubric of 'the international integration of financial markets' — comes into play. Like a child leaving home, the company encounters new and sometimes tougher rules of behaviour that in turn influence corporate governance wherever in the world the firm is, including its home base. Corporate governance in a global setting is tilting toward the outsider model.

Japan

Japan presents an intriguing case in the development of corporate governance systems and illustrates how national idiosyncrasies can establish significant barriers to the international integration of industry.

The ownership and governance of Japanese national industry is characterised by complex interlocking shareholding relationships. While there are variations on this theme, one particular version — the *keiretsu* — has come to typify the seemingly impenetrable system that runs Japanese industry.

A *keiretsu* is essentially an enterprise group. There are horizontal *keiretsu* (across different industries) and vertical *keiretsu* (between a manufacturer and its suppliers along with its wholesale distributors, dealers, and retailers). Central to a *keiretsu* is its 'core' company — either a powerful industrial firm or a 'main bank' — to which all member firms relate in some industrial or financial respect (discussed further below). *Keiretsu* members hold each other's shares, an arrangement that effectively protects each member from hostile take-over. The implicit pooling of risk also tends to relieve members of the short-term exigencies that might otherwise pressure more independent firms to pursue short-term profits at the expense of longer term development.

Experts on industrial systems have never been unanimous on the merits — in terms of productive and economically efficient organisation — of the Japanese way. Critics tended to be relatively quiet in, say, the 1970s and 1980s when Japan achieved impressive growth through increasing technological sophistication, moving to world dominance in a number of select industries such as electronics. More recently, however, the bloom is off the Japanese rose. The real estate collapse of the late 1980s precipitated a more general economic malaise that persists through to the present. There is some question of whether the Japanese system of corporate governance added undue risk to the economy by suppressing the revelation of bad news and thereby delaying constructive action and generally frustrating the flexibility that is crucial to economic recovery.

Such problems come into even sharper relief when one considers the role of Japanese banks and their sometimes smothering relationship with industry. Strong long-term relationships between banks and firms can be a source of strength for Japanese industry. Typically, a firm develops a relationship with a particular bank — its main bank — and relies on its financial support over the long term. The bank not only provides loans to the firm but also holds shares in it. In return, the firm retains the bank for major transactions from which the bank earns profits.

As a facet of corporate governance, the main bank acts as an agent for investors and lenders to the firm, examining the viability of investment projects and monitoring the performance of management. Individual stockholders do not monitor management efforts, and Japanese institutional investors tend not to exercise the kind of monitoring power, such as pressing for higher dividends, that investors exert in the outsider model. Insofar as a main bank takes a long-term view, an industrial firm under its umbrella may be more confident of the funding commitment required for long-term investment projects.

Alas, when industry is closely tied to banks, the difference between a strong, long-term relationship and crony capitalism may be a matter of degree.

Accentuating the negative, Fukao (1999) exposes the inherently weak and precarious relations between banks and industry in modern Japan. Japanese banks hold enormous amounts of the stock of domestic industrial companies. The insidious point is that banks are agents for outside investors while they (the banks) are also owners and creditors in their own right! Although banks are prohibited (by Article 11 of the Antimonopoly Law) from holding more than 5 percent of the outstanding shares of any one domestic company, there is no restriction on the total amount of stock that they may hold. By holding shares of many different companies, the Japanese banks build up very large portfolios of industrial equities.

Jun-Koo Kang and Rene Stulz (1997) examine the stock price performance of Japanese corporations in the period 1990 to 1993. During this time, the typical firm on the Tokyo Stock Exchange lost more than half its value and banks experienced severe adverse shocks. Kang and Stulz discover that firms whose debt involved a higher fraction of bank loans at the start of the period performed significantly worse — their stock prices fell more — than those corporations that relied less on bank loans. Firms that depended more on banks also invested less than other firms during this time. This evidence points to an adverse effect of bank-centred corporate governance, in particular, suffered by firms when their banks experience difficulties.

Banks represent the financial underpinnings of the *keiretsu*. Banks hold shares in order to establish interlocking relationships, thus providing stable shareholders for themselves, and to cement relationships with client companies. The latter motive, which is perhaps most pertinent to the question of the traditional corporate governance of the Japanese industrials, is observed to be waning a bit of late. The large companies that used to be banks' main clients have shifted their capital source from bank borrowings to capital markets. Relationships with banks are not as strong as they once were. Indeed, Fukao

(1999) reports that declines in large companies' borrowings from banks have caused a significant shift toward smaller businesses in banks' loan portfolios.

The apparent trend in Japan away from *keiretsu* structured around main banks represents a shift from a governance structure historically based on institutions to arrangements that are shaped more by markets. The initiative for the change seems to lie less with the banks and more with the industrials. Indeed, banks are reluctant to sell shares of their interlocked industrial partners because they would likely lose a banking customer while definitely losing capital base.

The unwinding of interlocking shareholding relationships between Japanese banks and industrial companies will move funding of large companies away from bank borrowings in favour of capital markets. In spite of the declining importance of bank borrowings, however, most companies still have a strong desire to maintain tight relationships with a main bank or a small group of core banks. In a survey by the Fuji Research Institute (1993), many industrial firms reported that they expected their main or core banks to provide emergency lending and other assistance in the event of crisis. In exchange for this, industrial companies keep deposits in excess of their operating needs, they concentrate their payments, payrolls and employee transactions with the chosen bank, and they pay high bond-underwriting fees.

These somewhat optimistic expectations perhaps reflect older managers' memory of being bailed out by their banks when they ran into trouble in the past. These days, companies are increasingly developing a more dispassionate attitude toward bank transactions as a new generation of managers takes control, especially as the virtuous cycle of financial market development takes effect — the markets continue to improve as industry makes more demand on them.

In terms of the international dimensions of corporate governance in Japan and the question that motives this review — whether a nation's system of corporate governance creates special difficulties for foreign investors — one might reasonably assume that the complex interlocking industrial and financial structures that govern the domestic players in Japan are mysterious to and impenetrable by outsiders. While Japan's post–World War II economic revival industrial reconstruction involved little inward foreign direct investment, in recent years macroeconomic factors — such as massive trade surpluses and a strong yen — have tended to discourage foreign direct investment. In addition, foreign investors generally found it difficult, costly, and burdensome to establish operations in Japan.

The positive moves of late suggest that the complex interlocking share system is beginning to erode for domestic firms. In time, the general relaxation of the rigidities of the Japanese financial/industrial culture will be relaxed for foreign direct investors as well.

Outsider and Insider Models Compared

Table 12.1 presents a summary of the distinguishing features of the outsider and insider models of corporate governance under several key headings. In this comparative listing, the table highlights the differences between the two systems. As the discussion above illustrates, individual countries moved to one or the other or a blend of the outsider or insider models as a result of specific historical, institutional, and industrial circumstances. Corporate governance is only part of the larger economic and legal context in which firms operate, which include, for example, macroeconomic policy and the degree of competition in the markets for products, technology, capital, and labour. Insofar as a variety of factors affect the governance and decision-making processes of firms, it is reasonable to search for common elements of good governance that span differences among countries and provide guidance to countries intent on developing legal, institutional, and regulatory policies consistent with strong, resourceful, and productive industry.

The Organisation for Economic Co-operation and Development (OECD) (1999) recently released the *OECD Principles of Corporate Governance*, The document focusses on the rights of shareholders, the role of stakeholders in governance, the importance of disclosure and transparency, and the responsibilities of the board.

Principles of corporate governance are evolutionary in nature. A specific and explicit set of principles, such as those issued by the OECD, ought to be reviewed in light of significant changes in circumstances. Nevertheless, as an initiative to guide policy development in a variety of countries with substantially different histories, industrial priorities, and business/government relations, the OECD's principles are usefully focussed, albeit remarkably measured. Most importantly, they recognise that to remain competitive, corporations must innovate and adapt their governance structures so as to meet new demands and to grasp new opportunities, especially in a world in which some markets — such as financial markets — develop more rapidly and with greater complexity than others. Similarly, governments have the responsibility to shape an effective regulatory framework with sufficient flexibility to allow markets to function effectively and to respond to the expectations of shareholders and other stakeholders. It is up to governments

Table 12.1 The Outsider and the Insider Models of Corporate Governance Compared

	Outsider	Insider
Ownership	• Providers of equity finance play dominant role in business and economic life • Generally large	• Power concentrated within families, bank, and government • Tend to be small to medium sized
Primary source of finance	• Widely held with emphasis on equity held by financial institutions	• Closely held with emphasis on retained earnings and debt as source of finance
Performance evaluation	• Short term • Emphasis on value creation • Predominantly 'financial' thinking based on achievement of growth/profit	• Long term • Emphasis on development of company and industry over the long term
Primary accountability	• To company shareholders • Command and control	• To broadly defined groups of stakeholders
Decision-making style	• Focussed with directors of corporation	• Collective achievement/ consensus
Level and type of external communication	• Disclosure • Substantial accountability and scrutiny; disclosure in detail concerning financial performance and strategy	• Little disclosure • Incomplete picture provided to select group of insiders and financial institutions

and industry broadly defined to decide how to apply the fundamental principles of corporate governance — a commitment to efficiency, responsibility, and security while in pursuit of innovation and growth — in developing their own frameworks for corporate governance, taking into account the costs and benefits of regulation.

As this chapter has stressed, the degree to which corporations observe basic principles of corporate governance is an increasingly important factor for investment decisions. Of particular relevance is the relation between corporate governance practices and the increasingly international character of investment. Companies can draw finances from a world market for capital, or capital — along with technology and management skill — moves across borders to enhance growth wherever it goes, usually to sites that offer legal, regulatory, and market-oriented policies consistent with good corporate governance. If countries are to enjoy the full benefit of being part of an integrated world economy, both as an attractive site for in-bound investment and as a home of market-expanding outward investment, corporate governance must be well understood and credible across borders.

Conclusions and a Long-Range Prediction

Ultimately, a review — even a brief, selective review — of a system in evolution demands prognostication. Where is the system going? What is the best guess of the future course of corporate governance? How will the world's industry be governed at the end of the twenty-first century?

Most signs point to increasing reliance on the outsider market-based system along with continued refinement of that system. And for good reason. The benefits that individual nations derive — in terms of investment, technology, employment, income, exports, growth — from international economic integration come with a corresponding institutional imperative. That imperative, a commitment to market principles, is more reflective of what we have described as the outsider model than the insider version.

Institutional initiatives everywhere are pushing in that direction. Almost every multilateral institution with an involvement in economic affairs, including the OECD, the International Monetary Fund, the World Trade Organisation, and the G7, endorses the principles of transparency, enforceable contracts, and the rule of commercial law. Competition law universally calls for less embrace, more arm's length. To the extent that the world's industry adopts 'standards' in business, such as for accounting and disclosure and onward to product quality and managerial best practice, such standards will inform and shape a more or less common corporate ideology consistent with the outsider model of corporate governance. The international standardisation of the rules and tools of business is the industrial side of 'deeper' integration, an expression in the argot of international politics.

There is also a techno-managerial class emerging from business and technical schools. Trained managers learn the same lessons concerning the objective of maximising shareholder value along with the importance of retaining flexibility in all matters of production and finance that prevails against the constraining rigidity of the insider system.

There is real impetus from international industrial reorganisation. The volume and value of international corporate mergers are growing exponentially — 20-fold in the past 10 years. At some point soon international mergers will cease to be viewed as novel phenomena. They will be the norm. While corporate governance may persist as problematic, the types of problems will not differ substantially among nations as they do today, e.g., insider problems in one place, outsider problems in another.

Perhaps one industry serves as a harbinger. The US$1.1 trillion global automobile industry represents an industrial organisation shaped by market forces more powerful than the provincial interests of any one particular place. The industry is mature, consisting essentially of one product, one technology, and one market. The pairing of the players — DaimlerChrysler, General Motors and Fiat, Nissan-Renault, etc., surely to be followed by other alliances — suggests a truly stateless industry. While each new merger reflects the pursuit of production and marketing efficiency, the process as a whole underscores the role of the product market in good corporate governance.

It is not surprising that the same type of international industrial consolidation — and a corresponding convergence of governance — is occurring in the aircraft industry as reflected in Airbus Industrie linking up with Mitsubishi or Boeing's close ties with a number of Japanese aerospace manufacturers. An airplane, it would seem, is merely a car with wings.

Similar motives for production efficiencies, marketing synergies, and co-ordinated research and development are spurring global industrial reorganisation and cross-border corporate consolidation in banking, electronics, entertainment, telecommunications, pharmaceuticals, and petrochemicals. In each case, an international corporate merger gives two thrusts in the direction of the outsider or market model of corporate governance. First, almost every new corporate relationship comes to be governed by the rules and regulations of the more commercially liberal, more market-oriented side of the deal. The common ground for governance is in the light, not in the shadow. Second, a corporate suitor or prospective partner to an international merger that comes from an insider system will find that the intimate associations that it enjoys domestically — co-ordinated by the house or main bank or *keiretsu* or even the home government — cannot be extended abroad to a new partner or to another country. This further suggests that foreign direct investment from a country with the insider system to a country with an outsider system — for example, Honda setting up in the U.S. or Bayer entering the UK — requires the (newly transnational) firm to commit to greater disclosure via international standards of accounting and disclosure. This has perhaps its greatest impact in financial dealings such as share exchanges, securities issues in New York or London, cross-border listings, and so on, wherein extensive standardised disclosure is not merely *de rigueur* but *de règle*.

Within individual countries currently characterised by the insider system, corporate governance likewise appears to be moving in a direction of something akin to the outsider structure. The path of change is less direct than that suggested above for the governance of transnational enterprise. While domestic institutions, customs, laws, and regulations change rather slowly, change is occurring nonetheless. The issue is not whether the world of commerce is being enveloped in a *Pax Americana* but whether certain common fundamental aspects of business — and corporate governance — are likely to emerge in all countries. Paul Halpern (1999), for example, does not foresee corporate governance systems designed by a template but rather anticipates what might be termed the 'functional convergence' of corporate governance:

> Convergence will require changes in ownership structures, a relaxation of cultural constraints on certain types of behaviour and development of markets that require very basic changes in financial systems. We can expect convergence in decisions intended to improve markets, to improve monitoring for the benefit of shareholders and directly to improve operations that will lead to better financial performance of relevance to shareholders. Therefore we anticipate changes to occur in the companies in countries with bank-based governance systems leading to a convergence of corporate structure and managerial decisions and less so in governance systems.

If this view is correct, corporate behaviour, as opposed to corporate governing systems *per se*, is becoming increasingly similar in functionally important respects — in terms of responsible and responsive decisions on the part of management — especially as a result of the strong disciplining forces of internationally integrated financial markets and competition in product markets.

Does it all matter, this international institutionalisation of *laissez-faire* and the seemingly inexorable world homogenisation of business and corporate governance? What does it imply for a nation's sovereignty over its industry and especially the rather mixed attitudes to international investment?

Several years ago, in a pair of provocative articles entitled 'Who Is Us?' and 'Who Is Them?', Robert Reich (1990, 1991) made the compelling case that a nation's economic gain from business does not necessarily require that the nation own the business. Likewise, we might add, the security of a nation's economic gain from international business does not require the nation to protect its interests by direct control of industry *per se* but rather through strong and enforceable commercial, corporate, and contract law.

In a more recent book, the popular *The Lexus and the Olive Tree*, Thomas Friedman (1999) puts the economic and cultural integration of nations into a context that, when applied to the theme of this review, suggests that the emergence of one system of corporate governance is the only logical prediction. The title of Friedman's book reflects the new and the technological juxtaposed with the old and the traditional. In 1992, while on assignment for the *New York Times*, Friedman visited the Lexus factory south of Tokyo and marvelled at robots that assembled cars with minimal human supervision. Later, on the bullet train to Tokyo, he read about the Middle East conflict and the age-old feuds about who owned the rights to which particular patch of land and which olive trees. Olive trees are important, he writes, 'they represent everything that roots us, anchors us, identifies us and locates us in this world ... At worst, though, when taken to excess, an obsession with our olive trees leads us to forge identities, bonds and communities based on the exclusion of others' (p. 27).

The challenge facing the world is to find the proper balance between the forces of globalisation — the Lexus — and the more traditional impulses — the olive tree. With respect to corporate governance, the forces that are moving us inexorably toward a market-based system for controlling industry do not do so by grand design, but they are moving us in a predictable direction nonetheless. National, social, political, and insider corporate interests will shape the outcome. But they will not deny it.

Notes

1   Furthermore, the conflicts are not restricted to management vis-à-vis disparate shareholders. Interested and vulnerable stakeholders also include workers, suppliers, and consumers.
2   For an excellent review of the theory and empirical evidence of corporate mergers and acquisitions, see Hirshleifer (1995).
3   As required by the *Codetermination Act* of 1976, German companies with fewer than 2000 but more than 500 employees have a supervisory board with one third of the members allocated to labour. Firms with fewer than 500 employees are not required to have a supervisory board.

References

Friedman, Thomas L. (1999), *The Lexus and the Olive Tree*, Farrar, Strauss, & Giroux, New York.
Fuji Research Institute (1993), *Survey of the Main Bank System and Interlocking Shareholding Relationships*, Fuji Bank, Tokyo.
Fukao, Mitsuhiro (1999), 'Japanese Instability and Weaknesses in the Corporate Governance Structure', Paper presented to the Organisation for Economic Co-operation and Development Conference on 'Corporate Governance in Asia: A Comparative Perspective', Seoul, Korea, 3–5 March.
Halpern, Paul J. (1999), 'Systemic Perspectives of Corporate Governance Systems', University of Toronto, mimeographed.
Hirshleifer, David (1995), 'Mergers and Acquisitions: Strategic and Informational Issues', in Robert A. Jarrow, V. Maksimovic, and W. T. Zeimba (eds.), *Finance*, Handbooks in Operations and Management Science, vol. 9, North-Holland Elsevier, Amsterdam, pp. 838–886.
Kang, Jun-Koo, and Rene Stulz (1997). 'Is Bank-centred Corporate Governance Worth It?', Ohio State University, mimeographed.
Nestor, Stilpon, and John Thompson (1999), 'Corporate Governance Patterns in OECD Economics: Is Convergence Under Way?', Paper presented to the Organisation for Economic Co-operation and Development Conference on 'Corporate Governance in Asia: A Comparative Perspective', Seoul, Korea, 3–5 March.
Organisation for Economic Co-operation and Development (1999). *OECD Principles of Corporate Governance*, Organisation for Economic Co-operation and Development, Paris, <www.oecd.org//daf/governance/principles.htm> (September 2000).
Reich, Robert B. (1990), 'Who Is Us?', *Harvard Business Review*, vol. 68, no. 1, pp. 53–64.
Reich, Robert B. (1991), 'Who Is Them?', *Harvard Business Review*, vol. 69, no. 2, pp. 77–88.

13 Creating Sustainable Global Governance

PIERRE MARC JOHNSON[1]

If people, especially young people, say unemployment is too high, they are right. If unions want better wages and conditions for working people, they are right. If environmentalists say that growth must be sustainable — and not destroy the planet's ecological balance — they are right. When developing countries say they are not getting fair access and economic justice, they too are absolutely right.

Mike Moore, Director General, World Trade Organization
29 November 1999

Introduction

These words, pronounced by Mike Moore on the eve of the World Trade Organization (WTO) ministerial meeting in Seattle in November 1999, were almost an advance warning of the tumultuous events that would take place in the days to follow. Seattle saw major groups of global civil society converging, and in the case of the most articulate, demanding democracy, transparency, and a new consideration for environmental and developmental issues. To paraphrase Alexander Dubcek, civil society was asking for 'globalization with a human face' (United Nations Development Programme [UNDP] 1999, p.1). Their message was clear: Let us get on board, or we will block the train. The events in Seattle almost derailed the train, and it has travelled at a considerably slower pace since. Officials and analysts attending the Davos World Economic Forum and the Bangkok United Nations Conference on Trade and Development (UNCTAD X) in early 2000 struggled to find new strategies for the train to regain its pre-Seattle speed.

Globalisation came to a crossroads in Seattle. Either the globalisation agenda will now be broadened from its almost exclusive focus on trade and financial issues to include human and sustainable development, or it will face increasing hostility from civil society and developing countries. Such hostility

245

246 Guiding Global Order

will continue to be a drag on commercial and financial globalisation as it is expressed in international fora and will result in diminishing political support for trade and financial liberalisation at the domestic and local levels. The lesson from Seattle may be that continuing on the current course could well lead to a halt in trade liberalisation and a return to regionalism and protectionism, with a considerable negative impact on the world economy, and on the broader human values it sustains.

The post-Seattle situation raises fundamental questions about global governance. At the same time, it opens new windows of opportunity for defining innovative governance structures. Governance can be defined broadly as a 'framework of rules, institutions and established practices that set limitations and give incentives for the behaviour of individuals, organisations and firms' (UNDP 1999, p. 8) and, one should add, the governments of nation-states. Never has the need to reconcile the trade and non-trade agendas of globalisation been felt with such urgency. It is clear that the WTO was not designed to deal with such dramatic changes on its own and therefore cannot address these new challenges in isolation. New approaches to governance are needed that include the WTO but that go beyond it.

This chapter develops the case for these new approaches and identifies some of their key features. It first analyses the multiple facets of globalisation and identifies the ensuing tensions between the trade and non-trade agendas, demonstrating that the North-South divide is not only trade-related but also linked to demographic pressures, natural resources depletion, access to technology, and financial vulnerabilities. Second, it briefly examines the divisions that led to failure in Seattle, with special attention to the need to resolve the trade and environment agendas and co-ordination issues under the WTO governance system. Here it argues that beyond a review of these issues, comprehensive adjustments to the WTO system are required to link it better with the system of Multilateral Environmental Agreements (MEAs) developed over the last 15 years. The third section describes and explores the global governance activities and tools developed outside the WTO system, including issues stemming from various international conventions, covenants, and action plans in the 1990s. The final section explores policy avenues for renewing the North-South bargain and for reconciling globalisation's multiple agendas. Above all, this chapter makes the case for a call to the highest authorities in the G7/8 and G20 to integrate their agendas for trade, finance, the environment, and social globalisation, and to do so in a way that brings these agendas effectively together.

The Multiple Faces of Globalisation: The Diversity of Change²

It is factually wrong to portray globalisation as a new phenomenon. The world has experienced extensive economic and political integration in past centuries. The early sixteenth century and late nineteenth century were, most notably, two 'golden eras' of commerce, characterised by open markets and extensive international trade. The current globalisation process, however, is fundamentally different in its scope, depth, and institutional characteristics. The process of economic integration today is truly global, as well as multidimensional. It is market-based, driven by powerful economic forces, and accelerated by a technological revolution. It is also supported and shaped by an extensive web of international organisations and rules, both formal and informal, public and private.

The Growth of Trade

The last 50 years have seen unprecedented economic growth, with considerable impacts on societies around the world:
- Global gross domestic product (GDP) multiplied more than six times in real terms between 1950 and 2000, while per capita GDP expanded almost three times.
- During the same period, international trade multiplied more than 14 times.
- In 1998, international trade represented 14 percent of the world GDP (US$39 300 billion), compared to only 6 percent in 1950.
- In the decade from 1987 to 1997, the share of trade in global GDP jumped from 10 percent to 15 percent. This trend was dampened only in 1998 by the onset of the Asian crisis.
- Trade currently represents 19 percent of the GDP of countries that are members of the Organisation for Economic Co-operation and Development (OECD) and 40 percent of Canada's, the smallest G7/8 member.
- The trade share of Canada's GDP increased by 56 percent over the 12 years leading up to 1999.
- In the United States, the G7/8's largest member, exports accounted for more than a quarter of economic growth and the creation of 20 million jobs in the ten years leading up to 1999.

The stakes in ensuring a rules-based, predictable, multilateral, open-trade regime for Canada and many other G7/8 and OECD countries are thus simply overwhelming. International trade does not, however, always lead to international development. For example, sub-Saharan countries export

30 percent of their combined GDP, yet this brings few benefits as debt-servicing costs absorb all these hard-currency revenues. As a result, these countries continue to be among the world's poorest. Trade can definitely be one engine of economic growth, but other factors are necessary to translate this economic activity into development.

The Explosion of Mobile Capital

A second economic driver of globalisation is the world-wide explosion of financial flows. In 1970, US$10 to US$20 billion were exchanged every day in the world's currency market. Today, more than US$1500 billion changes hands daily (UNDP 1999, p.1). Financial markets are characterised by the anonymity and the non-accountability of many actors involved in these massive flows and almost unlimited instantaneous transactions; many financial actors can elude state control by using powerful technologies. This new situation has considerable influence on both national and global governance as financial markets have become more and more difficult to regulate.

The increasing volume and speed of transactions have also increased the volatility of capital flows in the international financial system.[3] The Asian financial crisis demonstrated the devastating impact of this volatility on world trade and domestic economies. In 1996, net capital flows into Indonesia, Korea, Malaysia, the Philippines, and Thailand totalled US$93 billion. In 1997, these countries faced a net outflow of US$12 billion. This swing in financial flows of US$105 billion represents 11 percent of their combined GDP. As a result, real wages fell by 40 percent to 60 percent and 13 million people lost their jobs. The proportion of poor people in Indonesia rose from 11 percent to 40 percent in less than a year, feeding social and political instability. The international financial community mobilised more than US$170 billion from 1997 to 1999, which stabilised the financial markets in these countries as well as those of Russia and Brazil and apparently averted a similar situation in other countries (Kaiser, Kirton, and Daniels 2000). Economic growth in developing countries fell to 2 percent in 1997 and 1998 as a result of the crisis. World trade growth collapsed from 10 percent in 1997 to 3.7 percent in 1998.

Foreign Direct Investment (FDI), the other major component of financial flows, has grown faster than international trade in recent years. It has thus become an important driver of economic globalisation. Total FDI reached US$644 billion in 1998 — a gain of 39 percent over the previous year — driven by cross-border mergers and acquisitions. The share of FDI inflows to developing countries in 1998 was 42 percent, up from 18 percent in the mid 1980s. However, of the total FDI going to developing countries and Eastern Europe in the 1990s, more than 80 percent went to only 20 countries. More than one quarter went to China alone. In 1998, the top five developing countries received 55 percent of total FDI inflows to the developing world (United Nations Conference on Trade and Development [UNCTAD] 1999c). FDI has considerable impact on economic growth in the countries where it is massively channelled; indeed, FDI has become much more important than Official Development Assistance (ODA) in major developing countries, with obvious structural effects on their economies. At the same time, capital and money markets have demonstrated through their volatility that they can be disruptive and increase the vulnerability of host countries.

Increased Demographic Pressures

The world's population increased almost four-fold in the twentieth century, growing from 1.6 to 6 billion (UNDP 1999). Eighty million people, or the equivalent of Germany, are added to the global population each year. The 'middle scenario' of the United Nations forecasts the world population will grow by 38 percent more in the next 25 years to reach 8.3 billion by 2025. This growth will be concentrated in developing countries. Ninety percent of it will occur in cities. This will put considerable pressure on urban infrastructures, development strategies, the environment, and social stability.

Demographic growth is accompanied by increasing migration. Forty-two million people migrate temporarily for work each year. Six million migrate permanently. World-wide, 130 to 145 million legally registered migrants permanently live outside their own countries at this time. There are four million internal refugees and 15 million external refugees in the world. Globally, the number of international travellers has risen to 590 million every year. These movements of populations are unprecedented in human history. They can contribute to the instability of borders; they also demand tremendous growth to attain increased per capita income. At the same time, they drive the market expansion and increased consumption that is steadily putting pressure on natural resources and ecosystems. All these factors contribute to reciprocal interdependencies, new linkages among groups across borders, and a changing world social fabric.

The Information Revolution

The world is currently witnessing another unprecedented transformation with its development into an information-based society, driven by major technological changes in communications and computers. The number of television sets per 1000 people doubled between 1980 and 1995, from 121 to 235. In 1990, there were 33 billion minutes of international telephone communications; that figure had more than doubled by 1996, reaching 70 billion minutes. The number of computers with a direct connection to the internet rose from 100 000 in 1988 to 36 million in 1998. There were 140 million internet users in 1998. This number will increase to 700 million in 2002. The volume of data traffic on the internet has been doubling every 100 days as the twentieth century gives way to the twenty-first (UNDP 1999).

An unprecedented volume of information and ideas is now circulating in real time, often beyond the reach of direct state control. This has a considerable impact on democracy and governance. It thwarts authoritarian state practices to restrict the free flow of ideas. It also allows for the efficient action of non-governmental organisations through unlimited access to networking, thus facilitating democratic processes at the local and international levels. It also contributes to a wider circulation of knowledge among populations, thus putting pressure on local and national policies.

This technological revolution also has a deep structural effect on the world economy. The internet economy now represents US$300 billion or 5 percent of the American GDP. It generates almost a third of U.S. economic growth and employs 1.2 million workers. The internet sector is now equivalent to the automobile industry in the U.S. in terms of labour force and market. The value of electronic commerce totalled US$2.6 billion in 1996. It may reach, by some accounts, as much as US$300 billion in 2002 (UNDP 1999, p. 60). The share of high-technology products in international trade doubled from 12 percent to 24 percent over the 1990s. Clearly, a new wave in technological and social development has begun.

The Divided World: A New North-South Perspective

These figures on globalisation trends hide an increasingly divided world, where a North-South gulf has taken the place of the traditional East-West divide. The richest fifth of the world's population now controls 86 percent of world GDP and 82 percent of world exports. It is responsible for 92 percent of FDI outflows and receives 68 percent of FDI inflows. The poorest fifth accounts for less than 1 percent of these indicators. Income disparities between the richest and poorest fifths of the world's population increased from 30 to 1 in 1960 to 74 to 1 in 1997.

The World Bank estimates that 1.2 billion people live on less than US$1 a day, a number that is likely to remain stable until 2008 (Wolfensohn 2000). Some 840 million are malnourished world-wide. Since 1971, the number of countries considered by the United Nations to be extremely poor — Less Developed Countries (LDCs) — has risen from 25 to 48. These countries, representing 13 percent of world population, accounted for 0.4 percent of world exports and 0.6 percent of world imports in 1997. This represents a 40 percent decline since 1980. More than 80 countries have seen their per capita GDP fall during the 1990s. Only 33 countries sustained a GNP per capita growth of 3 percent in the 1980–96 period. During the cold war, the developed countries could further their geopolitical and strategic interests by supporting some of the poorest countries. The security interest to do the same in a depolarised world is still ill defined. This has considerable consequences for many of the poorest countries.

In addition, many indicators are announcing a technological or digital divide.[4] The OECD countries, representing 17 percent of world population, have 74 percent of all telephone lines and 88 percent of internet users. In contrast, 25 percent of the world's countries have fewer than 1 telephone for 100 inhabitants. Thailand has more cellular telephones than the entire African continent. The United States has more computers than all other countries combined (UNDP 1999, p. 62). In the high-technology sectors, OECD countries in 1993 accounted for 84 percent of global research and development expenditures and held 97 percent of world patents.

However, global co-operation has succeeded in raising the literacy rate from 64 percent to 76 percent, and access to safe drinking water increased from 40 percent to 72 percent during the 1990s. Food production per capita increased 25 percent over the same period. Economic growth kept pace with rapid demographic growth, as world GDP per capita rose by 1 percent annually in the 1990s. Yet the persisting inequalities are a testimony to the considerable challenge of translating growth into human development. Issues of social equity point to the need for global governance institutions to identify and implement innovative ways of disseminating knowledge and technology, including giving masses access to the powerful instrument of the internet.

The Vertical Loss of Sovereignty: More Room for More New Actors

Nation-states have suffered a vertical loss of power in the globalisation process, mainly as a result of the combination of the fiscal crisis of the state and the internationalisation of governance. The fiscal crisis has produced devolution of power to local authorities while states have also delegated aspects of their sovereignty to international regimes. This process has weakened the state and given prominence to new actors. Most notably, transnational corporations (TNCs)[5] have become the main drivers of FDI and world trade. In 1970, there were about 700 TNCs. In 1998, there were 60 000 TNCs with 500 000 foreign affiliates. TNCs accounted for 25 percent of the world's GDP and one third of world exports in 1997. They have become highly integrated and powerful actors rivalled only by the richest nation-states. General Motors' equivalent GDP of US$164 billion, for example, would place it among the 25 most important economies of the world, ranking between Thailand and Norway. The strength and influence of TNCs is compounded by the concentration of production in many economic sectors. The top ten companies in each sector control 86 percent of the market in telecommunications, 85 percent in pesticides, 70 percent in computers, 60 percent in veterinary medicine, 35 percent in pharmaceuticals, and 32 percent in commercial seeds.

Non-governmental organisations (NGOs) have also become influential actors. They have developed into a highly organised and diversified web of organisations, creating a truly global civil society. There were a mere 176 international NGOs in 1909. By 1993, there were 28 900. Human rights, environmental protection, and human development are all causes advocated by global civil society by way of NGOs. Civil society also plays an important role in education and community capacity-building in developing countries. While TNCs are the drivers and actors of economic globalisation, organised civil society represents the emerging voice of an evolving global democracy.

Although they differ from nation-states as actors in the global system in terms of accountability and responsibility, neither NGOs nor TNCs can be ignored. Their power, influence, and relevance, both at the local and international levels, demand that they be linked into various formal processes of globalisation.

The Environmental Challenge

Increased environmental pressures accompany this change in critical economic and demographic processes. Natural ecosystems are under high stress around the world as a result of increased pollution, natural resource overexploitation, and habitat destruction. Scarcities caused by the exhaustion of natural resources and the destruction of ecosystems pose an enormous challenge to economic growth and development and create serious tensions and displacements of populations.

Freshwater resources are a key component of these overall structural trends. Water withdrawals, mainly for agricultural purposes, grew seven-fold in the twentieth century. One third of the world's population, or 2 billion people in 80 countries, experiences moderate to high water stress. By 2025, two thirds of the world population could be in this situation if nothing is done.[6] Water scarcity, combined with the increased pollution of watercourses, constitutes an imminent threat to human health, food security, and social and political stability, and therefore to development and economic growth. Water scarcity could generate numerous international tensions, since shared international river basins drain 47 percent of the world's lands — excluding Antarctica — and are home to 40 percent of the world's population.

Natural ecosystems that provide essential resources for economic development are under stress everywhere. According to the World Conservation Union, 34 percent of freshwater fish species are threatened with extinction (Baillie and Groombridge 1996), while 6 out of 14 commercial sea fisheries are seriously depleted. Forest ecosystems are also threatened, as 200 million hectares of forest cover was lost between 1980 and 1995. Deforestation affects 12 million hectares annually, an area half the size of the United Kingdom. Desertification — the degradation of agricultural land in arid, semi-arid, and sub-humid territories — is threatening 40 percent of global lands, which are home to more than a billion humans (World Resources Institute *et al.* 1998).

Industrialisation has also affected natural macro systems such as climate and the ozone layer. In 1997, the hole in the ozone layer over Antarctica was twice the size of Europe. The ozone layer might not be restored until 2050. In addition, evidence confirms that global warming is not only a process created by human activities, but also that it has been accelerating in recent years (Intergovernmental Panel on Climate Change 1995). The warmest year ever recorded in modern history was 1998. The ten warmest years in history have been recorded in the 15 years leading up to 1999. The economic costs of implementing the Kyoto protocol commitments to reduce greenhouse gas emissions will be considerable. But weather-related damages have been exploding in recent years, reaching US$92 billion in 1998, a 53 percent increase in only two years (Brown, Renner, and Halweil 1999). The costs of inaction are thus overwhelming.

Economic growth, environmental degradation, and human development are intimately linked, as was recognised at the Earth Summit in 1992. This recognition led the international community to develop a series of international instruments to protect the global environment and promote a sustainable model for globalisation. As noted in a 1999 WTO report on trade and environment, the 'ongoing dismantling of economic borders reinforces the need to cooperate on environmental matters, especially on transboundary and global environmental problems that are beyond the control of any individual nation' (Nordstrom and Vaughan 1999). Accordingly, the rising number of international environmental agreements has paralleled the acceleration of trade liberalisation since 1985. There are currently 216 effective Multilateral Environmental Agreements (MEAs) in the world (Nordstrom and Vaughan 1999, p. 5), with eight major global MEAs signed since 1985.[7] These developments create a new need for consistency in governance. As the centre of world trade governance, the WTO cannot escape this new trade and environment/ development nexus.

The WTO and the Environmental Challenge: Trade and Sustainable Development Can Be Reconciled

Seattle: Confronting the Divisions

In many ways the events of Seattle can be attributed to the convergence of a series of underlying tensions that have characterised world governance since the end of the cold war. While they surely contributed to the tensions, circumstantial causes such as timing, inadequate preparation, U.S. electoral politics, demonstrations, and riots do not explain the Seattle setback. Seattle's failure is rooted in underlying weaknesses in the WTO, such as a lack of transparency, inadequate participation by developing countries, sharp divisions of opinions on the scope of the new round, flawed negotiation procedures, unresolved implementation issues, and conflict over the liberalisation of agricultural markets. The issues at stake are huge: the OECD has estimated that a new round of trade liberalisation would generate annual growth of 3 percent or US$1200 billion in global economic activity (Moore 1999). But the dividends of growth ought to be more fairly shared among the WTO's 135 members. The next round will have to be oriented toward development.

Environmental protection and related competitiveness issues are also fundamental aspects of the multilateral trade liberalisation process. As Esty and Geradin (1998, p. 46) have argued, 'if freer trade is to achieve the full measure of social welfare gain it promises and avoid the allocative inefficiency of environmental market failures, competitiveness concerns must be tackled head on. Moreover, continued public support for trade and investment liberalisation in many parts of the world depends on public confidence that other values about which people care (including environmental protection) are not being sacrificed at the altar of free trade'. The WTO has therefore launched many initiatives to develop a trade liberalisation model that brings a significant environmental dividend and does not foster downward competitive pressures on domestic environmental regulations.

The WTO has invested considerable energy in analysing trade and environment links over the last five years. In 1995, the organisation created the Committee on Trade and Environment, which produced a useful body of work on trade and environment issues and contributed to the development of closer ties with secretariats of MEAs. But the Committee on Trade and Environment was plagued by disagreements over basic principles, and has been unable to produce any concrete recommendations since its creation.

While a comprehensive legal analysis of environment and trade issues at the WTO would be beyond the scope of this chapter, it is essential to take a closer look at some of the core elements of the debate. Several issues pertaining to the consistency of trade and environmental agendas contributed to the Seattle failure and will have to be addressed in the next round of negotiations. Here are key pressures that must be addressed.

Environmental Regulations and Market Access

There is asymmetry between the advanced state of liberalisation of trade in goods and services that is of interest to OECD countries and the barriers to trade that persist for labour-intensive goods exported by developing countries. Commodities — especially food and fibre, and their processed products — that constitute most of developing countries' exports continue to face high barriers to import in OECD countries. In 1992, the Human Development Report estimated the cost for developing countries of these trade restrictions to be US$500 billion annually in lost export revenues, almost ten times the amount those countries receive in aid every year.

While all quantitative restrictions on developing countries' exports of textiles and clothing should be removed by 2005 under the Uruguay Round regime, developing countries will continue to face tariffs as well as non-tariff barriers in the form of standards, regulations, labelling, and other environmental measures. Developing countries have come to consider environmental regulations as disguised protectionist measures designed to restrict access to OECD markets. They also tend to perceive the inclusion of environmental and social protection issues under trade negotiations as threats to their national sovereignty. For these reasons, countries such as India, Brazil, China, and many others repeatedly oppose any discussions on environmental standards in trade liberalisation talks. Clearly, the issues of fair market access and environmental protection cannot be separated because developing countries fear the latter is a threat to the former.

Trade-Related Aspects of Intellectual Property

The Trade-Related Aspects of Intellectual Property (TRIPs) agreement came into force in 1995. This agreement is intended to protect intellectual property and therefore constitutes an important tool for promoting research and development activities, as well as technological innovation. Although each country implements its own regime of intellectual property rights, these regimes are subject to the TRIPs agreement, which imposes minimal standards on patents, copyrights, trademarks, and trade secrets. While TRIPs promises to bring important technological and economic dividends, its implementation poses considerable problems for many developing countries and for the protection of biological diversity.

The TRIPs regime's relationship with the Convention on Biological Diversity is complex and muddled. TRIPs allows, through patenting, for the appropriation by transnational corporations of traditional knowledge and biological or genetic diversity. Yet Article 15 of the Convention focusses on the equitable sharing of benefits of biological diversity and the Convention contains many provisions for protecting indigenous knowledge. TRIPs can also considerably raise the price of technology transfers to developing countries. Private appropriation of contents and knowledge within the TRIPs regime carries the seeds of a future division of the world between the knows and the know-nots, compounding the separation of the haves and have-nots. Many analysts have concluded that modifications to the TRIPs regime are necessary to create a system that gives developing countries access to knowledge and technology and protects biodiversity and traditional knowledge.

The Precautionary Principle and its Relationship with Multilateral Environmental Agreements

The inclusion of the precautionary principle in trade agreements also complicates the reconciliation of trade and environmental agendas. A widely recognised version of this principle states that 'where there are threats of serious or irreversible damage, lack of full scientific certainty shall not be used as a reason for postponing cost-effective measures to prevent environmental degradation' (United Nations General Assembly 1992). It constitutes a powerful preventive tool in the service of environmental protection. Its coherent operationalisation into a rules-based multilateral trade regime remains problematic: the fear that it could serve as an umbrella for a series of disguised protectionist measures is legitimate and must be properly addressed.

The precautionary principle was integrated into the Cartagena Protocol on Biosafety, which was negotiated in Montreal under the Convention on Biological Diversity in January 2000. This integration brings to the forefront the issue of the relationship between MEAs and the WTO. While some instruments such as North American Free Trade Agreement (NAFTA) or the Montreal Protocol on the Protection of the Ozone Layer clearly establish the paramountcy of trade-restricting practices contained in a series of MEAs,[8] the WTO's founding texts remain silent on this issue. The Cartagena protocol, which considers a series of trade issues in the biotechnology sector, has an equal 'and mutually supportive' relationship with trade agreements.[9] This situation could eventually lead to a clash between the trade and environmental regimes in the case of a trade dispute. It is clear that the general relationship between the two regimes will have to be clarified.

Trade-Distorting and Environmentally Damaging Subsidies

The elimination of trade-distorting and environmentally damaging subsidies constitutes a key strategy to link the trade and environment agendas. The United Nations Commission on Sustainable Development has estimated the total amount of these subsidies to be US$1000 billion a year (Runnals 1996, p. 13). For example, subsidies in the world fisheries total US$54 billion annually and provide 20 percent to 25 percent of revenues in this sector, with half of this amount spent in OECD countries (Nordstrom and Vaughn 1999 p. 3). These subsidies contribute to overexploitation of fisheries resources, sometimes to the point of near exhaustion, and constitute distortions to trade that are detrimental to developing countries. It is estimated that the elimination of these subsidies would reduce the world fishing fleet by half and thus allow for the regeneration of endangered fisheries resources. Developing countries would benefit considerably from the massive reduction of OECD countries subsidies in this sector. Significant gains could also be made in such sectors as energy, forestry, nonferrous metals, textiles, and clothing. The politics of subsidies elimination, however, will make it difficult to bring about such rational treatment of the issue.

The elimination of such subsidies would constitute a triple-win strategy: that is, a strategy that has the potential to benefit trade liberalisation, sustainable use of natural resources, and economic development. Such elimination would normally benefit developing countries more than the introduction of new environmental standards or regulations. The 1999 WTO report on trade and the environment identified the elimination of remaining trade barriers on environmental goods, services, and environmental management systems, as well as the reduction of trade-distorting/environmentally damaging subsidies as two key ways the WTO could promote sustainable development (WTO 1999).

Transparency and Participation

Lack of transparency and inadequate representation result in credibility problems, which undermine support for trade liberalisation processes both at the national and international levels. Transparency, effective participation of civil society, and adequate representation of developing countries are fundamental areas in which the WTO has tried to improve its credibility and secure support. While the WTO has made some efforts to expand participation in its work, its actions fell short of an effective strategy to integrate NGOs and intergovernmental organisations (IGOs) — especially MEA secretariats — in its decision-making and dispute resolution processes.

The WTO opens its doors to civil society mostly in the form of informal consultations and improved communications with NGOs and IGOs. However, the core of its work remains strictly intergovernmental in nature and in camera in method. In 1996, the WTO adopted guidelines for the participation of NGOs that focussed on improved communication channels and open meetings such as the Symposia on Trade and Environment. While they were intellectually productive and fostered a fruitful dialogue, the symposia were not policy oriented and no attempt was made to summarise issues or generate consensus. Their influence on negotiation processes was therefore very limited.

The effective participation of developing countries constitutes another challenge. Many do not have the resources to participate in preparatory meetings. The issue of representation is made more acute by the absence of 50 countries that do not have a seat at the WTO, including major trading countries such as China. At its General Council meeting in February 2000, members of the WTO agreed to improve and regularise funding for its technical co-operation activities and to co-operate more actively with other agencies such as UNCTAD to support effective participation by developing countries and facilitate implementation of key trade and investment liberalisation provisions and policies.

The WTO needs to make sustainable development a core part of its agenda. Integrating sustainable development into the WTO's trade disciplines, negotiation groups, and dispute resolution panels remains a considerable challenge. This could mean amending or reopening some treaties and reforming negotiation processes and dispute resolution procedures, as well as welcoming the expertise of new actors from civil society and international organisations.[10] It is now clear that the WTO cannot address the trade and sustainable development relationship alone and will therefore have to co-ordinate more closely with secretariats of MEAs, various UN organisations, and NGOs. Facilitating the presence of developing countries and opening up meaningful channels of substantive communication with NGOs and IGOs is of capital importance for the success of further negotiations.

The Need for Institutional Reform and a New North-South Bargain

Seattle destroyed any hope for a quick start of a new round of multilateral trade liberalisation. Negotiations on agriculture and services resumed in January 2000 without much hope of an early resolution. In February 2000, addressing the UNCTAD X delegates, Moore declared that the WTO would work on a confidence-building agenda in the next few months, recognising that the WTO will need to build the next negotiation round on a new North-South bargain. However, while it can do much to improve its institutional framework, the WTO also needs to broaden its agenda and co-operate with other organisations to work out new integrative governance models that will allow for the reconciliation of trade and non-trade agendas of globalisation. In short, the WTO must elaborate both an in-house plan and a strategy for external presence. Ultimately, the success or failure of the WTO will depend on this reconciliation of trade, environment, and development agendas under a broadened system of global governance. In the words of Moore, the cost of failure could be a stop to the multilateral liberalisation wheel and a return to trade-distorting and development-slowing regionalism.

Links Between Governing Instruments: Charting the Non-Trade World

Trade-accelerating international negotiations have not been accomplished in isolation. Parallel to this activity catering to the prosperity of nations, a large set of international instruments has been developed that responds to other goals and aspirations. These environmental, socioeconomic, and scientific conventions are part of a wider movement to secure balanced development, to ensure stability, and, ultimately, to secure peace. Increased participation by civil society and new governance initiatives are intimately linked to this.

Implementing the 1990s Conferences, Action Plans, and Environmental Conventions

In one of his last interventions before stepping down as the director of the International Monetary Fund (IMF), Michel Camdessus addressed UNCTAD X delegates and called for international mobilisation to implement the action plans of the 1990s United Nations conferences and summits. This important statement recognises the need for active co-operation to raise environmental and social standards and achieve a sustainable globalisation model. The 1990s global summits and conferences were instrumental in reaching consensus on a series of issues related to human and sustainable development, and establishing priorities that were assembled in coherent and extensive action plans. An impressive number of conferences collectively contributed to the articulation of the non-trade agenda for globalisation. These include:

- The World Summit on Children (1990)
- The Conference on Environment and Development (Rio, 1992)
- The Conference on Human Rights (Vienna, 1994)
- The International Conference on Population and Development (Cairo, 1994)
- The World Summit for Social Development (Copenhagen, 1995)
- The World Conference on Women (Beijing, 1995)
- The Global Conference on Human Settlement (Istanbul, 1996)
  Moreover, many MEAs have been concluded in the last 15 years, including:
- The Vienna Convention for the Protection of the Ozone Layer (1985)
- The Montreal Protocol on Substances that Deplete the Ozone Layer (1987)
- The Basel Convention on the Transboundary Movement of Hazardous Waste (1989)
- The Framework Convention on Climate Change (1992)
- The Convention on Biological Diversity (1992)

- The Convention to Combat Desertification in Countries Experiencing Serious Drought and/or Desertification, Particularly in Africa (1994)
- The Kyoto Protocol on Climate Change (1997)
- The Cartagena Protocol on Biosafety (2000)

In addition, instruments have been elaborated in the forests and water sectors.[11]

Most of these multilateral instruments contain common strategies and principles that will have to be fully implemented if their substance is to be given meaning. These strategies include international co-operation, scientific and technological transfers, capacity building, differentiated commitments, and the principle of equity between developed and developing countries.

International Co-operation: The Need to Co-ordinate Among Institutions

Institutional co-ordination is of particular importance, given the growing number of international instruments and organisations world-wide. In the words of Klaus Toepfer (1999, p. 1), 'the development of conventions and action plans, in particular, has been incremental, rather than strategic. It has not been based on an over-arching blueprint for the evolution of international law and institutions into the 21st century. Meanwhile, environmental problems and their solutions are becoming ever more complex and interlinked. A more coherent strategy is needed for policy making, scientific and technical assessment, and programming. In the current circumstances, one of the essential steps that can now be taken to advance the international environmental regime is to strengthen collaboration among the relevant agencies and conventions. Joining together is essential to ensuring that the voice of the environment is not drowned out in the debate over development, trade, and social issues. It is also vital to maintaining momentum and getting the most out of our scarce resources'.

Agenda 21 had already recognised this situation in 1992 by advocating better co-ordination of UN development and environment agencies in its section on international institutional arrangements (United Nations Conference on Environment and Development 1992). MEA secretariats and UN agencies have begun intensifying their collaboration through joint initiatives and joint-implementation programs. For example, the secretariats of the Convention of Biological Diversity and the Ramsar Convention on Wetlands have developed joint initiatives and action plans in the last two years. The United Nations Environmental Programme (UNEP) organised nine informal meetings of MEA secretariats between 1994 and 2000. In addition, UNEP is supporting joint implementation and co-ordinated reporting activities in developing countries to facilitate the implementation of MEA commitments.

Another important aspect of institutional co-ordination is the articulation of an integrated environmental position to serve as an input to the WTO's trade regime. UNEP has also developed an agreement between MEA secretariats and the WTO. It has been examining possibilities to establish an environmental database at the WTO to avoid conflicts between the two regimes. While the WTO administers 24 multilateral trade agreements in a centralised fashion, the environmental field is characterised by a fragmented structure. Some, such as Renato Ruggiero, former director of the WTO, have argued for the creation of a world environmental organisation that would act as a counterpart to the WTO. Fearing that the creation of a new organisation would contribute to more fragmentation — as it would simply be added on to existing structures — and that the structure of a new intergovernmental organisation would not be productive and efficient, the World Conservation Union and the International Institute for Sustainable Development have proposed the creation of the Standing Conference on Trade and the Environment.

This conference would be an open forum that would allow for the full participation of IGOs, NGOs, MEAs, International Financial Institutions (IFIs), and nation-states. Its mandate would be to articulate environmental policy as it relates to trade and to enter into a permanent dialogue with the WTO. The conference's influence would derive from its large representation and from the implementing capabilities of its member organisations. The World Conservation Union and the International Institute for Sustainable Development thus support the creation of a powerful and well co-ordinated forum that would allow energies and resources to cumulate effectively.[12]

Scientific and technological transfers Scientific knowledge transfers are promoted throughout international action plans, often discussed in both capacity-building and technological-transfer measures. Spreading knowledge is key to economic development, especially in light of the transition to an information-based economy and of the looming digital divide. As noted in the UNCTAD X (1999b, p. 27) report of the Secretary General, 'in a world economy in which knowledge is the critical component of economic success, countries without the skills to manipulate knowledge-based processes and to benefit from changes in technology fall behind even when the world economy grows vigorously'.

Technological transfer is another related strategy for sustainable development, especially in the area of environmentally friendly technologies.

UNCTAD X stressed that there needs to be a better understanding of the various channels for transfers of technology, such as FDI and trade. This position highlights the intimate relationship between the implementation of technology-transfer commitments on one side, and various provisions of the trade and investment regimes on the other. The international community is just beginning to address these links in order to facilitate technology transfers.

Capacity building Under most UN action plans and instruments, developing countries are to be given the financial resources, technologies, and institutional capacity to achieve the essential and complementary goals of economic development and environmental protection. This implies a series of technological and financial transfers, as well as sharing knowledge on environmental management strategies. A World Resources Institute study on the forestry sector has demonstrated that trade liberalisation should be accompanied by capacity-building strategies to strengthen the framework for environmental protection. UNEP and UNCTAD recently launched a joint program to integrate trade and environment policies in developing countries. A major part of this program will consist of capacity-building activities such as training sessions, seminars, and workshops designed to teach policymakers, civil servants, and private-sector actors how to maintain essential resources and maximise benefits of increased trade.

Differentiated commitments The action plans developed by MEAs and UN conferences contain common but differentiated commitments for developed and developing countries. For example, under the Kyoto protocol, developed countries have agreed to substantial reductions in greenhouse gas emissions, while developing countries did not — reflecting a traditional approach of the G77. On the other side, developing countries must bear most of the costs of adaptation to climate change, and developed countries have the obligation under the Convention on Climate Change to co-operate with them to facilitate adaptation. In all negotiated agreements since Rio, developing countries asked developed countries to commit to the transfer of new and additional financial resources to support them in the implementation of these conventions.

Common but differentiated commitments are a fundamental principle of environmental regimes, a reality that trade regimes also take into account. But the establishment of different statuses under some agreements at times leads to North-South conflict. For example, the United States has been pressuring developing countries such as India and China to take a stiffer stance on air emissions reduction commitments under the Kyoto protocol.

Competitiveness and development issues are often closely related to these conflicts. As a result, differentiated commitments must be co-ordinated with trade provisions, development co-operation activities, and development assistance programs.

Equitable sharing of benefits Issues of equity are fundamental in all major international instruments. In the regime of the Convention on Biological Diversity, the equitable sharing of benefits of biological diversity constitutes an essential part of the bargain. Developed countries are given access to developing countries' biological and genetic resources, in exchange for which they agree to share equitably the benefits of commercial and non-commercial use of these resources. This principle is a central component of North-South relations, but its operationalisation constitutes a demanding challenge as it often implies a transfer of obligations to the private sector. It is also difficult to reconcile this principle with the WTO's TRIPs agreement. Equitable sharing of benefits is likely to be integrated into the WTO's next round of negotiations and become one of the items that will underpin a new North-South bargain.

From Official Development Assistance to an Integrated Approach to Financial Transfers

In the current globalisation process, it has become clear that the traditional ODA model cannot fulfil its promise of development. More innovative strategies must be employed. In the words of Kanbur and Sandler (1998, p. 15), 'the aid delivery system of the last 50 years needs a change. It faces two challenges at the dawn of a new century. The first is disenchantment with conventional country-focused assistance, based on the perceived failure of that aid in fulfilling the objectives of economic growth, development, and poverty reduction. The second is the rise of transnational problems as major factors in global relations and the very process of development'. Before outlining new strategies for the integration of development financing policies, it is useful to look at the current situation of financial transfers to developing countries.

Official Development Assistance and other financial transfers Total ODA fell to US$49.6 billion in 1997, down from a 1992 high of US$65 billion. In real terms, this constitutes a 30 percent reduction. The share of ODA in the GDP of donor countries has fallen to 0.22 percent in 1997, below the 0.33 percent average maintained in the 1970s and 1980s, and well under the OECD countries' commitment to allocate 0.7 percent of their GDP to ODA, of which 0.2 percent should go to the Less Developed Countries (LDCs). Currently, total ODA is US$20 billion less than it would have been if this average level had been maintained (OECD 2000). On the positive side, the part of ODA that is 'tied aid' — that is, bilateral aid conditional on securing procurements from the donor country — has fallen from 50 percent of total ODA in 1979 to 20 percent in 1996, thus allowing for an allocation of resources increasingly driven by the domestic priorities of recipient countries. About three fifths of current aid volume is bilateral and two fifths is multilateral. The World Bank has estimated that the current volume of aid can lift 10 million people out of poverty every year.

While ODA had been reduced in the 1990s as a result of fiscal crisis, investment flows have undergone impressive growth in recent years as a consequence of financial market liberalisation. In 1990, total flows from developed to developing countries totalled US$100 billion, of which 57 percent was traditional official development assistance. In 1996, these flows had grown to US$338 billion, of which $299 billion came from private investment (Botchwey 2000). By 1998, private capital flows were five times higher than ODA (Global Environment Facility 1998). Clearly, private investment has become the most important source of financial transfers to developing countries.

Debt-relief initiatives The LDCs' external debt burden amounts to 90 percent of their combined GDP. Debt servicing consumes an important share of their export revenues and state budget. Tanzania spends nine times more on debt servicing than on health care, and four times more than on education (UNCTAD 1999b, p. 15). In doing so, it sacrifices investment in human resources, which are the basis for future growth and development. In 1996, the World Bank and the IMF launched a special initiative for 41 Highly Indebted Poor Countries (HIPCs), of which 33 are African. At the 1999 G7/8 Köln Summit, this initiative was taken further by broadening admissibility, accelerating the pace of debt relief, and linking debt relief more closely to poverty alleviation. It could still be improved; the international community has shown its ability in the case of the Asian crisis to act decisively when the need arises.

Special needs of Less Developed Countries The share of ODA going to LDCs fell from 33 percent in 1995 to 24 percent in 1997. For 14 out of 21 OECD donor countries, ODA to these countries was lower in 1996 than it was in 1990 (UNCTAD 1999b, pp. 22–23). A UN conference on LDCs is to be held in Brussels in 2001. Many development analysts argue that ODA should be targeted at LDCs. The WTO's February 2000 General Council adopted a package of measures to assist these countries with the objective of developing an integrated approach by all donors and international agencies. But many analysts argue that the largest potential gains for LDCs lie not in improved ODA but in better market access. Reflecting this view, Moore put forward a proposal for duty-free and quota-free market access for the 48 LDCs to attract foreign investment and sustain their economic development. Similarly, in Seattle, the European Union proposed free access to essentially all products from LDCs but failed to reach consensus with Japan, Canada, and the United States, which wanted to exclude textiles from the deal.

The financing for development initiative The United Nations will hold the Global Conference on Financing for Development in 2001. Representatives from nation-states, Bretton Woods institutions, UN agencies, NGOs, and the private sector will attend. They will consider domestic financial resources, international resources (including FDI and other private flows), and international financial co-operation (including ODA and debt relief). Special attention will be given to the needs of African countries, LDCs, and small island states. The conference will aim at improving the coherence and consistency of the international monetary, financial, and trade regimes. To achieve this goal, it will consider market access, governance, and innovative sources of funding. The conference will for the first time address financial transfers in a broad and integrative manner, thereby constituting a unique opportunity to define new avenues for future financial structures designed to support non-trade agendas of globalisation.

Good Governance

Trade and economic growth are more likely to promote sustainable and human development if they are backed by appropriate governance policies. As mentioned in the UNCTAD X (2000, p. 5) action plan, 'Democracy, rule of law, transparent and accountable governance and administration, including combating and eliminating corruption, are indispensable foundations for the realization of people-centred sustainable development'. A WTO study has similarly concluded that accountability and good governance are critical variables that condition the impact of trade (Nordstrom and Vaughan 1999, p. 52).

Good governance is, for example, important to drawing in foreign investment. FDI is attracted by sound policies that allow for long-term predictability and stability, such as strong property rights, low levels of corruption, openness to foreign trade and investment, and macroeconomic stability. The development of policies that maximise the impact of foreign direct investment in terms of knowledge and skills development, and access to technologies, is also of key importance.

The articulation of national and international policies is another important aspect of good governance. As mentioned in the UNCTAD (1999a, p. 7) report on economic governance, 'a capacity-building approach focusses attention on the importance of reconciling the task of institution-building at the national level and the challenge of constructing governance institutions at the global level'. This is especially true for the multilateral trade regime as the 'effective operation of the WTO regime depends on encouraging and strengthening the growth of organizational capacities at the national level'. The way in which trade and environmental policies are articulated at the domestic level is also important to achieving sustainable economic development. Particular attention should be given to interdepartmental co-ordination within countries and to environmental reviews of trade agreements.

Good governance also entails fighting corruption and organised crime. This is not an easy task, as international crime syndicates generate US$1500 billion in revenues annually (UNDP 1999, p. 42). Many have argued for an international convention on international organised crime. Such an instrument could include provisions to support developing countries that wish to combat corruption and crime and to raise transparency standards. It is becoming clear that repressive measures alone cannot succeed in eliminating this growing problem. Efforts are increasingly needed to address this part of the informal economy.

New Responses to World-wide Governance Issues

Rubens Ricupero (2000), Secretary General of UNCTAD, presented UNCTAD X, where 190 countries were represented, as a kind of 'world parliament' where the post-Seattle 'healing process' was to begin. But North-South divisions were still very apparent in February 2000. Developed countries made it clear that they would refuse to strike a trade-oriented deal outside the WTO system, while developing countries showed hostility and cynicism toward the WTO. Moreover, OECD countries' top officials did not show up in Bangkok, highlighting the organisation's lack of support among developed countries. Consequently, Supachai Panitchpakdi, Thailand's deputy prime minister and chair of UNCTAD X, and designated successor to Mike Moore as the WTO's director in 2002, abandoned plans to convene an informal meeting of trade ministers. In his closing statement, Ricupero said that UNCTAD X had been 'instrumental in creating an atmosphere of greater mutual understanding of the complexities of the globalization process. But much remains to be done in translating this into practical moves for institutional change at the international level' (p. 7).

Many actors share the view that institutional change and new governance structures are needed to promote sustainable and human development in an increasingly integrated and complex world. The current governance system suffers from a lack of clear jurisdictions, insufficient participation, and transparency, as well as from incoherence and lack of co-ordination. It also faces the persistent issue of the non-accountability of UN and UN-related bureaucracies. The 1999 Human Development Report prepared by the United Nations Development Programme, has tried to answer some of these problems by putting forward an ambitious plan to reform the international governance architecture.

Others argue that appropriate institutional structures are already in place but that they lack openness and proper co-ordination mechanisms. Opening existing institutions and creating new fora that would foster synergies within current structures are strategies that may have a better chance of success in the near term. Before resigning as IMF managing director, Camdessus called for the creation of a G30 summit, uniting the heads of states that sit as executive directors on the boards of the World Bank and IMF, and the Bretton Woods institutions and various UN agencies.

The recently created G20 brings together 18 countries (including the G7/8 and major developing countries), the Bretton Woods institutions, and the European Union (see Chapter 9). It is a promising organisation that could play a significant role in global governance. The G20 represents about 80 percent of world GDP and 65 percent of the world population, giving it considerable potential influence. As is the case for the G7/8, the G20 is the responsibility of the economic and finance departments of represented countries, a key feature that gives it special strength and influence. Its mandate focusses on good governance in financial markets and the reduction of vulnerability to international financial crises. But Paul Martin, Canada's finance minister and chair of the G20, has stressed the flexible and comprehensive mandate of the group: 'There is virtually no major aspect of the global economy or international financial system that will be outside of the group's purview' (Finance Canada 1999). The G20 will expand its focus and consider poverty reduction strategies at its next meeting in Canada in the autumn of 2000.

A New Deal for Globalisation: Mapping an Integrated Agenda for Policymakers

In a keynote address at the WTO High-Level Symposium on Trade and Environment in March 1999, UNEP's executive director Klaus Toepfer stressed 'that trade and environment policy cannot be isolated from the impact of international debt, the need to alleviate poverty, the equitable imperative to transfer technology, or the need to enhance capacity of developing countries to face the challenges of sustainable development' (International Institute for Sustainable Development 1999, p. 2). The UNCTAD X (1999b, p. 19) report also insisted that there was an 'urgent need to rethink the processes, mechanisms and policies that underpin the functioning of the world economy, and in particular those that link developing countries to the forces of globalization'. These statements were echoed at UNCTAD X in Bangkok in February 2000 when several delegations called for an international new deal.

Part of this new deal should embrace renewing the Rio North-South agenda. As early as 1996, analysts argued that the basic post-Rio North-South bargains were already dead and needed to be revived to avoid regionalism or protectionism and to promote effective multilateral trade liberalisation (see Bergsten 1996 and Runnals 1996). A new North-South bargain similar to Rio could be struck outside the WTO system (which is perceived as too northern-oriented by many developing countries). This bargain would involve two undertakings. First, developing countries would fully implement their trade liberalisation commitments and also consider environment and labour issues in a new round of trade liberalisation. Second, OECD countries would agree to increase financial and technological transfers significantly to developing countries and to support capacity-building activities, and would open their markets to the South faster than currently planned. Only the most important stakeholders of foreign policy and international trade can craft such a bargain.

The 'new deal' should be accompanied by the following policies. Efforts should be made to harmonise the trade and non-trade agendas through a systematic reform of the WTO regime in an integrative, transparent, and participatory manner to make it consistent with the objectives of human and sustainable development. Co-operation programs would be intensified — including a significant increase and better co-ordination in ODA deployment — to support developing countries in implementing trade and environmental agreements, as well as implementing action plans from the major UN conferences of the 1990s. This intensification of co-operation and implementation activities would be supported by a definite improvement of the interface between agendas and actors through reinforced inter-institutional co-operation. Furthermore, global governance would be broadened by the creation of new structures and practices (fora, formal and informal networks, organisations) that would allow for the full participation of developing countries and for a comprehensive consideration of globalisation agendas. Institutional intergovernmental practices would also be made more transparent and open to allow for the participation of civil society and the private sector.

Harmonising the Trade and Non-Trade Agendas in the WTO Regime

Conducting a comprehensive environmental review A comprehensive environmental review of the WTO system should be conducted to clarify the relationship between MEAs and the multilateral trade regime. This review should produce recommendations for ministerial approval and be followed by significant reforms. As a starting point, Canada tabled a paper in Seattle that called for each negotiation group to 'take environmental issues into consideration to make certain that liberalised trade is consistent with, and supportive of, the achievement of sustainable development'.[13]

Such a review would be mutually beneficial to trade and environment regimes. By supporting the establishment of multilateral environmental standards regimes under MEAs, the WTO should avoid the pitfalls of unilateralism and protectionism in the field of environmental regulation. Harmonisation of provisions of the multilateral trade system with trade measures adopted for environmental purposes, both at the national and international level, would support the implementation of both regimes. This would also be true in the area of subsidies. A reduction in energy subsidies, for instance, would certainly be an effective tool to support commitments to reduce carbon dioxide emissions adopted under the Kyoto protocol. The consequences for the global environment of certain practices related to trade should be a WTO priority.

Developing inter-institutional co-operation with MEAs The WTO and MEA secretariats should establish permanent co-ordination structures to make their regimes consistent and to develop mutually supportive policies. They could work on voluntary codes for minimal process and production methods standards, a range of common interpretations about the precautionary principle, and the operationalisation of the polluter-pays principle (Principle 16 of the Rio Declaration). They could also conduct an environmental review of the TRIPs agreement and elaborate a comprehensive plan to phase out trade-distorting and environmentally damaging subsidies. Attention could be given to full-cost pricing of natural resources to avoid market failures in their allocation.

Improving transparency and participation   Regarding transparency and participation issues, many share the view that 'the WTO should adopt thoroughgoing procedural reforms to improve the transparency of its decision-making processes to both the public and non-governmental organizations' (Schoenbaum 1997, p. 313). Significant reforms should be implemented to support the participation of civil society and developing countries in WTO activities, including dispute resolution panels and negotiation groups. There is a need to ensure solid real-time information and communication with civil society representatives where this is feasible and useful.

Implementing the 1990s Action Plans and Programs

Intensifying international co-operation activities   International environmental instruments still have untapped potential that could be exploited through the intensification of bilateral and multilateral co-operation and joint implementation activities. A systematic process to implement these instruments in an integrated manner is needed. This process could culminate with a conference of the heads of UN organisations, MEAs, the World Bank, and the IMF, as well as country representatives. It should also involve TNCs and civil society representatives. This conference would aim at integrating agendas and designing permanent co-ordination mechanisms that would ensure consistency in the implementation of major UN and MEA action plans and programs. Bilateral co-operation activities can also be made consistent with multilateral activities by closely following these action plans and programs and by working through the focal-point mechanisms.[14] Strong action is needed from OECD countries to implement their commitments at this level. Resorting to Sahel-Club–like activities in a more engaging way can be a practical approach.

An integrated approach to financing   The rise of FDI, the fall of ODA, the role of trade in financing development, and a series of other factors make an integrated approach to financial transfers more necessary than ever. The financing for development initiative should be strongly supported as the key to a comprehensive review of financing sources and channels, and as a way of developing innovative sources and solutions to financing challenges.

The OECD's Development Assistance Committee also has a key role to play by renewing its member countries' commitment to allocate 0.7 percent of their GDP to ODA, with 0.2 percent targeted to LDCs. The OECD countries and Bretton Woods institutions also need to co-ordinate and integrate their approaches more closely. There is also a need to better target public and private resource flows to countries that have sound economic policies (Kanbur and Sandler 1998). This good governance environment is more likely to lead to an efficient use of aid and private resources, and to have structuring impacts on development and poverty alleviation. In addition to better targeting, a common pool approach should be adopted, when appropriate, to aggregate donors' resources for development priorities that would be regionally or domestically defined.[15] Using the 'chef de file' approach is likely to achieve better efficiencies in co-ordination efforts in the national settings of recipient countries.

Supporting inter-institutional activities An effort should be made to systematically identify and support inter-institutional activities and mechanisms that can be gradually developed over the next few years. The UNEP/MEA secretariats meetings should be made into a permanent structure that meets annually and includes other UN organisations, multilateral financing institutions, and key representatives from civil society such as the World Conservation Union. Such meetings could produce a comprehensive framework for the joint implementation of major MEAs, as well as a permanent and systematic framework for collaboration between secretariats and UN institutions that would allow for synergies and a better allocation of scarce financial and human resources. Better funding for MEA secretariats and UNEP would support such initiatives. In the trade and environment area, the creation of the Standing Conference on Trade and Environment should be supported as a key mechanism for the co-ordination of environmental policy as it relates to trade.

Broadening the Governance Table

New mechanisms for developing countries' representation: A role for the G20 At their December 1999 meeting, members of the G20 reaffirmed the importance of the WTO's trade liberalisation process. By addressing some of the issues discussed above, the G20 could play a significant role in elaborating a new North-South bargain that would serve as a basis for resuming talks on a new round of trade liberalisation. This would require expanding the mandate of the group to trade, environment, and development issues in the same way that the G7/8 has gradually expanded its mandate to international security matters. The G20 could serve as a forum to design and foster the establishment of a new global governance for the multiple and necessarily interrelated agendas of globalisation. It could thus be instrumental in seizing the current window of opportunity and breaking the Seattle impasse.

Integrating civil society and the private sector NGOs and TNCs have become fundamental actors in the globalisation process whose contributions to evolving global governance models should be facilitated. Inconsistency — almost whimsicality — affects the decisions and orientations of international institutions when it comes to effective participation of civil society in the definition and implementation of agendas. This could be addressed more systematically through a high-level conference on the role and means of civil society in a better-integrated global governance system.

NGOs can play a major role in capacity-building and implementation activities at the local level. They should identify and articulate new issues to be addressed by international governance structures. NGOs have a strong capacity to synthesise and disseminate information, and to mobilise civil society. Governance structures are gradually opening to allow NGOs and civil society to play their roles fully. As argued by Mark Halle (2000, p. 13), 'It is time to recognise that there is an emerging global standard for transparency, participation and access to judicial processes, which cannot be ignored. It is the basis of the new global governance'. Parliamentarians, who have many transnational co-operative institutions and forums (the Commonwealth, la Francophonie, and regional/sub-regional organisations), can contribute to bridging the gap between governance structures and civil society.

TNCs have a major, but largely unexplored, potential to contribute to sustainable development. Channelling investment toward sustainable development is a very complex issue that requires some innovative approaches. To tap the TNCs' potential, the international community needs to bring them into the new framework of world governance. Transparency and accountability, formal obligations and informal habits, must be reinforced, especially in the environmental sector. Appropriate international policies must also be put into place to guide and influence TNCs' behaviour. The careful use of regulations, standards, economic incentives, and disincentives must be promoted to reach this objective. Voluntary codes of conduct or OECD guideline approaches can also generate useful dynamics.

Seizing Upcoming Opportunities

The next few years will offer many international opportunities to bring about the new approaches and strategies needed in the current post-Seattle context. Annual G7/8 meetings will continue to expand and deepen their focus from economic and financial matters to security, as well as to social and environmental concerns, thereby opening new opportunities for broadened governance. They could benefit from a wider North-South perspective on these issues that could be developed at the G20's meetings in the fall of 2000 and beyond.

In the coming months, the WTO will experience a phase of introspection and analysis that will give it time for systematic analyses and reforms. The Summit of the Americas (April 2001) could help resolve some environmental and social issues that plague North-South relations and imperil further multilateral trade liberalisation. The two processes should feed into one another and contribute to resolving some of the harmonisation issues still to be addressed.

Also in the spring of 2001, the Financing for Development Conference will be a unique opportunity to assess the world aid system and to develop an integrated approach to financial transfers that could boost development and contribute to restoring North-South confidence. The outcome of this conference could have a major impact on financial issues that will be addressed at the Rio+10 Conference scheduled for 2002. Multilateral work at the UN Commission on Sustainable Development will be of central importance. Meanwhile, UNEP's efforts to strengthen the institutional framework supporting the global environmental regime hold the potential for new synergies that could feed into these processes and lead to new efficiency standards. The G7/8 and G20 should systematically prepare for these events so they become meaningful stepping stones toward a new international governance structure.

Conclusion: A New and Determined Approach

It is paradoxical that Seattle's failure highlighted the deficiencies of WTO governance while it opened a new window of opportunity for developing innovative strategies of global governance. Global governance has become more complex and the need to integrate various agendas of globalisation into a coherent structure is more apparent than ever. As stated in the Human Development Report (UNDP 1999, p. 2): 'The challenge of globalisation in the new century is not to stop the expansion of global markets. The challenge is to find the rules and institutions for stronger governance — local, national, regional and global — to preserve the advantages of global markets and competition, but to provide enough space for human, community and environmental resources to ensure that globalization works for people — not just for profits'.

The values behind such an approach rest on a broadly shared concern in Western democracies about the need to provide domestically for the larger number, and the projection of this concern outward to the global community. The rationale at a global level is the importance of achieving the widest participation possible in the trade liberalisation process. In order to secure a commitment from reluctant developing countries that will allow the trade agenda to go forward, it is imperative to craft understandable and clear priorities that encompass the wider globalisation agenda. Addressing developing countries' needs, advancing environmental protection, and conserving threatened natural resources are core elements to integrate in this new global agenda. Opening up the decision processes of global governance systems and allowing systematic innovations by hybrid creatures such as the G20 are also part of the meeting of minds and interests that is needed to reconcile developed and developing countries.

This exercise requires an uncommon resilience in giving the multiple non-trade agendas their place in foreign policy efforts by adopting integrated rather than fragmented approaches. Establishing the multilateral structures and fora required to make renewed North-South bargains a reality constitutes a worthy ideal for Canadian foreign policy and that of its G7/8 partners. Canada's ability to articulate interests in multilateral fora and to develop consensual policies would serve this approach well. Canada can also put its credibility to good use by playing a mediatory role between the North and South, helping restore confidence and forging basic bargains. Moreover, Canadian foreign policy has long worked to integrate civil society and can thus work very comfortably with the open, transparent processes this entails. Canada has a seat in the G20, the UN Security Council, and the Summit of the Americas, and is also member of the G7/8, la Francophonie, the Commonwealth, and the trade ministers quadrilateral. These positions give it considerable influence. It can also make substantive contributions in the UN Commission for Sustainable Development as trade liberalisation talks regain momentum.

To do so efficiently and make a meaningful contribution that gives a direction to these changes, foreign policy, international financial, and trade talks, as well as summitry mechanics, must all be part of defining this new coherence and consistency. There are considerable obstacles on the way to efficiently integrating such complex issues.

Increased trade is unrealistic outside of a peaceful and secure setting. Population growth, natural resources depletion, and poverty-related social instability in an increased number of countries can affect peace and security. To face this evolving paradigm responsibly, the links between social and environmental realities and the international trade, peace and security agendas must be clearly recognised, addressed, and acted upon.

As with any change of course, the obstacles to change cannot be overcome without meaningful leadership at the highest level of foreign policy, international finance, international trade, and the security apparatus. The steering of globalisation forward in a direction that is more humanistic ultimately rests not on administrative personnel and international bureaucracies, but on the heads of governments and their ministers, who must elaborate and implement the necessary vision.

Notes

1   The author would like to thank his research assistant, Karel Mayrand, for his exceptional contribution. He also wishes to express his appreciation to André Beaulieu and Peter Watson for their comments and input, as well as Élizabeth Camiré for documentary support.
2   This section draws on the UNDP (1999) as well as Mike Moore (1999) and the United Nations Conference on Trade and Development (UNCTAD) (1999b, 1999c, 1999d).
3   This phenomenon was analysed in Toward a New International Architecture: Report of the Task Force of the Executive Committee on Economic and Social Affairs of the United Nations (United Nations 1999).
4   The term 'digital divide' was coined by James Wolfensohn (2000), President of the Word Bank, at UNCTAD X.
5   Most international publications refer to transnational corporations without defining the concept, thus avoiding academic debates over different definitions. However, a simple, widely agreed definition is a company that 1) engages in foreign production through its affiliates located in several countries, 2) exercises direct control over the policies of its affiliates, and 3) implements business strategies in production, marketing, finance, and staffing that transcend national boundaries (Iowa State University 2000).
6   Moderate water stress occurs when more than 20 percent of available renewable freshwater resources are used. High water stress refers to a situation in which more than 40 percent of available resources are used (World Meteorological Organization 1997).

7   They are the Vienna Convention for the Protection of the Ozone Layer (1985), the Montreal Protocol on Substances that Deplete the Ozone Layer (1987), the Basel Convention on the Transboundary Movement of Hazardous Waste (1989), the Framework Convention on Climate Change (1992), the Convention on Biological Diversity (1992), the Convention to Combat Desertification in Countries Experiencing Serious Drought and/or Desertification, Particularly in Africa (1994), the Kyoto Protocol on Climate Change (1997), and the Cartagena Protocol on Biosafety (2000). In addition, Agenda 21, the action plan of the Rio Conference on Environment and Development, was adopted in 1992, with a Non-Legally Binding Authoritative Statement of Principles for a Global Consensus on the Management, Conservation, and Sustainable Development of All Types of Forests.

8   The following MEAs are listed in NAFTA: Convention on International Trade in Endangered Species of Wild Fauna and Flora (CITES), Montreal Protocol on Substances that Deplete the Ozone Layer, Basel Convention on the Control of Transboundary Movements of Hazardous Waste (Johnson and Beaulieu 1996).

9   Without explicitly specifying the relationship between the Cartagena protocol and trade agreements, the protocol's preamble establishes the parameters of this relationship by recognising that trade and environment agreements should be mutually supportive with a view to achieving sustainable development, and emphasises that this protocol shall not be interpreted as implying a change in the rights and obligations of a party under any existing international agreements.

10   Many analysts argue that the interpretation of GATT's Article XX, sanitary and phytosanitary provisions, as well as processes and production methods, will have to be revised under WTO's dispute resolution procedures. In their view, the interpretative framework should be generally more open to environmental protection measures, which implies the reversal of the burden of proof in certain cases. For a more detailed analysis, see Schoenbaum (1997).

11   The Fourth Session of the Intergovernmental Forum on Forests produced a comprehensive action plan on forest protection in February 2000 that will be studied by the UN Commission on Sustainable Development. In the water sector, the second World Water Forum and Ministerial Conference on Water (The Hague, March 2000) has produced 'A Vision for Water for the 21st Century', to be followed by a framework for action that will serve as a plan of action for states, NGOs, and IGOs in the next 25 years.

12   For a more detailed analysis of the proposal of the Standing Conference on Trade and the Environment, see Mercer (1999).

13   The document was entitled 'Canadian Approach to Trade and Environment in the New WTO Round'.

14   Focal-point mechanisms are national or regional institutions that centralise incoming funding and co-ordinate implementation activities related to the Convention to Combat Desertification.

15   The Sahel Club has the potential to create such a pathway in the case of West Africa, but it would need more consistent support from senior foreign-policy personnel and decision makers of key countries.

References

Baillie, J., and B. Groombridge (eds.) (1996), *1996 IUCN Red List of Threatened Animals*, World Conservation Union (IUCN), Cambridge/Gland.
Bergsten, F. (1996), 'Globalizing Free Trade', *Foreign Affairs*, vol. 75, no. 3.
Botchwey, K. (2000), *Financing for Development: Current Trends and Issues for the Future*, United Nations Conference on Trade and Development, TD(X)/RT.1/11.
Brown, L., M. Renner, and B. Halweil (eds.) (1999), *Vital Signs 1999: The Environmental Trends That Are Shaping Our Future*, Worldwatch Institute, W. W. Norton and Company, New York.
Esty, D. C., and D. Geradin (1998), 'Environmental Protection and Environmental Competitiveness: A Conceptual Framework', *Journal of World Trade*, vol. 32, no. 3, pp. 5–46.
Finance Canada (1999), 'Finance Minister Paul Martin Chosen as Inaugural Chairperson of New Group of Twenty', Press Release 99-080, 25 September, <www.fin.gc.ca/newse99/99-080e.html> (September 2000).
Global Environment Facility (1998), *GEF Lesson Notes*, no. 2, April.
Halle, M. (2000), 'Seattle and Sustainable Development', *Bridges: Between Trade and Sustainable Development*, International Center on Trade and Sustainable Development, year 4, no. 1, pp. 13–14.
Intergovernmental Panel on Climate Change (IPCC) (1995), 'IPCC Second Assessment Report: Climate Change', World Meteorological Organisation and United Nations Environment Programme, Geneva.
International Institute for Sustainable Development (1999), *Sustainable Developments*, vol. 12, no. 2 (rev.), 22 March.
Iowa State University, Department of Economics (2000) 'Multinational Corporations', <www.econ.iastate.edu/classes/econ355/choi/mnc.htm> (September 2000).
Johnson, P. M., and A. Beaulieu (1996), *The Environment and NAFTA: Understanding and Implementing the New Continental Law*, Island Press, Washington DC.
Kaiser, K., J. Kirton, and J. Daniels (eds.) (2000), *Shaping a New International Financial System*, Ashgate, Aldershot.
Kanbur, R., and T. Sandler (1998), 'A Radical Approach to Development Assistance', *Development Outreach*, vol. 1, no. 2.
Mercer, M. (1999), *International Trade and the Environment: Addressing the Co-ordination Challenge*, World Conservation Union (IUCN), Canada Office, Montreal.
Moore, Mike (1999), 'Address to NGOs in Opening the Seattle Symposium on International Trade Issues in the Next Decade', 29 November 1999, Social Development Review, vol. 3, no. 4, pp. 24–26.
Nordstrom, H., and S. Vaughan (1999), *Special Studies 4: Trade and Environment*, World Trade Organization, Geneva.

Organisation for Economic Co-operation and Development (OECD) (2000), 'Development Co-operation Report 1999: Efforts and Policies of the Members of the Development Assistance Committee', *Development Assistance Committee Journal*, vol. 1, no. 1.

Ricupero, Rubens (2000), 'From the Washington Consensus to the Spirit of Bangkok', Closing Statement at United Nations Conference on Trade and Development, Tenth Session, Bangkok, 19 February, p. 7.

Runnals, D. (1996), 'Shall We Dance? What the North Needs to Do to Fully Engage the South in the Trade and Sustainable Development Debate', Working Paper, Trade and Sustainable Development Program, International Institute for Sustainable Development, Winnipeg.

Schoenbaum, T. J. (1997), 'International Trade and Protection of the Environment: The Continuing Search for Reconciliation', *American Journal of International Law*, no. 91, pp. 268–313.

Toepfer, K. (1999), 'UNEP's Convention Priorities', *Synergies: Promoting Co-operation on Environmental Treaties*, vol. 1, no. 1.

United Nations (1999), 'Toward a New International Architecture: Report of the Task Force of the Executive Committee on Economic and Social Affairs of the United Nations', ECSA/9/1, New York, 21 January.

United Nations Conference on Environment and Development (1992), *Agenda 2*, United Nations, Rio de Janeiro, chap. 38.

United Nations Conference on Trade and Development (1999a), *High-Level Round Table on Trade and Development Governance: Summary*, United Nations, New York.

United Nations Conference on Trade and Development (UNCTAD) (1999b), *Report of the Secretary General to UNCTAD X*, TD 380, United Nations, New York.

United Nations Conference on Trade and Development (UNCTAD) (1999c), *Trade and Development Report 1999*, United Nations, New York.

United Nations Conference on Trade and Development (UNCTAD) (1999d), *World Investment Report: Foreign Direct Investment and the Challenge of Development*, New York, United Nations.

United Nations Conference on Trade and Development (UNCTAD) (2000), *Plan of Action*, Tenth session, New York, United Nations, 2000.

United Nations Development Programme (UNDP) (1999), *Human Development Report 1999*, Oxford University Press, New York.

United Nations General Assembly (1992), *Rio Declaration on Environment and Development*, A/CONF.151/26, vol. 1.

Wolfensohn, James (2000) 'Summary of the Debate', United Nations Conference on Trade and Development, Tenth Session, 16 February, <www.unctad-10.org/interactive_debate/id_sum_wolfensohn.en.htm> (September 2000).

World Meteorological Organization (1997), *Comprehensive Assessment of Freshwater Resources of the World*, United Nations, New York.

World Resources Institute, United Nations Environment Programme, United Nations Development Programme, and World Bank (1998), *World Resources 1998–99: A Global Guide to the Human Environment*, Oxford University Press, New York.

World Trade Organization (1999), 'Trade Liberalization Reinforces the Need for Environmental Co-operation', Press Release 140, 8 October, <www.wto.org/english/news_e/pres99_e/pr140_e.htm> (September 2000).

Part IV
Conclusion

14 The G8's Contributions to Twenty-First Century Governance

JOHN J. KIRTON, JOSEPH P. DANIELS, AND ANDREAS FREYTAG

Introduction

As the twenty-first century opens, is a new global order emerging and is the G7/8 at the centre of it? There is no reason, of course, that the marking of a millennial moment in itself should convey a presumption that a fundamental transformation is underway in the international system, nor in the international institutions and principles, norms, and rules that govern it. Moreover, the preceding decade of the 1990s, prompted by the end of the European cold war and the onset of rapid 'globalisation', witnessed major changes, a veritable outpouring of new paradigms and an even richer debate about what an emerging new system would be (Boyer *et al.* 2000).

Nonetheless, there are several powerful and pervasive phenomena that suggest that the emergence of a genuinely new system and the search for an order to govern it are underway. The intensity, global contagion, and domestic impact of the 1997–99 financial crisis, when juxtaposed against the triumph of the booming 'Goldilocks' economy in the U.S. and vibrant growth in most other G7 countries revealed how interconnected the old nation-state–based system and international economy was, how vulnerable even the most powerful members were, and how fragile the inherited international institutions, largely conceived and constructed for the world of half a century ago, could be (Kaiser, Kirton, and Daniels 2000). The pervasive impact of accessible electronic technologies, now rapidly spreading from finance to the entire economy, information, education, and political mobilisation, and from the U.S. and G7 countries to much of the world, produced a penetrated nation-state and an instrument that all citizens, every day, can experience and employ (Deibert 1997). Largely as a result, there is a much greater demand from a broad array of civil society actors and citizens for direct access to and participation in international institutions. There is also a broad call for the revision or rejection of the principles, norms, rules and decision-making procedures that have guided the entrenched galaxy for so long.

The chapters in this volume suggest that in many instances a new system is emerging, and with it, at least in embryonic form, the new principles and processes of global governance that respond to its central features. At the same time, the degree of change and the depth and form of the emerging and required normative and institutional responses remain highly contested. Indeed, there are those whose values and analytical tools suggest that amidst the apparent novelty and confusion of the post-crisis years, the longstanding fundamentals of governance based on the nation-state and classic liberal precepts do and should endure. Others applaud the signs of success already apparent amidst the ongoing struggle to develop and embed a more socially safeguarded, legitimate, inclusive global order. Still others call for a much more wide-ranging and aggressive program to redesign global governance on the foundation of democratic principles and processes (Held 1995; Archibugi, Held, and Köhler 1998). And still others, with fresh memories of the 1997–99 crisis and the continuing economic, educational, ecological, and human impoverishment and insecurity in much of the world warn of coming chaos and collapse (Arrighi and Silver 1999).

Amidst this diversity, the chapters in this volume contribute in various ways to the large and ongoing debate about the desirable and feasible approach to constructing, or more modesty guiding, a new global order (Dewitt, Haglund, and Kirton 1993; Cox 1996). Yet, despite this diversity, these analyses provide a foundation for an independent judgement about the move toward a new global order and the role of the G8 in this process. They also identify some common themes to guide future work. This concluding chapter thus examines, first, the achievements of the 1999 G7/8 Cologne Summit in international policy co-ordination on key issues, as its accomplishments appeared at the Summit's end and over the following year. It then similarly explores the contribution of the Cologne Summit in putting in place a new set of principles — a Cologne consensus on socially sustainable globalisation — that marked a sharp departure from the prevailing neoliberal orthodoxy dominant in the G8 in the past and that set an appropriate foundation for global governance in the twenty-first century. It next offers a more sceptical view of the achievements of Cologne in particular and the G8 process of policy co-ordination in general, particularly as an approach to guiding global order in the future. It ends by summarising the judgements of the authors in this volume on these issues, and the agenda and approach they see as appropriate for the G8 and global governance as the new century unfolds.

The Achievements of the 1999 Cologne Summit

Assessments of the contribution of any individual G7/8 Summit have classically rested on judgements regarding the Summit's performance on its core function of reaching timely, well-tailored, ambitious, concrete, and often comprehensive agreements to co-ordinate policy in regard to the major issues faced by the G8 and the international community at the time and in future years (Putnam and Bayne 1987, Bayne 2000).[1] While the Summits also perform valuable roles by allowing leaders to deliberate among themselves and set directions to guide global order (Baker 2000), it is in the realm of taking decisions to co-ordinate policy that they are judged in the first instance. And while each Summit faces a different configuration of challenges, from fast-breaking crises of the moment, through compounding problems that have gone unsolved over the past several years, to forward-looking efforts to prevent crises and build a new order that anticipates and shapes the future, all are, by the prevailing standard, equally capable of making a major historical mark.

By these stringent standards, most informed observers concluded that the Cologne Summit was one of high achievement. Sir Nicholas Bayne (2000, p, 195), who, with Robert Putnam is the historic master grader of Summit co-operative achievements, awarded Cologne a grade of B+ by virtue of its accomplishments on debt, Kosovo, and finance. By this calculus, Cologne ranked equally with Birmingham in 1998, Halifax in 1995, Paris in 1989, and the two Tokyo Summits of 1979 and 1986. In the quarter-century history of the Summit, only Rambouillet, France, with an A– in 1975, and the legendary Bonn I in 1978 with an A surpassed Cologne. Even a usually sceptical media, pronouncing on Cologne as the Summit ended, offered a more charitable conclusion of its value than usual.

Similarly, John Kirton (1999a), assisted by the G8 Research Group, awarded the leaders' collective performance a grade of A– at the immediate conclusion of the Cologne Summit. Over the five-year period that the G8 Research Group has been assessing overall G7/8 performance by its distinctive calculus, this placed Cologne as the most successful Summit of the second half of the 1990s. It was tied with Denver 1997 at A–, and ranked ahead of Lyon 1996, Birmingham 1998, and Okinawa 2000, which each received a B+.

Such conclusions are indeed sound. Seldom before has a G7 and now G8 Summit been forced to address — and asked to resolve — the largest issues facing the world in both the political security and economic domains, while simultaneously dealing with the many issues, once domestic, that are now a routine part of G7/8 governance. In addition, Cologne featured an unusually comprehensive and demanding agenda. It was the first time the preparation for the G7 Summit occurred while most of its members were at war, and it was the first to open when the G8 had to conclude the peace and to plan and finance a post-war reconstruction effort. At the same time, it took place as a still fragile global economy was emerging from a two-year succession of financial crises that threatened at one point to engulf even the vibrant U.S. economy. As a result, the international community had to make critical decisions on the shape of an international financial system appropriate to the needs of a increasingly globalised world and its anxious citizens. In response, the G7/8 at Cologne put forward a set of recommendations designed to resolve both these central issues, and to do so in ways that strengthened its seminal mission of forwarding the principles of democratic governance, social protection, and market-oriented economies in a rapidly changing world (see G7 1975).

The major achievements of the Cologne Summit and the grades awarded by John Kirton are summarised in Table 14.1 and examined individually by issue area below.[2]

1. Russia (A)

The crowning overall achievement of Cologne, seen across several issue areas, was the inclusion of Russia as a full member of the G8, in terms of psychological self-definition as well as of formal status. Having participated in bringing an end to the war in Kosovo and pledging to help in the task of reconstruction, Russia asked to become a full member of the G7 at the opening dinner attended by Prime Minister Sergei Stepashin. Russia thus showed that

Table 14.1 The Achievements of the 1999 Cologne Summit

Overall Assessment:	A–
1. Russia	A
2. Peace in Kosovo	A
3. Reconstruction in the Balkans	A–
4. International Financial Architecture	A–
5. Debt Relief for the Poorest	B+
6. Trade Liberalisation	A
7. Environmental Issues	C+
8. Education and Human Capital	B–
9. Transnational Issues	C–
10. Political Issues	B–

it saw where its future lay and that it was a future in which it was at one with its seven colleagues. They in turn responded with signals that they would individually provide further financial support to Russia and seek ways to include it in the World Trade Organization (WTO). For a Russia whose prime minister had turned his plane away from the International Monetary Fund (IMF) and Washington as the war to liberate Kosovo began on 24 March, it was striking that both Prime Minister Stepashin and the ailing President Boris Yeltsin flew to the G8 in Germany to join in the task of ending the war and starting the reconstruction. A Russia that found it easy to be a member of an emerging G8 when the big issue was securing money and membership for itself from its G7 partners now proved it was a full member when it was called on to make its first substantive contribution to the process and take the political lead in getting Serbia to end the war on the G7's terms.

2. Peace in Kosovo (A)

The spirit of solidarity was evident in the conclusion of the final details of the peace plan in Kosovo in the hours following the opening dinner of the Summit on Friday night. The plan itself, in terms of the command and control structure and the deployment of Russian troops in various zones, was completed by ministers in other European capitals. But it was clearly the pull of and parameters set by the Cologne Summit that produced the final result. That result affirmed the core G7 desires — it integrated NATO-based command and control, and offered no separate zone for the Russians in which Serbian Kosovars might congregate and harm the process of producing a flourishing democratic multi-ethnic polity in the wake of the war. But it was a result that showed sensitivity to Russia's great-power status, its internal political difficulties, and its right to play a full part as a G8 member in the Kosovo operation.

It was, in fact, the G8 that produced the peace in Kosovo, on the G7's terms rather than those of Russia or its historic affiliate Serbia's. At a meeting of the G8 political directors in the lead-up to Cologne, Russia had stunned its G8 colleagues by declaring, after many weeks of firm opposition to its G7 colleagues actions, that it now wanted to work through the G8 to find a way to end the war. While Russia's partners calculated that Yeltsin had changed his position on the basis of a cold calculus of Russia's self-interest, they eagerly took up the offer and devoted their full energies, and subsequently those of their foreign ministers, to finding a formula that all could accept.

Simultaneously, amidst mounting frustration with the slow and partial results of the air war, G7 leaders had decided that they would have their first face-to-face collective discussion about the war at Cologne. Moreover, they would decide to move to the next stage by authorising the introduction of their own ground forces and those of the North Atlantic Treaty Organization (NATO), in a nonpermissive environment, into Kosovo itself. The consensus, led by the U.S. and Britain, was one that a committed Canada and the other G7 members found it relatively easy to embrace.

The deliberate intent of this diplomatic brinksmanship was to force Russia to cross the critical divide — to see if it would 'hang together' with its G8 colleagues in an historic reorientation of Russian foreign policy, or if it would remain wedded to its traditional role as defender of the Serbs. In the end, the pull of G8 membership and all that comes with it, along with other factors, proved decisive. On the eve of the Summit, the Russians informed the Serbian authorities of their impending decision. Milosevic immediately decided to withdraw his troops rather than fight a ground war he was sure to lose and risk losing the armed forces that were essential to keeping him in power in Serbia itself.

3. Reconstruction in the Balkans (A–)

Russia was also an active participant in the Friday night G8 discussion on how to shape and fund a relief and reconstruction effort for Kosovo itself, for the rest of the former Yugoslavia and its neighbours, and for Southern and Eastern Europe as a whole. Russia stood with the G8 in sending a clear message that there would be no funds offered to reconstruct Serbia itself while Milosevic remained in power and while the ideal of a fully democratic Serbia and Europe thus remained unfulfilled. For Kosovo itself, a framework and funding level were established to encourage the Kosovars to return home and rebuild their society as soon as possible. In an example of balanced G8 burden sharing, among the finance ministers in particular, the European Union (EU) and the World Bank agreed to lead in the effort, with all G8 members making their contribution in support. Many countries would be asked to give, and the G8 would serve as the steering committee to guide the effort. The precise level of the effort remained elusive at the conclusion of the Cologne Summit. However, with teams for damage assessment starting to enter the region, such figures were expected to come relatively soon. They did so at a subsequent conference involving many additional countries, and so began the long, slow difficult task of rebuilding Kosovo, in the first instance to meet essential needs such as security, civil administration, housing, electricity, and water through the coming winter.

4. International Financial Architecture (A–)

In the economic domain, G7 leaders, meeting on Friday afternoon just prior to the G8's opening dinner, built on the work of their finance ministers to give high-level confirmation of several new principles and processes for a new financial architecture for the twenty-first century (Kaiser, Kirton, and Daniels 2000). G7 leaders affirmed the principle of private-sector participation in response to future financial crises. No longer would private investors be allowed to reap the gains while times were good but rely on governments and their taxpayers to bail them out and foot the bill when crisis erupted and losses came. A second core principle was the need to build a new financial architecture and introduce crisis-response programs that gave priority attention to the social impact of the crisis and the need to protect ordinary citizens in afflicted societies from the ravages of forces not of their own making. In the realm of process, G7 leaders expanded the membership of the recently created Financial Stability Forum (FSF) to include emerging countries. Perhaps most important, they declared that the centre of the new system would not only be the IMF of 1945 with an improved Interim Committee but would also be a new forum — soon formalised as the G20 — with the forward-looking flexibility and membership more appropriate to the twenty-first century.

As the leaders left Cologne, however, they still faced the challenge of how to translate the principle of private-sector burden sharing into practice, through such tools as an emergency standstill mechanism or other means. They also confronted the formidable task of how to convince the private sector to play its part, how to stop the flight of capital from domestic investors when crises erupted, and how finally to stop the financial haemorrhaging in Russia. Obvious solutions, notably the relaunch of negotiations for a Multilateral Agreement on Investment (MAI) to encourage the flow of long-term, capital, and the management, technology, distribution systems, and markets that came with it, remained largely off the agenda (Rugman 1999). Nonetheless, the results of the G7 finance ministers in September 1999, January 2000, April 2000, July 2000, and September 2000 showed that steady progress was being made.

Another achievement came from something that did not happen – the end of any effort to fix the exchange rates of the three major currencies (Euro, U.S. dollars, yen) in target zones. Until early 1999 this issue had been strongly advocated by the German government against the advice of almost the entire economic profession. However, it was suddenly dropped after the German Minister of Finance, Oskar Lafontaine, resigned. In the views of many economists, exchange rate agreements between these currencies do not make sense since, as in the presence of divergent inflation rates, they usually exert costs on those who run sound economic and above all monetary policies. This holds true particularly if the burden to adjust to potential exchange rate changes is to be shared. Furthermore, the question remains of which is the proper and sustainable exchange rate target and reference range, and who if not the markets knows best what it is (see Chapter 3, 'Challenges for the Global Financial System'). The experience of the depreciation of the Euro in 2000 strengthens this point, as it certainly would not have been predicted by an exchange-fixing committee a year ago. To summarise, the leaders were prudent not to pretend to have better knowledge than the markets. In addition, even those more sympathetic to active currency co-ordination in cases of extreme volatility or misalignment could see little case for co-ordinated action in 1999, given the relatively stable record of the major currencies, even amidst the 1997–99 global financial crisis and the major growth differentials among G7 countries, throughout the 1990s (Kirton 1999b).

5. Debt Relief for the Poorest (B+)

The Cologne Debt Initiative had long been conceived to be the centrepiece 'deliverable' of the Summit. The only question was how large the package would be. A discussion of whether debt relief for Highly Indebted Poor Countries (HIPCs) does solve the most urgent problem did not take place. Rather, this was taken for granted by the leaders. In addition, the issue of moral hazard remained politically underexposed, as there was no discussion of it in the political arena.

In the end, the leaders at Cologne promised enough relief to write off much of the debt of the poorest to hasten the return of these countries to a sustainable growth track. There was a further commitment to have three quarters of the 41 eligible HIPC countries into the debt-relief process by the end of 2000. Equally importantly, in keeping with a strengthening G7 conviction during the 1990s (Gill 1993, p. 8; Clayton 2000), the money would flow with strong conditionality, so that the new funds would not be wasted on military spending and other excesses but would be devoted to education, social infrastructure, the health of women and children, and the other programs that are required to generate real sustainable social capital and growth. Led by Britain's Tony Blair, the G7 leaders sought to involve the private sector in the effort.

Despite the importance of this advance at Cologne, however, the leaders missed an opportunity to go even further. Some countries were prepared to grant even more funds to the relief effort if other G7 partners would do more.

But those partners proved reluctant, and the high-level bargain slipped away. Moreover, the pace was not as rapid as many, notably civil society advocates joined in Jubilee 2000, had hoped. The process was handed back to the International Financial Institutions before the G7 would return to it in the fall.

The Cologne Debt Initiative also demonstrated how civil society representatives and ordinary citizens could effectively influence democratic leaders within the G7 to inspire far-reaching changes (Dent and Peters 2000). Present in the many thousands at Cologne, as they had been in Birmingham a year earlier, representatives of Jubilee 2000 had a consequential role in producing the decision for faster, broader, and deeper debt relief for the poorest that Cologne affirmed. By April 2000, most G7 members had announced a full writeoff of their HIPC loans. However, the process of actually getting the relief to the recipients remained rather slow. Virtually none proved able to meet the stringent conditions set for eligibility. The U.S. Congress refused to authorise the sum necessary for the U.S. to bear its fair share of the overall debt-relief burden. And at the IMF and G7 meetings in Washington in April 2000, German officials prevented the rest of the G7 from moving forward to grant Uganda its desired eligibility for debt relief. The subsequent decision of Uganda to invade its neighbour diminished the enthusiasm of others in the G7 to proceed with generous debt relief, especially for the dozen or so HIPC countries involved in military conflict. By the time, the G7/8 Okinawa Summit opened on 21 July 2000, there appeared to be little hope that the ambitious targets and timetables set at Cologne would be met.

6. Trade Liberalisation (A)

G7 Summits have been at their best when launching and concluding rounds of multilateral trade liberalisation. Cologne offered a chance to keep this tradition alive. Here, it not only lived up to expectations but also set a new standard. Urged on by U.S. president Bill Clinton at the G8's opening dinner, the leaders endorsed the launch of the Millennium Round of negotiations for multilateral trade liberalisation. This round would have a comprehensive agenda and be concluded quickly — within three years. Most importantly, it would come with social protections and democratic participation built in from the start. A regime to incorporate labour and environmental standards would be included and civil society groups would be given their chance to participate and improve the result. In the past, it has taken as long as eight years to launch a new round and eight years to conclude it, and several Summits have failed in getting the job done (Bayne 2000). Cologne, however, launched a new round after only five years from the successful conclusion of the previous one and suggested that it would be concluded within three years.

The easy launch and schedule for concluding this comprehensive round suffered a setback in November/December 1999. At the WTO ministerial meeting in Seattle, a combination of President Clinton's ill-timed, politically oriented call for the use of trade sanctions to enforce environmental and labour standards, developing country dissatisfaction with the results of the previous Uruguay Round, and the disruptions caused by protesters engaged in acts of arson and violence meant that a fast start for a full new round was stalled. Immediately after the multilateral WTO had failed, the G7 quadrilateral trade ministers began to work to get the launch of the Millennium Round back on track. However, continuing trade rows between the U.S. and the EU over bananas, hormone-tainted beef, and export tax programs, as well as the failure of the G7 to address the concerns of developing countries, impeded these efforts.

7. Environmental Issues (C+)

Somewhat surprisingly for a German-hosted Summit, environmental issues received little attention and not much of global significance was achieved. The leaders did agree that the potentially deadly Chernobyl nuclear reactors would be finally closed — a full 14 years after the 1986 explosion — by the year 2000. The host, Chancellor Gerhard Schroeder, was dispatched to Ukraine to get the job done. But the G8 largely passed on an ambitious French proposal to deal with the critical emerging issue of biosafety, even though it did give impetus to a process that produced a biosafety protocol at Montreal within the year. There was little more than lip service on the key global issues of climate change, biodiversity, oceans, and forests.

This was the more disappointing as international cross-border pollution is one of the few political problems that inevitably demands international co-operation for progress. Furthermore, a consensus across all camps has been reached after years of severe disagreement that the scarce environment can be well allocated with the help of the price mechanism. Proposals range from an international ban of certain emissions, through taxes to the international trade of emission quotas. It is theoretically reasonably clear that international environmental issues have to be addressed internationally. The policy response has to be clarified and organised politically. The Cologne Summit missed the opportunity to give important impetus here.

8. Education and Human Capital (B–)

The microeconomic agenda of the Summit had a new twist on a subject with an old Summit pedigree. The leaders issued a separate statement on education, underscoring the need for international exchanges, high standards, and innovation, including the use of electronic technologies. This was the Cologne equivalent of the emphasis that Birmingham 1998 had placed on employment — with life-long learning and the formation of human capital identified as the keys to employability and growth. The statement contained meaningful principles that extended into the difficult domains of domestic politics and areas where sub-national governments within federal systems usually jealously guard their prerogatives. But there was little concrete on new programs or processes.

Implementation proved to be more successful, and the legacy of Cologne quite robust. For in April 2000, the Japanese hosted the first ever meeting of G8 education ministers, in part to develop proposals to take to leaders in Okinawa in July.

However, it is questionable whether the Cologne charter on lifelong learning can be much more than an important and well-conceived reminder. Education policy is an entirely domestic issue that does not lead to clear international spillovers. Thus international co-ordination is not directly productive. Indirectly, it well may be of utmost use for national governments. If they want to take measures to implement new education schemes — in particular, the rise in primary and secondary school enrolment in developing countries — they can quote the charter, which then serves the function of a scapegoat. As long as the charter remains general in nature and does not give one-size-fits-all recommendations, it makes perfect sense.

9. Transnational Issues (C–)

Crime was a central subject at Birmingham (Hodges, Kirton, and Daniels 1999). It all but disappeared at Cologne, giving ammunition to G7/8 critics who point to the episodic nature of the leaders' attention span. The finance ministers did some useful ground work on financial crime. But the leaders added little, even on key subjects such as the way organised crime in Russia was preventing the advent of financial stability and sustainable growth in an economy on G7 and IMF life support. Nor was there any major move forward on crime following the Summit, despite the continuing importance of the subject in the world.

10. Political Issues (B–)

Cologne's contribution to the political agenda came largely in the week before the Summit when the G8 foreign ministers met. They made important advances regarding conflict prevention and human security, and agreed to meet again in December to continue their work. But even as the conflict between India and Pakistan escalated, there was little that the leaders themselves did to address the pressing issue of weapons proliferation or regional instability beyond the Balkans.

One success was the authorisation of a G8 ministerial meeting in Berlin in December 1999 on the theme of conflict prevention. That conference did good work on an ambitious agenda, even if it failed to authorise an explicit follow-up action plan. Yet, the mere fact that the meeting was held marked a modest move toward having G8 foreign ministers provide more frequent and year-round governance, if not to the level that their finance and trade counterparts have long had. Moreover, Berlin did identify seven specific subjects for follow-up on conflict prevention and pledged to institute a culture of prevention throughout the activities of each of their members. The list of priorities and normative commitment generated pressure on the G8 to convert principles into concrete actions for Okinawa, often in ways that represented major intrusions into the domestic affairs of sovereign states. This momentum led the G8 political directors to come to consensus just before the July meeting of their foreign ministers and leaders that action would be taken in five of the seven areas Berlin had singled out.

The New Cologne Consensus on Socially Sustainable Globalisation: An Optimistic View

In addition to these extensive concrete achievements on the core issues at the centre of the international agenda, the Cologne Summit made a much broader and potentially much more enduring contribution. In the largest terms, it went beyond merely revising the existing rules and norms of the international system to construct the first stages of a new set of principles to replace the neoliberal consensus that had dominated during the past few decades. These new principles moved beyond the foundation of liberal democratic governance and collective market-based economic management proclaimed in 1975, and even the consensus of embedded liberalism established in the 1940s. In essence, the Cologne Summit marked a sharp and substantial shift to a new consensus on socially sustainable globalisation. The new consensus directly addressed the anxieties of citizens about the pace and path of apparently unguided globalisation, and gave social safeguards an equal place alongside the market liberalisation and democratic governance that had long formed the foundation of the G7/8's *raison d'être*. It also, in the realm of process, for the first time promised a meaningful role for civil society actors in working with governments to foster a response that took social values into account.[3] Whereas the Birmingham Summit of 1998 had first identified the serious anxieties about globalisation felt by many, Cologne went beyond to put in place much more boldly a potentially convincing response.

The process had begun on the road to Cologne, in the immediate aftermath of the peak of the global financial crisis of 1997–99 when G7 leaders issued an unprecedented separate statement on 30 October 1998 (Kirton 2000). This statement focussed directly on the social dimensions of the financial crisis. It started by declaring that all the leaders' deliberations and decisions, for the short term and longer, were conducted with a singular concern for the impact of their actions on the poor and the most vulnerable. It promised to strengthen the international financial system in ways that better protected the most vulnerable and that would minimise 'the human costs of financial crises' (G7 Finance Ministers 1998). It specifically endorsed an emergency facility in the World Bank to offset the social damage caused by financial failure for the most vulnerable groups and called for principles of good practice in social policy to protect the most vulnerable social groups.

The start of this new Cologne consensus was the clear statement by G8 leaders in their Cologne communiqué of five founding precepts that were almost entirely new.[4] The first was the frank acknowledgement that amidst its many benefits, 'globalization has been accompanied by a greater risk of dislocation and financial uncertainty for some workers, families and communities across the world'. It secondly noted the need 'to respond to concerns about a lack of control over its effects'. Thirdly, it proceeded with a target that gave equal place to distributional concerns as well as growth ones: 'sustain and increase the benefits of globalization and ensure that its positive effects are widely shared by people all over the world'. Fourthly, it identified an inclusive, multistakeholder process for creating a future order. This was one, fifthly, in which social progress and environmental protection were assigned equal value to the prosperity which had dominated for so long. The Communiqué issued read: 'We therefore call on governments and international institutions, business and labor, civil society and the individual to work together to meet this challenge and realize the full potential of globalization for raising prosperity and promoting social progress while preserving the environment' (see Appendix B).

The first sign that these five founding precepts were more than preambular exhortations came in the inclusion in the Communiqué of an entirely new section on 'Strengthening Social Safeguards'. This section stood equally alongside those on the traditional subjects of the world economy, trade, employment, education, development, debt, environmental protection, arms control, and global challenges. It noted that globalisation had indeed resulted in some dislocation, particularly in developing countries, and that the institutional and social infrastructure must be strengthened to produce widely shared prosperity. It identified 'enhancing social cohesion' as an overarching target, and spoke of the need for balance between social support programs and personal responsibility. It declared social infrastructure, notably investment in basic social services during times of crisis, to be an important cause of speedy recovery, and respect for core labour standards to be 'indispensable prerequisites for social stability'. It called on the IMF to design polices and practices that 'ensure the protection of the most vulnerable', for the implementation of standards of rights at work and child labour, and for the International Financial Institutions (IFIs) and WTO to co-operate in this regard.

This new social sensitivity was carried forward into individual sections in related realms. In addition to those protections for nonmarket values proclaimed in previous communiqués, there were several new provisions focussed on social policy itself. The treatment of the world economy highlighted social reform in Russia and the social impact of economic transformation. The section on trade noted that liberalisation had promoted social progress but that the WTO needed to be more responsive to civil society, to find a more effective way to promote social welfare world-wide, and to co-operate more with labour organisations. The employment passage endorsed the need to 'provide social safety nets that support employment' and 'take forward the social dialogue'. Treatment of development pointed to the important role of non-governmental organisations (NGOs) and civil society, the need to 'mobilize sufficient means for social services' and to achieve social development. The debt passage spoke of releasing resources to invest in social needs. Finally, the section on global issues asserted that social inequality was a cause of violent conflict and civil wars, and that transnational crime constituted a threat to social stability.

Despite these many significant advances, the vision of a socially sustainable and directed process of G8-guided globalisation and governance remained highly limited in several respects. References to social values were absent from three of the communiqué's ten sections. It was absent in regard to education, although the special Cologne Charter — Aims and Ambitions for

Lifelong Learning — emphasised the role of education in achieving social cohesion. Equally surprising was the lack of attention afforded in the passage on the natural environment, despite the well-known importance of social organisation in shaping the environmental effects of trade (Commission for Environmental Cooperation 1999, Kirkpatrick and Lee 1999). Perhaps more understandable was its inability to penetrate the difficult domain of arms control.

These silences were joined by other omissions and imbalances. There was a tendency to treat the social impact of globalisation as a perception to be managed rather than as an objective reality to be changed. Social values tended to be treated as a utilitarian instrument to achieve the ultimate desired goal of liberalisation and other market values, as well as being conceived as a valued end in their own right. There was a bias toward equating social actors with the organised labour movement and the venerable United Nations–centred international organisation, the International Labor Organization. And gender remained entirely absent as a concern.

As the G8 moved from Cologne to the Year 2000 Okinawa Summit, there were important concerns about how deep and durable this new social sensitivity would prove to be. It was possible that it was but a transitory, tactical response to the global financial crises of 1997–99 (and thus destined to disappear with the return of stability and growth), or to the particular shock of the failure of the MAI. Moreover, it was unclear whether the Japanese hosts in 2000 would be as naturally sympathetic in that Asian setting to such concerns as the 'red-green' governing coalition of Germany in 1999. As their preparations for their Okinawa Summit moved from spring into early summer, there were no clear signs that strengthening social safeguards would again be an overarching theme (Hajnal and Kirton 2000, Akaneya 2000, Weilemann 2000). Yet, the slow and tentative recovery in Japan and the rest of Asia, the jarring protests at the WTO ministerial meeting in Seattle in December 1999 and at the United Nations Conference on Trade and Development (UNCTAD) in Bangkok in February 2000 suggested these concerns would stay alive.

There was, however, some evidence that the G8's new social sensitivity might endure and even expand. The relationship between the leaders and ministerial levels of the G7/8 process can sometimes be tenuous. G7 finance ministers, meeting without Russia, have a much narrower mission than their leaders, and one that is among the least likely across portfolios in G7 governments to embrace social concerns. Yet on 25 September 1999, in Washington, the G7 finance ministers and central bank governors gave extensive emphasis to social concerns in their treatment of the two central economic pillars of the Cologne

Summit — debt of the poorest and the international financial architecture. On debt, they underscored that budgetary resources should be targeted to specified social priorities, that poverty reduction programs should involve public participation, and that barriers to access by the poor should be reduced (G7 Finance Ministers 1999). In the annex on financial architecture, they included as a priority for further work the task of ensuring that 'social policies are in place to ease adjustment during times of crisis and prevent the burden of adjustment from falling disproportionately on the poorest and most vulnerable groups in society'. They affirmed the World Bank's work to develop principles and good practices in social policy, called on them to be given operational effects, and asked that 'IMF and World Bank programs take full account of the social dimensions' (G7 Finance Ministers 1999).

At Berlin in December 1999, at their special meeting to discuss conflict prevention, the G8 foreign ministers concluded that the prevention of armed conflict required an integrated, comprehensive approach in which social policies had an equal place with political, security, economic, financial, environmental, and development policies. They also included social justice as a principle on which this approach was to be based (G8 Foreign Ministers 1999).

There was, however, some diminution of concern, as the chair passed from Germany to Japan, as the subject of ministerial meetings altered and as time went on. The Communiqué of the G8 Ministerial Conference on combating transnational organised crime, held in Moscow on 19–20 October 1999, made no mention of the social dimension, despite the links between the two subjects made by G8 leaders in the Cologne Communiqué (see Appendix B). More importantly, the G7 finance ministers, meeting in Tokyo on 22 January 2000, did not refer to the social dimension of their work.

In sharp contrast, the first G8 meeting of education ministers, held in Japan on 1–2 April 2000 gave strong emphasis to the social themes highlighted at Cologne. The ministers took social development and social cohesion, along with economic development, as their overall goals, and, at the individual level, emphasised social needs, social success, and social life. They called for educational initiatives to be implemented in engagement with society as a whole and with local communities. They also pointed to the new social pressures on individuals, amidst both affluence and poverty. They highlighted the problems of poverty and social neglect and called for strong safety nets for those at risk of marginalisation. They emphasised that social and economic policy must work together equally to address these problems and shrink the 'digital divide' between the more and less advantaged members of society.

From Cologne through Okinawa toward Genoa: Defects and Disappointments

The view presented in the forgoing section is an optimistic one with respect to the governments' ability to incorporate social objectives into global governance. Despite an indisputable agreement on the desirability of social cohesion and increasing welfare across the world among all schools of thought, there are other views of global leadership that are more critical of the prospects for, and desirability of moving along the path of building in social safeguards from the start. Economists especially are very sceptical, as has been shown elsewhere in this volume. Their case falls into two lines of arguments.

The first is a public choice or political economy view. The following passage gives a very brief overview of its main reasoning. It does not strive for perfection or completeness, but does give a feeling of the concerns economists usually have. Governments do not operate in isolation from different interest groups, and they depend on re-election to implement their political objectives. These two constraints are responsible for the deviation of political rationality from economic rationality. It sometimes pays for governments to favour certain groups at the expense of others and to think in a short-term way rather than within a long-term perspective. Thus, it often occurs that economic policy does not allow for the economy to explore all potential efficiency gains.

Examples of such behaviour are legion. To name just one that has been raised in this volume, the European Community's trade policy very much reflects the fact that agriculture in the EU is highly subsidised and protected from foreign competition. The Common Agricultural Policy (CAP) is extremely costly, not only for the EU's citizens but also for third countries, and it recurrently gives rise to international conflict. Therefore, an economically rational policy would rely on the international division of labour. However, the respective interest groups in the EU are politically important and prevent an economically superior policy from prevailing. To be sure, the behaviour of the responsible European politicians is not perceived as being evil in this view. Public choice is rather about rationality in that it makes very clear the rationality behind certain policies. Furthermore, it shows that leaders — be they on a national or an international scale — are not benevolent dictators. Instead, they have their own objective functions that are, technically speaking, to be maximised.

The second argument is related to the knowledge and information that governments and markets can generate and fruitfully explore. Given that there are bits and pieces of information emerging very quickly and spontaneously all over the world that are relevant for the decision making of individuals and governments, it seems to be a good strategy to use markets as the proper place to use this information. In this view, governments should avoid as much as possible engaging in the process of setting the division of labour, be it as market participant, wage setter, or price setter. The latter includes the fixing of exchange rates. Economists are aware of the fact that a 'pretence of knowledge' is likely to occur.

In other words, the best way to make the optimum use of information about changing scarcities is to rely on decentralised activities as observable in markets. In addition, this view implies that political action should always take place on the lowest possible political level — following the subsidiarity principle. It must be acknowledged that the subsidiarity principle can be interpreted very differently. Indeed, it even can become completely meaningless, if every political action is justified with it. Nevertheless, it should be the guide for agenda setting, in particular in the international arena.

Again, governments are assumed to act with the best of intentions. The problem here is the lack of relevant information that increases with a rising political level. This holds in many policy fields, among them social policy. Thus, to summarise, economists are sceptical as to the ability of international organisations, fora, summits, and such to care adequately for social concerns. What does this mean for global governance? Should the role of G8, G20, and other international gatherings be cut down? Not at all. Global governance is both necessary and useful. There is no disputing that in a world of increasing globalisation there is an increasing need for international co-ordination. Private and public activities in one country influence the situation in other countries — to an ever increasing extent. This volume has highlighted several fields where international spillovers are on the rise: trade in goods and services, financial flows, environmental problems, crime, and, last but certainly not least, international and even internal conflict.

Increasing globalisation calls for a new shaping of responsibilities. For instance, one field not extensively covered in this volume is the competition order. A huge debate is going on about whether international mergers and acquisitions call for international competition law. This certainly must be considered in the coming years and will enter the agenda of forthcoming summits. The same can be said for the need to devise an international regime and appropriate international institution to govern information technology on a global scale. And the need for a strong central global environmental organisation or co-ordinating mechanism and for regimes for freshwater and forests are becoming apparent. This shows that international agencies should also be flexible so they can both respond to new developments and be changed or even dissolved if old tasks become obsolete. Ever increasing structural change does not exclude these bodies. A large task of ensuring effectiveness and coherence in global governance for the twenty-first century lies ahead.

However, given the existence of political considerations as well as the relevance of decentralised information, there is one extremely important restriction on the scope of international summits. They should be used exclusively to set the rules of the game. These include international trade rules, banking regulation rules, the rules affirming independent central banks, and the like. There is no economic justification for the forthcoming summits to allow the G8 or other bodies to play in the game itself by setting prices, defining minimum wages, or minimum ecological standards that would be valid all over the world. The clear lesson of the recent history of international relations is that rules rather than discretion are a device to enhance economic growth, social justice, and high environmental standards. The WTO can be quoted as the one success story in international relations. The G8 process is the second, as long as it is used to work on rules, as it largely has done in the past.

Conclusion

Throughout this volume, the assessments of the G8 approach to global governance have been diverse. They range from cautious optimism and reasonable confidence in the leaders' ability to address and solve the relevant problems of global governance to a more critical view that does not question the need for international co-ordination but sees a limited role for the kind of co-ordination that should take place. Whereas the former sees some scope for discretionary action, the latter insists on the restriction of international fora to set the rules of the game. The issues covered as this debate unfolds span and integrate a broad range of issues, embracing trade policy, international financial architecture, environmental policy, and social cohesion.

There is much to be gained from the dialogue among different, if not entirely controversial, perspectives, and policy recommendations. They make it clear for researchers from different social science disciplines and traditions that there is a variety of standpoints justified by thorough analysis. The variety presented here in *Guiding Global Order* will contribute to a deeper understanding of the G8 process and will, one hopes, contribute, at least at the margin, to an improved and adequate system of global governance in the future.

Notes

1 Those employing this decision-based, liberal-optimising policy co-ordination (package deal) referent tend to award lower grades to individual Summits for failing to live up to this high ideal standard in practice. Those starting from a concert conception of G8 governance, which gives greater weight to direction-setting and deliberative functions, to disasters avoided and to the *status quo* defensively pursued, tend to grade individual achievements with higher marks, consistent with more conservative conceptions of what any international institution can achieve in an anarchic work of sovereign states (see Kirton 1989). Others, such as von Furstenberg and Daniels (1993), Kokotsis (1995, 1999), and Kokotsis and Daniels (1999), rate the Summit's achievements on the compliance of the actual members with the collective commitments in the year after they were made, rather than rating the agreements reached at the Summit itself. One thus needs to wait to see if the agreements made at Cologne were actually fulfilled in order to assign a definitive grade or characterise it as 'Summit of high achievement'. Here, the 1999/2000 compliance assessment of the G8 Research Group, assessing compliance by the nine G8 members (including the European Union) with six priority issues at Cologne, embracing economic, transnational, and political-security (terrorism) domains, offer an average compliance score of +0.39 (G8 Research Group 2000). This is marginally below the +0.45 of Birmingham 1998, but above the +0.15 of Denver 1997 and +0.36 of Lyon 1996. It is also above the traditional +0.30 yielded by the seminal von Furstenberg and Daniels analysis of the economic and energy commitments of the G7 Summits form 1975 to 1989.

2 This section is based on John Kirton, 'An Assessment of the 1999 Cologne G7/G8 Summit by Issue Area', as assisted by the G8 Research Group, 20 June 1999, available at <www.g7.utoronto.ca>. It has been updated to take account of new information and subsequent developments, although in general terms the initial judgements largely stand.

3 For a sceptical view see Carothers (1999–2000).

4 The G7 leaders' statement, released at Cologne on 18 June 1999, emphasised promoting social policies to protect the poor and most vulnerable, the need to invest in basic social needs, and declared: 'Social policies are the cornerstone of a viable international financial architecture. Economic development and reform must benefit all members of society' (G7 1999a). It also noted the Cologne Debt Initiative should proceed in consultation with civil society and be directed at social needs.

References

Akaneya, T. (2000), 'The View from Japan: Tasks for the G8 Kyushu-Okinawa Summit Meeting', *NIRA Review*, vol. 7, no. 2, pp. 11–15.

Archibugi, D., D. Held, and M. Köhler (eds.) (1998), *Re-imagining Political Community: Studies in Cosmopolitan Democracy*, Polity Press, Cambridge.

Arrighi, G., and B. Silver (1999), *Chaos and Governance in the Modern World System*, University of Minnesota Press, Minneapolis.

Baker, A. (2000), 'The G-7 as a Global 'Ginger Group': Plurilateralism and Four-Dimensional Diplomacy', *Global Governance*, vol. 6, pp. 165–190.

Bayne, N. (2000), *Hanging in There: The G7 and G8 Summit in Maturity and Renewal*, Ashgate, Aldershot.

Boyer, M., M. Caprioli, R. Denemark, E. Hanson, and S. Lamy (2000), 'Visions of International Studies in a New Millennium', *International Studies Perspectives*, vol. 1 (April), pp. 1–9.

Carothers, Thomas (1999/2000), 'Civil Society', *Foreign Policy*, Winter, pp. 18–24.

Clayton, J. (2000), *The Global Debt Bomb*, M. E. Sharpe, Armonk, NY.

Commission for Environmental Cooperation (1999), 'Assessing Environmental Effects of the North American Free Trade Agreement (NAFTA): An Analytic Framework (Phase II)', in Commission for Environmental Co-operation (ed.), *Assessing Environmental Effects of the North American Free Trade Agreement (NAFTA): An Analytic Framework (Phase II) and Issue Studies*, Commission for Environmental Co-operation, Montreal, pp. 1–43.

Cox, D., with T. Sinclair (1996), *Approaches to World Order*, Cambridge University Press, Cambridge.

Deibert, R. (1997), *Parchment, Printing, and Hypermedia: Communication in World Order Transformation*, Columbia University Press, New York.

Dent, M., and B. Peters (2000), *The Crisis of Poverty and Debt in the Third World*, Ashgate, Aldershot.

Dewitt, D., D. Haglund, and J. Kirton (eds.) (1993), *Building a New Global Order: Emerging Trends in International Security*, Oxford University Press, Toronto.

G7 (1975), 'Declaration of Rambouillet', Rambouillet, 17 November, <www.library.utoronto.ca/g7/summit/1975rambouillet/communique.html> (September 2000).

G7 (1999a), 'G7 Statement', Cologne, 18 June, <www.library.utoronto.ca/g7/summit/1999koln/g7statement_june18.htm> (September 2000).

G7 Finance Ministers (1998), 'Declaration of G7 Finance Ministers and Central Bank Governors', 30 October, Washington DC, <www.library.utoronto.ca/g7/finance/fm103098.htm> (September 2000).

G7 Finance Ministers (1999), 'Statement of G-7 Finance Ministers and Central Bank Governors', Washington DC, 25 September, <www.library.utoronto.ca/g7/finance/fm992509state.htm>, (September 2000).

G8 Foreign Ministers (1999), 'Conclusions of the Meeting of the G-8 Foreign Ministers Meeting in Berlin', 16–17 December, Berlin, <www.library.utoronto.ca/g7/foreign/fm991216.htm> (September 2000).

G8 Research Group (2000), *Assessment of Compliance with the 1999 Cologne Commitments*, <www.g7.utoronto.ca/analytic studies/2000> (September 2000).

Gill, S. (1993), 'Gramsci and Global Politics: Towards a Post-Hegemonic Research Agenda', in Stephen Gill (ed.), *Gramsci, Historical Materialism, and International Relations*, Cambridge University Press, Cambridge.

Hajnal, P., and J. Kirton (2000), 'The Evolving Role and Agenda of the G7/G8: A North American Perspective', *NIRA Review*, vol. 7, no. 2, pp. 5–10.

Held, David (1995), *Democracy and the Global Order: From the Modern State to Cosmopolitan Governance*, Stanford University Press, Stanford.

Hodges, M., J. Kirton, and J. Daniels (eds.) (1999), *The G8's Role in the New Millennium*, Ashgate, Aldershot.

Kaiser, K., J. Kirton, and J. Daniels (eds.) (2000), *Shaping a New International Financial System: Challenges of Governance in a Globalizing World*, Ashgate, Aldershot.

Kirkpatrick, Colin, and Norman Lee (1999), 'WTO New Round: Sustainability Impact Assessment Study, Phase Two, Main Report', Institute for Development Policy and Management and Environmental Impact Assessment Centre, University of Manchester, 18 November.

Kirton, J. (1989), 'Contemporary Concert Diplomacy: The Seven-Power Summit and the Management of International Order', Paper prepared for the annual meeting of the International Studies Association and the British International Studies Association, London, 29 March–1 April, <www.library.utoronto.ca/g7/scholar/kirton198901/index.html> (September 2000).

Kirton, J. (1999a), 'An Assessment of the 1999 Cologne G7/G8 Summit by Issue Area', with the G8 Research Group, <www.library.utoronto.ca/g7/evaluations/1999koln/issues/kolnperf.htm> (September 2000).

Kirton, J. (1999b), 'Economic Cooperation, Summitry, Institutions and Structural Change', in Gavin Boyd and John Dunning (eds.), *Structural Change and Cooperation in the Global Economy*, Edward Elgar, Cheltenham, pp. 1–38.

Kirton, J. (2000), 'The G7 and Concert Governance in the Global Financial Crisis of 1997–99', Paper prepared for the annual conference of the International Studies Association, Los Angeles, 15–19 March.

Kokotsis, E. (1995), 'Keeping Sustainable Development Commitments: The Recent G7 Record', in John Kirton and Sarah Richardson (eds.), *The Halifax Summit, Sustainable Development, and Institutional Reform*, National Round Table on the Environment and the Economy, Ottawa, pp. 117–133, <www.library.utoronto.ca/g7/scholar/kirton199503/kokotsis/index.html> (September 2000).

Kokotsis, E. (1999), *Keeping International Commitments: Compliance, Credibility, and the G7, 1988–1995*, Garland Publishing, New York.

Kokotsis, E., and J. Daniels (1999), 'G8 Summits and Compliance', in Michael Hodges, John Kirton, and Joseph Daniels (eds.), *The G8's Role in the New Millennium*, Ashgate, Aldershot, pp. 75–94.

Putnam, R., and N. Bayne (1987), *Hanging Together: Cooperation and Conflict in the Seven-Power Summits*, Harvard University Press, Cambridge, MA.

Rugman, A. (1999), 'Negotiating Multilateral Rules to Promote Investment', in M. Hodges, J. Kirton, and J. Daniels (eds.), *The G8's Role in the New Millennium*, Ashgate, Aldershot, pp. 143–158.

von Furstenberg, George M., and Joseph Daniels (1992), 'Can You Trust G-7 Promises?', *International Economic Insights*, vol. 3 (September/October), pp. 24–27.

Weilemann, P. (2000), 'The Summit Meeting: Diplomacy at its Highest Level', *NIRA Review*, vol. 7, no. 1, pp. 16–20.

Appendices

A New Challenges for the International Monetary System

HELMUT SCHIEBER

During the past few years, monetary aggregates and monetary turnover have grown much faster worldwide than the real economy. Similarly, the process of integration towards a global market (known as 'globalisation') has probably taken place even more quickly in the financial sector than in the real economy.

Whereas in the real economy, volatility — in the sense of fluctuations in output — has tended to decrease in recent years (*inter alia* due to a rising government spending ratio to gross domestic product (GDP), the stabilisation of incomes due to growing government transfers, an increasing share of services with a tendency for demand to be more stable), volatility in the financial sector has tended to increase (examples: increase in short-term cross-border capital movements, growing importance of institutional investors with a leaning to short-termism, increasing spillover effects between financial market segments, asset price bubbles, unstable financial sectors in emerging markets).

In view of the resulting global systemic risks, the task of building and maintaining sound and resilient financial institutions and markets assumes a crucial importance. Extending international and cross-sector co-operation among prudential supervisors — embracing the emerging markets — must be given a high priority (examples: drawing up international standards such as the Basle 'Core Principles'; involving the International Monetary Fund (IMF) and World Bank in the implementation of these standards; setting up the Financial Stability Forum (FSF) and a new training centre for banking supervisors at the Bank for International Settlements (BIS); further extending the network of memos of understanding with a view to improving the co-ordination of prudential activities).

Short-term cross-border capital links with their high-maturity transformation and currency risks have played a major role in the financial crises of recent years. This has rightly triggered an intensive international debate about the scale, conditions and timing of the liberalisation of capital flows, especially for emerging markets. My propositions:

a) Priority of liberalising long-term capital movements (including direct investment) over liberalising the more volatile short-term capital movements.
b) Precautionary control of capital imports better than crisis-triggered moves to prevent capital exports (capital flight).
c) Linking the liberalisation of capital movements to progress made in creating a sound, resilient, and well-supervised financial sector.
d) Use of international prudential standards to prevent maturity transformation and currency risks in the financial sector.

The efforts already under way to prevent and — where unavoidable — to resolve financial crises (new financial architecture) must be vigorously pursued. The International Financial Institutions (the IMF, World Bank, regional development banks, and the BIS) play a key role. It is particularly important in this respect to strengthen the policy-improving role especially of the IMF and the World Bank (examples: appropriate economic policy, good governance, compatible exchange rate systems, promotion of stable financial systems).

In averting crises, the key concept is transparency and disclosure. This especially concerns improving debtor information (e.g., IMF standards, Article IV consultations), creditor statistics (BIS), and ensuring a more intensive exchange of information between official agencies and the private sector at both the national and international level. Creditor banks need to pay particular attention to the subject of risk management and risk controlling.

When it comes to solving financial crises, the IMF needs to concentrate more than it has done in the past on its role as a catalyst. Massive injections of financial aid are if anything counterproductive, given the moral hazard they engender and the immense international financial potential; it is imperative to involve private creditors in the task of resolving crises. That goes not only for banks and financial institutions but also for bondholders. The problems that need to be tackled in this context are admittedly diverse and complex; but that makes it all the more necessary to discuss the issues and make headway. One thing is certain, however: a unilateral transformation of the IMF and the other International Financial Institutions into international lenders of last resort would have disastrous consequences.

B G8 Communiqué Köln 1999

Final, June 20, 1999

1. We, the Heads of State and Government of eight major democracies and the President of the European Commission, met in Köln for the 25th Economic Summit. On the threshold of the new millennium we discussed growing opportunities as well as forward-looking solutions to the challenges facing our nations and the international community.
2. Globalization, a complex process involving rapid and increasing flows of ideas, capital, technology, goods and services around the world, has already brought profound change to our societies. It has cast us together as never before. Greater openness and dynamism have contributed to the widespread improvement of living standards and a significant reduction in poverty. Integration has helped to create jobs by stimulating efficiency, opportunity and growth. The information revolution and greater exposure to each others' cultures and values have strengthened the democratic impulse and the fight for human rights and fundamental freedoms while spurring creativity and innovation. At the same time, however, globalization has been accompanied by a greater risk of dislocation and financial uncertainty for some workers, families and communities across the world.
3. The challenge is to seize the opportunities globalization affords while addressing its risks to respond to concerns about a lack of control over its effects. We must work to sustain and increase the benefits of globalization and ensure that its positive effects are widely shared by people all over the world. We therefore call on governments and international institutions, business and labor, civil society and the individual to work together to meet this challenge and realize the full potential of globalization for raising prosperity and promoting social progress while preserving the environment.

I. Getting the World Economy on Track for Sustained Growth

4. Since we met last year in Birmingham, the world economy has faced major challenges. Progress has been achieved in addressing the crisis and laying the foundations for recovery. Policy steps aimed at supporting growth in the major industrialized countries and important policy actions leading to stronger performance in some emerging markets have improved the economic outlook. A number of substantial challenges still remain. We therefore renew our commitment to pursue appropriate macroeconomic policies and structural reforms. These will contribute to more balanced growth in the world economy, thereby reducing external imbalances.

5. The world economy is still feeling the effects of the financial crises that started in Asia two years ago. Without an open, rules-based world trading system and the beneficial flows of goods and services it encourages, the countries affected would be having much greater difficulty recovering from these crises and stabilizing their economies.

6. We welcome the outline agreements recently reached by Russia with the IMF and the World Bank and look forward to their speedy implementation as a further important step in Russia's reform program. Once an IMF agreement is in place, we encourage the Paris Club to act expeditiously to negotiate a debt rescheduling agreement with Russia. In order to support Russia's efforts towards macroeconomic stability and sustainable growth, we encourage the Paris Club to continue to deal with the problem of the Russian debt arising from Soviet era obligations, aiming at comprehensive solutions at a later stage once Russia has established conditions that enable it to implement a more ambitious economic reform program.

7. We agreed to intensify our dialogue within the G8 structures on the longer term social, structural and economic reform in Russia. To this end, we have instructed our personal representatives to ensure the overall continuity and cohesion of the work among the G8 on this subject. Particular emphasis should be given to concrete areas of cooperation such as small business development, strengthened cooperation with regions, health, the social impact of economic transformation. We agreed to deepen our cooperation on law enforcement, fighting organized crime and money laundering, including as they relate to capital flight.

II. Building a World Trading System That Works for Everyone

8.   The multilateral trading system incorporated in the World Trade
     Organization (WTO) has been key to promoting international trade and
     investment and to increasing economic growth, employment and social
     progress. We therefore renew our strong support for the WTO and our
     commitment to an open trade and investment environment. We call on all
     nations to resist protectionist pressures and to open their markets further.
     We encourage those states not yet members of the WTO to join it, by
     accepting its principles.

9.   Given the WTO's vital role, we agree on the importance of improving its
     transparency to make it more responsive to civil society while preserving
     its government-to-government nature. We pledge to work for a successful
     ministerial meeting in Seattle in order to launch the new round. We will
     also seek a more effective way within the WTO for addressing the trade
     and environment relationship and promoting sustainable development and
     social and economic welfare worldwide.

10. We therefore call on all nations to launch at the WTO Ministerial
     Conference in Seattle in December 1999 a new round of broad-based and
     ambitious negotiations with the aim of achieving substantial
     and manageable results. All members should have a stake in the process.
     We encourage all members to make proposals for progress in areas where
     developing countries and in particular least developed countries can make
     solid and substantial gains; all countries should contribute to and benefit
     from the new round. An effective new round of trade negotiations should
     help pave the way for the further integration of the developing countries
     into the world economy. In this context we reaffirm our commitment made
     in Birmingham last year to the least developed countries on improved
     market access. We also urge greater cooperation and policy coherence
     among international financial, economic, labor and environmental
     organizations.

11. Because trade is increasingly global, the consequences of developments
     in biotechnology must be dealt with at the national and international levels
     in all the appropriate fora. We are committed to a science-based, rules-
     based approach to addressing these issues.

III. Designing Policies for More Employment

12. One of the most urgent economic problems is the high level of unemployment in many countries. We reaffirm the importance of intensified international cooperation and enhanced efforts at the national level to design the right policies for more employment. To strengthen the foundations for sustainable growth and job creation, we strongly emphasize a two-tiered approach:
    - promoting structural reforms to enhance the adaptability and competitiveness of our economies and to help the long-term unemployed to return to the labor market;
    - pursuing macroeconomic policies for stability and growth and ensure that monetary and fiscal policies are well balanced.
13. The greater the adaptability of our economies, the greater the likelihood that economic growth will result in more employment. We therefore strongly support the elimination of structural rigidities in labor, capital and product markets, the promotion of entrepreneurship and innovation, investment in human capital, reform of the tax/benefit systems to strengthen economic incentives and encourage employment, and development of an innovative and knowledge-based society.
14. We also endorse the G8 Labor Ministers' conclusions at their conference in Washington last February, namely to provide social safety nets that support employment, to prevent long-term unemployment by early action, to facilitate job search by offering labor market information and employment services, to promote lifelong learning and new forms of work organization, to ensure equal access to the labor market for all workers, including job entrants and older workers, and to take forward the social dialogue.

IV. Investing in People

15. Basic education, vocational training, academic qualifications, lifelong upgrading of skills and knowledge for the labor market, and support for the development of innovative thinking are essential to shape economic and technical progress as we move towards a knowledge-based society. They also enrich individuals and foster civic responsibility and social inclusion.
16. In support of these goals, we agree to pursue the aims and ambitions set out in the Köln Charter.

17. Adaptability, employability and the management of change will be the primary challenges for our societies in the coming century. Mobility between jobs, cultures and communities will be essential. And the passport to mobility will be education and lifelong learning for everyone.

18. To this end, we support an increase in exchanges of teachers, administrators and students among the nations of the Eight and with other nations and invite our experts to identify the main obstacles to increased exchanges and to come forward with appropriate proposals before the next Summit. We call upon the and the United Nations Educational, Scientific and Cultural Organization (UNESCO) to study how different countries are attempting to raise education standards, for example by looking at best practices in the recruitment, training, compensation and accountability of the teaching profession internationally. We commit ourselves to explore jointly ways to work together and through international institutions to help our own countries as well as developing nations use technology to address learning and development needs, for example, through distance learning.

V. Strengthening Social Safeguards

19. As the process of globalization has gained momentum, it has brought with it important social and economic progress. At the same time, rapid change and integration has left some individuals and groups feeling unable to keep up and has resulted in some dislocation, particularly in developing countries. We therefore need to take steps to strengthen the institutional and social infrastructure that can give globalization a 'human face' and ensure increasing, widely shared prosperity.

20. Social security policies, including social safety nets, must be strong enough to encourage and enable individuals to embrace global change and liberalization and to improve their chances on the labor market, while enhancing social cohesion. We recognize that faced with financial constraints, it is vital to strike a sustainable balance between social support programs and greater personal responsibility and initiative.

21. We are convinced that the countries most seriously affected by the recent economic and financial crises will sustain a speedier recovery if they create and improve the necessary social infrastructure. It is therefore particularly important to maintain investment in basic social services during times of crisis. Budgetary priorities and flexibility should enhance the quality of social infrastructure and investment.

22. Democracy, the rule of law, good governance and respect for human rights and for core labor standards are further indispensable prerequisites for social stability. The development of well-functioning and corruption-free institutions that are cost-effective, transparent and accountable to the public must complement the process of liberalization.

23. We call on the International Financial Institutions (IFIs) to support and monitor the development of sound social policy and infrastructure in developing countries. We commend actions already being taken in this regard. We urge the International Monetary Fund (IMF) to give more attention to this issue in designing its economic programs and to give particular priority to core budgets such as basic health, education and training to the extent possible, even during periods of fiscal consolidation. We welcome the efforts of the World Bank, in collaboration with the UN, to develop principles of good practice in social policy and their work to strengthen partnerships with borrower countries through the comprehensive development network. We invite the World Bank and the IMF to work together to develop a set of policies and practices that can be drawn upon, by donors and borrowers alike, in the design of adjustment programs that ensure the protection of the most vulnerable.

24. We support improved exchange of information, including analysis of the cost and benefits of social safety nets, within the UN, the OECD, and in other appropriate fora on the design and implementation of social reforms.

25. We commit ourselves to promote effective implementation of the International Labor Organization's (ILO) Declaration On Fundamental Principles and Rights at Work and its Follow-up. We also welcome the adoption of the ILO Convention on the Elimination of the Worst Forms of Child Labor. We further intend to step up work with developing countries to improve their capacity to meet their obligations. We support the strengthening of the ILO's capacity to assist countries in implementing core labor standards.

26. We also welcome the increasing cooperation between the ILO and the IFIs in promoting adequate social protection and core labor standards. We urge the IFIs to incorporate these standards into their policy dialogue with member countries. In addition, we stress the importance of effective cooperation between the WTO and the ILO on the social dimensions of globalization and trade liberalization.

VI. Deepening the Development Partnership

27. Developing countries are essential partners in a globalized world. We are committed to working with them, especially with the poorest countries, to eradicate poverty, launch effective policies for sustainable development and develop their capacity to integrate better into the global economy, thus benefiting from the opportunities offered by globalization.

    – We will continue to provide substantial support and assistance to developing and transition economies in support of their own efforts to open and diversify their economies, to democratize and improve governance, and to protect human rights.

    – We will strive gradually to increase the volume of official development assistance (ODA), and to put special emphasis on countries best positioned to use it effectively.

    – To ease future debt burdens and facilitate sustainable development, we agree to increase the share of grant-based financing in the ODA we provide to the least developed countries.

    – Non-governmental organizations also have an important role to play.

    – While international assistance and debt relief are clearly important, their positive effects depend on sound national efforts towards economic and structural reform and good governance, where the private sector and civil society are able to play productive roles.

    – We intend to step up work with developing countries and multilateral institutions to improve developing country capacity to exercise their rights and meet their obligations in the global trading system so as to ensure that they derive the full benefits of liberalized trade and thus contribute to global economic growth.

    – We call on the UN and the IFIs to help developing countries mobilize sufficient means for social services and basic infrastructure and continue to support and to mainstream democratization, good governance and the rule of law into country development strategies.

    – We reaffirm our support for the OECD mandate to finalize a recommendation on untying aid to the least developed countries. We call on OECD members to bring this effort to a successful conclusion as soon as possible.

28. We reaffirm our commitment to contribute to the achievement of economic and social development in Africa, Asia and Latin America. We will review the situation in that regard every year, on the basis of reports by the IFIs and the relevant regional development banks, on the alleviation of poverty.

VII. Launching the Köln Debt Initiative

29. We have decided to give a fresh boost to debt relief to developing countries. In recent years the international creditor community has introduced a number of debt relief measures for the poorest countries. The Highly Indebted Poor Countries (HIPC) framework has made an important contribution in this respect. Recent experience suggests that further efforts are needed to achieve a more enduring solution to the problem of unsustainable debt burdens. To this end we welcome the 1999 Köln Debt Initiative, which is designed to provide deeper, broader and faster debt relief through major changes to the HIPC framework. The central objective of this initiative is to provide a greater focus on poverty reduction by releasing resources for investment in health, education and social needs. In this context we also support good governance and sustainable development.

30. We are aware that new proposals will require additional substantial financing. While several means of financing are under consideration, credible progress in identifying additional funding possibilities is needed, and we stand ready to help with financing solutions. In this context we recognize the importance of fair burden sharing among creditors.

VIII. Redoubling Efforts to Protect the Environment

31. To underscore our commitment to sustainable development we will step up our efforts to build a coherent global and environmentally responsive framework of multilateral agreements and institutions. We support the outcome of the G8 Environment Ministers' meeting in Schwerin and will expedite international cooperation on the establishment, general recognition and continual improvement of environmental standards and norms. We agree that environmental considerations should be taken fully into account in the upcoming round of WTO negotiations. This should include a clarification of the relationship between both multilateral environmental agreements and key environmental principles, and WTO rules.

32. We agree to continue to support the Multilateral Development Banks in making environmental considerations an integral part of their activities and we will do likewise when providing our own support. We will work within the OECD towards common environmental guidelines for export finance agencies. We aim to complete this work by the 2001 G8 Summit.

33. We reaffirm that we consider climate change an extremely serious threat to sustainable development. We will therefore work towards timely progress in implementing the Buenos Aires Plan of Action with a view to early entry into force of the Kyoto Protocol. In particular, we encourage decisions on the operation of the Kyoto mechanisms and on a strong and effective compliance regime. We underline the importance of taking action to reduce greenhouse gas emissions through rational and efficient use of energy and through other cost-effective means. To this end, we commit ourselves to develop and implement domestic measures including under the UN Framework Convention on Climate Change. We also agreed to exchange experience on best practices. We will also promote increasing global participation of developing countries in limiting greenhouse gas emissions. We welcome the action already taken by developing countries and stress the need to support their efforts through financial mechanisms, the development and transfer of technology, and capacity-building. We note the important role that the Clean Development Mechanism (CDM) can play in these areas. We also welcome the intention announced by some developing countries in Buenos Aires to undertake further commitments to abate their greenhouse gas emissions.

IX. Promoting Non-proliferation, Arms Control and Disarmament

34. Strengthening the international non-proliferation regime and disarmament measures is one of our most important international priorities. We intend to build a broad international partnership on expanded threat reduction to address security, arms control, decommissioning and non-proliferation requirements while reducing risks to the environment. This will build on efforts currently being undertaken and planned by G8 countries and others. We are committed to increased resources for these purposes and encourage all other interested countries to join us.

35. We recognize the continuing need to protect and manage weapons-grade fissile material, especially plutonium. In past years, G8 countries have worked on the issue of managing weapons-grade nuclear material no longer required for defense purposes. We affirm our intention to establish arrangements for the safe management of such fissile material. We strongly support the concrete initiatives being undertaken by G8 countries and others for scientific and technical cooperation necessary to support future large-scale disposition programs. We invite all interested countries to

support projects for early implementation of large-scale programs and urge establishment of a joint strategy. We recognize that an international approach to financing will be required involving both public and private funds, and we will review potential increases in our own resource commitments prior to the next G8 Summit.

36. We are deeply concerned about recent missile flight tests and developments in missile proliferation, such as actions by North Korea. We undertake to examine further individual and collective means of addressing this problem and reaffirm our commitment to the objectives of the Missile Technology Control Regime (MTCR).

37. Effective export control mechanisms are essential for achieving a broad range of our arms control and non-proliferation objectives. We will continue to look for ways to strengthen these mechanisms. At the same time we stress the role of the Nuclear Suppliers' Group in preventing nuclear proliferation.

38. One year after the nuclear tests by India and Pakistan, we reiterate our concerns and reaffirm our statement from the Birmingham Communiqué. Recent missile tests have further increased tension in the region. We encourage both countries to follow first positive steps already undertaken by joining international non-proliferation and disarmament efforts and taking the steps set out in UN Security Council resolution 1172.

X. Tackling Global Challenges

39. In many countries, violent conflicts and civil wars continue to be an obstacle to making good use of the opportunities of globalization. Effective crisis prevention and management must address the root causes of these conflicts. These causes include the political manipulation of ethnic tensions, economic and social inequality, and extreme poverty as well as the absence of democracy, the rule of law and good political and economic governance. They are often exacerbated by human rights violations, environmental degradation, scarcity of resources, rapid population growth and the rapid spread of diseases.

40. In order to improve our ability to prevent crises, it is necessary, consistent with the principles and purposes of the UN Charter, to:
    – enhance the capacity to recognize and address the potential for conflict at an early stage. Risks and causes of violent conflicts must be more effectively monitored and the information shared to forestall them;

- ensure that our security, economic, environmental and development policies are properly coordinated and are conducive to the prevention of violent conflict. We will, in our dialogue with other countries and international institutions, work to coordinate our policies;
- recognize the important role the United Nations plays in crisis prevention and seek to strengthen its capacity in this area;
- monitor systematically military expenditures in the larger context of public expenditure patterns and in the macroeconomic context for growth and development;
- encourage and support the efforts of regional organizations and arrangements to expand their jurisdictional and operational ability, in accordance with international law, to help control and resolve conflict in their area;
- promote a free press, establish fair electoral processes, help improve the democratic accountability and functioning of legislatures, of judicial systems and of the military and the police forces, and improve human rights monitoring and advocacy.

41. We are concerned at the continuing global spread of AIDS. We reaffirm the need to continue efforts to combat AIDS at the national and international level through a combined strategy of prevention, vaccine development and appropriate therapy. We welcome and support the coordinating and catalytic role of UNAIDS in the fight against AIDS. We call on co-sponsors and other partners to cooperate in the formulation of clear goals, strategies and initiatives at both the global and regional level.

42. We also pledge to continue our national and international efforts in the fight against infectious and parasitic diseases, such as malaria, polio and tuberculosis, and their drug-resistant forms. In particular we will continue to support the endeavors of the World Health Organization and its initiatives 'Roll Back Malaria' and 'Stop TB'. We call on governments to adopt these recommended strategies.

43. In light of the increasing importance of issues concerning food safety we invite the OECD Working Group on Harmonization of Regulatory Oversight of Biotechnology and the OECD Task Force for the Safety of Novel Foods and Feeds to undertake a study of the implications of biotechnology and other aspects of food safety. We invite OECD experts to discuss their findings with our personal representatives. We ask the latter to report to us by the next Summit on possible ways to improve our approach to these issues through international and other institutions, taking into account the reflections underway in other fora.

44. We welcome the growing recognition by the international community of the damaging effects of all forms of corruption and the coming into force of the OECD Anti-Bribery Convention in February 1999. We hope that more countries will ratify the Convention. We applaud the results and planned follow-up of the international conference on anti-corruption efforts, attended by over 80 countries including all G8 partners, and the OECD conference on anti-corruption efforts, both held in the United States in February 1999. In the context of the UN Crime Convention, we urge that acts of corruption involving public officials be made criminal offenses.

45. We will sustain the momentum of international efforts to combat transnational organized crime and the threat it represents to political, financial and social stability worldwide. We commend the work of the Senior Experts Groups on Transnational Organized Crime and on Terrorism and urge them to continue their work, in particular for an early conclusion of the negotiations of UN conventions and protocols on organized crime. We also call for more rapid progress of negotiations on the UN Convention on the Financing of Terrorism. We ask the two expert groups to report back to us next year. We reaffirm our commitment to tackle the drug issue, in particular through active implementation of the conclusions of the 1998 UN General Assembly Special Session on the World Drug Program. We welcome the upcoming Ministerial Meeting on Crime to be held in Moscow this fall.

46. We renew the commitment we made at the 1996 Moscow Summit to safety first in the use of nuclear power and the achievement of high safety standards worldwide. In this regard, we attach great importance to the results of the Nuclear Safety Convention peer review meeting and to the International Atomic Energy Agency Conference on Strengthening Nuclear Safety in Eastern Europe.

47. We reaffirm our commitment to strengthen cooperation in the field of nuclear safety. We welcome the concerted efforts to address the Year 2000 computer problem ('Millennium Bug') in this area. With regard to the Nuclear Safety Account, we continue to attach great importance to full and timely implementation of the grant agreements.

48. There has been real progress since the Birmingham Summit in tackling the 'Millennium Bug'. But there is still much to do. We will maintain vigorous programs of action to ensure our own Year 2000 readiness and to minimize the potential impact on our countries and on the world as a whole. We urge all other governments to do the same. In these efforts, high priority should be given to the key infrastructure sectors * energy,

telecommunications, financial services, transport and health * as well as to defense, the environment and public safety. Public confidence will be crucial and will depend heavily upon transparency and openness as to the state of preparation in critical sectors. Governments, international organizations, infrastructure providers and information technology suppliers will need to ensure a regular flow of reliable information to the general public. It will be important, as the date approaches, for responsible bodies to have in place contingency plans to cope with system failures that may occur in the most sensitive areas despite intensive preparations. We urge third countries to do the same. We will maintain close cooperation among ourselves and with others on this as well as other aspects of the problem. We shall convene a special G8 conference on contingency planning later this year.

Next Summit

49. We have accepted the invitation of the Prime Minister of Japan to meet in Okinawa (Kyushu) on 21–23 July next year.

C G8 Statement on Regional Issues

June 20, 1999

Kosovo

We welcome the decisive steps already taken and now underway to end violence and repression in Kosovo, to establish peace and to provide for the safe and free return of all refugees and displaced persons to their homes. In this regard, we particularly welcome the adoption on June 10 of United Nations Security Council Resolution (UNSCR) 1244, and commend the intensive efforts of our Foreign Ministers and others, including the Special Envoys of the European Union and the Russian Federation, to restore peace and security.

We reaffirm strong support for the international civil and security presences in accordance with UNSCR 1244. We welcome the leadership of the United Nations in the international civil presence, and pledge to collaborate closely to ensure the United Nations' success in carrying out its complex mission. We also welcome the agreement reached between NATO and Russia on the international security presence, and the relevant Military Technical Agreement. In that regard, we insist that all parties to the conflict in Kosovo respect the cease-fire and fully abide by the terms of UNSCR 1244 and the Military Technical Agreement concerning the withdrawal of all Yugoslav and Serb military, police, and paramilitary forces from Kosovo and the demilitarization of the KLA and other armed Kosovo Albanian groups.

We expect all residents of Kosovo to contribute to the creation of a democratic, multi-ethnic Kosovo. The return of refugees and displaced persons to their homes, and the assurance of security for all persons including Serb and all other minorities in Kosovo will be high priorities of the international community. To ensure the wellbeing of the refugees and displaced persons, their return must be undertaken in a safe, orderly, and organized fashion. We will work cooperatively with each other, the United Nations, the European Union, the OSCE, and other international organizations to facilitate safe return including demining.

We will fully cooperate with the work of the International Criminal Tribunal for the Former Yugoslavia. We affirm our commitment to a meeting of the international donor community in July to address short-term humanitarian and other needs for Kosovo, and a subsequent meeting in the fall after a full assessment of needs has been developed pursuant to the assistance coordination process chaired by the European Commission and the World Bank.

We stress the importance of the civil implementation and, given the key role the G8 has played in the Kosovo crisis, we invite our Foreign Ministers to review on a regular basis the progress achieved thus far in this process and to provide further guidance.

South Eastern Europe Stability Pact and Donor Coordination

We welcome the adoption of the Stability Pact on June 10 in Cologne, an initiative of the European Union which will continue to play the leading role. This Stability Pact has launched a process for South Eastern Europe with the objective of a positive mid- and long-term perspective for the countries in the region to achieve lasting peace as well as political and economic stability. We take note that countries in the region participating in the Stability Pact commit themselves to continued democratic and economic reforms, as well as bilateral and regional cooperation amongst themselves to advance their integration, on an individual basis, into Euro-Atlantic structures. We consider this stabilization process to be one of the major political and economic challenges ahead of us. We declare our readiness to take strong action to achieve all the objectives of the Stability Pact. In regard to the above, the Federal Republic of Yugoslavia must demonstrate a full commitment to all of the principles and objectives of the Pact.

We underline that, in order to achieve the goals of the Stability Pact, the countries of the region bear a primary responsibility. Assistance from outside can help, but not replace the countries' own efforts. Therefore we call on the countries of South Eastern Europe to cooperate with each other and within the international community to develop a shared strategy for stability and growth of the region. In recognition of the principle of fair burden sharing, we also call on the international donor community to undertake the necessary measures in order to give the countries in the region a strong signal of active international support and solidarity and to organize donor conferences as early as feasible.

We welcome the progress made through the chairmanship of the European Commission and the World Bank towards establishing a donor coordination process to develop a coherent international assistance strategy for the region opening the door for all donor opportunities as well as to mobilize additional financial support for reconstruction, regional integration, economic recovery and reform and to promote sound macroeconomic and structural policies by the countries concerned. This process will be guided by the High Level Steering Group, in which the Special Coordinator of the Stability Pact will play an important role.

The High Level Steering Group will be co-chaired by the European Commission and the World Bank and include the Special Coordinator of the Stability Pact, the IMF, the EIB and the EBRD which will be active in the region, plus one UN representative and the Finance Ministers of major donor countries and, where appropriate, Development Ministers.

Middle East Peace Process

We reaffirm our support for a negotiated settlement in the Middle East, that should be based on the full implementation of existing commitments and on the principles of land for peace, UNSC resolutions 242 and 338, the Madrid and Oslo Agreements, UNSC resolution 425, and secure and recognized boundaries. We welcome recent encouraging statements by the Prime Minister-elect of Israel and call upon all parties to pursue the Middle East Peace Process with resolve, renewed efforts and good faith, leading to a comprehensive, just and lasting peace.

We urge both Israel and the Palestinians to implement fully and promptly the Wye River Memorandum, to combat terror, to fight violence and incitement to violence and to refrain from all activities that prejudge the outcome of the Permanent Status negotiations. We call upon both sides to resume immediately the Permanent Status negotiations. We believe that the parties should set a goal of concluding the Permanent Status negotiations within a target period of one year.

We also call for an early resumption of negotiations between Israel and Syria and Lebanon in order to achieve peace agreements. In the meantime, we urge all parties concerned strictly to respect the provisions of the April 26, 1996, understanding and to contribute actively to the work of the monitoring group in South Lebanon.

We equally underline the importance of resuming the multilateral track of the peace process and encourage the working groups and steering group to pursue their activities, supporting the bilateral negotiations and enhancing regional cooperation and economic integration.

326 Guiding Global Order

We remind all parties that sustained economic development and improved living standards for the Palestinian people are real factors in securing peace and enhancing stability in the region.

We are convinced that peace and security and the fulfillment of the rights of all the people of the Middle East, including the Palestinians, are vital to a lasting, just and negotiated settlement that provides for the Palestinians to live as a free people on their own land.

Jordan

We welcome King Abdullah's reaffirmation of Jordan's long-standing support for the Middle East Peace Process. We are committed to enhancing stability by supporting Jordan's economic reform during this critical period. We recognize the importance that Jordan attaches to alleviating its debt burden and call on the international community to provide economic assistance, including, where appropriate, debt relief.

Nigeria

The G8 warmly welcomes Nigeria's return to civilian rule and democracy. It recognizes that the strong backing of the international community will be needed to help the new government implement the necessary political and economic reforms. The G8 will assist positive change in Nigeria by continued support for democracy and human rights, good governance, transparency and accountability and the reduction of poverty.

Kashmir

We are deeply concerned about the continuing military confrontation in Kashmir following the infiltration of armed intruders which violated the Line of Control. We regard any military action to change the status quo as irresponsible. We therefore call for the immediate end of these actions, restoration of the Line of Control and for the parties to work for an immediate cessation of the fighting, full respect in the future for the Line of Control and the resumption of the dialogue between India and Pakistan in the spirit of the Lahore Declaration.

Cyprus

The Cyprus problem has gone unresolved for too long. Resolution of this problem would not only benefit all the people of Cyprus, but would also have a positive impact on peace and stability in the region.

Both parties to the dispute have legitimate concerns that can and must be addressed. The members of the G8 are convinced that only comprehensive negotiations covering all relevant issues can do this.

The members of the G8, therefore, urge the UN Secretary-General in accordance with relevant UN Security Council resolutions to invite the leaders of the two parties to negotiations in the fall of 1999. They call upon the two leaders to give their full support to such a comprehensive negotiation, under the auspices of the UN Secretary-General.

In accepting this invitation, the two parties/leaders should commit themselves to the following principles:
- No pre-conditions;
- All issues on the table;
- Commitment in good faith to continue to negotiate until a settlement is reached;
- Full consideration of relevant UN resolutions and treaties.

The members of the G8 undertake to give their full and sustained backing to the negotiating process and hope that it will prove possible for its outcome to be reported to the meetings of Heads of State and Government at the OSCE Summit this November.

Source: Released at the Köln Summit 1999

D Report of G7 Finance Ministers on the Köln Debt Initiative to the Köln Economic Summit

Cologne, Germany, 18–20 June, 1999

1. Launched in 1996, the initiative to reduce the debt overhang of heavily-indebted poor countries (HIPC Initiative) has already yielded positive results, bringing together for the first time multilateral, Paris Club, and other official bilateral creditors in a comprehensive framework for debt relief. Nonetheless, recent developments and experience have highlighted the vulnerability of many HIPCs to exogenous shocks. At the threshold of a new millennium, it is now time to reinforce the initiative so as to enhance the prospects for a robust and lasting exit for qualifying countries from recurrent debt problems.

2. We therefore support faster, deeper and broader debt relief for the poorest countries that demonstrate a commitment to reform and poverty alleviation. If implemented, the debt stock of countries possibly qualifying under the HIPC Initiative would be reduced, from some $71 billion in Net Present Value (NPV) remaining after traditional debt relief, by an additional $27 billion. These measures, together with forgiveness of debts arising from Official Development Assistance (ODA), of which some $20 billion in nominal terms are owed to G 7 countries, would lower countries' debt service burden significantly and free resources for priority social spending.

A Framework for Poverty Reduction

3. While enhanced debt relief will reinforce debtor countries' scope for policy action, sound economic policies must continue to be pursued, and renewed unproductive expenditure must be avoided. At the same time, it is important that the benefits of debt relief are targeted to assist the most vulnerable segments of population. Hence, there will have to be a strong link between

debt relief, continued adjustment, improved governance and poverty alleviation. Both better governance in budgetary matters and financial savings derived from debt relief should allow for targeted expenditure on basic social services.

4. The pursuit of sound social policies should be integrated with structural adjustment programs that debtor countries are expected to implement. The new HIPC initiative should be built on an enhanced framework for poverty reduction, developed by the International Financial Institutions (IFIs). This is critical to ensure that more resources are invested in health, education and other social needs, which are essential for development.

5. To that effect, the World Bank and the IMF should adapt their support under the 'Policy Framework Papers' (PFP), in particular the IMF's programs under the Enhanced Structural Adjustment Facility (ESAF). Integrating their efforts, the World Bank and IMF should help qualifying countries with the drafting and implementation of poverty reduction plans for the effective targeting of savings derived from debt relief, together with increased transparency of budgetary procedures to protect social expenditures. Throughout program design and implementation, there should be consultations with broader segments of the civil society. Such dialogue will be the basis for deepening the sense of 'ownership' with governments and citizens in debtor countries when necessary adjustment programs are to be adopted.

6. We call upon the World Bank and the IMF to develop by the time of the Annual Meetings specific plans for such an enhanced framework for poverty reduction.

Faster Debt Relief

7. While implementation of debt relief must continue to be predicated on sound economic policies over two stages, debtor countries should be allowed to advance the 'completion point' through improved performance. The second stage could thus be shortened significantly if a country meets ambitious policy targets early on ('floating completion point'). This mechanism should lay out specific priority steps needed to deepen structural reforms and enhance social sector investment, focusing in particular on poverty reduction.

8. In addition to addressing the debt overhang, the HIPC Initiative should focus more on significantly reducing the cash-flow burden of debt service

payments, in order to release resources for poverty reduction. The debt service burden of qualifying countries should be alleviated more quickly through provision of 'interim relief' by the IFIs even before debt reduction is implemented at the 'completion point'. This is already current practice in the Paris Club for bilateral debts, and the IFIs should provide comparable treatment. Furthermore, after the 'completion point', the IFIs could frontload debt stock reduction in a way to reduce debt service payments more strongly in the early years.

9. In order both to make the HIPC process more predictable and to simplify the modalities of earlier cash-flow relief, the amount of debt reduction should be determined at the 'decision point' on the basis of the situation prevailing at that time. This will provide greater certainty about the level of debt relief.

10. A number of the very poorest countries with heavy debt burden have not yet embarked on the HIPC process. We call on the IFIs and the Paris Club to make it a priority to assist them to begin the process.

Deeper and Broader Debt Relief

11. In order to achieve lasting debt workouts for qualifying HIPCs and to support their efforts to alleviate poverty, the international community should commit to new steps to free up resources. Target ratios indicating the level where debt sustainability can be assumed, should be reassessed and lowered. Thus, we support bringing down the debt/exports ratio from a current 200-250 percent range to 150 percent. In addition, the alternative debt/revenue ratio should be given more attention and be lowered from currently 280 percent to 250 percent. This suggests also a revision of the sub-criteria designed to avoid moral hazard under this alternative and describing the minimum GDP ratios of exports and tax revenues; these sub-criteria could be lowered from 40 percent and 20 percent, respectively, to 30 percent and 15 percent. These combined revisions would result in deeper debt forgiveness, take greater account of debtor countries' fiscal positions and broaden the HIPC Initiative to more countries.

12. While bilateral creditors in the Paris Club currently grant countries qualifying for the HIPC Initiative debt forgiveness of up to 80 percent on commercial debt, we support an even deeper degree of cancellation. To achieve debt sustainability, we would be prepared to forgive up to 90 percent and more in individual cases if needed, in particular for the very poorest among these

countries. For poor countries not qualifying under the HIPC Initiative, the Paris Club could consider a unified 67 percent reduction under Naples terms and, for other debtor countries, an increase of the existing limit on debt swap operations with due regard to appropriate transparency.

13. While many bilateral creditors have forgiven debt arising from Official Development Assistance and/or extend ODA to poor countries only in the form of grants, remaining ODA debt continues to be a source of the debt overhang in many countries. We therefore call on all creditor countries to forgive bilaterally, through a menu of options, all ODA debt of qualifying countries on top of the amounts required to achieve debt sustainability. We are aware that such forgiveness would present a special burden on some creditor countries. In order to help ensure that HIPCs do not face new debt problems in the future, new ODA should preferably be extended in the form of grants.

Financing

14. We recognise that these changes will entail significant costs, in particular arising from debt owed to the IFIs. However the final costs of the initiative are subject to many uncertainties, and actual outlays will be spread over a long period of time. We are prepared to support a number of mechanisms to meet these costs, recognising the importance of maintaining an adequate concessional lending capacity by the IFIs:

   – To meet the IMF's costs, the Fund should mobilise its resources, while maintaining an appropriate level of reserves, through: the use of premium interest income; possible use of reflows from the special contingency account or equivalent financing; and use of interest on the proceeds of a limited and cautiously-phased sale of up to 10 million ounces of the IMF's gold reserves.

   – The multilateral development banks should build on the work they have begun to identify and exploit innovative approaches which maximise the use of their own resources.

   – The costs to the IFIs will also require bilateral contributions. We have pledged substantial contributions to the existing HIPC Trust Fund. We will consider in good faith contributions to an expanded HIPC Trust Fund.

   – In meeting the costs, we call for appropriate burden sharing among donors taking into account all relevant aspects, including the magnitude and quality of ODA already extended and past ODA forgiveness, and recognising the contributions of countries with high ODA loans outstanding relative to GDP.

15. On the basis of this framework, we call upon the IFIs and the Paris Club to provide faster, deeper and broader debt relief. Concrete proposals should be agreed by the time of the next Annual Meetings of the IMF and World Bank.

Bibliography

Akaneya, T. (2000), 'The View from Japan: Tasks for the G8 Kyushu-Okinawa Summit Meeting', *NIRA Review*, vol. 7, no. 2, pp. 11–15.

Alesina, A., and G. Tabellini (1988), 'Credibility and Politics', *European Economic Review*, pp. 542–550.

Alogoskoufis, George, and Richard Portes (1991), 'The Euro, the Dollar, and the International Monetary System', in Paul R. Masson *et al.* (eds.), *EMU and the International Monetary System*, International Monetary Fund, Washington DC, pp. 58–78.

Archer, Clive (1992), *International Organizations*, second edition, Routledge, New York.

Archibugi, D., D. Held, and M. Köhler (eds.) (1998), *Re-imagining Political Community: Studies in Cosmopolitan Democracy*, Polity Press, Cambridge.

Arrighi, G., and B. Silver (1999), *Chaos and Governance in the Modern World System*, University of Minnesota Press, Minneapolis.

Baig, Taimur and Ilan Goldfajn (2000), 'The Russian Default and the Contagion to Brazil', mimeographed, Pontificia Universidade Catolica, Brazil.

Baillie, J., and B. Groombridge (eds.) (1996), *1996 IUCN Red List of Threatened Animals*, World Conservation Union (IUCN), Cambridge/Gland.

Bainbridge, T., and A. Teasdale (1995), *Penguin Companion to the European Union*, Penguin, London.

Baker, A. (2000), 'The G-7 as a Global 'Ginger Group': Plurilateralism and Four-Dimensional Diplomacy', *Global Governance*, vol. 6, pp. 165–190.

Baltensperger, Ernst (1999), 'Monetary Policy under Conditions of Increasing Integration', in Deutsche Bundesbank, *Fifty Years of the Deutsche Mark*, Oxford University Press, Oxford, pp. 439–524.

Banco de México (1999), *The Mexican Economy*, Dirección de Organismos y Acuerdos Internacionales of Banco de México, Mexico.

Barro, R. J. (1999), 'Let the Dollar Reign from Seattle to Santiago', *Wall Street Journal*, Midwest edition, 8 March, p. A18.

Bayne, Nicholas (1995), 'The G7 Summit and the Reform of Global Institutions,' *Government and Opposition* vol. 30 (Autumn), p. 497.

Bayne, Nicholas (1998), Jobs, Crime and Money: Challenges for the G8 Summit in 1998, <www.library.utoronto.ca/g7/evaluations/1998birmingham/impression/index.html> (September 2000).

Bayne, Nicholas (2000), *Hanging in There: The G7 and G8 Summit in Maturity and Renewal*, Ashgate, Aldershot.

Beattle, Alan (1999), 'New Forum to Supplement G7 Work', *Financial Times*, 27 September, p. 5.

Beauchesne, Eric (1999), 'Martin Warns against Complacency', *Montreal Gazette*, 26 September, p. A9.

Beddoes, Z. M. (1999), 'From EMU to AMU?', *Foreign Affairs*, July/August.

Belke, A. (1996), *Politische Konjunkturzyklen in Theorie und Empirie: Eine kritische Analyse der Zeitreihendynamik in Partisan-Ansätzen*, Mohr, Tübingen.

Berg, Andrew, and Catherine Patillo (1998), 'Are Currency Crises Predictable? A Test', IMF Working Paper, No. 98/145, International Monetary Fund, Washington DC.

Bergsten, F. (1996), 'Globalizing Free Trade', *Foreign Affairs*, vol. 75, no. 3.

Bergsten, F. (1998), 'The New Agenda with China', *International Economic Policy Briefs*, vol. 98, no. 2, pp. 1–2.

Bergsten, F. C. (1997), 'The Impact of the Euro on Exchange Rates and International Policy Cooperation,' in Paul R. Masson *et al.* (eds.), *EMU and the International Monetary System*, International Monetary Fund, Washington DC, pp. 17–48.

Bergsten, F. C., and R. C. Henning (1996), *Global Economic Leadership and the Group of Seven*, Institute for International Economics, Washington DC.

Bergsten, F., *et al.* (1997), 'G7: Going, Going...', *International Economy*, vol. 11, no. 4.

Bildt, Carl (1998), 'Holbrook's History', *Survival*, vol. 40, no. 3, pp. 187–191.

Bildt, Carl (1999), *Peace Journey, The Struggle for Peace in Bosnia*, Weidenfeld and Nicholson, London.

Blackburn, K., and M. Christensen (1989), 'Monetary Policy and Policy Credibility: Theories and Evidence', *Journal of Economic Literature*, vol. 27, pp. 1–45.

Boote, Anthony R. and Kamau Thugge (1998), 'Debt Relief for Low-Income Countries: The Enhanced HIPC Initiative', IMF Pamphlet Series No. 51.

Bordo, Michael, Barry Eichengreen, and Douglas Irwin (1999), 'Is Globalization Today Really Different Than Globalization a Hundred Years Ago?', National Bureau of Economic Research Working Paper No. 7195.

Botchwey, K. (2000), *Financing for Development: Current Trends and Issues for the Future*, United Nations Conference on Trade and Development, TD(X)/RT.1/11.

Boudevaix, Francine (1997), *Une Diplomatie informelle pour l'Europe*, Le Groupe de Contact Bosnie, Paris.

Boyer, M., M. Caprioli, R. Denemark, E. Hanson, and S. Lamy (2000), 'Visions of International Studies in a New Millennium', *International Studies Perspectives*, vol. 1 (April), pp. 1–9.

Brown, L., M. Renner, and B. Halweil (eds.) (1999), *Vital Signs 1999: The Environmental Trends That Are Shaping Our Future*, Worldwatch Institute, W. W. Norton and Company, New York.

Bryant, Ralph C. (1995), *International Coordination of National Stabilization Policies*, Brookings Institution, Washington DC.

Bryant, Ralph C., *et al.* (eds.) (1989), *Macroeconomic Policies in an Interdependent World*, Brookings Institution, Centre for Economic Policy Research, and International Monetary Fund, Washington DC.

Brzezinski, Zbigniev (1996), 'Let's Add to the G-7', *New York Times*, 25 June, p. A11.

Buiter, W. (1997), 'The Economic Case for Monetary Union in the European Union', *Review of International Economics*, Special Supplement, vol. 5, no. 4.

Calic, Janine-Marie (1996), *Krieg und Frieden in Bosnien-Hercegovina*, second edition, Suhrkamp, Frankfurt.

Calomiris, Charles (1998), 'The IMF's Imprudent Role As Lender of Last Resort', *Cato Journal*, Special Issue on Money and Capital Flows in a Global Economy, vol. 17, no. 3.

Calvo, G. (1978), 'On the Time Consistency of Optimal Policy in a Monetary Economy', *Econometrica*, vol. 46, pp. 1411–1428.

Camdessus, Michel (2000), 'Development and Poverty Reduction: A Multilateral Approach,' Address at the Tenth United Nations Conference on Trade and Development, Bangkok, 13 February.

Canada (1999), 'Finance Minister Paul Martin Chosen as Inaugural Chairperson of New Group of Twenty', Press Release 99-080, Department of Finance, 25 September, <www.fin.gc.ca/newse99/99-080e.html> (September 2000).

Canada (1999), 'New G-20 Forum: Backgrounder', Department of Finance, Ottawa, <www.library.utoronto.ca/g7/g20/g20backgrounder.htm> (September 2000).

Canada (2000), 'Speech to the House of Commons Standing Committee on Foreign Affairs and International Trade: The Honourable Paul Martin', Department of Finance, Ottawa, 18 May, <www.fin.gc.ca/newse00/00-041e.html> (September 2000).

Canada (2000), 'Statement by the Honourable Paul Martin, Minister of Finance for Canada, to the Institute for International Economics', Washington DC, 14 April, <www.fin.gc.ca/newse00/00-031e.html> (September 2000).

Canzoneri, Matthew B., and Dale W. Henderson (1991), *Monetary Policy in Interdependent Economies: A Game-Theoretic Approach*, MIT Press, Cambridge, MA.

Carothers, Thomas (1999/2000), 'Civil Society', *Foreign Policy*, Winter, pp. 18–24.

Claessens, Stijn, Michael P. Dooley, and Andrew Warner (1995), 'Portfolio Capital Flows: Hot or Cold?', *World Bank Economic Review*, vol. 9, pp. 153–174.

Clayton, J. (2000), *The Global Debt Bomb*, M. E. Sharpe, Armonk, NY.

Cohen, Benjamin (1998), *The Geography of Money*, Cornell University Press, Ithaca, NY.

Cohen, Lenard J. (1995), *Broken Bonds: Yugoslavia's Disintegration and Balkan Politics in Transition*, second edition, Westview Press, Boulder, CO.

Cohn, Theodore (2000), *Global Political Economy: Theory and Practice*, Longman, New York.

Cologne European Council (1999), 'Conclusions of the Presidency', 3–4 June, Cologne, <www.europarl.eu.int/dg7/summits/en/kol2.htm> (September 2000).

Cologne European Council (1999), Presidency Conclusions, Document 150/99 (Presse 0), 3 to 4 June, <ue.eu.int/en/Info/eurocouncil/index.htm> (September 2000).

Commission for Environmental Cooperation (1999), 'Assessing Environmental Effects of the North American Free Trade Agreement (NAFTA): An Analytic Framework (Phase II)', in Commission for Environmental Co-operation (ed.), *Assessing Environmental Effects of the North American Free Trade Agreement (NAFTA): An Analytic Framework (Phase II) and Issue Studies'*, Commission for Environmental Co-operation, Montreal, pp. 1–43.

Commission of European Communities (1997), 'External Aspects of Economic and Monetary Union', *Euro Papers*, no. 1, European Commission, Brussels, <europa.eu.int/comm/economy_finance/document/europap/eup01en.htm> (September 2000).

Commission of European Communities, Directorate-General for Economic and Financial Affairs (1990), *One Market, One Money: An Evaluation of the Potential Benefits and Costs of Forming an Economic and Monetary Union*, Office for Official Publications of the European Communities, Luxembourg.

Commission on Global Governance (1995), *Our Global Neighbourhood: The Report of the Commission on Global Governance*, Oxford University Press, New York.

Contact Group (1999), 'Press Briefing by the Contact Group Negotiators', Rambouillet, 18 December, <www.diplomatie.fr/actual/evenements/ramb28.gb.html> (September 2000).

Corden, Max (1994), *Economic Policy, Exchange Rates, and the International System*, University of Chicago Press, Chicago.

Courchene, T. J., and Harris, R. G. (1999), 'From Fixing to Monetary Union: Options for North American Currency Integration', *C. D. Howe Institute Commentary*, vol. 19, Toronto.

Cox, D., with T. Sinclair (1996), *Approaches to World Order*, Cambridge University Press, Cambridge.

Craig, P., and Gráinne de Búrca (1998), *EU Law: Text, Cases, and Materials*, second edition, Oxford University Press, Oxford.

Crane, David (1997), 'Asia Crisis Brings Global Powershift', *Toronto Star*, 30 November, p. D2.

Cukierman, A. S. (1992), *Central Bank Strategy, Credibility, and Independence: Theory and Evidence*, MIT Press, Cambridge, MA.

Currie, David (1998), 'Will the Euro Work?', Research Report Number P526, Economist Intelligence Unit, London.

Cutter, W. B., J. Spero, and L. D. Tyson (2000), 'New World, New Deal: A Democratic Approach to Globalization', *Foreign Affairs*, vol. 79, no. 2, pp. 80–98.

Davanne, Olivier, and Pierre Jacquet (2000), 'Practising Exchange Rate Flexibility', in Karl Kaiser, John Kirton, and Joseph Daniels (eds.), *Shaping a New International Financial System: Challenges of Governance in a Globalizing World*, Ashgate, Aldershot.

De Grauwe, Paul (1996), *International Money: Postwar Trends and Theories*, second edition, Oxford University Press, Oxford.

De Grauwe, Paul (1998), 'The Design of the European Central Bank', in Hans-Hermann Francke Eberhart Ketzel, and Hans-Helmut Kotz (eds.), *Europäische Währungsunion: von der Konzeption zur Gestaltung*, Duncker und Humblot (Kredit und Kapital), Berlin, vol. 14, pp. 295–316.

De Gregorio, José, Sebastian Edwards and Rodrigo O. Valdés (2000), 'Controls on Capital Inflows: Do they Work?', *Journal of Development Economics*, forthcoming.

Deibert, R. (1997), *Parchment, Printing, and Hypermedia: Communication in World Order Transformation*, Columbia University Press, New York.

Dent, M., and B. Peters (2000), *The Crisis of Poverty and Debt in the Third World*, Ashgate, Aldershot.

Dewitt, D., and J. Kirton (1983), *Canada as a Principal Power: A Study in Foreign Policy and International Relations*, John Wiley, Toronto.

Dewitt, D., D. Haglund, and J. Kirton (eds.) (1993), *Building a New Global Order: Emerging Trends in International Security*, Oxford University Press, Toronto.

Die Zeit (1999), 'Wie Deutschland in den Krieg geriet', no. 20, 12 May.

Dixit, Avinash (1996), *The Making of Economic Policy: A Transaction-Cost Politics Perspective*, MIT Press, Cambridge, MA.

Dluhosch, Barbara, Andreas Freytag, and Malte Krüger (1996), *International Competitiveness and the Balance of Payments: Do Current Account Deficits and Surpluses Matter?*, Edward Elgar, Cheltenham and Lyme.

Economist (1998), 'Welcome to China, Mr. Clinton', vol. 347, no. 8074, p. 17.

Edwards, Sebastian (1984), 'The Order of Liberalization of the External Sector in Developing Countries', *Essays in International Finance*, no. 156.

Edwards, Sebastian (1995), 'Comments', in Stephen Haggard, *Developing Countries and the Politics of Global Integration*, Brookings Institution, Washington DC.

Eichengreen, Barry, and Fabio Ghironi (1997), 'How Will Transatlantic Policy Interaction Change with the Advent of EMU?', Discussion Paper No. 1643, Centre for Economic Policy Research, London.

Elrod, Richard (1976), 'The Concert of Europe: A Fresh Look at an International System', *World Politics*, January, pp. 159–174.

Erlanger, Steven (1997), 'Russia Sits with Big 8, Party Crasher No More,' *New York Times*, 22 June.

Esty, D. C., and D. Geradin (1998), 'Environmental Protection and Environmental Competitiveness: A Conceptual Framework', *Journal of World Trade*, vol. 32, no. 3, pp. 5–46.

Evans, G., and J. Newnham (1998), *Dictionary of International Relations*, Penguin Books, London.

Finance Canada (1999), 'Finance Minister Paul Martin Chosen as Inaugural Chairperson of New Group of Twenty', Press Release 99-080, 25 September, <www.fin.gc.ca/newse99/99-080e.html> (September 2000).

Financial Stability Forum (1999), 'First Meeting of the Financial Stability Forum,' *Press Release*, 6 April, <www.fsforum.org/Press/P19990406.html> (September 2000).

Financial Times (2000), 'Chinese Chequers,' 15 February.

Folkerts-Landau, David, and Lindgren, Carl-Johan (1998), *Toward a Framework for Financial Stability*, International Monetary Fund, Washington DC.

Frankel, Jeffrey A. (1999), 'Dollarization: Fad or Future for Latin America?', www.imf.org/external/np/tr/1999/TR990624.HTM (September 2000).

Frankel, Jeffrey A., and Katharine E. Rockett (1989), 'International Macroeconomic Policy Coordination When Policymakers Do Not Agree on the True Model', *American Economic Review*, vol. 78, no. 3, pp. 318–340.

Freytag, A. (1995), 'The European Market for Protectionism: New Competitors and New Products', in L. Gerken (ed.), *Competition among Institutions*, Macmillan, Houndmills, pp. 231–258.

Freytag, A., and R. Sally (forthcoming), 'Globalisation and Trade Policy: 1900 and 2000 Compared', *Jahrbuch für Neue Politische Ökonomie*, vol. 19, Mohr Siebeck, Tübingen.

Friedman, Thomas L. (1999), *The Lexus and the Olive Tree*, Farrar, Strauss, & Giroux, New York.

Frowick, Robert (1997), 'Concept of Mutually Reinforcing Institutions: Lessons Learned in Bosnia and Herzegovina', Paper presented at the Organization for Security and Co-operation in Europe Seminar on Co-Operation among International Organizations and Institutions: Experience in Bosnia and Herzegovina, Portoroz, Slovenia, 30 September.

Fry, Michael, John Kirton, and Mitsuru Kurosawa (eds.) (1998), *The North Pacific Triangle: The United States, Japan, and Canada at Century's End*, University of Toronto Press, Toronto.

Fuji Research Institute (1993), *Survey of the Main Bank System and Interlocking Shareholding Relationships*, Fuji Bank, Tokyo.

Fukao, Mitsuhiro (1999), 'Japanese Instability and Weaknesses in the Corporate Governance Structure', Paper presented to the Organisation for Economic Co-operation and Development Conference on 'Corporate Governance in Asia: A Comparative Perspective', Seoul, Korea, 3–5 March.

Funabashi, Yoichi (1988), *Managing the Dollar: From the Plaza to the Louvre*, Institute for International Economics, Washington DC.

G7 (1975), 'Declaration of Rambouillet', Rambouillet, 17 November, <www.library.utoronto.ca/g7/summit/1975rambouillet/communique.html> (September 2000).

G7 (1991), 'Chairman's [British Foreign Secretary Douglas Hurd] Statement', London, 16 July, <www.library.utoronto.ca/g7/summit/1991london/chairman.html> (September 2000).

G7 (1992), 'Chairman's [German Foreign Minister Klaus Kinkel] Statement', Munich, 7 July, <www.library.utoronto.ca/g7/summit/1992munich/chairman.html> (September 2000).

G7 (1995), 'Chairman's Statement', Halifax, 17 June, <www.library.utoronto.ca/g7/summit/1995halifax/chairman.html> (September 2000).

G7 (1997), 'Communiqué', Denver, 22 June, <www.library.utoronto.ca/g7/summit/1997denver/g8final.htm> (September 2000).

G7 (1997), 'Confronting Global Economic and Financial Challenges: Denver Summit Statement by Seven', 21 June, Denver, <www.library.utoronto.ca/g7/summit/1997denver/confront.htm> (September 2000).

G7 (1998), 'Declaration of G7 Finance Ministers and Central Bank Governors', 30 October, Washington DC, <www.library.utoronto.ca/g7/finance/fm103098.htm> (September 2000).

G7 (1998), 'Transcript "A" of the Press Conference Given by Prime Minister, Mr. Tony Blair', Birmingham, 17 May, <www.library.utoronto.ca/g7/summit/1998birmingham/blaira.html> (September 2000).

G7 (1999), 'G7 Statement', Cologne, 18 June, <www.library.utoronto.ca/g7/summit/1999koln/g7statement_june18.htm> (September 2000).

G7 (1999), 'Statement of G-7 Finance Ministers and Central Bank Governors', 25 September, Washington DC, <www.g7.utoronto.ca/g7/finance/fm992509state.htm> (September 2000).

G8 (1996), 'Lyon Summit: Decisions Concerning Bosnia and Herzegovina', 29 June, Lyon, <www.ohr.int/docu/d960629a.htm> (September 2000).

G8 (1997), 'Denver Summit of the Eight: Statement on Bosnia and Herzegovina', 22 June, Denver, <www.ohr.int/docu/d970622a.htm> (September 2000).

G8 (1998), 'Birmingham Summit of the Eight: Statements on FRY/Kosovo and Bosnia and Herzegovina', 17 May, Birmingham, <www.orh.int/docu/d980517a.htm> (September 2000).

G8 (1999), 'Conclusions of the Meeting of the G-8 Foreign Ministers Meeting in Berlin', 16–17 December, Berlin, <www.library.utoronto.ca/g7/foreign/fm991216.htm> (September 2000).

G8 Research Group (2000), *Assessment of Compliance with the 1999 Cologne Commitments*, <www.g7.utoronto.ca/analytic studies/2000> (September 2000).

Garavoglia, Guido (1984), 'From Rambouillet to Williamsburg: A Historical Assessment', in Cesare Merlini (ed.), *Economic Summits and Western Decision-Making*, St. Martin's Press, London, pp. 1–42.

Garavoglia, Guido and Pier Carlo Padoan (1994), 'The G-7 Agenda: Old and New Issues', *International Spectator*, vol. 29, no. 2, <www.library.utoronto.ca/g7/scholar/garavoglia1994/index.html> (September 2000).

Gavin, Michael, and Dani Rodrik (1995) 'The World Bank in International Perspective', *American Economic Review Papers and Proceedings*, vol. 85, pp. 329–334.

Gerster, Richard (1998). 'Der Internationale Währungsfonds und Nachhaltige Entwicklung: Institutionelle Voraussetzungen und Wirtschaftliche Implikationen', *Aussenwirtschaft*, vol. 53, pp. 347–361.

Giavazzi, Francesco, and Fabio Ghironi (1997), Out in the Sunshine? Outsiders, Insiders, and the United States in 1998, Discussion Paper No. 1547, Centre for Economic Policy Research, London.

Giersch, Carsten (1998), *Konfliktregulierung in Jugoslawien 1991–1995, Die Rolle von OSZE, EU, UNO und NATO*, Nomos, Baden-Baden.

Gill, S. (1993), 'Gramsci and Global Politics: Towards a Post-Hegemonic Research Agenda', in Stephen Gill (ed.), *Gramsci, Historical Materialism, and International Relations*, Cambridge University Press, Cambridge.

Global Environment Facility (1998), *GEF Lesson Notes*, no. 2, April.

Glöckler, G., L. Junius, G. Scappucci, S. Usherwood, and J. Vassallo (1998), *Guide to EU Policies*, Blackstone Press Limited, London.

Goldstein, Morris (1997), *The Case for an International Banking Standard, Institute for International Economics*, Washington DC.

Gow, James (1997), *Triumph of the Lack of Will: International Diplomacy and the Yugoslav War*, Hurst & Company, London.

Gray, John (1998), *False Dawn: The Delusions of Global Capitalism*, Granta Books, London.

Gros, Daniel (1998), Delivering Price Stability in EMU: The European System of Central Banks, Hans-Hermann Francke, Eberhart Ketzel, and Hans-Helmut Kotz (eds.), *Europäische Währungsunion: von der Konzeption zur Gestaltung*, Duncker und Humblot (Kredit und Kapital), Berlin, vol. 14, pp. 341–364.

Haggard, Stephen (1995), *Developing Countries and the Politics of Global Integration*, Brookings Institution, Washington DC.

Hainsworth, Susan (1990), 'Coming of Age: The European Community and the Economic Summit', Country Study No. 7, Centre for International Studies, University of Toronto, Toronto, <www.library.utoronto.ca/g7/scholar/hainsworth1990/bisfor.htm> (September 2000).

Hajnal, Peter (1989), *The Seven-Power Summit: Documents from the Summits of Industrialized Countries, 1975–1989*, Kraus International Publications, Millwood, NY.

Hajnal, Peter (1991), *The Seven-Power Summit: Documents from the Summits of Industrialized Countries: Supplement: Documents from the 1990 Summit*, Kraus International Publications, Millwood, NY.

Hajnal, Peter (1999), *The G7/G8 System: Evolution, Role, and Documentation*, Ashgate, Aldershot.

Hajnal, Peter, and John Kirton (2000), 'The Evolving Role and Agenda of the G7/G8: A North American Perspective', *NIRA Review*, vol. 7, no. 2, pp. 5–10.

Halle, M. (2000), 'Seattle and Sustainable Development', *Bridges: Between Trade and Sustainable Development, International Center on Trade and Sustainable Development*, year 4, no. 1, pp. 13–14.

Halpern, Paul J. (1999), 'Systemic Perspectives of Corporate Governance Systems', University of Toronto, mimeographed.

Hausmann, R. (1999), 'Exchange Rate Debate' and other short articles, Inter-American Development Bank, *Latin American Economic Policies*, vol. 7 (Second Quarter).

Hausmann, R. (1999), 'Should There be Five Currencies or One Hundred and Five?', *Foreign Policy*, vol. 116.

Hayek, Friedrich A. von (1944), *The Road to Serfdom*, Routledge, London.

Hayek, Friedrich A. von (1960), *The Constitution of Liberty*, Routledge, London.

Hayek, Friedrich A. von (1974), 'The Pretence of Knowledge', in Nobel Lectures (Nobel Memorial Lecture) in Bank of Sweden, *Nobel Lectures: Economic Science*, World Scientific Publishing Company, Singapore.

Held, David (1995), *Democracy and the Global Order: From the Modern State to Cosmopolitan Governance*, Stanford University Press, Stanford.

Henderson, David (1993), 'International Economic Co-operation Revisited', *Government and Opposition*, vol. 28, no. 1.

Henderson, David (1998), 'International Agencies and Cross-Border Liberalisation: The WTO in Context', in Anne O. Krueger (ed.), *The WTO as an International Organisation*, World Trade Organisation, Geneva.

Henderson, David (1998), *The Changing Fortunes of Economic Liberalism: Yesterday, Today, and Tomorrow*, Institute of Economic Affairs, London.

Henderson, David (1999), 'The Changing International Economic Order: Rival Visions for the Coming Millennium', *International Finance*, vol. 2, no. 3.

Henderson, David (1999), *The MAI Affair: A Story and Its Lessons*, Royal Institute of International Affairs, London.

Henning, C. Randall (1994), *Currencies and Politics in the United States, Germany, and Japan*, Institute for International Economics, Washington DC.

Henning, C. Randall (1997), *Cooperating with Europe's Monetary Union*, Policy Analysis in International Economics Series, no. 49, Institute for International Economics, Washington DC.

Hetzel, R. L. (1990), 'The Political Economy of Monetary Policy', in T. Mayer (ed.), *The Political Economy of American Monetary Policy*, Cambridge University Press, Cambridge, pp. 99–114.

Hirschman, Albert O. (1958), *The Strategy of Economic Development*, Yale University Press, New Haven.

Hirshleifer, David (1995), 'Mergers and Acquisitions: Strategic and Informational Issues', in Robert A. Jarrow, V. Maksimovic, and W. T. Zeimba (eds.), *Finance, Handbooks in Operations and Management Science*, vol. 9, North-Holland Elsevier, Amsterdam, pp. 838–886.

Hodges, Michael, John Kirton, and Joseph Daniels (eds.) (1999), *The G8's Role in the New Millennium*, Ashgate, Aldershot.

Holbrooke, Richard (1998), *To End a War*, Random House, New York.

Holle, P. (1999), 'Canadians Wonder Whether the Loonie is for the Birds', *Wall Street Journal*, 6 August, p. A11.

Intergovernmental Panel on Climate Change (IPCC) (1995), *IPCC Second Assessment Report: Climate Change*, World Meteorological Organisation and United Nations Environment Programme, Geneva.

International Institute for Sustainable Development (1999), *Sustainable Developments*, vol. 12, no. 2 (rev.), 22 March.

International Monetary Fund and World Bank (1999), 'Modifications to the Heavily Indebted Poor Countries (HIPC) Initiative', <www.imf.org/external/np/hipc/modify/hipc.htm> (September 2000).

International Monetary Fund Executive Board (1999), 'IMF Executive Board Reviews HIPC Initiative Modifications', Public Information Notice (PIN) No. 99/76, Washington DC, 13 August.

Iowa State University, Department of Economics (2000) 'Multinational Corporations', <www.econ.iastate.edu/classes/econ355/choi/mnc.htm> (September 2000).

Ipsen, K. (1990), *Völkerrecht*, third edition, Beck, Munich.

Irwin, Douglas (1998), 'Comments on the Paper by David Henderson', in Anne O. Krueger (ed.), *The WTO as an International Organisation*, World Trade Organisation, Geneva.

Issing, Otmar, and Bernhard Winkler (1999), 'On the Credibility of Co-ordination', in Otto G. Mayer and Hans-Eckart Scharrer (eds.), *Transatlantic Relations in a Global Economy*, Nomos, Baden-Baden, pp. 95–99.

Issing, Otmar (1996), 'Reform des Weltwährungssystems?', *Zeitschrift für Wirtschaftspolitik*, vol. 45, pp. 316–322.

Iversen, Torben (1999), *Contested Economic Institutions: The Politics of Macroeconomics and Wage Bargaining in Advanced Countries*, Cambridge University Press, Cambridge.

Ize, A., and Levy-Yeyati, E. (1998), 'Dollarization of Financial Intermediation: Causes and Policy Implications', *International Monetary Fund Working Paper*, WP/98/28.

Jayawardena, L. (1989), 'World Economic Summits: The Role of Representative Groups in the Governance of the World Economy', *Journal of the Society for International Development*, vol. 4, pp. 17–20.

Jeanne, Olivier (1997), 'Are Currency Crises Self-fulfilling? A Test', *Journal of International Economics*, vol. 43, pp. 263–286.

Jervis, Robert (1983) 'Security Regimes', in Stephen D. Krasner (ed.), *International Regimes*, Cornell University Press, Ithaca, NY, pp. 173–194.

Jervis, Robert (1985), 'From Balance to Concert: A Study of International Security Co-operation', *World Politics*, October, pp. 58–79. (Also in Kenneth Oye (ed.), *Co-operation Under Anarchy*, Princeton, New Haven, 1986.)

Johnson, P. M., and A. Beaulieu (1996), *The Environment and NAFTA: Understanding and Implementing the New Continental Law*, Island Press, Washington DC.

Kaiser, Karl, John Kirton, and Joseph Daniels (eds.) (2000), *Shaping a New International Financial System: Challenges of Governance in a Globalizing World*, Ashgate, Aldershot.

Kanbur, R., and T. Sandler (1998), 'A Radical Approach to Development Assistance', *Development Outreach*, vol. 1, no. 2.

Kang, Jun-Koo, and Rene Stulz (1997). 'Is Bank-centred Corporate Governance Worth It?', Ohio State University, mimeographed.

Karns, Margaret P. (1987), 'Ad Hoc Multilateral Diplomacy: The United States, The Contact Group, and Namibia', *International Organization*, vol. 41, no. 1. pp. 93–123.

Katzenstein, Peter, Robert Keohane, and Stephen Krasner (1998), 'International Organization and the Study of World Politics', *International Organization*, vol. 52, no. 4, pp. 645–685.

Kaul, Inge, Isabelle Grunberg, and Marc Stern (eds.) (1999), *Global Public Goods: International Co-operation in the Twenty-first Century*, Oxford University Press, New York.

Kawamoto, A. (1997), 'A Regulatory Reform on the International Trade Policy Agenda', *Journal of World Trade Law*, vol. 31, no. 4.

Kenen, Peter B. (1989), *Exchange Rates and Policy Coordination*, Manchester University Press, Manchester.

Kenen, Peter B. (1995), *Economic and Monetary Union in Europe: Moving Beyond Maastricht*, Cambridge University Press, Cambridge.

Kenen, Peter B. (1999), 'EMU and Transatlantic Economic Relations', in Otto G. Mayer and Hans-Eckart Scharrer (eds.), *Transatlantic Relations in a Global Economy*, Nomos, Baden-Baden, pp. 77–94.

Kennedy, Ellen (1991), *The Bundesbank: Germany's Central Bank in the International Monetary System*, Royal Institute of International Affairs, London.

Keohane, Robert O. (1982), 'The Demand for International Regimes', *International Organization*, vol. 36, no. 2.

Keohane, Robert O. (1984), *After Hegemony: Cooperation and Discord in the World Political Economy*, Princeton University Press, Princeton.

Keohane, Robert O. (1989), *International Institutions and State Power: Essays in International Relations Theory*, Westview Press, Boulder, CO.

Keohane, Robert O., and Joseph Nye (1989), *Power and Interdependence*, second edition, Scott, Foresman, Glenview, IL.

Kirkpatrick, Colin, and Norman Lee (1999), 'WTO New Round: Sustainability Impact Assessment Study, Phase Two, Main Report', Institute for Development Policy and Management and Environmental Impact Assessment Centre, University of Manchester, 18 November.

Kirshner, Jonathan (1995), *Currency and Coercion: The Political Economy of International Monetary Power*, Princeton University Press, Princeton.

Kirton, John (1997), 'Canada, the G7, and the Denver Summit of the Eight: Implications for Asia and Taiwan,' *Canadian Studies* 3 (1998).

Kirton, John (1997), 'Le rôle du G7 dans le couple intègration regionale-securité globale', *Études Internationales*, vol. 28, pp. 255–270.

Kirton, John (1989), 'Contemporary Concert Diplomacy: The Seven-Power Summit and the Management of International Order', Paper prepared for the annual meeting of the International Studies Association and the British International Studies Association, London, 29 March–1 April, <www.library.utoronto.ca/g7/scholar/kirton198901/index.html> (September 2000).

Kirton, John (1999), 'An Assessment of the 1999 Cologne G7/G8 Summit by Issue Area', with the G8 Research Group, <www.library.utoronto.ca/g7/evaluations/1999koln/issues/kolnperf.htm> (September 2000).

Kirton, John (1999), 'Economic Cooperation, Summitry, Institutions and Structural Change', in Gavin Boyd and John Dunning (eds.), *Structural Change and Cooperation in the Global Economy*, Edward Elgar, Cheltenham, pp. 1–38.

Kirton, John (1999), 'What Is the G20?', <www.library.utoronto.ca/g7/g20/g20whatisit.html> (September 2000).

Kirton, John (2000), 'The G7 and Concert Governance in the Global Financial Crisis of 1997–99', Paper prepared for the annual conference of the International Studies Association, Los Angeles, 15–19 March.

Kitterer, Wolfgang (1999), 'Public Finance and the Central Bank', in Deutsche Bundesbank (ed.), *Fifty Years of the Deutsche Mark*, Oxford University Press, Oxford, pp. 165–218.

Kiuchi, Takashi (2000), 'The Asian Crisis and its Implications', in Karl Kaiser, John Kirton, and Joseph Daniels (eds.), *Shaping a New International Financial System: Challenges of Governance in a Globalizing World*, Ashgate, Aldershot, pp. 37–46.

Klodt, Henning. (1999), *Internationale Politikkoordination: Leitlinien für den globalen Wirtschaftspolitiker*, Institut für Weltwirtschaft, Kiel.

Köck, H. F., and Fischer, P. (1997), *Internationale Organisationen*, third edition, Linde Verlag Vienna.

Kohler-Koch, Beate (1989), 'Zur Empirie und Theorie internationaler Regime', in Beate Kohler-Koch (ed.), *Regime in den Internationalen Beziehungen*, Nomos, Baden-Baden, pp. 17–85.

Kokotsis, E. (1995), 'Keeping Sustainable Development Commitments: The Recent G7 Record', in John Kirton and Sarah Richardson (eds.), *The Halifax Summit, Sustainable Development, and Institutional Reform*, National Round Table on the Environment and the Economy, Ottawa, pp. 117–133, <www.library.utoronto.ca/g7/scholar/kirton199503/kokotsis/index.html> (September 2000).

Kokotsis, E. (1999), *Keeping International Commitments: Compliance, Credibility, and the G7, 1988–1995*, Garland Publishing, New York.

Krasner, S. (1978), *Defending the National Interest: Raw Materials Investments and U.S. Foreign Policy*, Princeton University Press, Princeton.

Krasner, Stephen D. (1982) 'Structural Causes and Regime Consequences: Regimes as Intervening Variables', *International Organization*, vol. 36, no. 2.

Krasner, Stephen D. (ed.) (1983), *International Regimes*, Cornell University Press, Ithaca, NY.

Krueger, Anne O. (1990), 'Trade Policy as an Input to Development', in *Perspectives on Trade and Development*, Harvester Wheatsheaf, New York.

Krueger, Anne O. (1997), 'Trade Policy and Economic Development: How Do We Learn?' *American Economic Review*, vol. 87, pp. 1–22.

Krueger, Anne O. (1998), 'Whither the World Bank and the IMF?', *Journal of Economic Literature*, vol. 36, pp. 1983–2020.

Krugman, P. A. (1997), 'What Should Trade Negotiators Negotiate About?', *Journal of Economic Literature*, vol. 35, pp. 113–120.

Kupchan, Charles, and Clifford Kupchan (1991), 'Concerts, Collective Security, and the Future of Europe', *International Security*, vol. 16, pp. 114–161.

Kydland, F., and C. Prescott (1977), 'Rules Rather Than Discretion: The Inconsistency of Optimal Plans', *Journal of Political Economy*, vol. 85, pp. 473–491.

Lafontaine, Oskar, and Dominique Strauss-Kahn (1999), 'Europa-sozial und stark', in *Die Zeit*, 14 January, p.17.

Laidler, D. (1999), 'Canada's Exchange Rate Options', *Canadian Public Policy*, vol. 25, no. 3, pp. 324–332.

Lamy, Pascal (1988), 'The Economic Summit and the European Community', Bissell Paper No. 4, Centre for International Studies, University of Toronto, Toronto, <www.library.utoronto.ca/g7/scholar/lamy1988/lamtext4.htm> (September 2000).

Landes, David S. (1998), *The Wealth and Poverty of Nations: Why Some Are So Rich and Others So Poor*, Norton, New York.

Landmann, Oliver (1991), 'Alternative Währungsordnungen im Lichte des Zuordnungsproblems,' in Jürgen Siebke (ed.), *Monetäre Konfliktfelder der Weltwirtschaft*, Duncker and Humblot, Berlin.

Larosière, Jacques de (1985), 'Interrelationships between Protectionism and the Debt Crisis', *Aussenwirtschaft*, vol. 40, pp. 219–228.

Laubach, Thomas, and Adam Posen (1997), *Disciplined Discretion: Monetary Targeting in Germany and Switzerland*, International Finance Section, Department of Economics, Princeton University, Princeton.

Lewis, Flora (1991), 'The "G7½" Directorate', *Foreign Policy*, vol. 85, pp. 25–40.

Loisel, Olivier and Philippe Martin (1999), 'Coordination, Cooperation, Contagion and Currency Crises', CEPR Discussion Paper, No. 2075, Centre for Economic Policy Research, London.

Lucas, Robert E. (1990), 'Why Doesn't Capital Flow from Rich to Poor Countries?', *American Economic Review*, vol. 80 (Papers and Proceedings).

Mack, C. (1999), 'Time to Reap the Dollar's Reward', *Financial Times*, 16 December, p. 15.

Martin, Hans-Peter, and Harald Schumann (1997), *The Global Trap: Globalisation and the Assault on Prosperity and Democracy*, Zed Books, New York.

Martin, Philippe (1997), The Exchange Rate Policy of the EURO: A Matter of Size?, Working Paper 97-06, Centre d'études prospectives et d'informations internationales, Paris, <www.cepii.fr/ANGLAIS/DOCW9706.HTM> (September 2000).

Mayer, T. (ed.) (1990), *The Political Economy of American Monetary Policy*, Cambridge University Press, Cambridge.

McCallum, B. T. (1997), 'Crucial Issues Concerning Central Bank Independence', *Journal of Monetary Economics*, vol. 39, pp. 99–112.

Meltzer, Allan (1998), 'Asian Problems and the IMF', *Cato Journal*, Special Issue on Money and Capital Flows in a Global Economy, vol. 17, no. 3.

Mercer, M. (1999), *International Trade and the Environment: Addressing the Co-ordination Challenge*, World Conservation Union (IUCN), Canada Office, Montreal.

Meyer, L. H. (1999), 'The Euro in the International Financial System', *Federal Reserve Bank of Minneapolis The Region*, vol. 13, no. 2, pp. 25–27, 58.

Michaelis, Jochen (1994), 'DM-Exchange Rate Policymaking', in Hans-Eckart Scharrer (ed.), *Economic and Monetary Policy Cooperation*, Nomos, Baden-Baden, pp. 75–100.

Moore, Mike (1999), 'Address to NGOs in Opening the Seattle Symposium on International Trade Issues in the Next Decade', 29 November 1999, *Social Development Review*, vol. 3, no. 4, pp. 24–26.

Morck, Randall and Bernard Yeung (1995), 'The Corporate Governance of Multinationals', in Ronald J. Daniels and Randall Morck (eds.), *Corporate Decision Making in Canada*, Industry Canada Research Series, University of Calgary Press, Calgary.

Morris, Stephen and Hyun Song Shin (1998), 'Unique Equilibrium in Self-Fulfilling Currency Attacks', *American Economic Review*, vol. 88, pp. 587–597.

Müller, Harald (1993), *Die Chance der Kooperation. Regime in den internationalen Beziehungen*, Wissenschaftliche Buchgesellschaft, Darmstadt.

Müller, Henrik, and Thomas Straubhaar (1999), 'Das trojanische Pferd der Währungsunion: Dem Euro droht die Politisierung durch die Hintertür des Außenwerts', *Frankfurter Allgemeine Zeitung*, 5 June, no. 127, p.15.

Murphy, Kevin M., Andrei Shleifer, and Robert W. Vishny (1989), 'Industrialization and the Big Push', *Journal of Political Economy*, vol. 97, pp. 1003–1026.

Myrdal, Gunnar (1957), *Economic Theory and Underdeveloped Regions*, Duckworth, London.

Nestor, Stilpon, and John Thompson (1999), 'Corporate Governance Patterns in OECD Economics: Is Convergence Under Way?', Paper presented to the Organisation for Economic Co-operation and Development Conference on 'Corporate Governance in Asia: A Comparative Perspective', Seoul, Korea, 3–5 March.

Neville-Jones, Pauline (1996), 'Dayton, IFOR, and Alliance Relations in Bosnia', *Survival*, vol. 38, no. 4, pp. 45–65.

Newlyn, W. T. (1962), *Theory of Money*, Clarendon Press, Oxford.

Nordstrom, H., and S. Vaughan (1999), *Special Studies 4: Trade and Environment*, World Trade Organization, Geneva.

North Atlantic Treaty Organization [NATO] (1999), 'Press Statement' (011), 28 January, <www.nato.int/docu/pr/1999/p99-011e.htm> (September 2000).

North Atlantic Treaty Organization [NATO] (1999), Press Statement (040), 23 March, <www.nato.int/docu/pr/1999/p99-040e.htm> (September 2000).

Nurkse, Ragnar (1958), *Problems of Capital Formation in Underdeveloped Countries*, Blackwell, Oxford.

Obstfeld, Maurice (1996), 'Models of Currency Crises with Self-fulfilling Features', *European Economic Review*, vol. 40, pp. 1037–1047.

Odom, William (1995), 'How to Create a True World Order', *Orbis*, vol. 39, no. 2, pp. 155–172.

Office of the High Representative [OHR] (1995), 'Conclusions of the Peace Implementation Conference Held at Lancaster House', 8–9 December, <www.ohr.int/docu/d951208a.htm> (September 2000).

Office of the High Representative [OHR] (1995), 'The General Framework Agreement for Bosnia and Herzegovina', 14 December, <www.ohr.int/gfa/gfa-home.htm> (September 2000).

Office of the High Representative [OHR] (1998), 'Contact Group: Statement on Kosovo', 25 March, Bonn, <www.ohr.int/docu/d980325b.htm> (September 2000).

Office of the High Representative [OHR] (1998), 'Contact Group: Statement', 29 April, Rome, <www.ohr.int/docu/d980429a.htm> (September 2000).

Office of the High Representative [OHR] (1999), 'Conclusions', London, 29 January, <www.ohr.int/docu/d990129a.htm> (September 2000).

Office of the High Representative [OHR] (1999), 'Rambouillet Accords: Co-Chairmen's Conclusions', Rambouillet, 23 February, <www.ohr.int/docu/d990223a.htm> (September 2000).

Ohr, Renate (1999), 'Gefährliche Therapie: Eine Schwankungsbremse durch Zielzonen bringt mehr Schaden als Nutzen', *Rheinischer Merkur*, Bonn, 19 February.

Olson, M. (1965), *The Logic of Collective Action*, Harvard University Press, Cambridge, MA.

Olson, Mancur (1982), *The Rise and Decline of Nations*, Yale University Press, New Haven.

Organisation for Economic Co-operation and Development (1998), *Open Markets Matter: The Benefits of Trade and Investment Liberalisation*, Organisation for Economic Co-operation and Development, Paris.

Organisation for Economic Co-operation and Development (1999), *EMU Facts, Challenges and Policies*, Organisation for Economic Co-operation and Development, Paris.

Organisation for Economic Co-operation and Development (1999). *OECD Principles of Corporate Governance*, Organisation for Economic Co-operation and Development, Paris, <www.oecd.org//daf/governance/principles.htm> (September 2000).

Organisation for Economic Co-operation and Development (OECD) (2000), 'Development Co-operation Report 1999: Efforts and Policies of the Members of the Development Assistance Committee', *Development Assistance Committee Journal*, vol. 1, no. 1.

Ortiz, G. (1999), 'Dollarization: Fad or Future for Latin America?', <www.imf.org/external/np/tr/1999/TR990624.HTM> (September 2000).

Ostry, Sylvia (1990), 'Canada, Europe, and the Economic Summits', Paper presented at the All-European Canadian Studies Conference, The Hague, 24–27 October, <www.library.utoronto.ca/g7/scholar/ostry1990/ost1.htm> (September 2000).

Owen, David (1995), *Balkan Odyssey*, Victor Golancz, London.

Persson, T., and G. Tabellini (1990), *Macroeconomic Policy, Credibility, and Politics*, Harwood, Chur, Switzerland.

Pöhl, Karl Otto (1987): 'You Can't Robotize Policymaking', *International Economy*, vol. 1, no. 6, pp. 20–26.

Porter, Tony (2000), 'The G-7, the Financial Stability Forum, the G-20, and the Politics of International Financial Regulation', Paper prepared for the International Studies Association Annual Meeting, Los Angeles, California, 15 March.

Putnam, R., and N. Bayne (1987), *Hanging Together: Cooperation and Conflict in the Seven-Power Summits*, Harvard University Press, Cambridge, MA.

Rawls, John (1971), *A Theory of Justice*, Harvard University Press, Cambridge, MA.

Reich, Robert B. (1990), 'Who Is Us?', *Harvard Business Review*, vol. 68, no. 1, pp. 53–64.

Reich, Robert B. (1991), 'Who Is Them?', *Harvard Business Review*, vol. 69, no. 2, pp. 77–88.

Reimann, Winfried (1999), 'Fixkurs-Nostalgie', *Börsen-Zeitung*, 24 February.

Reszat, Beate (1994), 'Germany's Role in International Macroeconomic Policy Co-operation', in Hans-Eckart Scharrer (ed.), *Economic and Monetary Policy Cooperation*, Nomos, Baden-Baden, pp. 47–74.

Ricupero, Rubens (2000), 'From the Washington Consensus to the Spirit of Bangkok', Closing Statement at United Nations Conference on Trade and Development, Tenth Session, Bangkok, 19 February, p. 7.

Rittberger, Volker (1994), *Internationale Organisationen*, Leske u. Budrich, Opladen.

Robbins, Lionel (1937), *Economic Planning and International Order*, Macmillan, London.

Robbins, Lionel (1958), *Robert Torrens and the Evolution of Classical Economics*, Macmillan, London.

Rodrik, Dani (1997), 'Trade Policy and Economic Performance in Sub-Saharan Africa', Study commissioned by the Swedish Ministry of Economic Affairs, <www.ksg.harvard.edu/rodrik/papers.html> (September 2000).

Rodrik, Dani (1997), *Has Globalisation Gone Too Far?*, Institute for International Economics, Washington DC.

Roessler, Frieder (1998), 'Domestic Policy Objectives and the Multilateral Trade Order: Lessons from the Past', in Anne O. Krueger (ed.), *The WTO as an International Organisation*, World Trade Organisation, Geneva.

Rogoff, Kenneth (1985), 'Can International Policy Co-ordination Be Counterproductive?', *Journal of International Economics*, vol. 18, no. 3/4, pp. 199–217.

Röpke, Wilhelm (1954), *Internationale Ordnung – Heute*, Rentsch Verlag, Stuttgart.

Röpke, Wilhelm (1959), *International Order and Economic Integration*, Reidel, Dordrecht.

Rose, Andrew K. (1998), 'Limiting Currency Crises and Contagion: Is there a Case for an Asian Monetary Fund?', Lecture delivered at the Reserve Bank of New Zealand.

Rosenstein-Rodan, Paul (1943), 'Problems of Industrialization in Eastern and South-Eastern Europe', *Economic Journal*, vol. 53, pp. 202–211.

Rugman, A. (1999), 'Negotiating Multilateral Rules to Promote Investment', in M. Hodges, J. Kirton, and J. Daniels (eds.), *The G8's Role in the New Millennium*, Ashgate, Aldershot, pp. 143–158.

Runnals, D. (1996), 'Shall We Dance? What the North Needs to Do to Fully Engage the South in the Trade and Sustainable Development Debate', Working Paper, Trade and Sustainable Development Program, International Institute for Sustainable Development, Winnipeg.

Sachs, Jeffrey (1998), 'Global Capitalism — Making it Work,' *Economist*, vol. 348, no. 8085, pp. 23–25.

Sachs, Jeffrey (1999), 'Helping the World's Poorest', *Economist*, 14 August, pp. 17–20.

Sachs, Jeffrey (forthcoming), 'Do We Need a Lender of Last Resort?' Graham Lecture, Princeton International Finance Series.

Sachs, Jeffrey, and Andrew Warner (1995), 'Economic Reform and The Process of Global Integration', in William C. Brainard and George L. Perry (eds.), *Brookings Papers on Economic Activity*, vol. 1.

Sachs, Jeffrey, and Andrew Warner (1995), 'Economic Reform and the Process of Global Integration', *Brookings Papers on Economic Activity*, vol. 1, no. 95.

Sachs, Jeffrey, and F. Larrain (1999), 'Why Dollarization is More Straitjacket Than Salvation', *Foreign Policy*, vol. 116, pp. 80–92.

Sachverständigenrat zur Begutachtung der gesamtwirtschaftlichen Entwicklung [Council of Economic Experts] (1986/87), *Weiter auf Wachstumskurs, Jahresgutachten 1986/87*, Kohlhammer, Stuttgart.

Sachverständigenrat zur Begutachtung der gesamtwirtschaftlichen Entwicklung [Council of Economic Experts] (1987/88), *Vorrang für die Wachstumspolitik*, Metzger-Poeschel, Stuttgart.

Sachverständigenrat zur Begutachtung der gesamtwirtschaftlichen Entwicklung [Council of Economic Experts] (1995/96), *Im Standortwettbewerb*, Metzger-Poeschel, Stuttgart.

Sally, Razeen (1998), *Classical Liberalism and International Economic Order: Studies in Theory and Intellectual History*, Routledge, London, pp. 54–60.

Sally, Razeen (1999), 'National Trade Policy Reform, The WTO and the Millennium Round: The Case of Developing Countries and Countries in Transition', Paper prepared for the World Trade Organization seminar, Cato Center for Trade Policy Studies, Washington DC, 17 November.

Sally, Razeen (2000), 'Globalisation and Policy Response: Three Perspectives', *Government and Opposition*, vol. 35, no. 2, pp. 239–253.

Sally, Razeen (2000), 'Hayek and International Economic Order', *ORDO*, vol. 51.

Scheide, Jochen, and Stefan Sinn (1989): 'How Strong is the Case for International Coordination?', in J. A. Dorn and W. A. Niskanen (eds.), *Dollars, Deficits, and Trade*, Kluwer Academic Publishers, Boston, pp. 397–422.

Schneider, F., and A. Wagner (1999),' The Role of International Monetary Institutions after the EMU and after the Asian Crisis: Some Preliminary Ideas Using Constitutional Economics', Paper presented at the Annual Meeting of the Public Choice Society, New Orleans, March 13–15.

Schoenbaum, T. J. (1997), 'International Trade and Protection of the Environment: The Continuing Search for Reconciliation', *American Journal of International Law*, no. 91, pp. 268–313.

Segal, Gerald (1999), 'Does China Matter?', *Foreign Affairs*, vol. 78 (September/October), pp. 24–36.

Shaw, M. N. (1997), *International Law*, fourth edition, Cambridge University Press, Cambridge.

Shleifer, Andrei, and Robert W. Vishny (1993), 'Corruption', *Quarterly Journal of Economics*, vol. 108, pp. 599–617.

Siebert, Horst (1989), 'The Half and the Full Debt Cycle', *Weltwirtschaftliches Archiv*, vol. 125, pp. 217–229.

Silguay, Y.-T. de (1997), 'The Impact of the Creation of the Euro on Financial Markets and the International Monetary System', Address to the Institute of International Finance, Washington DC, 29 April 29.

Smith, Adam (1976 [1776]), *An Inquiry into the Nature and Causes of the Wealth of Nations*, Book IV, University of Chicago Press, Chicago.

Smyser, W. R. (1993), 'Goodbye, G-7', *Washington Quarterly*, vol. 16, no. 1, pp. 15–28.

Snidal, D. (1989), 'The Limits of Hegemonic Stability Theory', *International Organization*, vol. 39, no. 4, pp. 579–614.

Soros, George (1998), *The Crisis in Global Capitalism: Open Society Endangered*, BBS/Public Affairs, New York.

Stein, E. (1999), 'Financial Systems and Exchange Rates: Losing Interest in Flexibility', *Inter-American Development Bank Latin American Economic Policies*, vol. 7 (Second Quarter), pp. 2, 8.

Strange, Susan (1998), *Mad Money*, Manchester University Press, Manchester.

Suk, Sarah (1999), 'Schroeder Hopes China Will Join G-8, Learn from Japan,' *Kyodo*, Tokyo, 2 November.

Tietmeyer, Hans (1989), 'Anmerkungen zu den neuen internationalen Kooperations-bemühungen seit der Plaza-Verabredung 1985', in Bub Norbert (ed.), *Geldwertsicherung und Wirtschaftsstabilität: Festschrift für Helmut Schlesinger*, Knapp, Frankfurt, pp. 479–497.

Tietmeyer, Hans (1999), 'International Co-operation and Co-ordination in the Area of Financial Market Supervision and Surveillance', Report to the Finance Ministers and Central Bank Governors of the G-7 Countries (26 February 1999).

Tinbergen, J. (1952), *On the Theory of Economic Policy*, North-Holland, Amsterdam.

Tindemans, Leo, *et al.* (1996), *Unfinished Peace: Report of the International Commission on the Balkans*, Aspen Institute, Berlin; Carnegie Endowment, Washington DC.

Toepfer, K. (1999), 'UNEP's Convention Priorities', *Synergies: Promoting Co-operation on Environmental Treaties*, vol. 1, no. 1.

Tumlir, J. (1979), 'The New Protectionism, Cartels and the International Order', in R. C. Amacher, G. Haberler, T. D. Willett (eds.), *Challenges to a Liberal International Economic Order*, American Enterprise Institute, Washington DC, 1979.

Tumlir, J. (1980), 'National Sovereignty, Power, and Interest', *ORDO*, vol. 31.

Tumlir, J. (1981), 'Evolution of the Concept of International Economic Order, 1914–1980', in Frances Cairncross (ed.), *Changing Perspectives of Economic Policy: Essays in Honour of Sir Alec Cairncross*, Methuen, London.

Tumlir, J. (1983), 'International Economic Order and Democratic Constitutionalism', *ORDO* 34, pp. 71–83.

Tumlir, J. (1983), 'Need for an Open Multilateral Trading System', *World Economy*, vol. 6, no. 4.

Tumlir, J. (1984), *Economic Policy as a Constitutional Problem*, Institute of Economic Affairs, London.

Tumlir, J. (1985), *Protectionism: Trade Policy in Democratic Societies*, American Enterprise Institute, Washington DC.

U.S. Senate Banking Committee on Banking, Housing, and Urban Affairs (1999), *Citizen's Guide to Dollarization*, Committee Documents Online, 106th Congress, <www.senate.gov/~banking/docs/reports/dollar.htm> (September 2000).

ul Haq, M. (1994), 'The Bretton Woods Institutions and Global Governance', in Peter Kenen (ed.), *Managing the World Economy*, Institute for International Economics, Washington DC, pp. 409–418.

Ullrich, H., and A. Donnelly (1998), 'The Group of Eight and the European Union: The Evolving Partnership', *G7 Governance*, vol. 5, <www.library.utoronto.ca/g7/governance/gov5> (September 2000).

United Nations (1999), 'Toward a New International Architecture: Report of the Task Force of the Executive Committee on Economic and Social Affairs of the United Nations', ECSA/9/1, New York, 21 January.

United Nations 1999, 'Statement by the Secretary-General Kofi Annan', Press Release SG/SM/6878, Brussels, 28 January.

United Nations Conference on Environment and Development (1992), *Agenda 2*, United Nations, Rio de Janeiro, chap. 38.

United Nations Conference on Trade and Development (1999), *High-Level Round Table on Trade and Development Governance: Summary*, United Nations, New York.

United Nations Conference on Trade and Development (1999), *Report of the Secretary General to UNCTAD X*, TD 380, United Nations, New York.

United Nations Conference on Trade and Development (1999), *Trade and Development Report 1999*, United Nations, New York.

United Nations Conference on Trade and Development (1999), *World Investment Report: Foreign Direct Investment and the Challenge of Development*, New York, United Nations.

United Nations Conference on Trade and Development (2000), *Plan of Action*, Tenth session, New York, United Nations, 2000.

United Nations Development Programme (1999), *Human Development Report 1999*, United Nations, New York.

United Nations General Assembly (1992), *Rio Declaration on Environment and Development*, A/CONF.151/26, vol. 1.

Vasquez, Ian (1998), 'Official Assistance, Economic Freedom, and Policy Change: Is Foreign Aid Like Champagne?', *Cato Journal*, vol. 18, no. 2.

Vaubel, Roland (1983), 'Coordination or Competition Among National Macroeconomic Policies?', in Fritz, Machlup, Gerhard Fels, and H. Muller-Groeling (eds.), *Reflections on a Troubled World Economy: Essays in Honour of Herbert Giersch*, St. Martin's Press, London.

Vaubel, R. (1991), 'A Public Choice View of International Organizations', in R. Vaubel and T. D. Willett (eds.), *The Political Economy of International Organizations*, Westview Press, Boulder, CO, pp. 27–45.

Viner, Jacob (1951), *International Economics*, The Free Press, Glencoe, IL.

von Furstenberg, George M. (2000), 'Does North America Need an Amero?', *Policy Options/Options politiques*, vol. 21, no. 7, pp. 55–58.

von Furstenberg, George M., and Joseph Daniels (1992), 'Can You Trust G-7 Promises?', *International Economic Insights*, vol. 3 (September/October), pp. 24–27.

Wallace, William (1984), 'Political Issues at the Summits: A New Concert of Powers', in Cesare Merlini (ed.), *Economic Summits and Western Decision-making*, St. Martin's Press, London.

Weber, Axel A. (1996), 'Foreign Exchange Intervention and International Policy Co-ordination: Comparing the G3 and EMS experience', in Matthew B. Canzoneri, Wilfred J. Ethier, and Vittorio Grilli (eds.), *The New Transatlantic Economy*, Cambridge University Press, New York, pp. 54–113.

Weilemann, P. (2000), 'The Summit Meeting: Diplomacy at its Highest Level', *NIRA Review*, vol. 7, no. 1, pp. 16–20.

Weller, Marc (1999), 'The Rambouillet Conference on Kosovo', *International Affairs*, vol. 75, no. 2, pp. 221–251.

Whyman, William (1995), 'We Can't Go On Meeting Like This: Revitalizing the G-7 Process', *Washington Quarterly*, vol. 18, no. 3, pp. 139–165.

Wijk, Rob de (1998), 'De Contactgroep: een Europese Veiligheidsraad?', *Internationale Spectator*, April.

Williamson, John (1985), *The Exchange Rate System*, Policy Analyses in International Economics Series, vol. 5, Institute for International Economics, Washington DC.

Williamson, John, and Miller, Marcus M. (1987), *Targets and Indicators: A Blueprint for the International Coordination of Economic Policies*, Policy Analyses in International Economics Series, vol. 22, Institute for International Economics, Washington DC.

Wolfensohn, James (2000) 'Summary of the Debate', United Nations Conference on Trade and Development, Tenth Session, 16 February, <www.unctad-10.org/interactive_debate/id_sum_wolfensohn.en.htm> (September 2000).

World Bank (1997), *World Development Report 1997: The State in a Changing World*, World Bank, Washington DC.

World Bank (1999), *Global Development Finance 1999*, Washington DC, <www.worldbank.org/prospects/gdf99> (September 2000).

World Bank (1999), *HIPC Debt Tables in Global Development Finance 1999*, Washington DC, <www.worldbank.org/hipc/about/debt-table/debt-table.html> (September 2000).

World Bank (1999), *World Development Report 1999/2000: Entering the 21st Century*, World Bank, Washington DC.

World Meteorological Organization (1997), *Comprehensive Assessment of Freshwater Resources of the World*, United Nations, New York.

World Resources Institute, United Nations Environment Programme, United Nations Development Programme, and World Bank (1998), *World Resources 1998–99: A Global Guide to the Human Environment*, Oxford University Press, New York.

World Trade Organization (1999), 'Trade Liberalization Reinforces the Need for Environmental Co-operation', Press Release 140, 8 October, <www.wto.org/english/news_e/pres99_e/pr140_e.htm> (September 2000).

Yeager, Leland (1998), 'How to Avoid International Financial Crises', *Cato Journal*, Special Issue on Money and Capital Flows in a Global Economy, vol. 17, no. 3.

Young, Alwyn (1992), 'A Tale of Two Cities: Factor Accumulation and Technical Change in Hong Kong and Singapore', *NBER Macroeconomics Annual*, MIT Press, Cambridge, MA.

Young, Oran R. (1983), 'Regime Dynamics: The Rise and Fall of International Regimes', in Stephen Krasner (ed.), *International Regimes*, Cornell University Press, Ithaca, NY, pp. 93–114.

Index